ASSET ALLOCATION

Balancing Financial Risk

FIFTH EDITION

ROGER C. GIBSON

WITH CHRISTOPHER J. SIDONI

McGraw Hill Education

New York Chicago San Francisco Lisbon London
Madrid Mexico City Milan New Delhi San Juan
Seoul Singapore Sydney Toronto

1 2 3 4 5 6 7 8 9 0 DOC/DOC 1 9 8 7 6 5 4 3

ISBN 978-1-265-80197-7
MHID 1-26-580197-5

e-ISBN 978-0-07-180419-6
e-MHID 0-07-180419-6

Library of Congress Cataloging-in-Publication Data

Gibson, Roger C.
Asset allocation: balancing financial risk/by Roger Gibson.—Fifth Edition.
pages cm
Includes index.
ISBN-13: 978-1-265-80197-7
ISBN-10: 1-26-580197-5
1. Portfolio management. 2. Asset allocation. I. Title.
HG4529.5.G53 2013
332.6—dc23 2013002471

To Brenda, my wife and partner in all ways for always

The royalties from this book will be donated to the Roger and Brenda Gibson Family Foundation in memory of my parents, Don B. and Marianne A. Gibson.

Contents

Foreword to the Fifth Edition

Experienced investors all understand four wonderfully powerful truths about investing, and wise investors govern their investing by adhering to these four great truths:

1. The dominating reality is that the most important decision is your long-term mix of assets: how much in stocks, real estate, bonds, or cash.
2. That mix should be determined by the real purpose and time of use of money.
3. Diversify within each asset class—and between asset classes. Bad things do happen—usually as surprises.
4. Be patient and persistent. Good things come in spurts—usually when least expected—and fidgety investors fare badly. "Plan your play and play your plan," say the great coaches. "Stay the course" is also wise. So setting the right course is crucial—which takes you back to number 1.

Curiously, most active investors—who all say they are trying to get "better performance"—do themselves and their portfolios real harm by going against one or all of these truths. They pay higher fees, more costs of change, and more taxes; they spend hours of time and lots of emotional energy; and accumulate "loss leaks" that drain away the results they could have had from their investments if they had only taken the time and care to understand their own investment realities, develop a sensible long-term program most likely to achieve their goals, and stay with it.

The importance of being realistic about investing continues to increase because the markets are increasingly dominated by large, fast-acting, well-informed professionals who are armed with major advantages. During the past generation, to cite a few examples, the following basic changes have taken place:

- Institutions have gone from executing 10 percent of all trades to 95 percent.
- Exchange volume—using the NYSE as an example—has mushroomed from 3 million shares to 5 billion shares, and derivatives volume doubles that to 10 billion shares—a 3,000-fold increase.
- The 50 largest institutions now do half of all the trading, so when an individual buys or sells, half the time, she is trading against one of the fast, smart giants. Sure, she may win sometimes, but can she do it *regularly*? Not a chance.

Even the pros find it very hard to "beat the market." Over the last 5, 10, or 20 years, more than half got beaten by the market. For individuals, the grim reality is far worse.

"If you can't beat 'em, join 'em." That's why indexing has become so widely accepted. An even better reason for individuals to index is that they are then free to devote their time and energy to the one role where they have a decisive advantage: knowing themselves and accepting markets as they are—just as we accept weather as it is—designing a long-term portfolio structure or mix of assets that meet important tests:

1. The investor can and will live with it.
2. The long-term reasonably expectable results will meet the investor's own priority.

While some few investors are so skillful, so well supported, and so independent that they really can add value by actively changing their investments, the records show over and over again that their number is fewer than most investors are willing to believe. For individuals, the chances of identifying one of these Great Winners *before* its record has been established is very low.

Changing managers—firing one *before* disappointment and hiring a new one *before* success is shown—is virtually impossible. Such "dating" should be recognized as an expensive waste of time and energy and should be avoided by all serious investors.

So the great advantage of investors who are wisely concentrating on asset mix decisions is that it helps them avoid the "snipe hunt" of a vain search for "performance" and concentrates their attention on the most important decision in investing—long-term asset mix to minimize the odds of unacceptable outcomes caused by avoidable mistakes *and* maximize the chances of achieving priority investment objectives.

If, as the pundits say, "success is getting what you want and happiness is wanting what you get," investors—by concentrating on asset mix—can be both successful and happy with their investments by living with and investing by the four simple truths—so investments really do work for and serve them.

Of course, as all experienced investors also know, most individual investors take many, many years, make many mistakes, and have many unhappy experiences to learn these "simple but never easy" truths. Fortunately, there is a convenient alternative: We can all learn, as Harry Truman recommended so wisely, by reading history. Markets are markets and people are people, and together they have created or written a lot of history of the mistakes of others from which we can all learn valuable lessons at low cost.

Charles D. Ellis
January 2013

Foreword to the First Edition

After 49 years of professional investment counseling worldwide, I believe that successful investing is mainly common sense. It is common sense to search for an asset where you can buy the greatest value for each dollar you pay. This means bargain hunting. For example, it is wise to compare a multitude of similar investments in order to select that one which can be bought for the lowest price in relation to other similar assets. If you buy a share of a company for a small fraction of its intrinsic value, then there is less risk of a major price decline and more opportunity for a major price increase.

To diversify your investments is clearly common sense so that those that produce more profits than expected will offset those that produce less. Even the best investment professional must expect that no more than two-thirds of his decisions will prove to be above average in profits. Therefore, asset allocation and diversification are the foundation stones of successful long-term investing.

To diversify means that you do not put all of your assets in any one type of investment. Similarly, it is not wise to invest only in the shares of any one company, industry, or nation. If you search in all nations you are likely to find more good bargains and perhaps better bargains. Clearly you will reduce the risk because bear markets and business recessions occur at different times in different nations. Changing economic conditions also affect various types of investment assets differently. By diversifying among different types of assets, the value of your portfolio will not fluctuate as much.

To begin with modest assets and build a fortune obviously requires thrift. An investor seeking to become wealthy should adhere to an annual family expense budget that includes a large amount of savings.

For example, during my first 15 years after college, I made a game of adhering to a budget that included saving 50 cents out of every dollar of earnings. Those who are thrifty will grow wealthy, and those who are spendthrifts will become poor.

Also, there is a magic formula called *dollar-cost averaging* in which you invest the same amount of money at regular intervals in an investment whose price fluctuates. At the end of the investment period, your average cost will be below the average price paid for the investment. In other words, your dollars will buy more shares when prices are low and fewer shares when prices are high, so that your average cost is low compared with the average for the market.

John D. Rockefeller said that to grow wealthy you must have your money work for you. In other words, be a lender and not a borrower. For example, if you have a big mortgage on your home, the interest paid will more than double the cost of the home. On the other hand, if you own a mortgage on a house, the annual interest on that mortgage will compound and make a fortune for you. If you never borrow money, interest will always work for you and not against you. You will also have peace of mind and be able to live through the bear markets and business recessions that occur in most nations about twice every 10 years.

It is only common sense to prepare for a bear market. Experts do not know when each bear market will begin, but you can be certain that there will be many bear markets during your lifetime. Commonsense investing means that you should prepare yourself both financially and psychologically. Financially you should be prepared to live through any bear market without having to sell at the wrong time. In fact, your financial planning should provide for additional investment funds so that you can buy when shares are unreasonably low in price. Preparing psychologically means to expect that there will be many bull markets and bear markets so that you will not sell at the wrong time or buy at the wrong time. To buy low and sell high is difficult for persons who are not psychologically prepared or who act on emotions rather than facts.

When my investment counsel company began in 1940, on the front page of our descriptive booklet were these words: "To buy when others are despondently selling and to sell when others are avidly buying requires the greatest fortitude and pays the greatest reward."

Probably no investment fact is more difficult to learn than the fact that the price of shares is never low except when most people are selling and never high except when most are buying. This makes investing totally different from other professions. For example, if you go to 10 doctors all of whom agree on the proper medicine, then clearly you should take that medicine. But if you go to 10 security analysts all of whom agree that you should buy a particular share or type of asset then quite clearly you must do the opposite. The reason is that if 100 percent are buying and then even one changes his mind and begins selling, then already you will have passed the peak price. Common sense is not common; but common sense and careful logic show that it is impossible to produce superior investment performance if you buy the same assets at the same time as others are buying.

When selecting shares for purchase there are many dozens of yardsticks for judging value. A most reliable yardstick is how high is the price in relation to earnings. However, it is even more important to ask how high is the price in relation to probable earnings 5 to 10 years in the future. A share is nothing more than a right to receive a share of future earnings. Growth in earnings usually results from superior management. Even the best professionals have great difficulty in judging the ability of management. For the part-time investor, the best way is to ask three questions. Is this company growing more rapidly than its competitors? Is the profit margin wider than its competitors? Are the annual earnings on invested assets larger than for competitors? These three simple indicators will tell you much about the ability of management.

History shows frequent and wide fluctuations in the prices of many types of assets. Proper asset allocation helps to dampen the impact that these price swings will have on your portfolio. Asset price fluctuations may be even greater and more frequent in the future because all human activity is speeding up. This is one reason why you should not select a professional advisor based on short-term performance. For example, an advisor who takes the most risk is likely to have top performance in a bull market and the opposite in a bear market. Individual investors as well as managers of pension funds and university endowments should judge the ability of investment advisors over at least one full market cycle and preferably several cycles. This helps to balance out the element of luck and reveal which advisor has received the blessing of common sense.

I hope that almost every adult will become an investor. When I became an investment counselor there were only 4 million shareholders in America, and now there are 48 million. The amount of money invested in American mutual funds is now 1,000 times as great as it was 55 years ago. Thrift, common sense, and wise asset allocation can produce excellent results in the long run. For example, if you begin at age 25 to invest $2,000 annually into your Individual Retirement Account where it can compound free of tax, and if you average a total return of 10 percent annually, you will have nearly a million dollars accumulated at age 65.

Investment management requires the broad consideration of all major investment alternatives. In this book, Roger Gibson develops the principles of asset allocation which make for good commonsense investing in a rapidly changing world. In easily understood terms, he guides investment advisors and their clients step-by-step through a logical process for making the important asset allocation decisions. The broadly diversified investment approach Roger Gibson advocates should give investment advisors and their clients good investment results with increased peace of mind.

John M. Templeton
Chairman of the Templeton Foundations
April 11, 1989

Acknowledgments

First I want to thank my coauthor and associate, Christopher J. Sidoni. This edition was my first experience working with a coauthor. I can say without reservation that Chris made the project much more manageable and enjoyable for me and that the new material he contributed has made it a better book. Thanks also to Chad Hileman, an analyst for Gibson Capital, LLC, who provided research support to Chris and me and also prepared initial drafts of exhibits that appear throughout the book. I would also like to thank my wife, Brenda, who as chief executive officer is responsible for the daily challenges of managing Gibson Capital, LLC. Brenda also worked many evenings and weekends editing and formatting the manuscript and exhibits prior to submission to McGraw-Hill.

A book such as this is impossible without the work of many companies that provided research support and capital market performance data. I especially want to thank Don Phillips, president of Morningstar's Investment Research division. Don (also known as "Spike") has generously provided support for the fifth as well as prior editions of this book. I accordingly would like to thank Morningstar, Inc., and Ibbotson Associates, a wholly owned subsidiary of Morningstar, Inc. I also want to thank UBS Global Asset Management, Vestek, Thomson Reuters, Robert Shiller (http://www.econ.yale.edu/~shiller/data.htm), Dimensional Fund Advisors, and Wealthcare Capital Management, Inc.

I am very grateful to Darwin M. Bayston, past president and chief executive officer of the Association for Investment Management Research, who critiqued the draft of the first edition and made many helpful suggestions for improving the text. He also paved the way for the translation of the book into Japanese. I would also like to thank Nobel laureate Harry M. Markowitz, known as the father of modern portfolio theory, for his kind endorsement. His pioneering work is the foundation for the ideas discussed in this book.

I am especially thankful to the late Sir John M. Templeton, former chairman of the John Templeton Foundation, which endeavors to build spiritual wealth for the world. Mr. Templeton has been an inspiration to me both spiritually and professionally. I am very honored that a person who produced one of the world's best long-term investment track records wrote the Foreword to the first edition of this book.

I am very thankful to Charles D. Ellis, who wrote the excellent Foreword to the fourth and fifth editions. Dr. Ellis is a luminary in the investment profession whose words of wisdom beautifully set the stage for the book's major themes.

I want to thank my editors at McGraw-Hill, Zachary Gajewski and Janice Race, with whom it has been a pleasure to work. I appreciate their commitment to making the book the best it could be.

My thanks to the many investment and financial professionals from across the country who have attended the presentations on asset allocation and modern portfolio theory that I have been privileged to make at numerous conferences. The quality of dialogue at these lectures has been of great value in refining the ideas in this book.

This book is one of concepts. Some are original, but many are borrowed. If you are intrigued by a certain idea, you may want to know the source. Where possible, I have acknowledged the author. Unfortunately, much of my material no longer has an identifiable origin. Thus, I ask forgiveness from those who have shaped my thinking but are not directly given credit. I also want to deliver from possible blame those whose ideas I have borrowed and altered based on my own research and experience.

Finally, I would like to acknowledge and thank all the clients of Gibson Capital, LLC, present and future, who make our work as an investment advisor a challenging and rewarding experience.

Roger C. Gibson, CFA

Introduction

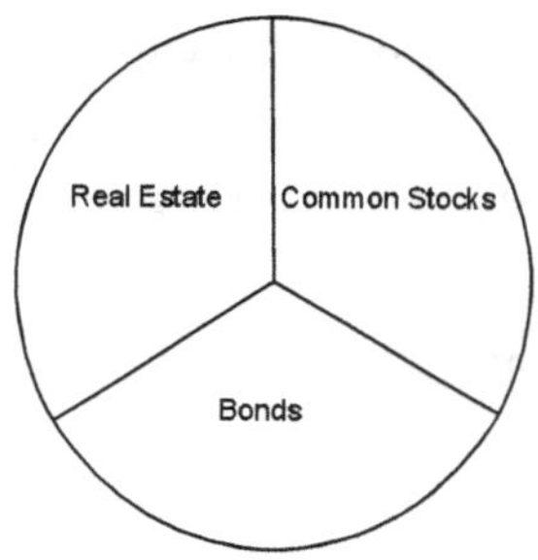

Let every man divide his money into three parts, and invest a third in land, a third in business, and a third let him keep in reserve.

—*Talmud (c. 1200 BC–AD 500)*

Asset allocation is not a new idea! The Talmud quotation above is approximately 2,000 years old. Whoever said it knew something about risk. He also knew something about return. He may have been the world's first proponent of asset allocation. Today we talk about asset allocation rather than diversification, but that is really just a new name for a very old and time-tested investment strategy. A more contemporary translation of the advice might read: "Let every investor create a diversified portfolio that allocates one third to real estate investments and one third to common stocks, with the remaining one third allocated to bonds."

Is this still good advice today? Let's examine the recommendation in more detail. The overall portfolio balance is one-third fixed-income investments and two-thirds equity investments. The third allocated to fixed income mitigates the high volatility risk inherent in the two-thirds allocated to equity investments. Diversification across two major forms of equity investing with dissimilar patterns of returns further reduces the equity risk. The result is a balanced portfolio, tilted toward equities, appropriate for an investor with a longer investment time horizon who is simultaneously concerned about both risk and return. It is a remarkably elegant and powerful asset allocation strategy. Imagine trying to develop a one-sentence investment strategy, knowing that a wide variety of investors, most of whom are not yet born, will follow the advice for the next 2,000 years. You would be hard-pressed to come up with something better!

The decade of the 2000s has been called the "lost decade." Over this 10-year period, even with full reinvestment of dividend income, U.S. large company stocks generated a compound annual loss of −0.95 percent. (See Exhibit I.1.) At that dismal rate of return, an initial $100,000 investment in U.S. large company stocks was worth less than $90,900 by the end of the decade. The Talmud strategy mitigated that downside risk in two ways. The first was bond diversification. During the 2000s, U.S. bonds earned a compound annual return of 6.33 percent. Even though, in the long run, bonds have lower expected returns than stocks, they can provide a valuable cushion against a period of poor U.S. stock performance. For example, Exhibit I.1 shows that, over the lost decade, an annually rebalanced portfolio that allocated one-third to U.S. bonds and two-thirds to U.S. stocks earned a compound annual return of 2.07 percent. Although this return was not sufficient to keep pace with the decade's 2.52 percent inflation rate, the return was at least positive.

The Talmud strategy, however, offered a second way to mitigate risk: diversification across two forms of equity investing with dissimilar patterns of returns. Even though U.S. stocks cumulatively lost money, real estate securities had a compound annual return of

Exhibit I.1
"Lost Decade" (2000–2009)

	Compound Annual Return*
Asset Class	
U.S. Bonds (Taxable, High Quality, Intermediate Term)	6.33%
U.S. Stocks (Large Company)	-0.95%
Real Estate Securities (REITs)	10.63%
Asset Allocation Strategy	
U.S. Bond and Stock Strategy:	
⅓ U.S. Bonds	
⅔ U.S. Stocks	2.07%**
Talmud Strategy:	
⅓ U.S. Bonds	
⅓ U.S. Stocks	6.13%**
⅓ Real Estate Securities	

* With full reinvestment of income

** With annual portfolio rebalancing

Data source: Morningstar® Principia®,

10.63 percent during the lost decade. Diversification across equity asset classes with dissimilar patterns of returns mitigated downside risk *without resorting to diversification into asset classes with lower expected returns*. Given its allocation of one-third U.S. bonds, one-third U.S. stocks, and one-third real estate securities, the Talmud strategy is equity oriented. It nevertheless generated a compound annual return of 6.13 percent, handily beating inflation. The Talmud strategy's return was particularly impressive given that U.S. stocks had their second worst 10-year holding period return since 1926. Of course, there is no assurance that the Talmud strategy will as easily negotiate the next "lost decade." With all the uncertainties facing investors, however, multiple-asset-class investing is a smart strategy.

The unknown author of the Talmud quote could not have possibly envisioned today's investment world. Over the past two decades, democracies and free enterprise have replaced many of the world's dictatorships and centrally directed economies. New capital markets are forming, and investment alternatives have proliferated. People from around the world exchange volumes of information instantaneously via the Internet, virtually without cost. The world has truly gotten smaller and increasingly interconnected, with economic events in one part of the world impacting markets on the other side of the globe.

In spite of all this change, investors are not that different today than they were a hundred years ago. They want high returns, and they do not want to incur risk in securing those returns. Unfortunately, when it comes to investments, everyone has an opinion, and misconceptions abound. These misconceptions are most prevalent and dangerous in the area of asset allocation decision making. For example, an investor may inappropriately reject a major investment asset class, perhaps bonds or stocks, even though that asset class may play an important role in developing the best strategy to reach his objectives. It is not surprising, therefore, that many investors have portfolio structures that accurately reflect their comfort levels and investment preferences, yet are not the best asset allocations for realizing their financial goals. In these situations it is not enough for an investment advisor to clearly evaluate a client's circumstances and develop an appropriate asset allocation strategy, as the client may not have the conceptual knowledge and frame of reference to understand that the strategy is in his best interest.

Often an advisor and client agree to sidestep such a problem through the client's abandonment of all aspects of the investment management process to the investment advisor's discretion. In essence, the client says to the investment advisor, "Investment management is your job, not mine. That's why I hired you. I trust you. Just tell me this time next year how we're doing." While trust is essential in a client-advisor relationship, it may not be sufficient to carry the client through extreme market conditions when the risk increases that emotions may override reason.

Most investors are notoriously susceptible to making poor decisions as they sell one investment to buy another. DALBAR, Inc., a

Boston-based firm that provides research to companies in the financial services industry, published an often-cited study entitled "Quantitative Analysis of Investor Behavior." The study compared the performance of the average investor in equity mutual funds with that of the S&P 500 index of U.S. large company stocks for the 20-year period between 1986 and 2005. An analysis of the timing of contributions to and withdrawals from the equity mutual funds showed that the average equity fund investor actually earned just 3.9 percent annually compared with an annual return of 11.9 percent for the S&P 500 Index. Much of the underperformance is due to investors periodically reallocating money from one fund to another in a counterproductive attempt to chase the performance of funds and markets that recently had performed well. The study concluded:

> Investment return is far more dependent on investor behavior than on fund performance. Mutual fund investors who hold their investments are more successful than those that time the market. . . . The most important role of the financial advisor is to protect clients from the behaviors that erode their investments and savings.[1]

In his book *Against the Gods: The Remarkable Story of Risk*, Peter L. Bernstein comments:

> A growing volume of research reveals that people yield to inconsistencies, myopia, and other forms of distortion throughout the process of decision-making. That may not matter much when the issue is whether one hits the jackpot on the slot machine or picks a lottery number that makes dreams come true. But the evidence indicates that these flaws are even more apparent in areas where the consequences are more serious.[2]

The good news here is that the problem has a solution. It involves educating clients regarding capital market behavior and the principles of investment portfolio management. With the proper frame of reference, an informed client can confidently develop an appropriate asset allocation strategy with the guidance of her investment advisor. Over time, the asset allocation decisions will be a primary determinant of a portfolio's risk and return characteristics. It is essential, therefore, that the client be actively involved in the design of her portfolio.

This book presents a disciplined framework within which investment professionals and their clients can make the most important decisions impacting portfolio performance. One of the book's major themes is that successful investment management requires successful management of the client's expectations. At the outset, I acknowledge that, for this decision-making framework to be successful in practice, it must:

- Be conceptually sound
- Be comprehensible to clients without requiring an inordinate time commitment on their part
- Facilitate the development of appropriate, individually tailored, all-weather strategies based on the client's unique needs and circumstances
- Be standardized with respect to the steps to be followed
- Continue to be relevant and effective in the future, throughout changing investment markets
- Help clients to consistently follow their asset allocation strategies with patience and discipline while simultaneously sleeping well at night

I will draw on and explore the concepts of modern portfolio theory for the purpose of enhancing the conceptual understanding of my subject matter. But my emphasis will be on the practical implications of these theories. As the gap between theory and practice narrows, the investment management process becomes more effective. It is my hope that this book contributes to the design of better portfolios for clients and that they have the confidence to remain committed to the path that leads them toward the realization of their financial goals.

Chapter 1

The Importance of Asset Allocation

> Not only is there but one way of doing things rightly, there is but one way of seeing them, and that is seeing the whole of them.
>
> —*John Ruskin (1819–1900),* The Two Paths, *1885*

The capital markets have changed dramatically over the last few decades, and investment management has undergone a concurrent evolution. In the early 1960s, the term *asset allocation* did not exist. The traditional view of diversification was simply to "avoid putting all your eggs in one basket." The argument was that if all your money was placed in one investment, your range of possible outcomes was very wide—you might win very big, but you also had the possibility of losing very big. Alternatively, by spreading your money among a number of different investments, you increased the likelihood that you would not be either right or wrong on all of them at the same time. Narrowing the range of outcomes created an advantage.

For the individual investor, those were the days when broad diversification meant owning several dozen stocks and bonds along with some cash equivalents. For pension plans and other institutional portfolios, the same asset classes were often used in a balanced fund with a single manager. Because the U.S. stock and bond markets constituted the major portion of the world capital markets, most investors did not even consider international investing. Bonds traded within a fairly narrow price range. Security analysis concentrated more on common stocks, the common belief being that a full-time skilled professional should be able to consistently "beat the market." The money manager's job was to add value through successful market timing and/or superior security selection. The focus was much more on individual securities than on the total portfolio. The *prudent man rule,* with its emphasis on individual assets, reinforced this type of thinking in the fiduciary community.

As time passed, large swings in interest rates dramatically increased price volatility, and bonds moved out of their narrow trading ranges. Multiple managers on both the fixed-income and the equity portions of institutional portfolios replaced the single balanced manager. With institutional trading on the rise, the full-time professionals were no longer competing against amateurs. They were now competing against each other.

Imagine for a moment the floor of the New York Stock Exchange. Willing buyers and sellers are generating millions of transactions. For any single transaction, the buyer has concluded that the security is worth more than the money, while the seller has concluded that the money is worth more than the security. Both parties to the transaction may be institutions that have nearly instantaneous access to all publicly available relevant information concerning the value of the security. Each has very talented, well-educated investment analysts who have carefully evaluated this information and have interestingly reached opposite conclusions. At the moment of the trade, both parties are acting from a position of informed conviction, though time will prove one of them right and the other wrong. Through free market dynamics, the security's transaction price equates supply with demand and thereby clears the market. A free market price is therefore a consensus on a security's intrinsic value.

In the investment management business, the stakes are high and the rewards are correspondingly great for successful money managers who are able to produce a consistently superior return. It is no wonder that so many bright, talented people are drawn to the profession. In such a marketplace, however, it is difficult to imagine that the market price for any widely followed security will depart meaningfully from its true underlying value. This is the nature of an efficient market.

In both investment management and academic communities, considerable, ongoing controversy exists regarding the degree to which the capital markets are efficient. The debate has far-reaching implications. To the extent that a market is inefficient, opportunities exist for individuals to exercise superior skill to produce an above-average return. While various market anomalies do seem to indicate that the capital markets are not perfectly efficient, most research supports the notion that the markets are reasonably efficient. The accelerating advances in information processing technologies will undoubtedly drive the markets to become even more efficient in the future. It thus will become increasingly unlikely that anyone will be able to consistently beat the market.

The tremendous growth in the use of index funds serves as tangible evidence that this issue is not solely one of academic curiosity. In an efficient capital market, the expectation is that active management, with its associated transaction costs, will result in below-average performance over time. If this is true, one way to win the game is never to play it at all. Those who have invested in index funds have chosen not to play the security selection game. It is ironic (yet logical) that the same high-powered money management talent that creates the efficiency of the marketplace likewise makes the achievement of an above-average return so exceedingly difficult. Even in those situations where a money management organization has a unique proprietary insight that enables it to produce a superior result, the advantage will erode over time if other money management organizations discover and exploit the process.

In 1952, Harry M. Markowitz published an article entitled "Portfolio Selection."[1] In this article, he developed the first mathematical model that specified the volatility reduction that occurs in a portfolio as a result of combining investments with different patterns of returns. The amazing thing about his accomplishment is that he developed his thesis over a half century ago, long before the advent of the modern computer. His influence on the world of modern finance and investment management has been so profound that he became known as the father of modern portfolio theory and was awarded the Nobel Prize in Economics in 1990.

Before modern portfolio theory, investment management was a two-dimensional process focused primarily on the volatility and return characteristics of individual securities. Markowitz's work resulted in the recognition of the importance of the interrelationships among asset classes and securities within portfolios. Modern portfolio theory added a third dimension to portfolio management that evaluates an investment's *diversification effect* on a portfolio. Diversification effect refers to the impact that the inclusion of a particular asset class or security will have on the volatility and return characteristics of the overall portfolio.

Modern portfolio theory thus shifted the focus of attention away from individual securities toward a consideration of the portfolio as a whole. The notion of diversification had to be simultaneously reconsidered. Optimal diversification goes beyond the idea of simply using a number of baskets in which to carry your eggs. It also places major emphasis on finding baskets that are distinctly different from one another. The differences are important because each basket's unique pattern of returns partially offsets the others, with the effect of smoothing overall portfolio volatility.

In an efficient capital market, security prices are always fair. Given this premise, modern portfolio theory stresses the wisdom of investing in a broad array of diverse investments. These concepts later received legislative endorsement in the Employee Retirement Income Security Act of 1974, which governs the management of corporate retirement plans. The act legislates the importance of diversification within a broad portfolio context.[2] In 1992, the basic rule governing the investment of trust assets, known as the *prudent investor rule*, was restated to "focus on the trust's portfolio as a whole and the investment strategy on which it is based, rather than viewing a specific investment in isolation."[3] Later, this thinking was incorporated into the Uniform Prudent Investor Act (1994), which governs fiduciary investing in most American states. John H. Langbein, the eminent legal historian and principal drafter for this legislation, wrote:

> The emphasis on diversification also underlies another prominent feature of the Uniform Act, the portfolio standard of care in section 2(b), which reads: "A trustee's investment and management decisions respecting individual assets must be evaluated not in isolation but in the context of the trust portfolio as a whole …" The official Comment says: "An investment that might be imprudent standing alone can become prudent if undertaken in sensible relation to other trust assets, or to other nontrust assets." This insistence on diversifying investments responds to one of the central findings of Modern Portfolio Theory (MPT), that there are huge and essentially costless gains to diversifying the portfolio thoroughly.[4]

He went on to comment:

> The other great lesson from MPT is the understanding of why individual stock selection is so perilous—why, that is, investors find it so hard to pick winners and avoid losers.[5]

Looking to the future, Langbein predicted:

> Increasingly, the main work of the fiduciary investor will be what has come to be called asset allocation. The trustee will form a

view of the needs, resources, and risk tolerances of the beneficiaries of the particular trust. The trustee will then decide what proportion of the portfolio to invest in what classes of assets. These choices will take the form of allocating the trust assets among large, diversified portfolios, primarily mutual funds and bank common trust funds.[6]

The investment world of today is indeed very different from that of the past. The number and the variety of investment alternatives have increased dramatically, and the once well-defined boundaries between asset classes often are blurred. We now deal in a global marketplace. Exhibit 1.1 shows that the non-U.S. capital markets are as large, and therefore as important, as the U.S. capital markets. Computer technology delivers relevant new information regarding a multitude of investment alternatives almost instantaneously to a marketplace populated by both retail and institutional investors. The traditionally diversified U.S. stock and bond portfolio will become increasingly inadequate in the investment world of the future.

Exhibit 1.1

Total Investable Capital Market (December 31, 2011)

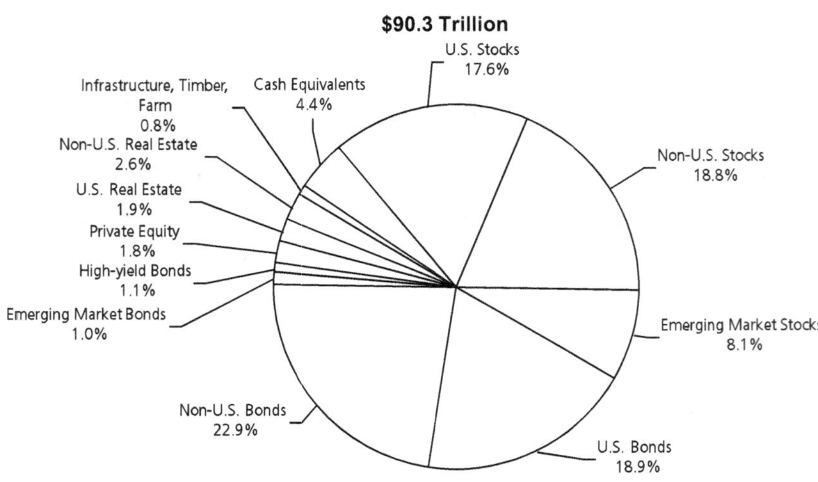

Source: Data provided by UBS Global Asset Management.

Designing an investment portfolio consists of several steps:

1. Deciding which asset classes will be represented in the portfolio
2. Determining the long-term target percentage of the portfolio to allocate to each of these asset classes
3. Specifying for each asset class the range within which the allocation can be altered in an attempt to exploit better performance possibilities in one asset class versus another
4. Selecting securities within each of the asset classes

The first two steps form the foundation for the portfolio's volatility and return characteristics and are often referred to as *investment policy decisions*. Traditionally, investment advisors have built diversified portfolios with three asset classes: cash equivalents, U.S. bonds, and U.S. stocks. They should, however, explicitly consider other asset classes—for example, non-U.S. bonds, non-U.S. stocks, real estate investments, and commodity-linked securities. To the extent that these various asset classes are affected differently by changing economic events, each will have its unique pattern of returns. It is the ability of one asset class's pattern of returns to partially offset another asset class's pattern that drives the power of diversification to reduce portfolio volatility. When considering which asset classes to include in the portfolio, the advisor should start from the premise that all major asset classes will be represented unless specific, sound reasons can be established for the exclusion of a particular class or classes.

The advisor can use a variety of methods to determine the target weights assigned to each of the various asset classes. Modern portfolio theory suggests that, in an efficient market, an investor with average volatility tolerance should hold a portfolio that mirrors the apportionment of the world's wealth among the various asset classes. This asset allocation would be similar to that shown in Exhibit 1.1.

In practice, however, clients vary considerably in their unique needs and circumstances. Thus, the use of one target allocation for all clients—"cutting the person to fit the cloth"—is not advisable. The client's investment objective, relevant time horizon, and volatility tolerance combine to determine whether the client should structure his portfolio for greater principal stability with correspondingly lower returns or, alternatively, for higher growth at the price of more volatility. In either case, the goal is to use the best allocation across the various asset classes in order to achieve the highest expected return relative to the volatility assumed.

For step 3, minimum and maximum limits are often set for each asset class's portfolio commitment. If, for example, stocks are judged to be unusually attractive relative to other asset classes, the proportion of stocks is moved to its upper limit. At other times, when stocks appear to be overvalued, the commitment is moved down to its minimum allocation. This represents the *market-timing* dimension of the investment management process. The success of market-timing activities presumes the existence of inefficiencies in the pricing mechanism among asset classes, coupled with the superior skill needed to identify and act on that mispricing. An extreme form of market timing allocates 100 percent of the portfolio to either cash equivalents or stocks, in an attempt to participate fully in common stock bull markets, while resting safely in cash equivalents during bear markets. The obvious danger of such an approach is that of being in the wrong place at the wrong time with 100 percent of one's capital. The minimum and maximum limits set for each asset class in step 3 act to minimize this risk by requiring that the portfolio avoid extreme allocations.

Market timers use various strategies in attempting to identify and exploit asset class mispricing. Technical analysis, for example, attempts to predict future price movements on the basis of the patterns of past price movements and the volume of security transactions. The overwhelming body of research evidence indicates that such approaches do not beat a naive buy-and-hold strategy. Other approaches rely on sophisticated forecasting procedures to determine the relative attractiveness of one asset class versus another. In essence, market timers claim to have the ability to identify asset class mispricing that everyone else misses and the decisiveness to act confidently on that foresight. A review of both the empirical evidence and the research done on the subject suggests that attempts to improve investment performance through market timing will most likely fail. In my judgment, the game is not worth playing.

For step 4, the advisor may recommend either active or passive security selection. If done passively, the advisor may recommend index funds for the various asset classes in order to obtain the desired breadth of diversification while minimizing transaction costs and management fees. Active security selection is predicated on the belief that exploitable inefficiencies, which can be identified through skilled analysis, exist at the individual security level. To add value, an active manager must produce an incremental return in excess of the transaction costs and associated fees—a very difficult though not necessarily impossible achievement.

The traditional viewpoint equates investment management with the third and fourth steps of the process—market timing and security selection. The probability for success in these areas is so low because of the tremendous intelligence and skill of the investment professionals engaging in these activities. Yet the first two steps in the process—the choice of asset classes and their respective weights in a portfolio—have had, and will continue to have, a large impact on future performance.

The focus of "value-added" investment advice is shifting decidedly in favor of fuller involvement by both investment advisors and their clients with proper asset allocation. By collaboratively exploring these issues and committing their decisions to writing in the form of an investment policy statement, both investment advisors and their clients gain the advantage of a shared frame of reference for evaluating investment performance and monitoring the progress being made toward the achievement of financial goals. Investment management is also demystified, and the likelihood increases that the client will adhere to a properly conceived, sound investment strategy during those phases of the market cycle when the temptation to depart from established policy is at its height.

If asset allocation is a major determinant of portfolio performance, why do investment advisors and investors obstinately focus so much attention on security selection and market timing? Part of the reason is historical. The money management profession is rooted in the notion that superior skill can beat the market. Many investment professionals secretly worry that, were it not for the expectation of superior results from security selection or market timing, they would be out of a job.

The realities of the marketplace, however, stubbornly persist. Research studies repeatedly show that most money managers underperform the market on average over time, and those who do outperform the market in one time period do not have a better-than-even chance of outperforming the market in the next time period. This conclusion is not surprising. Professionals populate the marketplace, and by definition, the majority cannot outperform the average. Given the transaction costs and management fees incurred in attempting to do so, most money managers will continue to underperform the markets in which they invest.

The hope offered through market timing and security selection has tremendous, seductive appeal. All investors want to enjoy the pleasures of a good market and avoid the pain of a bad market. As a result, many have never challenged the hypothesis that professional money managers can reliably add value through either successful market timing or security selection. As data emerge to refute the hypothesis, investors may either ignore the evidence or reflexively misinterpret the data in a way that continues to support the hypothesis. Given the desire to find money managers who will beat the market, investors easily can fall prey to misconceptions or succumb to wishful thinking. For example, an article appearing in an issue of a popular financial magazine screened several hundred mutual funds in an attempt to identify those with superior skill. The author advised against making a judgment based on one year's results. Instead, he suggested finding managers who maintained above-median performance results in each of the past five years. The reader could then choose from among these so-called better money managers. However, this approach does not adequately differentiate between above-median results produced by luck versus those produced by skill.

Consider, for example, that we have a group of 1,000 money managers, each of whom makes security selections on the basis of a random process, like rolling dice. At the end of the first year, we can rank these 1,000 money managers on the basis of their returns. By definition, 500 will be above the median, and 500 will be below the median. We eliminate those with below-median performance in the first year. The remaining above-median managers continue to roll dice to make security selections through the second year. Half of these will be above the median, and half will be below the median. Again, we eliminate from consideration those who underperform. Continuing in this manner, by the end of the fifth year, we will have a group of slightly more than 30 who had above-median performance in each of the five years. Because we know that these managers used a random process (rolling dice) to make security selections, we do not attribute superior skill to the results they achieved. In the real world, however, money managers promise superior results. Identifying 30 managers out of a universe of 1,000 who have outperformed a group of their peers in each of the preceding five years can lead investors to be too quick to assume that the performance was due to superior skill rather than simple luck.

Given the number and variety of securities available for investment, a diverse group of money managers will typically produce a wide dispersion of returns during any particular time frame. This dispersion produces an illusion that the skill levels of these managers vary as much as their results do. In reality, short-run variations in performance are heavily influenced by chance. Without realizing this, many investors continue to compare their performance against the results achieved by the latest investment guru. In the end, investors often chase those performance numbers by constantly reallocating money from one manager to another in their persistent search for the elusive money manager who will continue to produce superior performance tomorrow.

While managers with superior skill may exist, they are rare and extraordinarily difficult to identify conclusively. Barr Rosenberg developed a statistical approach to determine the length of time that above-average performance must continue in order for the appraiser to be confident that the incremental return is attributable to superior skill rather than to luck. His calculation indicates that very long periods of time are usually required, often several decades.

The expected payoff from superior skill will vary depending on where that skill is directed. Not all sectors of the capital markets may be equally efficient. For example, small company stocks do not command as much institutional research as large company stocks and may therefore be less efficiently priced. Similarly, various non-U.S. capital markets may not be as efficient as the U.S. capital market. Where inefficiencies exist, superior investment analysis may uncover exploitable opportunities to produce added value. We should not overlook these opportunities. Over time, however, we should expect that the increasing efficiency of the market will continue to narrow the possible incremental rewards from superior skill as more investors act to exploit these opportunities.

For centuries, scientists accepted without question Sir Isaac Newton's conception of the laws of nature. The universe followed deterministic, billiard ball–like laws of cause and effect. The work of Albert Einstein ended this worldview. Modern physics has changed our notions of time and space. Now we view the universe in a context in which all things are relative to everything else. Einstein's work did not invalidate Newton's laws of physics: It merely defined the limited context within which Newton's mechanistic laws are true. Likewise, modern portfolio theory has eclipsed traditional investment management, with its emphasis on individual security selection. In the spirit of Einstein, modern portfolio theory considers each asset class not as an end in itself but rather as it stands in relationship to all others in the portfolio. Modern portfolio theory does not invalidate traditional investment management approaches so much as it prescribes the limits within which they are valid and can add value. Indeed, without financial analysis and the buying and selling activities of intelligent investors, the marketplace would not be as efficient as it is!

The focus on asset allocation and investment policy is transforming investment management. Within this wider and more important context, less emphasis is placed on beating the market and more energy is directed to devising appropriate asset allocation strategies that will move clients toward their financial goals with the least amount of risk. These strategies do not fight the capital markets; they ride with them intelligently. Investment management today requires a holistic approach in its view of both the investment world and the client's situation. Investment advisors can be very valuable to their clients by helping them to devise appropriate asset allocation strategies designed to realize their objectives and then encouraging them to adhere to their strategies with discipline. Clients have been trained to look over their advisors' shoulders and evaluate the results. If clients *perceive* that a strategy is not working, they will look for a new advisor. In investment management, perceptions often differ from reality. For this reason it is vitally important that both the client and advisor share a common frame of reference regarding the capital markets and the investment management process.

It is easy to fall into the trap of presuming that clients have a grasp of basic investment concepts when in reality their understanding may be quite limited. At the risk of being rudimentary, it is advisable to avoid this danger by taking the time to define terms and explain investment concepts to new clients at the outset. In the next chapter, we will discuss the historical performance of the U.S. capital markets. Keep in mind that although the information may be familiar to you, it is unknown territory to many clients. For this reason, we will engage in this review of the basics in order to give investment professionals a methodology for developing a common frame of reference with their clients. Armed with knowledge, clients will be more comfortable with the investment policies most appropriate for them.

Chapter 2

U.S. Capital Market Investment Performance: A Historical Review

Hindsight is always 20/20.

—*Billy Wilder (1906–2002)*, Colombo's Hollywood

Life can only be understood backwards; but it must be lived forwards.

—*Søren Kierkegaard (1813–1855)*

An investment advisor and a new client often complete an extensive data questionnaire at the beginning of their work together. The advisor asks the client to describe the facts of his financial situation, state his investment objective, and specify his risk tolerance. Armed with this information, the investment advisor designs a suitable investment strategy. This data gathering process can have its problems, however. What assurance does the investment advisor have that the client has realistic expectations regarding investment performance? For example, how does an advisor work with a self-described conservative person who wants to earn a compound annual return of 15 percent but who doesn't want to take any chances with his principal? We generally can agree that, for a client's investment strategy to be successful, it must be consistent with his volatility tolerance. But what if the client's volatility tolerance is inordinately influenced by fears that have been triggered by a lack of investment knowledge? Here the problem lies not within the capital markets but rather within the client. How can the investment advisor be confident that the client clearly perceives all the risks involved in the investment management process and the relative dangers posed by those risks?

An investment advisory relationship inevitably will encounter difficulties if the client has a different investment worldview than the advisor. This situation is a time bomb waiting to explode. In October 1987, the U.S. stock market experienced the largest single-day decline in history, with prices falling by more than 20 percent. Following the crash, an advisory relationship would have been in trouble if the investment advisor's strategy was predicated on the notion that market timing is not possible, and yet the client believed that the investment advisor's job was to protect him from stock market declines.

Clients' investment performance expectations tend to be overly optimistic. Generally, people believe that higher returns are possible with less volatility than is actually the case. Therefore, an important rule in investment management is to first manage the client's expectations and only then manage the client's money. The client and the investment advisor must share a common investment worldview before implementing the investment strategy.

Realistic expectations are necessary for the development of realistic objectives. Clients must understand *all* types of risks and must accurately assess the relative importance of each type in their particular situations. The advisor must destroy the myth of the ideal investment. No liquid investment alternatives with stable guaranteed principal values exist that can provide real returns by consistently beating the combined impact of inflation and income taxes. Any misconceptions that remain uncorrected will tend to surface later, often to the detriment of the investment management process.

The advisor also needs to educate the client about the importance of his *time horizon* in establishing an appropriate investment strategy. These educational tasks can be accomplished with a thorough review of the historical performance of the capital markets. The worldview that emerges from this process serves as a foundation for the investment management approach used to help clients reach their financial goals.

The *2012 Ibbotson® Stocks, Bonds, Bills, and Inflation® Classic Yearbook*, published by Morningstar, Inc., is one of the best sources of up-to-date information regarding the performance of various U.S. capital market investment alternatives. The data cover the period from 1926 to the present. During these decades, the capital markets experienced periods of war and peace, inflation and deflation, and several cycles of economic expansion and contraction. Exhibit 2.1 traces the cumulative effect of compounded total returns on $1 invested at the end of 1925 for various investment alternatives. These performance figures are not adjusted for the impact of income taxes and generally do not take transaction costs into consideration. The vertical axis on the graph is a logarithmic scale, where a given vertical distance represents a specific percentage change, regardless of where it is measured. A logarithmic scale is often used to facilitate the comparison on the same graph of investments with widely varying performance results.

Inflation

The measure of inflation used in Exhibit 2.2 is the Consumer Price Index for All Urban Consumers (CPI-U), as compiled by the Bureau of Labor Statistics.[1] Some experts prefer the gross national product deflator as a better measurement of inflation, but the CPI-U is widely publicized and more commonly used. As a proxy for the cost of living, let us assume that a breakfast of bacon and eggs, toast, and coffee costs $1 at the end of 1925. During the following 86 years, inflation increased the cost of living over 12 times, pushing the price of this same breakfast to $12.59 by the end of 2011.

Exhibit 2.1
Wealth Indices of Investments in the U.S. Capital Markets (Year-End 1925 = $1.00)

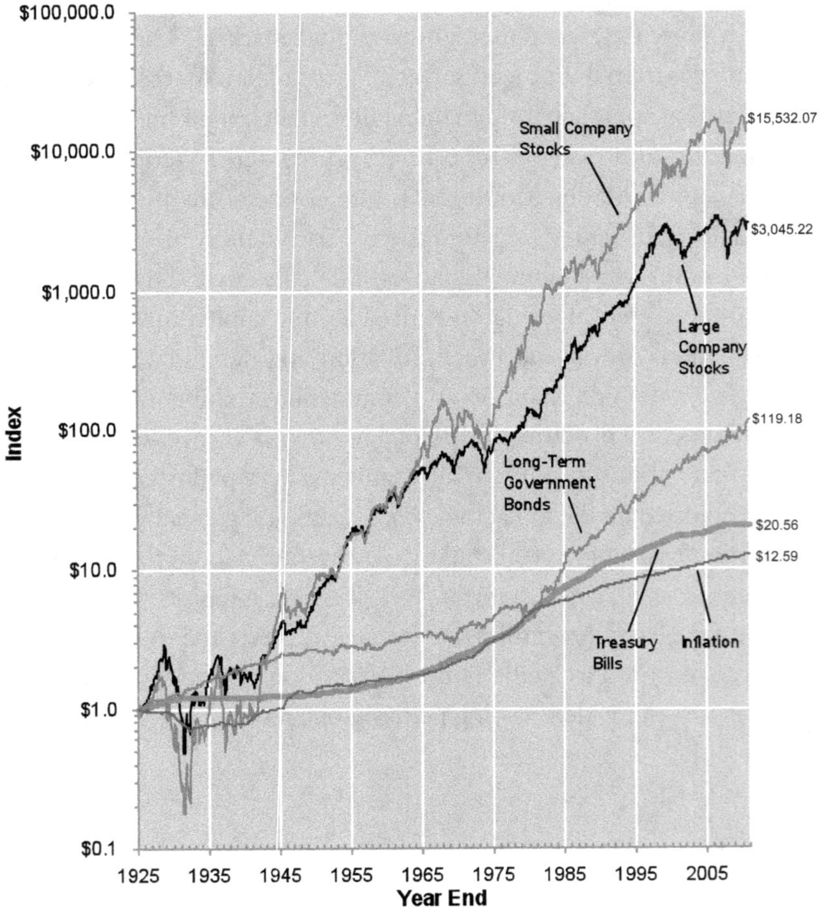

Data source: Calculated by Gibson Capital, LLC using data presented in *2012 Ibbotson® Stocks, Bonds, Bills, and Inflation® (SBBI®) Classic Yearbook*, © 2012 Morningstar. All rights reserved. Used with permission.

The first seven years of this period, however, were deflationary, averaging a 4.4 percent compound annual decline in the cost of living, reducing the price of our hypothetical breakfast to $0.73 by the end of 1932. Not until the end of 1945 did inflation push the cost of our breakfast back to $1. The over 12-fold increase in the cost of living

Exhibit 2.2
Inflation (Cumulative Index and Rates of Change)

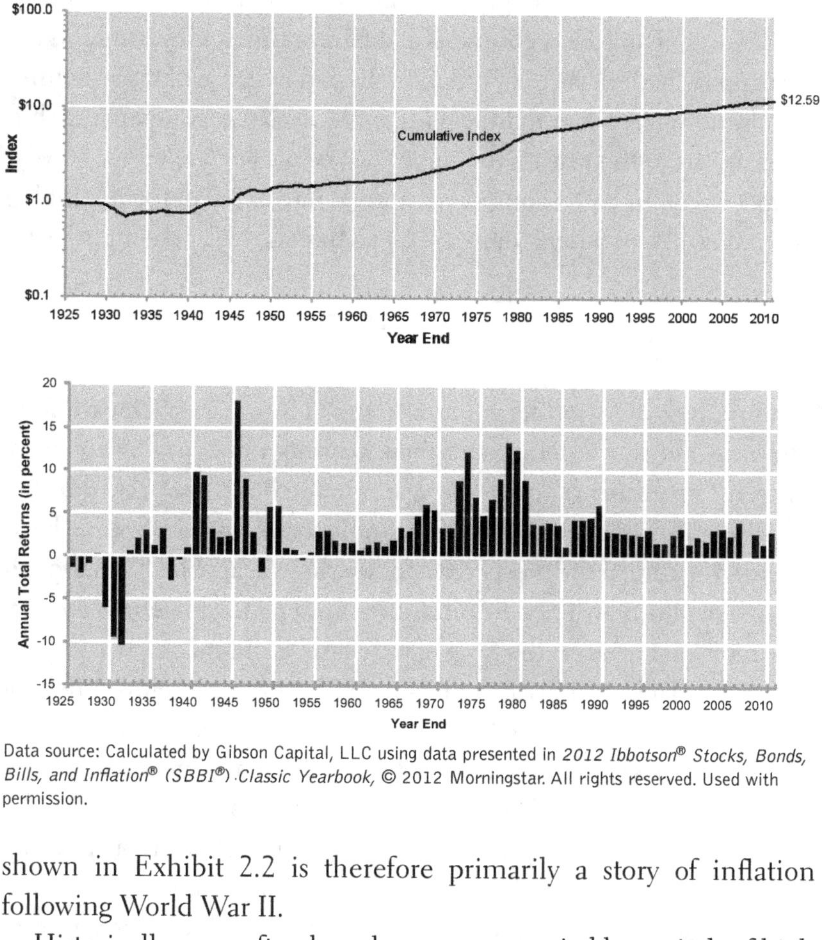

Data source: Calculated by Gibson Capital, LLC using data presented in *2012 Ibbotson® Stocks, Bonds, Bills, and Inflation® (SBBI®) Classic Yearbook,* © 2012 Morningstar. All rights reserved. Used with permission.

shown in Exhibit 2.2 is therefore primarily a story of inflation following World War II.

Historically, wars often have been accompanied by periods of high inflation, but usually a postwar deflation would bring price levels back down again. This deflation did not occur following World War II. Inflation continued, although at a modest compound annual rate of 2.8 percent, over the next two decades. From the mid–1960s through 1981, inflation became much more serious, compounding at an average annual rate of 7 percent. At this pace, the cost of living doubles approximately every decade. From 1982 through 2011, inflation returned to a more modest 3 percent compound annual rate.

The persistent inflation following World War II was not confined to the United States. The phenomenon occurred worldwide, to varying degrees, in different countries at different times. Governments are the primary beneficiaries of inflation, in part because of tax structures that tax nominal rather than real income, with an accompanying shift of wealth from the private to the public sector. For the entire 86-year period, inflation had a compound annual rate of 3.0 percent, ranging from a low of –10.3 percent in 1932 to a high of 18.2 percent in 1946.

Treasury Bills

Treasury bills are short-term loans to the U.S. Treasury Department. They are sold at a discount from their maturity value, pay no coupons, and have maturities of up to one year. Treasury bills are backed by the full faith and credit of the federal government and historically have been regarded as among the most creditworthy issues available. Even though the rate of return on Treasury bills varies from period to period, the specific return is known at the time of purchase. Exhibit 2.3 shows that $1 invested in Treasury bills at the end of 1925 grew, with reinvestment of interest, to be worth $20.56 by the end of 2011. The compound annual return over this 86-year period was 3.6 percent, compared with a compound annual inflation rate of 3 percent over the same period.

Exhibit 2.3 also shows the year-by-year pattern of returns on Treasury bills. From 1926 through 1932, the real returns were quite high because of the deflationary environment. During the 1940s, the federal government pegged Treasury bill yields at low levels during a period of higher inflation, resulting in negative real interest rates. Treasury bill yields were deregulated in 1951, and since then yields have followed inflation rates more closely. Over the entire 86-year period, returns ranged from a low of 0 percent to a high of 14.7 percent.

The Treasury bill's stability of principal value is its great virtue. The price paid for this advantage is a rate of return only marginally ahead of inflation. It should be noted that these rates of return are pretax performance numbers. Had the Treasury bill returns been

Exhibit 2.3
Treasury Bills (Return Index and Returns)

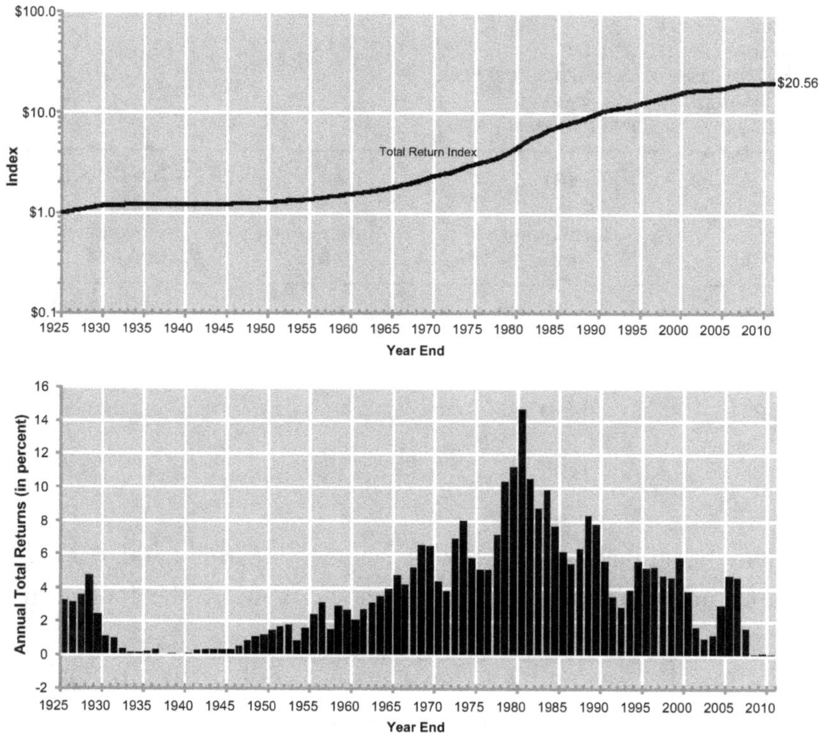

Data source: Calculated by Gibson Capital, LLC using data presented in *2012 Ibbotson® Stocks, Bonds, Bills, and Inflation® (SBBI®) Classic Yearbook,* © 2012 Morningstar. All rights reserved. Used with permission.

adjusted downward for payment of income taxes, their performance would have lagged considerably behind inflation. The investment implication is clear. For a Treasury bill investor to stay whole in real terms, he would have to live in a tax-free world and limit his withdrawals for living expenses to a small fraction of the interest earned.

When the combined effects of inflation and taxation are considered, Treasury bills and other forms of short-term, interest-bearing securities are not riskless investments. Consider the situation of a 54-year-old widow, as summarized in Exhibit 2.4. If she is of average health, she has a life expectancy of approximately 30 more years. Let us assume that certificate of deposit (CD) interest rates are at 4 percent, with an

Exhibit 2.4
The Impact of Inflation

Widow, Age 54
30-Year Life Expectancy
4% Certificate of Deposit Interest Rate
3% Average Inflation Rate
$2,500,000 Available for Investment

Year	(A) Capital Purchasing Power	(B) CD Interest Rate	(C) = (A) X (B) Real Yield
Now	$2,500,000	4%	$100,000
10	1,860,235	4%	74,409
20	1,384,189	4%	55,368
30	1,029,967	4%	41,199

underlying annual inflation rate of 3 percent. With $2,500,000 available for investment, CDs could provide her with $100,000 of annual income.

Assume that she never touches a penny's worth of the principal but uses the full interest income for her living expenses. Over the next decade, the cost of living will advance more than 34 percent, reducing the purchasing power of her $2,500,000 by more than 25 percent, to $1,860,235. Her $100,000 income stream likewise loses more than 25 percent of its value and can purchase only $74,409 worth of goods and services. Continuing in this same manner over the remaining two decades of her life expectancy, the purchasing power of her initial $2,500,000 drops to only $1,029,967, with an annual income stream capable of purchasing only $41,199 worth of goods and services!

Many investors who fear the risks associated with equity investments seek what they perceive to be a safe haven in short-term interest-generating investments. This illustration can be effectively used to underscore the purchasing power risk inherent in such investments. Often, investors are not sufficiently sensitive to the issue of inflation because of the insidious way it takes its toll. Although investors should be concerned primarily with their real returns (i.e., returns adjusted for inflation), they often seem more interested in their nominal results.

For example, during the high interest rate environment of 1979 through 1981, Treasury bill returns averaged 12.1 percent annually, producing an average after-tax return of 8.5 percent for a 30 percent marginal-tax-bracket investor. Inflation averaged 11.5 percent annually over the same period, producing a Treasury bill after-tax real *loss* of 3 percent per year. Three years later, many of these same investors were complaining as they saw the average annual Treasury bill returns from 1982 through 1984 decline to 9.7 percent, which equated to an average after-tax return of 6.8 percent for the same 30 percent marginal-tax-bracket investor. These returns were achieved, however, during a period when inflation averaged 3.9 percent, thus providing investors with a positive real return after taxes of nearly 3 percent per year. Investors need to clearly understand the money illusion of wealth accumulating, when in fact it may be eroding.

Of course, there are other ways to lend money at interest for short periods. *Commercial paper* is unsecured, short-term promissory notes issued by corporations. Historically, commercial paper yields have been approximately 0.5 percent higher than those of U.S. Treasury bills. In general, cash equivalents, defined as any short-term, higher-quality, interest-bearing security, share many of the same advantages and disadvantages possessed by Treasury bills. Although the real return from cash equivalents occasionally will turn negative, on average it is expected that they will produce pretax returns of approximately 1 to 1.5 percent above the average inflation rate.

Bonds

Bonds are negotiable promissory notes of a corporation or government entity. They usually pay a series of interest payments followed by a return of principal at maturity. The par value (face value) of a bond appears on the front of the bond certificate and is ordinarily the amount the issuing company initially borrowed and promises to repay at maturity. The coupon rate is the stated rate of interest on a bond that, when multiplied by the par value, determines the annual interest payments to be made. The market price of a bond is usually different from its face value. A variety of factors determines the market price of a bond, including the current interest rate environment and the bond's coupon rate, creditworthiness, maturity date, call provisions, and tax status. Bonds are often referred to as *fixed-income securities.* This term is somewhat misleading. Only the maximum payment is fixed, not the income paid. In the case of defaulted corporate bonds, for example, interest payments are not always paid as promised.

Bond prices depend in large measure on the prevailing interest rate environment. The fluctuation in bond prices, due to changes in interest rates, is referred to as *interest rate risk.* When first exposed to the concept, many clients may be puzzled by the inverse relationship between interest rate movements and bond prices. A simple illustration can clarify the concept. Suppose an investor purchases a newly issued 20-year corporate bond at its $10,000 par value. The bond has a 5 percent coupon rate, providing the investor with $500 in interest payments annually. Over the following year, the interest rate environment increases such that similar newly issued 20-year corporate bonds must provide a 6 percent coupon bond payment in order to entice investors to purchase them. If the holder of the 5 percent coupon bond wants to sell it in this higher interest rate environment, he will find that no one is willing to pay the original $10,000 purchase price. There is no incentive to buy a $500-per-year stream of interest payments when the same $10,000 will now buy a $600-per-year stream of interest payments, given the higher interest rates prevailing. The 5 percent coupon bond clearly has value, however, and its price in the marketplace would have declined until it reached a level where the $500 payment on the lower market value, coupled with the return of face value at maturity, is as attractive as the $600 annual interest payments on the newly issued $10,000 bond.

The discount rate that equates the present value of the bond's stream of future cash flows (interest payments plus return of principal) to the bond's current market value is the bond's *yield to maturity*. (Mathematically, it is the bond's internal rate of return.) The yield to maturity is often simply referred to as the *yield* and takes into consideration the annual interest payments, the number of years to maturity, and the difference between the bond's purchase price and its redemption value at maturity. The yield to maturity must be differentiated from the *current yield* of a bond, which is simply the annual interest payments divided by the current market value of the bond. The yield to maturity on a bond will be greater than the current yield when the market value of the bond is less than its par value, because the yield to maturity takes into consideration the average annual increase in the bond's value as it approaches full par value at maturity. Conversely, the yield to maturity on a bond will be less than the current yield when the market value of the bond is greater than its par value.

U.S. bond investors can choose from a wide variety of alternatives. Conventional bonds can most easily be described with three characteristics: interest-rate-risk sensitivity, creditworthiness, and tax status.[2] Interest-rate-risk sensitivity refers to the magnitude of price changes induced by movements in interest rates. As a first approximation, the maturity of a bond is a rough indicator of how sensitive its price will be to interest rate changes. All other things being equal, the longer the maturity, the more the bond price will fluctuate for a given interest rate movement.[3] The marketplace normally prices bonds with various maturities such that longer-maturity bonds with greater price sensitivity will have higher yields to maturity than shorter-maturity securities with more stable principal values. This market pricing gives rise to the normal upward-sloping yield curve, as shown in Exhibit 2.5. The yield curve plots the relationship between bond yields to maturity and corresponding maturities.

Exhibit 2.5
Nominal Yield Curve

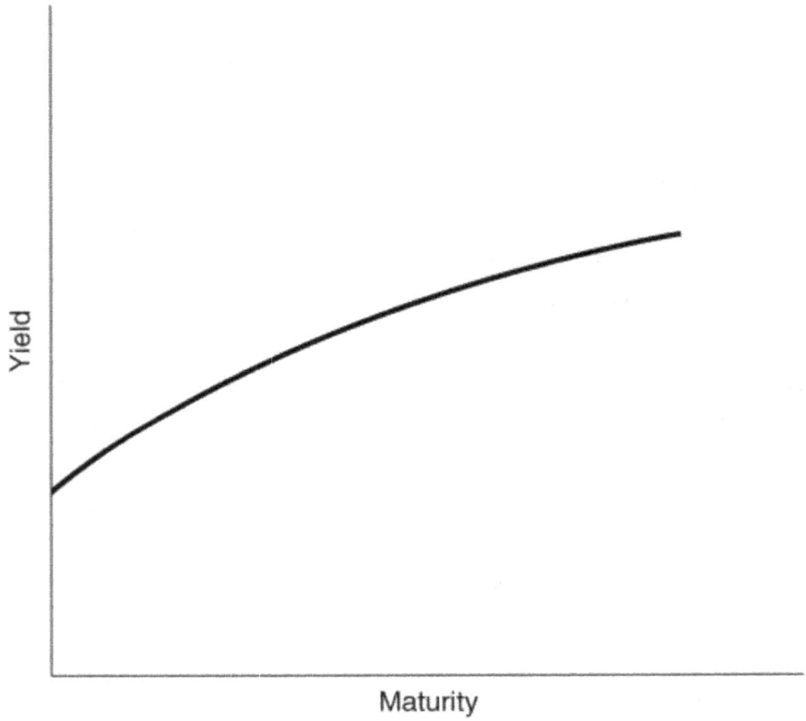

When we discussed the historical performance of Treasury bills, we commented that their returns tend to follow short-term movements in the inflation rate. Longer-term yields to maturity, however, are not as sensitive to changes in current inflation rates because the yield to maturity on a long-term bond reflects consensus expectations regarding inflation over the entire remaining life of the bond. As a result, the longer-maturity portion of the yield curve moves less as current inflation rates change. Interest-rate-risk sensitivity is an extremely important concept for a client to understand. It makes even U.S. government bonds risky and therefore is as important to consider as the creditworthiness of a bond.

The creditworthiness of a bond means the likelihood that payments of interest and return of principal will be made as promised. Direct U.S. government obligations, such as Treasury bills and Treasury bonds, are backed by the full faith and credit of the federal government and historically have been regarded as among the most creditworthy issues available. This high creditworthiness enabled the U.S. government to issue its debt obligations at lower interest rates than less-creditworthy borrowers. Corporate bonds have varying degrees of creditworthiness, and their yields to maturity vary accordingly, with the highest yields to maturity associated with those bonds that have the highest possibility of default.

The last characteristic concerns the tax status of the bond. Certain kinds of municipal bonds issued by local and state governments are free from federal income taxes and therefore can be issued at lower yields. Corporate and federal government bonds, however, generate interest income that is fully subject to federal income taxes. Investors in high tax brackets should consider municipal securities in addition to taxable obligations.

Let us now review the historical performance of long-term government bonds, intermediate-term government bonds, and long-term corporate bonds.

Long-Term Government Bonds

Long-term government bonds are direct obligations of the U.S. government and for most of the country's history were considered to be free of default risk. On August 5, 2011, however, Standard & Poor's downgraded the U.S. government's AAA sovereign credit rating on long-term U.S. debt to AA+. Standard & Poor's said that "political brinksmanship" in the debate over raising the debt ceiling made the U.S. government's ability to manage its finances "less stable, less effective, and less predictable." Standard & Poor's also stated that the bipartisan agreement reached earlier that week to find at least $2.1 trillion in budget savings over the following decade "fell short of what, in our view, would be necessary to stabilize the government's medium-term debt dynamics." At the time, despite Standard & Poor's downgrade of long-term U.S. debt, economic and political turmoil in Europe continued to drive investors toward U.S. Treasury bonds, thus preventing a possible increase in longer-term interest rates.

The following performance numbers are based on the construction of a portfolio containing one bond with a reasonably current coupon and a remaining term to maturity of approximately 20 years. Exhibit 2.1 traces the cumulative performance of a $1 investment in long-term government bonds as compared to other investment alternatives. Exhibit 2.6 shows the long-term government bonds' return indices for total returns versus capital appreciation only. The total return index shows the combined effect of bond price movements coupled with reinvestment of income. In measuring the total annual return from a government bond, the income earned from the bond is added to the change in the price of the bond before the resulting sum is divided by the value of the bond at the beginning of the period. The capital appreciation return is defined as the total return minus the bond's yield to maturity. The capital appreciation index accordingly reflects only bond price changes caused by interest rate movements. The only way an investor can be assured of receiving the current yield to maturity on a long-term government bond is by holding the bond until maturity. If the bond is sold prior to maturity, an intervening interest rate movement will produce a corresponding capital gain or capital loss, causing the investor's actual return to vary.

As we lengthen the time horizon over which we lend money to the government through the purchase of a long-term government bond, we leave behind the stable principal value characteristic of short-term Treasury bills. Interest rate risk now enters the equation. For bearing this risk, we expect to be compensated in the form of a higher yield to maturity on our invested dollar. In Exhibit 2.6, we see that $1 invested in long-term government bonds at the end of 1925 grew

Exhibit 2.6

Long-Term Government Bonds (Return Indices, Returns, and Yield to Maturity)

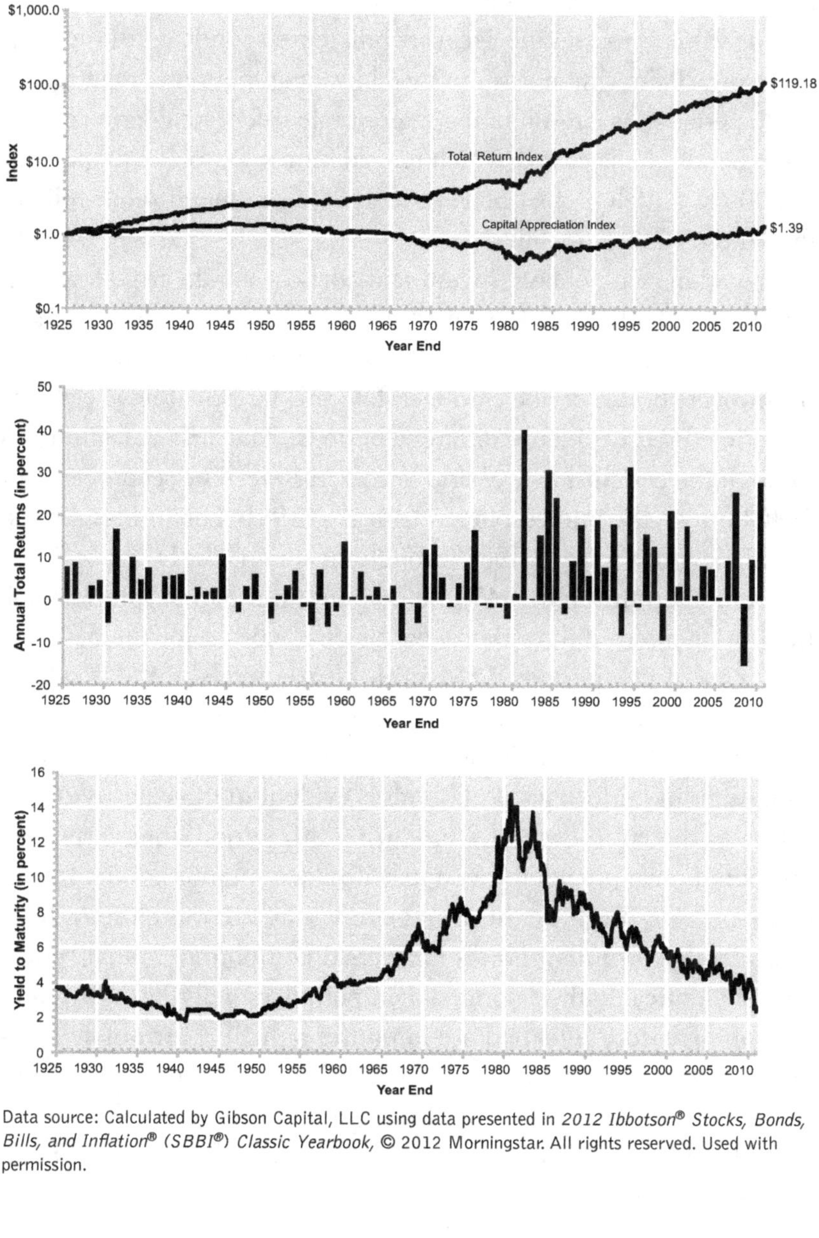

Data source: Calculated by Gibson Capital, LLC using data presented in *2012 Ibbotson® Stocks, Bonds, Bills, and Inflation® (SBBI®) Classic Yearbook,* © 2012 Morningstar. All rights reserved. Used with permission.

to be worth $119.18, with full reinvestment of income, by the end of 2011. The result is a compound annual return of 5.7 percent. This ending value surpasses the Treasury bills' corresponding 2011 ending value of $20.56, which was produced by a compound annual return of 3.6 percent. As a result of the interest rate risk of long-term government bonds, their returns, which ranged from a low of −14.9 percent in 2009 to a high of 40.4 percent in 1982, were much more volatile than those of Treasury bills.

In working with clients, investment advisors should avoid focusing too much attention on the relationships among long-term average returns without also discussing the variations in performance that occur over shorter periods. To facilitate this historical review, let us consider three decidedly different periods. The first is from 1926 through the conclusion of World War II in 1945. The second is from 1946 through the interest rate cycle peak of 1981. The third is the disinflationary period from 1982 through the end of 2011.

From 1926 through 1945, the compound inflation rate was less than 0.1 percent due to the deflation that existed for the first several years of this period. We see this clearly in Exhibit 2.2, which traces the CPI from its initial $1 value in 1926 down to its low of $0.73 in 1932 before rising again to just over $1 by the end of 1945. The superior performance of bonds is evident in their steady rise in value, as shown in Exhibit 2.6. During this period, long-term government bonds provided investors with a compound annual return of 4.7 percent. Because the average inflation rate was close to zero, long-term government bonds had a real compound annual return almost identical to their nominal compound annual return. By comparison, Treasury bills had a compound annual return of 1.1 percent. By the end of 1945, $1 invested in long-term government bonds with full reinvestment of income grew to be worth $2.51—more than twice as much as a $1 investment in Treasury bills that grew to be worth $1.24.

An examination of the bottom graph in Exhibit 2.6 shows that yields to maturity were relatively stable during this period and trended down within a relatively narrow range of 2 to 4 percent. The downward trend produced a corresponding appreciation in long-term government bond prices. This trend can be identified on the top graph in Exhibit 2.6, which shows the capital appreciation index reaching a maximum for the entire 86-year period of $1.42 by the end of 1945. The middle chart in Exhibit 2.6 shows the pattern of total annual returns and confirms the positive performance achieved during this period. With the notable exceptions of 1931 and 1933, when government bonds had total returns of −5.3 percent and −0.1 percent, respectively, total annual returns during these two decades were positive.

During the second period, which extends from the beginning of 1946 through the end of 1981, long-term government bonds experienced a prolonged bear market. Exhibit 2.2 shows that inflation increased sharply during a brief period following World War II, then leveled off for two decades before beginning its prolonged acceleration from the 1970s through the end of 1981. Over this period, the compound annual inflation rate was 4.7 percent. Short-term interest rates and Treasury bill returns lagged behind inflation during the first portion of this period as a result of the federal government's action in pegging interest rates at artificially low levels. Following deregulation of Treasury bill rates, however, Treasury bill returns closely mirrored the accelerating inflation and interest rate environments that characterized this period.

From 1946 through 1981, the bottom graph in Exhibit 2.6 shows a pattern of increasing yields to maturity pushed by an accelerating inflationary environment. The middle graph shows frequent occurrences of negative total annual returns during years when interest payments on the bond were not large enough to offset the bond's price loss for the year. Long-term government bonds' compound annual return with reinvestment of income for this period was 2 percent—less than half that of Treasury bills' compound annual return of 4.1 percent. Current yields obviously were much higher, indicating that the low total return was caused by a protracted capital loss.

Without the reinvestment of income, the investment experience of long-term government bondholders was devastating. The capital appreciation component of long-term government bonds' cumulative return had reached its peak of $1.42 at the end of 1945 and then declined to its 86-year low of $0.48 by the end of 1981. The decline resulted in a principal loss of nearly two-thirds, *before* considering the additional damage imposed by inflation. (Refer to the top graph in Exhibit 2.6.) The interest rate risk that worked for long-term government bondholders prior to 1946 worked against them from 1946 through the end of 1981.

A government bond's yield to maturity has three components: an inflation component, a real riskless interest rate, and a premium for bearing interest rate risk. A policy of consistently spending all three components is a prescription for long-term trouble. No period of history more clearly demonstrates the danger of buying supposedly safe long-term government bonds and spending the interest for living expenses than the period between 1946 and the end of 1981.

As Treasury bill returns peaked at a historical high of 14.7 percent in 1981, many investors swore that they would never again invest in long-term government bonds. These bonds failed to deliver the premium investors expected to receive for bearing interest rate risk. The deterioration in bond performance had been so dramatic by the end of 1981 that the post–1925 cumulative performance of Treasury bills actually surpassed that of long-term government bonds. Exhibit 2.1 shows where the inflation, Treasury bill, and long-term government bond indices converge at the end of 1981.

The final period begins in 1982, when inflation and interest rates both began to drop precipitously, producing huge gains in long-term government bond prices. The magnitude of these gains can be appreciated by examining the middle graph in Exhibit 2.6, which shows the pattern of total annual returns. During the 56-year period leading up to 1982, the total return on long-term government bonds exceeded 15 percent in only 2 years, 1932 and 1976. Then, in 1982, long-term government bonds produced a total return of 40.4 percent—the best return for the entire period from 1926 through 2011. The good news continued for long-term government bondholders, who enjoyed total annual returns in excess of 15 percent 12 more times by the end of 2011. During the period from 1982 through 2011, long-term government bonds had a spectacular compound annual return of 11.0 percent against the backdrop of a modest 3.0 percent compound annual inflation rate. Given the disinflationary environment, Treasury bill returns were declining as expected but were nevertheless high in real terms by historical standards.

A comparison of the performance of long-term government bonds for the first versus the second half of the decade ending with 1986 provides an interesting contrast of the good and bad aspects of interest rate risk, coupled with the impact of inflation. All long-term bond investors should sign statements indicating that they have seen and understand the information presented in Exhibit 2.7. In a changing interest rate environment, long-term fixed-income securities are definitely risky.

Over the whole 86-year period, long-term government bonds provided a compound annual return of 5.7 percent. This return is considerably ahead of Treasury bills and inflation, but it took the experience of several spectacular bond years since 1981 for these relative performance relationships to redevelop. We have seen that, during periods of deflation and disinflation, long-term government bonds provide excellent returns.

Exhibit 2.7
Comparative Bond Performance

	(A)	(B)	(C) = (A) – (B)
Five-Year Period	Long-Term Govt. Bond Compound Return	Compound Rate of Inflation	Long-Term Govt. Bond Compound Return Minus Compound Rate of Inflation
1977 through 1981	-1.1%	10.1%	-11.2%
1982 through 1986	21.6%	3.3%	18.3%

Data source: Calculated by Gibson Capital, LLC using data presented in *2012 Ibbotson® Stocks, Bonds, Bills, and Inflation® (SBBI®) Classic Yearbook,*

During periods of moderate inflation, returns are good provided that the inflation is anticipated. During periods of high inflation, however, long-term government bonds, as well as other long-term fixed-income securities, do poorly.

Intermediate-Term Government Bonds

The return indices, total annual returns, and yields to maturity for intermediate-term government bonds are shown in Exhibit 2.8. The data used for constructing this Exhibit describe the performance of a noncallable government bond with the shortest maturity of not less than five years. These bonds have less interest-rate-risk sensitivity than long-term government bonds because of their shorter maturities. The expectation, therefore, is that intermediate-term bonds should produce total returns less than those of long-term government bonds but more than those of Treasury bills. Exhibit 2.8 confirms this by showing that $1 invested in intermediate-term government bonds, with full reinvestment of income, grew to be worth $92.08 by the end of 2011. This growth corresponds to a compound annual return of 5.4 percent.

Although the upside potential of intermediate-term government bonds is less than that of long-term government bonds, the downside risk is also correspondingly smaller. For example, over the 86-year period from 1926 through 2011, intermediate-term government bonds had negative total returns in only 9 years, compared with 22 years of negative total returns for long-term government bonds. Against the backdrop of six interest rate hikes imposed by the Federal Reserve, 1994 was one of those loss years for both long-term and intermediate-term government bonds. Exhibit 2.9 graphically depicts the dramatic upward shift in the yield curve during 1994. The magnitude of these interest rate increases triggered a total return of −5.1 percent for intermediate-term government bonds—the largest annual loss for the 86-year period. For long-term government bonds, the 1994 loss of −7.8 percent was the fourth largest loss.

Not all Federal Reserve interest rate hikes trigger significant bond losses, however. For example, the Federal Reserve initiated 13

Exhibit 2.8

Intermediate-Term Government Bonds (Return Indices, Returns, and Yield to Maturity)

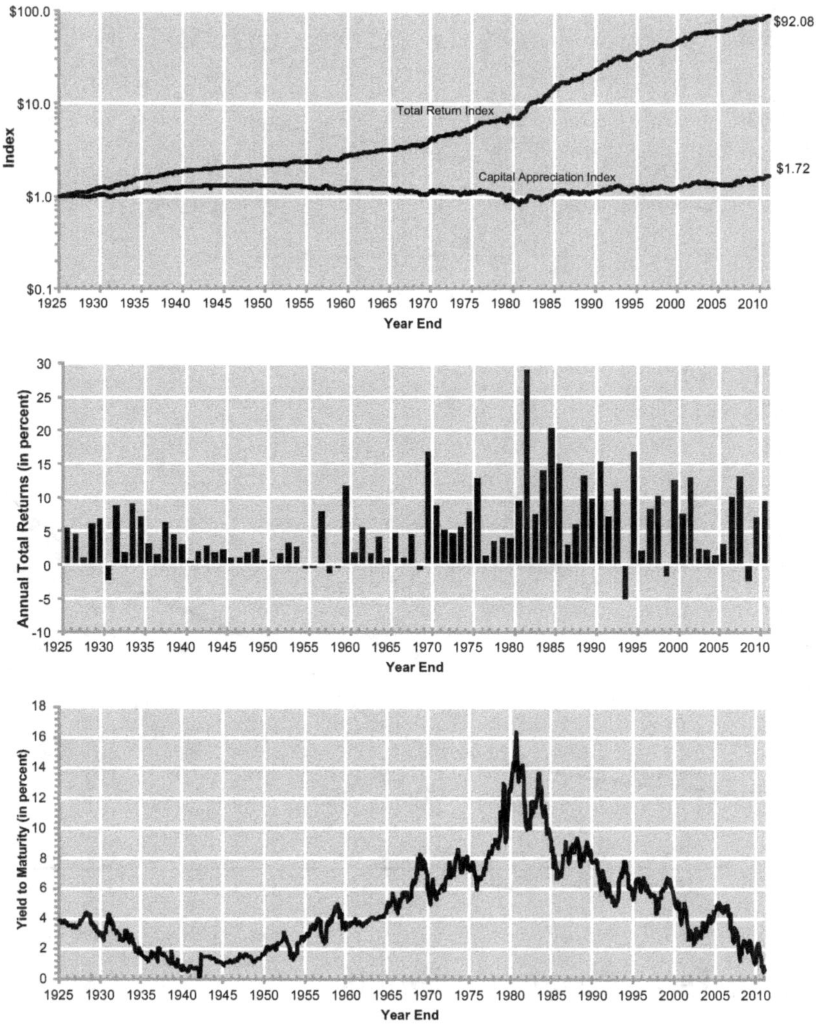

Data source: Calculated by Gibson Capital, LLC using data presented in *2012 Ibbotson® Stocks, Bonds, Bills, and Inflation® (SBBI®) Classic Yearbook*, © 2012 Morningstar. All rights reserved. Used with permission.

quarter-point interest rate increases between June 30, 2003, and December 31, 2005. Exhibit 2.10 shows the resulting yield curve shift. Shorter-term interest rates increased significantly, while 20-year rates were relatively unaffected.

Exhibit 2.9
Yield Curve Shift

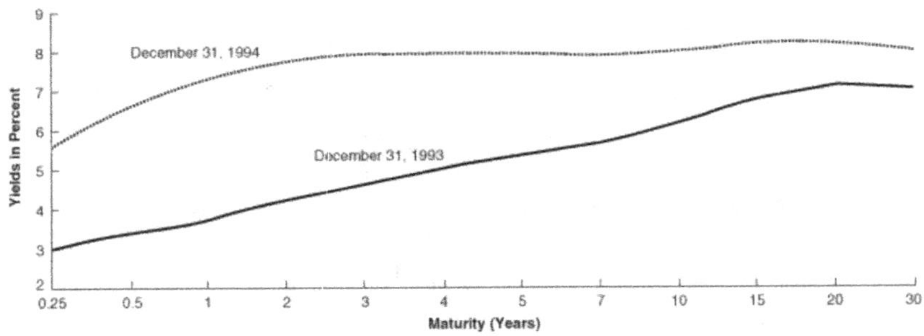

Exhibit 2.10
Yield Curve Shift

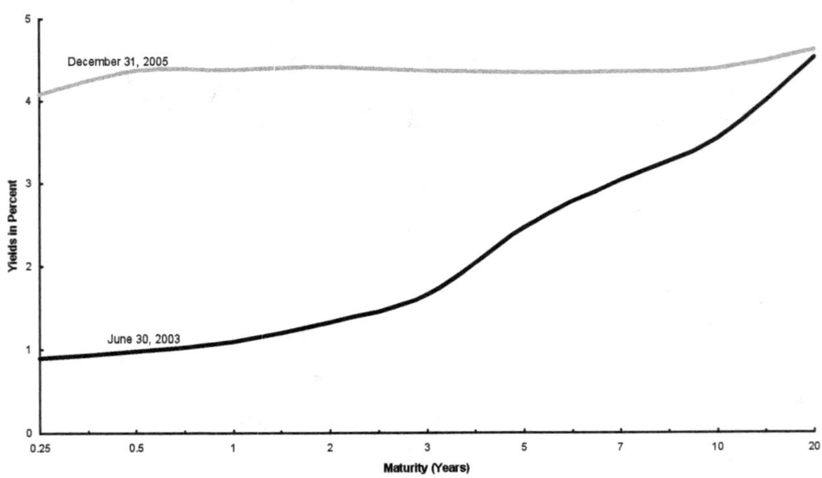

Long-Term Corporate Bonds

As with long-term government bonds, long-term corporate bonds have long maturities. They therefore are subject to interest rate risk, and investors deserve a corresponding horizon premium for bearing that risk. Long-term corporate bonds also carry credit risk. Investors lack complete certainty that all payments of interest and principal will be made as promised. If held to maturity, a government bond will provide an investor with a compound annual return equal to the bond's yield to maturity. But because corporate bonds have a possibility of default, an investor's probability-weighted compound return (adjusted for the likelihood of default) will be less than the yield to maturity. To compensate investors for bearing this credit risk, the return on corporate bonds, after adjustment for any defaults, should be in excess of the return available from higher-quality long-term government bonds. We will call this compensation the *default premium* and define it as the difference between the return on government bonds and the return on corporate bonds with similar maturity after any necessary adjustment for losses due to defaults.

Exhibit 2.11 shows the total return index, as well as the pattern of total annual returns, for long-term corporate bonds. The bonds used in compiling this data series are high-grade Aaa- and Aa-rated bonds with maturities of approximately 20 years. As with government bonds, total returns are equal to capital appreciation plus reinvested income. Based on the 86 years of data compiled by Ibbotson Associates, the default premium historically has been 0.4 percent compounded annually. We can approximate this default premium by subtracting the compound annual return of 5.7 percent for long-term government bonds from the 6.1 percent compound annual return produced by long-term corporate bonds.[4] This higher return from corporate bonds produced a 2011 ending value of $157.32 for an initial investment of $1 with reinvestment of income.

Corporate bonds vary widely in terms of their creditworthiness, with lower-quality bonds having higher expected returns than high-quality bonds. Returns on low-quality bonds are more volatile because of their greater sensitivity to movements in stock prices. Historically, medium- to lower-grade bonds have provided investors with higher net returns over time after adjustments for all capital losses.

Exhibit 2.11
Long-Term Corporate Bonds (Return Index and Returns)

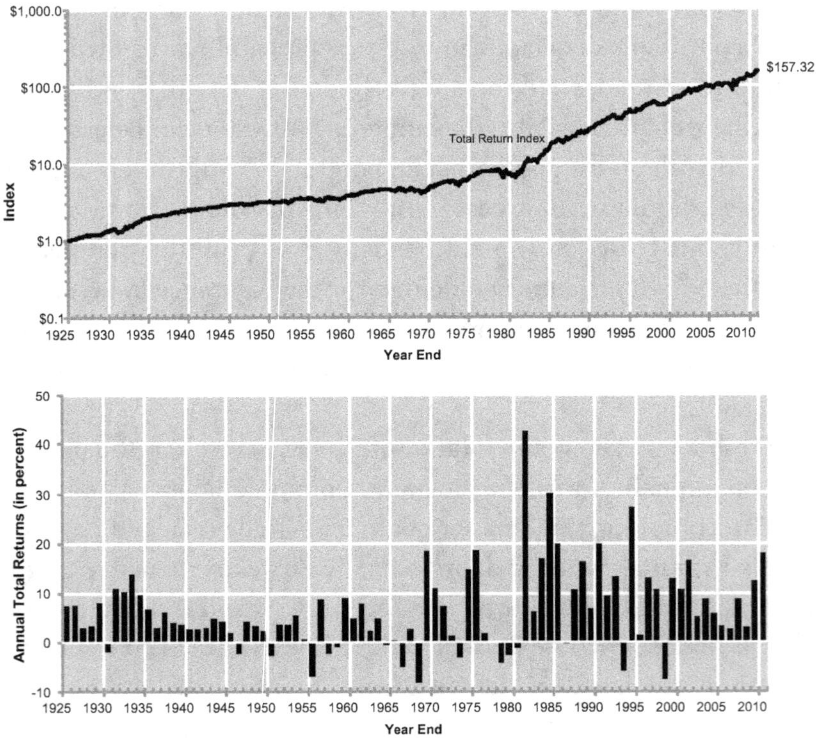

Data source: Calculated by Gibson Capital, LLC using data presented in *2012 Ibbotson® Stocks, Bonds, Bills, and Inflation® (SBBI®) Classic Yearbook*, © 2012 Morningstar. All rights reserved. Used with permission.

Large Company Stocks

Common stock represents ownership interest in a corporation. Investors who buy a share of common stock buy a piece of the company. Unlike fixed-income securities, common stocks have neither fixed maturity dates nor fixed schedules of promised payments. Out of its revenues, a corporation must first pay its expenses, including what it owes to bondholders and other creditors. A corporation's creditors therefore have greater certainty regarding their payment than do its shareholders, and common stocks are more risky than fixed-income securities. Because the bondholders and other creditors of a corporation have a prior claim to the corporation's revenues and assets, common stock shareholders are said to have a *residual ownership interest.*

The return to a shareholder takes the form of dividends and/or capital appreciation. Dividends are paid in accordance with the decisions of the board of directors, which is elected by the shareholders. The portion of earnings not paid out in dividends is available for reinvestment by the corporation and provides one source of financing for the future growth of the enterprise. Like any business owner, common stock shareholders share in both the upside potential and downside risk of the corporation. For assuming greater risk, common stock shareholders expect greater rewards over time. Stock market prices in general reflect investors' assessment of the state of the economy: The better the economic outlook for business, the higher the level of stock prices.

The large company stock performance numbers used for Exhibits 2.1 and 2.12 are based on the S&P 500 index which includes 500 blue chip, U.S. large company stocks. (Prior to March 1957 the index consisted of 90 stocks of the largest companies.) These stocks are those of leading companies in leading industries, and as a group they represent about 75 percent of the value of the total U.S. stock market as of December 31, 2011. An investment of $1 in large company stocks, with reinvestment of income, grew rapidly from the end of 1925 until it reached a value of $2.20 by the end of 1928. The stock market crash and Great Depression followed, taking stock prices down for the next 4 years. By the end of 1932, the total return index reached its 86-year low of $0.79. By comparison, government and corporate bonds were performing quite well.

By the end of 1944, large company stocks had made up their lost ground, with their total return index reaching $2.91, thereby surpassing the $2.82 total return index for the best-performing interest-generating alternative, long-term corporate bonds. From that point forward through the end of 2011, the total return index for large

Exhibit 2.12

Large Company Stocks (Return Indices and Returns)

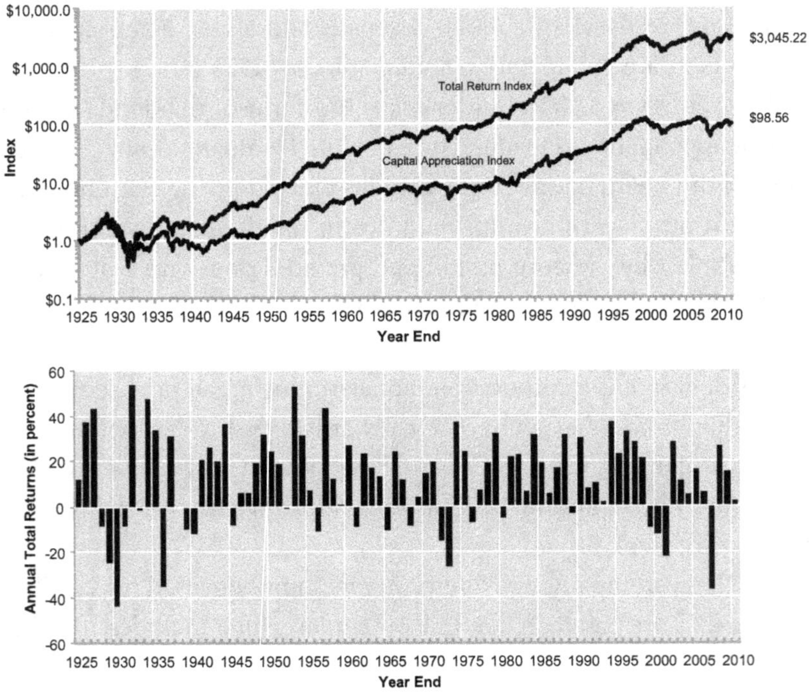

Data source: Calculated by Gibson Capital, LLC using data presented in *2012 Ibbotson® Stocks, Bonds, Bills, and Inflation® (SBBI®) Classic Yearbook*, © 2012 Morningstar. All rights reserved. Used with permission.

company stocks maintained its cumulative performance advantage over corporate bonds, government bonds, and Treasury bills. Although common stock bear markets periodically narrowed the lead, the long-term secular trend was one of an increasing performance advantage for common stocks.

Several years of this period are particularly noteworthy. The bull market, which began on August 12, 1982, produced a price-only cumulative advance of over 228 percent before peaking 5 years later on August 25, 1987. Although this advance was not the largest bull market advance on record, it was one of the most rapid prolonged gains. Measured from the trough to the peak, the total return on large company stocks was over 30 percent compounded annually. Another remarkable market event was just around the corner. On October 19, 1987, the stock market crashed. With prices falling more than 20 percent, it was the largest single-day decline on record. Although a dramatic loss, stock prices quickly recovered in the next bull market, which began on December 4, 1987. This bull market was by far both the longest in duration and largest in terms of advance in the last 100 years. By the time large company stocks peaked on March 24, 2000, the bull market had lasted over 12 years and produced a price-only cumulative gain of more than 582 percent. The extraordinary gains during this bull market were in part driven by investors' "irrational exuberance" that pushed stock prices to extremely high levels during the latter half of the 1990s.

The ensuing bear market lasted 30 months, during which the price/earnings ratio of large company stocks dropped significantly, accompanied by a market price decline of 49.15 percent before bottoming on October 9, 2002. Although the subsequent bull market took prices up 101.50 percent, the Global Financial Crisis of 2008 triggered another devastating large company stock price decline of 56.78 percent from October 9, 2007, to March 9, 2009. The decade of the 2000s has been called "the lost decade" because large company stocks generated a cumulative total return net loss of −9.1 percent. The timing was particularly bad for baby boomers entering their retirement years, many of whom had also seen the values of their homes drop during the financial crisis.[5]

At the end of 2011, the large company stock total return index had a value of $3,045.22, which was produced by an 86-year compound annual return of 9.8 percent. This performance completely dominates the compound annual returns of 6.1 percent, 5.7 percent, 5.4 percent, and 3.6 percent over the same period for long-term corporate bonds, long-term government bonds, intermediate-term government bonds, and U.S. Treasury bills, respectively.

The "miracle of compound interest" is quite apparent when one realizes that large company stocks had a compound annual return of only 6.2 percent in excess of Treasury bills, yet produced over 148 times the accumulated wealth during the 86-year period. The dramatic, superior long-term performance of large company stocks is matched by a correspondingly higher volatility in annual returns. This higher volatility is evident by a visual comparison of the total return indices for large company stocks versus Treasury bills in Exhibit 2.1. The bottom graph in Exhibit 2.12 also highlights this volatility by showing large company stocks' year-by-year pattern of total annual returns.

When we examined the historical performance of corporate bonds, government bonds, and Treasury bills, we saw that these investment alternatives could outpace inflation only by reinvesting their income returns. This was not true, however, of large company stocks. Exhibit 2.12 shows that the capital appreciation return index had a 2011 ending value of \$98.56, which is nearly eight times the \$12.59 CPI ending value. Thus, even if the dividend yield had been spent for living expenses, large company stocks' capital appreciation on average would have stayed ahead of inflation. In this sense, it is reasonable to consider large company stocks to be a long-term inflation-indexed investment. This is not surprising, given the long-term real growth of the U.S. economy.

For example, imagine a hypothetical economy with an annual inflation rate of 3.5 percent that results in a doubling of the prices of goods and services over the next two decades. If we presume that the corporations producing these goods and services maintain the same level of production over the next two decades and have the same profit margins and price/earnings ratios for their common stocks then as now, then corporate earnings, dividends, and share prices will likewise double, even if all earnings are paid out as dividends.

As with bonds, anticipated inflation is priced into the expected return of common stocks. But with common stocks our performance expectations are different. We expect a broadly diversified common stock portfolio to maintain its purchasing power (i.e., keep up with inflation) while simultaneously generating a stream of dividends, which may start out at a modest level but can likewise grow to maintain its purchasing power on average over time. By contrast, bonds promise only the return of principal in nominal terms, with a fixed-income return that is initially higher than the average dividend yield available from common stocks but that is fixed as to its upper limit. In essence, with bonds' other promises, you also have the assurance that your principal will lose to inflation.[6]

Historically, common stocks do much better in a low-inflationary environment in which consumer prices are relatively stable. They have performed poorly during periods of either deflation or high inflation. It is the *unanticipated* inflation that has been especially harmful to common stock performance—particularly in the short run. Over longer periods, corporations can make adjustments to inflation, but in the short run these adjustments are more difficult to accomplish. It is logical to project that, barring a catastrophic economic event, common stocks as an investment vehicle will provide a good alternative for the long-term preservation and enhancement of purchasing power.

Small Company Stocks

Exhibit 2.1 shows the long-term superior performance of small company stocks relative to all other investment alternatives that we have discussed thus far. The stocks used to compile this wealth index are those comprising the fifth (smallest) quintile of the New York Stock Exchange and similarly sized companies that trade on the American Stock Exchange and NASDAQ National Market System. The sizes of these stocks are measured by their market capitalization (market price times the number of shares outstanding).[7] An investment of $1 in small company stocks at the end of 1925 grew to be worth $15,532.07 with full reinvestment of income by the end of 2011. This growth represents a compound annual return of 11.9 percent, compared with the next best result of 9.8 percent achieved by large company stocks. We will call the 2.1 percent difference between small and large company stock performance the *small stock premium.*

The superior performance of small company stocks has several possible explanations. A comparison of the patterns of total annual returns, as shown on the bottom graph of Exhibit 2.13, reveals more volatility than is demonstrated by large company stock returns. An increased return for small company stocks is consistent with their higher volatility. Also, small company stocks tend to have higher betas, making them more susceptible to overall stock market movements and thereby again justifying higher returns. Finally, one could argue that large companies may tend to be in more mature businesses, with their periods of rapid growth behind and not ahead of them.

Exhibit 2.13
Small Company Stocks (Return Index and Returns)

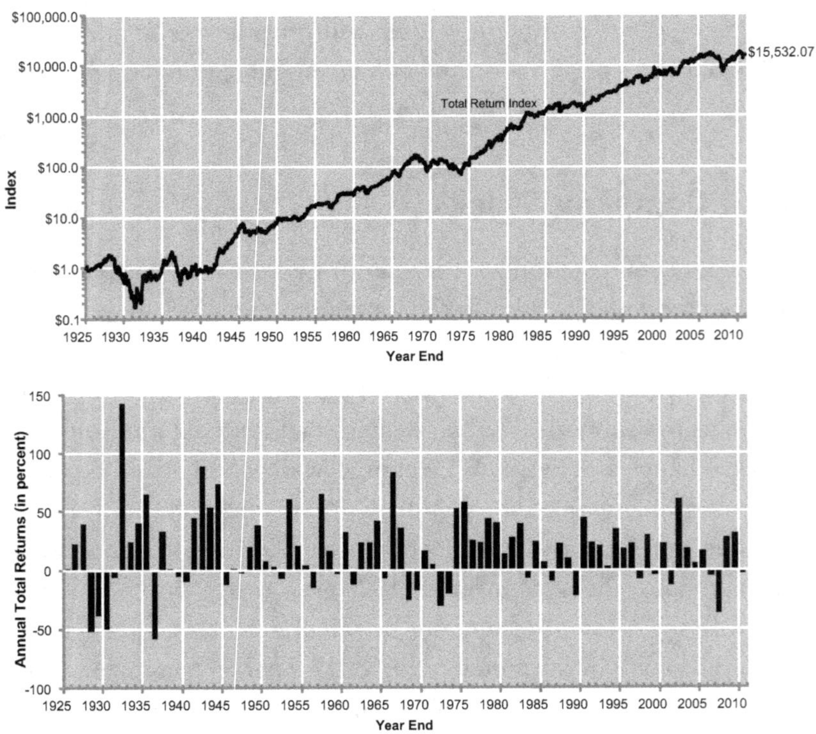

Data source: Calculated by Gibson Capital, LLC using data presented in *2012 Ibbotson® Stocks, Bonds, Bills, and Inflation® (SBBI®) Classic Yearbook*, © 2012 Morningstar. All rights reserved. Used with permission.

Appendix: Bond Duration

Maturity is not the preferred measure of interest-rate-risk sensitivity because it considers only the timing of repayment of principal upon maturity. Maturity accordingly ignores the timing and magnitude of interest payments made in the interim. Because a major portion of the present value of a bond may be attributed to the interest payments, a better measure would take these payments into consideration as well. A bond's *duration* is a measurement that accomplishes this. Duration is calculated as the weighted average of the lengths of time prior to receipt of interest payments and return of principal, where each payment's weight is determined by dividing its present value by the current market value of the bond. In short, it is the present-value weighted-average time that the bondholder has money owed to her.

Exhibit 2.14 shows the calculation of duration for a 5 percent coupon bond priced to provide a 4 percent yield to maturity. The

Exhibit 2.14
Calculation of Bond Duration

Par Value	$10,000
Coupon Rate	5%
Interest Payments	$500 annually
Years to Maturity	7
Current Market Value of Bond	$10,599
Yield to Maturity	4%

(1) Years From Now	(2) Payment	(3) Present Value of Payment at 4%	(4) Present Value of Payment as a Percentage of the Bond's Current Market Value	(5) Column (1) Times Column (4)
1	$ 500 I	$ 481	.045	.045
2	500 I	462	.044	.087
3	500 I	444	.042	.126
4	500 I	427	.040	.161
5	500 I	411	.039	.194
6	500 I	395	.037	.224
7	500 I	380	.036	.251
	10,000 P	7,599	.717	5.019
		$ 10,599	1.000	Duration = 6.107

I = Interest

P = Principal

duration of 6.107 years is less than the 7-year maturity because of the consideration given to the interim interest payments. Had we calculated the duration of a 7-year-maturity zero-coupon bond, we would have given 100 percent of the weighting to the single-payment return of principal at maturity, and accordingly the duration would have been equal to the maturity of 7 years.

Because duration is a better indicator of interest-rate-risk sensitivity, a group of bonds with the same duration but varying maturities will respond similarly to a given interest rate movement, whereas a different group of bonds with the same maturity but different durations will have varying price sensitivities. Duration most accurately reflects interest-rate-risk sensitivity for bonds whose prices are close to par. For example, for a bond with a 6-year duration, a 6 percent yield, and a market value equal to par, a 50 basis point decrease in the yield to 5.5 percent would cause the price of the bond to increase by approximately 6 times 50 basis points, or 3 percent, to $10,300.

Chapter 3

Comparative Relationships Among U.S. Capital Market Investments Alternatives

The best way to suppose what may come is to remember what is passed.

—*George Savile, Marquess of Halifax (1633–1695),* Political, Moral and Miscellaneous Reflections, *1750*

In this chapter, we will review the historical rewards for bearing different forms of risk: inflation, interest rate risk, credit risk, equity risk, and small company risk. The incremental returns earned for bearing these risks are called risk premiums. We will use these risk premiums as components of simple models to estimate the future long-term compound annual returns[1] for the U.S. capital market investment alternatives discussed in Chapter 2. Exhibit 3.1 summarizes the historical return and volatility statistics for these investments. For example, from 1926 through 2011, Treasury bills had a compound annual return of 3.6 percent, which is 0.6 percent more than the corresponding compound annual

Exhibit 3.1
Summary Statistics of Annual Total Returns (1926–2011)

	Compound Annual Return %	Simple Average Return %	Standard Deviation (Volatility) %	Serial Correlation
Inflation	3.0	3.1	4.2	0.64
Interest-Generating Investments:				
U.S. Treasury Bills	3.6	3.6	3.1	0.91
Intermediate-Term Gov't. Bonds	5.4	5.5	5.7	0.13
Long-Term Government Bonds	5.7	6.1	9.8	-0.11
Long-Term Corporate Bonds	6.1	6.4	8.4	0.08
Equity Investments:				
Large Company Stocks	9.8	11.8	20.3	0.02
Small Company Stocks	11.9	16.5	32.5	0.06

Data Source: Formatted by Gibson Capital, LLC using data presented in *2012 Ibbotson® Stocks, Bonds, Bills, and Inflation® (SBBI®) Classic Yearbook,* © 2012 Morningstar. All rights reserved. Used with permission.

inflation rate of 3.0 percent. Some researchers have concluded on this basis that the real (i.e., inflation-adjusted) riskless interest rate is therefore 0.6 percent.

The interest rate risk associated with long-term government bonds deserves compensation in the form of a higher yield than that available from Treasury bills. The incremental return for bearing interest rate risk is commonly referred to as the *horizon premium*. Historically, long-term government bonds have had a compound annual return of 5.7 percent, compared with the 3.6 percent compound annual return produced by Treasury bills. The difference is the historical compound annual horizon premium of 2.1 percent.

The pricing mechanism of the marketplace builds into the bond's yield compensation for the risks associated with the *anticipated* inflation rate and level of bond price volatility. Although investors expect that their bond portfolios will fluctuate in principal value, they do not expect long-term cumulative changes in the principal value of their bond portfolios. When modeling future bond returns based on historical data, it is important to examine whether any cumulative capital appreciation or loss has occurred in the data series. In this situation, the estimated horizon-premium must be adjusted for the bond portfolio's *unanticipated* gain or loss. If a cumulative capital gain has occurred, a downward adjustment is required to offset the effect of the unanticipated capital appreciation. If a cumulative capital loss has occurred, the estimated horizon premium should be adjusted upward. In the last chapter, the top graph in Exhibit 2.6 shows that long-term government bonds had a cumulative gain in the capital appreciation index from 1926 through 2011. This appreciation corresponds to a compound annual gain of 0.4 percent. For this reason, the historical compound annual horizon premium of 2.1 percent is higher than what would have been expected had bonds preserved their nominal values. An expected horizon premium can be inferred from the historical data by adjusting for long-term government bonds' appreciation in principal value. This adjustment indicates an expected horizon premium of 1.7 percent computed as follows:

5.7%	Compound annual return from long-term government bonds
− 3.6%	Minus the compound annual return from Treasury bills
2.1%	Historical compound annual horizon premium
− 0.4%	Minus an adjustment for the compound annual gain in principal value
1.7%	Estimated horizon premium

On this basis, it is reasonable to project that, on average, Treasury bills will provide a compound annual return of 0.6 percent in excess of the inflation rate, while long-term government bonds will have a compound annual return of 1.7 percent in excess of the current Treasury bill yield. We can now specify a model for the estimated compound annual return on long-term government bonds:

X%	Treasury bill yield
+ 1.7%	Plus horizon premium
(X + 1.7%)	Future compound annual return on long-term government bonds

Corporate bonds have higher yields than government bonds in order to compensate investors for the risk of possible default of payment of interest and/or principal. If we presume that the default premium will be the same in the future as it has been historically, our model for the estimated compound annual return on long-term corporate bonds is:

X%	Treasury bill yield
+ 1.7%	Plus horizon premium
(X + 1.7%)	Future compound annual return on long-term government bonds
+ 0.4%	Plus default premium
(X + 2.1%)	Future compound annual return on long-term corporate bonds

Over the period from 1926 through 2011, large company stocks had a compound annual return of 9.8 percent. At the beginning of 1926, large company stocks had a price/earnings ratio of 10.2. At the end of 2011, the price/earnings ratio was 14.0. This expansion of the price/earnings ratio accounts for 0.4 percent of large company stocks' 9.8 percent compound annual return. The expansion of the price/earnings ratio, however, is unrelated to the underlying economic growth of large companies. Rather it is simply a change in the price that investors are willing to pay for a dollar's worth of corporate earnings. Had there been no change in the price/earnings ratio, large company stocks would have had an 86-year compound annual return of 9.4 percent (i.e., 9.8 percent minus 0.4 percent).

As there is no reason to believe that the price/earnings ratio will continue to expand, our estimate of future returns for large company stocks will be based on the adjusted compound annual return of 9.4 percent. This return is 5.8 percent higher than the compound annual return of 3.6 percent from Treasury bills. The difference between the adjusted return from large company stocks and the return from Treasury bills is called the *equity risk premium.*[2] If we assume that the volatility inherent in large company stocks will not be materially different in the future than it has been in the past, and if we further assume that the market will price large company stocks such that the compensation for bearing that volatility will be the same in the future as it has been historically, then 5.8 percent will be a reasonable estimate of the equity risk premium in the future. We can thus build a simple model for the estimated compound annual return for large company stocks:

X%	Treasury bill yield
+ 5.8%	Plus equity risk premium
(X + 5.8%)	Future compound annual return on large company stocks

Finally, with the assumption that the historical small company stock premium is a good estimate of the future small company stock premium, our model for the estimated compound annual return on small company stocks is:

X%	Treasury bill yield
+ 5.8%	Plus equity risk premium
(X + 5.8%)	Future compound annual return on large company stocks
+ 2.1%	Plus small stock premium
(X + 7.9%)	Future compound annual return on small company stocks

It is important to emphasize that these models are based on long-term, historical relationships among the investment alternatives. Accordingly, the models represent averages of many distinctly different subperiods during which actual results were very different from what would be indicated by these models. For example, Exhibit 3.2 illustrates how the equity risk premium has varied during the past 86 years. Each point on the graph indicates the difference between the compound

Exhibit 3.2
Equity Risk Premium (1926–2011)

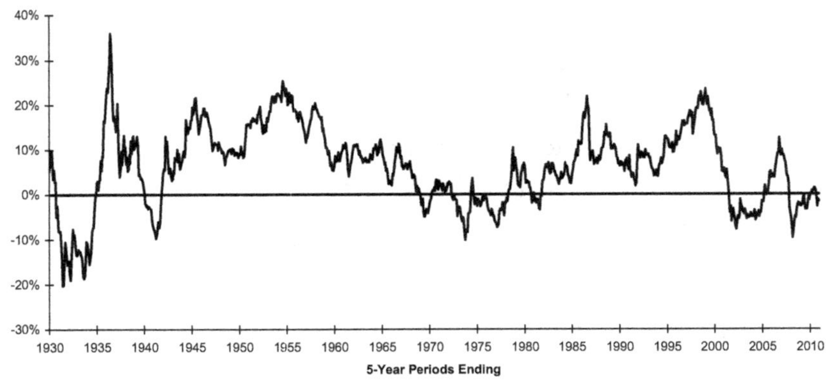

Data Source: Formatted by Gibson Capital, LLC using data presented in *2012 Ibbotson® Stocks, Bonds, Bills, and Inflation® (SBBI®) Classic Yearbook,*

annual return for large company stocks and the compound annual return for Treasury bills for the preceding 5-year period. The variability is quite apparent and serves as a strong reminder that these models provide only historically based, single-point estimates of future security returns. A better description of future performance would incorporate a description of a probabilistic range of outcomes. It is important to share this uncertainty in returns with clients in order to provide them with a context for evaluating subsequent investment performance.

The relationships described in these models are an important part of the foundation for developing the client's understanding of investment risk and return. They also provide valuable benchmarks that can help clients develop more realistic expectations regarding future investment performance.

Summary Comparisons and Implications

Clients often misperceive the risks they face in the investment of their money. If these misperceptions remain uncorrected, these clients very likely will make portfolio decisions that are not in their best interests. This highlights the value of providing to the client a detailed historical review of the capital markets. A client who fully understands inflation risk, interest rate risk, credit risk, and equity risk is in a much better position to make intelligent investment decisions appropriate for his financial goals.

Exhibit 3.1 provides an excellent summary of the comparative performance of the major investment alternatives we have reviewed.[3] By comparing the compound annual returns for the various investment alternatives, it is obvious that, over the long term, equity investments such as common stocks have had better returns than bonds, which in turn have outperformed Treasury bills. Correspondingly, we can see by comparing their respective standard deviations that the higher returns from equity investments have been obtained at the price of much greater volatility.

In comparing the returns of these investment alternatives, clients often are surprised by the impact that small, incremental returns have had on wealth accumulation. For example, Treasury bills, with a compound annual return of 3.6 percent, resulted in the growth of a $1 investment to $20.56 by the end of 2011. By contrast, large company stocks had a compound annual return of only 6.2 percent more, and yet the initial $1 investment grew to $3,045.22 over the same period. Similarly, small company stocks had an incremental compound annual return of only 2.1 percent in excess of the compound annual return of large company stocks, and yet this small additional return produced an astounding value of $15,532.07 by the end of 2011. These examples demonstrate the "miracle of compound interest."

Compared to these relatively modest incremental differences in compound annual returns, the standard deviations of returns among the various investment alternatives differ widely. For example, Exhibit 3.1 shows that Treasury bills not only had the lowest historical compound annual return but also had the lowest standard deviation. The historical variability of returns for Treasury bills, however, should not be interpreted as a short-run measure of uncertainty in return for two reasons: First, average Treasury bill returns had a multiple-decade upward trend from the late 1930s until their peak in 1981 and then trended downward over the following three decades. These long upward and downward secular movements in Treasury bill returns produced higher deviations around the long-term average than would be true around the average for a shorter period of time. In this sense, the long-term standard deviation of Treasury bills overstates their historical short-run volatility. Second, it is possible to completely eliminate the short-run uncertainty in return by purchasing a one-year maturity Treasury bill and thereby lock in the return. For these reasons, it is inappropriate to consider Treasury bills' long-term standard deviation as an indicator of short-run volatility.

Although the wide range of standard deviation numbers shown in Exhibit 3.1 provides a good comparison of relative volatility, a visual comparison is much more striking. Exhibits 3.3A and 3.3B show the patterns of annual total returns for the various investment alternatives compared directly with each other on a series of graphs with a common vertical scale. This method of presentation gives the client a much better sense of relative volatility.

The annual total returns for large company stocks can be divided into two components: income and capital appreciation. If we measured the standard deviation of each component, we would find that the capital appreciation component has a standard deviation of 19.6 percent compared with a much smaller standard deviation of only 1.6 percent for the income component. The variability of return associated with large company stocks therefore is attributable almost entirely to stock price movements, with a relatively stable dividend income component.

One possible explanation for large company stocks' stable income lies in the manner in which dividend policy is established for most corporations. A corporation's earnings will fluctuate from year to year. Rather than pay a dividend that fluctuates with earnings, however, corporations seek to set dividends at a rate that comfortably can be paid out of earnings through both good and bad years. Corporations do not want to cut a dividend unless it is absolutely necessary, and they generally raise dividends only when they are confident that a relatively permanent improvement in earnings justifies a higher payout.[4] This practice leads to a relatively stable and gradually increasing pattern of dividend payouts.

Exhibit 3.3A

Annual Total Returns in Percent (1926–2011)

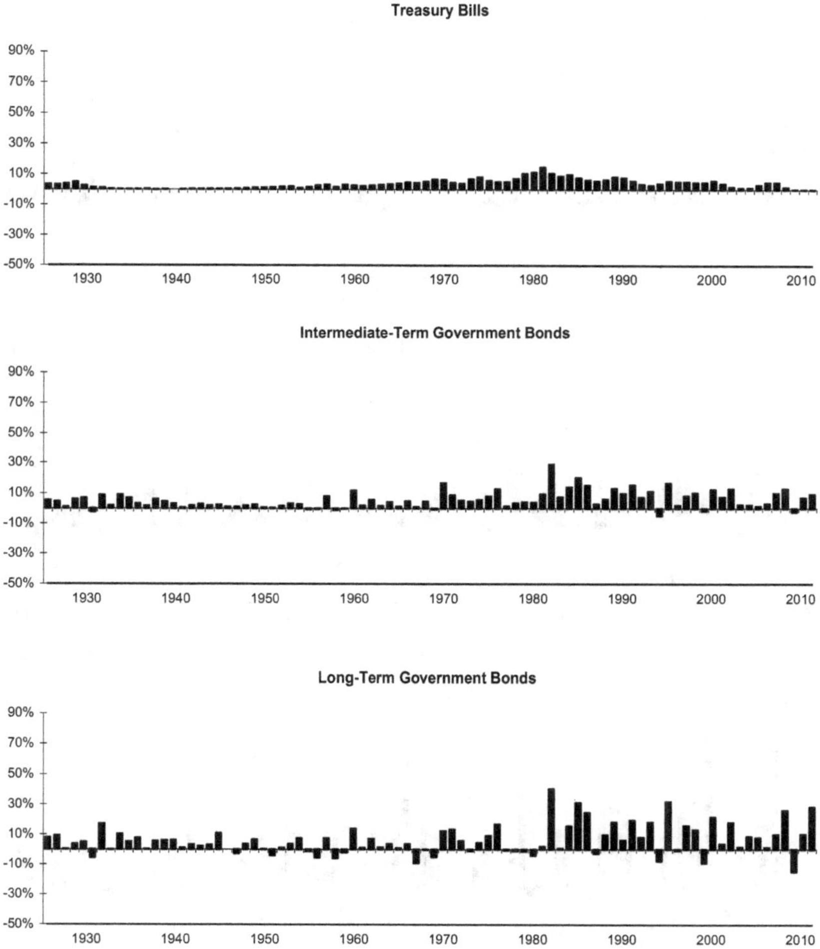

Data Source: Formatted by Gibson Capital, LLC using data presented in *2012 Ibbotson® Stocks, Bonds, Bills, and Inflation® (SBBI®) Classic Yearbook,* © 2012 Morningstar. All rights reserved. Used with permission.

The capital appreciation component for large company stock returns has a compound annual return of 5.5 percent. This return is just 0.6 percent less than the *total* return of the best-performing interest-generating alternative—long-term corporate bonds. In essence, a broadly diversified common stock investor historically has had long-term capital appreciation sufficient to not only maintain but also

Exhibit 3.3B
Annual Total Returns in Percent (1926–2011)

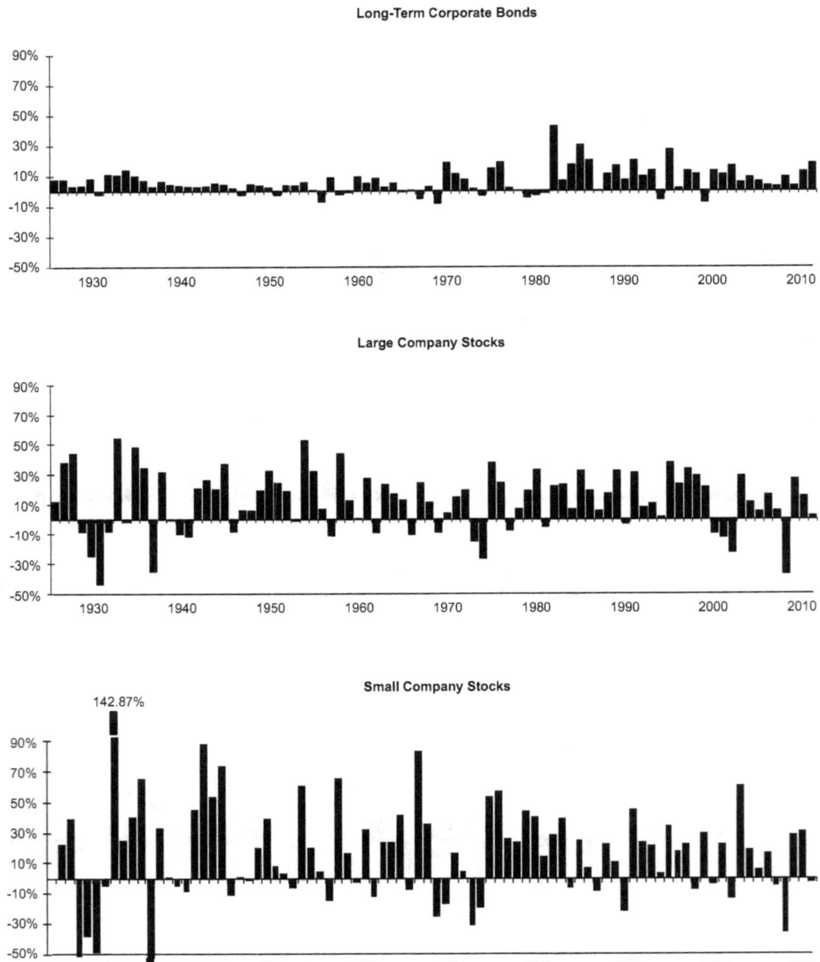

Data Source: Formatted by Gibson Capital, LLC using data presented in *2012 Ibbotson® Stocks, Bonds, Bills, and Inflation® (SBBI®) Classic Yearbook,* © 2012 Morningstar. All rights reserved. Used with permission.

enhance her purchasing power. This leaves the dividend stream available for consumption. Because the value of a broadly diversified common stock portfolio can keep up with inflation *on average over time,* so will its dividend stream. Emphasis is on the phrase *on average over time,* because in the short run the much higher volatility of common stocks produces great uncertainty in annual total returns. Therefore, short-term and intermediate-term results may diverge substantially from the average relationships indicated by examining performance over very long periods.

The capacity of a common stock portfolio to produce a relatively stable, growing dividend stream is important for an investor who wants to keep up with inflation. Had the 54-year-old woman previously described in Exhibit 2.4 allocated a portion of her money to common stocks, her portfolio would not have been so susceptible to the devastating impact of inflation.

When reviewing the information in Exhibit 3.1 with clients, it is important to emphasize that the return numbers should be evaluated in terms of their spreads relative to each other. For example, in comparing the 3.6 percent compound annual return of Treasury bills with the 9.8 percent compound annual return of large company stocks, the relationship is best described in terms of the 6.2 percent spread between the two. Occasionally, the relationship is erroneously considered multiplicatively. That is, it is misleading to think of large company stocks' 9.8 percent compound annual return as being 2.7 times that of Treasury bills' 3.6 percent compound annual return. (A review of the security return models we developed for each of the investment alternatives shows the relationships in terms of arithmetic differences or spreads.)

A similar problem involves looking at the returns outside their historical context. During the late 1970s and early 1980s, interest rates were at double-digit levels. At that time, clients often asked, "Why should I invest in risky common stocks for a compound annual return of 10 percent, when I can safely get 12 percent by investing in Treasury bills?" Again, explaining that the long-term 9.8 percent compound annual return of large company stocks corresponds to a compound annual return of only 3.6 percent for Treasury bills over the same multiple-decade period can clear up this misconception.

The last column in Exhibit 3.1 specifies *serial correlations.* This statistic describes the extent to which the return in one period is helpful in predicting the return in the following period. A series of returns with a serial correlation near 1.0, for example, would be highly predictable from one period to the next and indicative of a trend. If the serial correlation is near −1.0, the series is highly cyclical. If the serial correlation is near 0, then the series has no predictable pattern and is described as a *random walk*. The high serial correlations for inflation and U.S. Treasury bills indicate that each follows a trend from year to year. By contrast, large company stocks' highly volatile pattern of total returns closely resembles a random walk, as evidenced by a serial correlation that is near zero.

Although not shown in Exhibit 3.1, the serial correlation for the small stock premium is 0.36, which suggests that it tends to follow a trend. A review of the historical comparative performance of large company stocks versus small company stocks confirms that often one of these investment alternatives tends to outperform the other for multiple-year periods.

Appendix: Statistical Concepts

Compound Annual Return Versus Simple Average Return

The first column of data in Exhibit 3.1 displays the *compound annual return* for each of the investment alternatives listed. The second column displays the *simple average return* for each. An example will illustrate the difference. Assume we invest $100 in a stock that during the first year increases in value to $125, for a total return of +25 percent. During the second year, the stock has a total return of −20 percent, decreasing in value from $125 to the original $100. The simple average return of these two annual returns is their sum divided by 2:

25%	Year 1 return
+ −20%	Plus year 2 return
5%	
÷ 2	Number of years
2.5%	Simple average return

The compound annual return, however, is 0 percent—that is, a $100 investment that is worth $100 two years later has a compound annual return of 0 percent. For any series of returns, the simple average return always will be greater than or equal to the compound annual return. The difference between the simple average return and compound annual return is larger for highly volatile returns. Only in the situation where the annual returns are constant will the simple average return and compound annual return be equal. The disparity between these two measures arises from the fact that it requires a larger percentage of above-average performance to offset a given percentage of below-average performance.

The simple average return is the appropriate measure of typical performance for a single period. The compound annual return is more appropriate when comparing returns over multiple periods, as it represents the growth rate for an investment that is continually compounded. Often, models that describe the expected returns for various investment alternatives are single-period models, which accordingly utilize simple average returns.[5] Because the purpose of this chapter is to develop a framework for establishing long-term (i.e., multiple-period) investment policies, the comparison of relative historical performance and models of future investment returns will utilize compound annual returns.

Risk Premiums and Inflation-Adjusted Returns

Throughout this book, in order to derive a risk premium or inflation-adjusted return, the compound annual return of one investment alternative is *arithmetically* subtracted from another, or from inflation. For example, the compound annual return of 5.7 percent for long-term government bonds is subtracted from the compound annual return of 6.1 percent for long-term corporate bonds to derive the historical default premium of 0.4 percent. Ibbotson Associates, a wholly owned subsidiary of Morningstar, Inc., which provided the historical data on

Treasury bills, bonds, and stock returns used in Chapters 2 and 3 of this book, prefers to state risk premiums and inflation-adjusted returns as the geometric difference between various return series. For example, the geometric difference between 4 and 10 percent is not 6 percent but 5.8 percent, computed as follows:

$$\frac{1.10}{1.04} - 1 = 0.058 = 5.8\%$$

The models developed in this book are to be used to provide a *conceptual* understanding of investment performance for both advisor and client. For this reason, when developing models, the arithmetic difference rather than the geometric difference is used in order to be consistent with the way a client typically thinks. (Most people think of the difference between 4 and 10 percent as being 6 percent, not 5.8 percent.) This simpler approach does not impair the conceptual value of the model and avoids the problem of getting sidetracked in explanations of geometric versus arithmetic differences.

Expected Return and Standard Deviation

The *expected return* of an investment is calculated as the weighted average of its possible returns, where the weight for each return is its corresponding probability. Thus, this single statistic incorporates both the value of each outcome and its probability of occurrence.

For example, Exhibit 3.4 describes an investment in common stock XYZ that, depending on three alternative economic scenarios, will have a return of either −5 percent, 10 percent, or 25 percent. We can express the probability of each economic scenario in decimal form. For example, the first scenario has a 25 percent likelihood of occurrence and is therefore assigned a probability of 0.25. Exhibit 3.5 shows the mathematics for calculating the 10.75 percent expected return from an investment in common stock XYZ.

Exhibit 3.4
Probability of Various Returns from an Investment in Common Stock XYZ

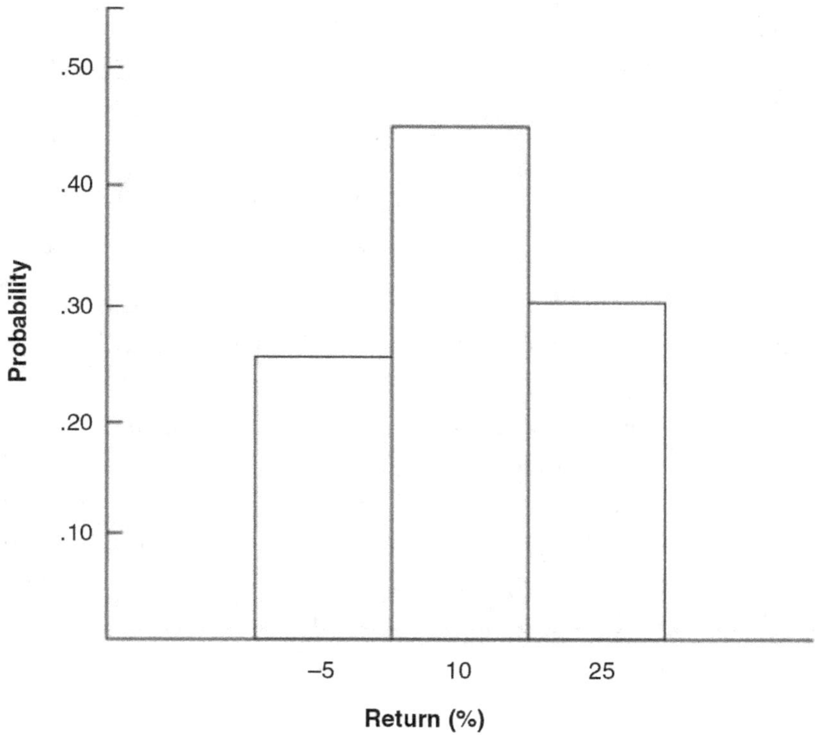

Exhibit 3.5
Calculating the Expected Return of Common Stock XYZ

(1)	(2)	(3)	(4) = (2) X (3)
Economic Scenario	**Probability of Occurrence**	**Return**	**Calculation of Expected Return**
1	0.25	-5%	-1.25%
2	0.45	10%	4.50%
3	0.30	25%	7.50%
	1.00		Expected Return = 10.75%

Different investments vary in terms of their expected returns, but an investment's expected return is only one aspect of future performance. It is equally important to simultaneously consider the volatility of an investment's returns. The more widely an investment's returns

Exhibit 3.6
Calculating the Standard Deviation of Returns for Common Stock XYZ

(1)	(2)	(3)	(4) = (3) – 10.75%	(5) = (4)^2	(6) = (2) X (5)
Economic Scenario	Probability of Occurrence	Return	Deviation	Deviation Squared	Probability Times Deviation Squared
1	0.25	-5%	-15.75%	248.06	62.02
2	0.45	10%	-0.75%	0.56	0.25
3	0.30	25%	14.25%	203.06	60.92
				Variance =	123.19
			Standard deviation = Square root of variance =		11.10

vary from its expected return, the more volatile it is. The *standard deviation* is a commonly used measure of this volatility. To calculate the standard deviation, deviations are derived by subtracting the expected return from each possible return. These deviations are then squared and multiplied by their corresponding probabilities before being added together. The resulting sum is the *variance* (or probability-weighted average squared deviation). The square root of the variance is the standard deviation. In our example, the standard deviation of returns is 11.1 and is calculated as shown in Exhibit 3.6.

Probability Distribution

In the real world, the possible returns from an investment usually cannot be divided into three discrete possibilities as in the previous example. Rather, the range of possible returns forms a continuous curve, or *probability distribution*, similar to that shown in Exhibit 3.7. Because the distribution of returns is continuous, probabilities are described for various ranges of outcomes. For example, the probability that the return from common stock ABC will fall between 5 and 10 percent can be determined by calculating what portion of the total area under the curve lies between 5 and 10 percent on the horizontal axis. If, for example, the blackened area represents 9 percent of the area underneath the curve, then there is a 9 percent likelihood (or 0.09 probability) that the return from common stock ABC will fall between 5 and 10 percent.

Exhibit 3.7
Probability of Various Returns from an Investment in Common Stock ABC

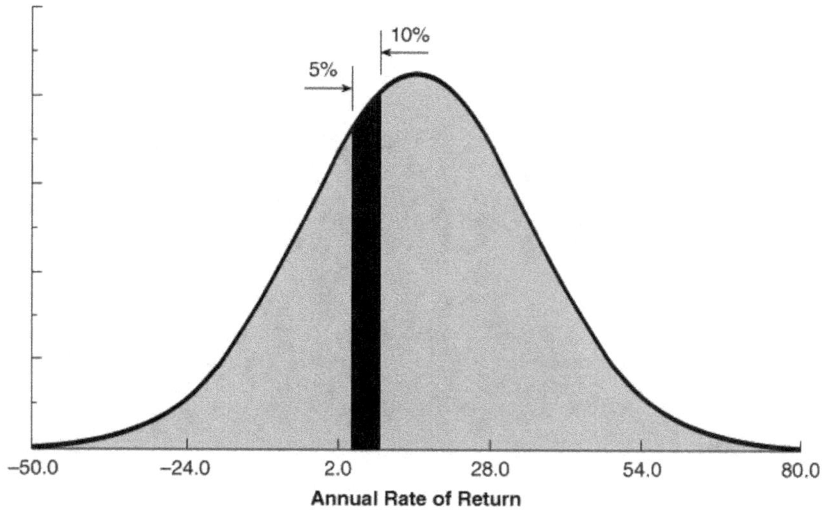

Source: Figure produced using Vestek Systems, Inc. software.

The probability distribution shown in Exhibit 3.7 is the familiar bell-shaped curve, or *normal distribution.* A normal distribution has attractive statistical properties. For example, it can be completely specified using only two numbers: the mean and the standard deviation. That is, given only these two numbers, anyone would draw the same bell-shaped curve. The curve is symmetrically centered on its mean, with 68 percent (approximately two-thirds) of the area underneath the curve lying within one standard deviation of the mean and 95 percent lying within two standard deviations of the mean.

In the example of common stock ABC in Exhibit 3.7, the mean is the expected return of 15 percent, and the standard deviation of 20 percent is the measure of volatility, which describes the dispersion of possible returns around the expected return. Given the properties of a normal distribution, we know that the chances are roughly 2 out of 3 (i.e., a probability of 0.68) that the realized return will be between −5 and 35 percent (i.e., 15 percent ± 20 percent), and the chances are roughly 95 out of 100 that the realized return will be between − 25 and 55 percent (that is, 15 percent ± 40 percent).

Chapter 4

Dispersion and the Limits of Prediction

It is far better to foresee even without certainty than not to foresee at all.

—*Henri Poincaré (1854–1912)*

We are convinced that the average investor cannot deal successfully with price movements by attempting to forecast them.

—*Benjamin Graham (1894–1976)*

In the previous chapter, we explored the long-term historical rewards for bearing various forms of risk. Relative to the stable principal value of Treasury bills, the horizon premium entices long-term government bond investors to accept the variability of bond prices caused by changes in interest rates. Long-term corporate bond investors bear default risk in order to capture a premium return relative to long-term government bond returns. The equity risk premium compensates investors for the high price volatility inherent in common stock ownership. Lastly, we know that investors in small company stocks historically have earned a premium return relative to investing in large company stocks.

These risk premiums represent differences between the historical compound annual returns of various investment alternatives. While knowledge of the historical returns of different investment alternatives helps to build context for a client engaged in a portfolio design process, the advisor should acknowledge the limitations of such single-point statistics. Clients should be concerned not only about an asset class's historical return but also about the dispersion of annual returns that they will experience and the likelihood that future returns will be higher or lower than historical returns.

A dice-rolling example is a simple way to introduce the concept of dispersion. With each roll of two dice, there are 11 possible outcomes: 2, 3, 4, 5, 6, 7, 8, 9, 10, 11, and 12. Which outcome is most likely? Exhibit 4.1 illustrates all the possible outcomes in a histogram. Note that 7 is both the mean (i.e., simple average) and the median (half of the outcomes above and half below) of this distribution. Likewise, 7 is also the mode (highest frequency) of this distribution. A roll of 7 is more likely than any other possible outcome: 1 + 6, 6 + 1, 2 + 5, 5 + 2, 3 + 4, 4 + 3. If you are betting on the outcome of any given roll, you should pick 7. Yet given that 7 is the most likely outcome with one roll of the dice, is it smarter to bet on a roll of 7 or *not* on a roll of 7? The histogram in Exhibit 4.1 demonstrates that there are cumulatively more ways to roll numbers other than 7 than a 7 itself. Ironically, 7 is the simple average outcome, the median outcome, the most likely outcome, and yet an unlikely outcome, all at once.

Armed with the information from Chapters 2 and 3, clients often will anchor their return expectation to an investment alternative's long-term historical return. An advisor should seek to detach a client's expectations somewhat from this single-point statistic. Like the dice-rolling example, the average return may in fact be an unlikely outcome. In Exhibit 3.1, we see that, from 1926 through 2011, the simple average return for large company stocks was 11.8 percent. For the following illustration, let us round this average to 12 percent and create a range around that average of plus or minus 4 percent (i.e., between 8 and 16 percent). How frequently has the annual total

Exhibit 4.1
Histogram of Dice-Rolling Outcomes

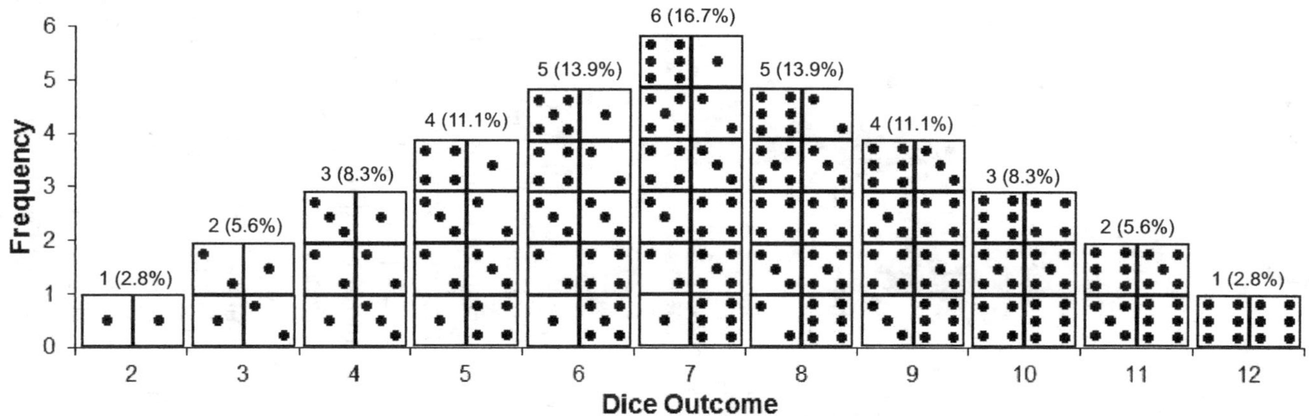

Due to rounding, percentages do not sum to 100%.

Exhibit 4.2
Frequency of Annual Total Returns for Large Company Stocks (1926–2011)

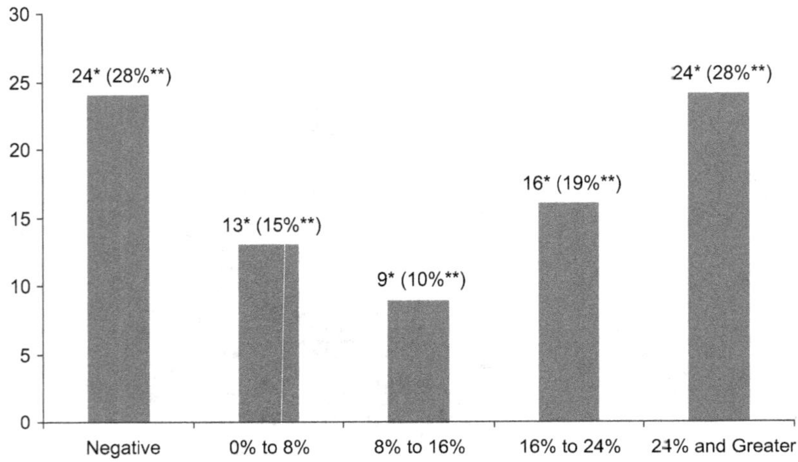

* Number of observations
** Percentage of observations

Data source: Calculated by Gibson Capital, LLC using data presented in *2012 Ibbotson® Stocks, Bonds, Bills, and Inflation® (SBBI®) Classic Yearbook*, © 2012 Morningstar. All rights reserved. Used with permission.

return for large company stocks fallen between 8 and 16 percent? The answer is presented in Exhibit 4.2. Only nine times during the past 86 years has the annual total return fallen between 8 and 16 percent. Fewer than half of all annual total returns have landed within the even wider range of 0 to 24 percent. To most investors, this result is surprising and a little unsettling. Large company stock investors seldom experience average returns. Instead, they endure returns that vary widely from year to year.

Let us return for a moment to the dice-rolling example in Exhibit 4.1. The histogram of dice-rolling outcomes is symmetrical around the average outcome of 7. The likelihood that the next roll will be above 7 is equal to the likelihood that it will be below 7. There is therefore no way to predict whether an above-average outcome or below-average outcome is more likely. Are we in the same dilemma when we try to predict future asset class returns? In other words, unlike with the dice-rolling example, is it possible to know whether the future returns of an asset class are more likely to be higher or lower than they have been in the past?

The relevance of the above questions goes beyond merely setting appropriate return expectations for clients. Money has a purpose. Regardless of the uncertainty regarding future returns over a planning horizon, clients must nonetheless make important decisions regarding appropriate savings rates and spending rates. Providing advice on these issues requires the development of reasonable asset class return assumptions, and long-term historical returns often are not the best estimates of future returns. We now turn to the challenges of forecasting returns over an assumed 10-year horizon. The forecasting approaches vary for the three investments we have chosen for this discussion: Treasury bills (a short-term interest-generating investment), long-term government bonds (a long-term interest-generating investment), and large company stocks (an equity investment).

Treasury Bills

Historically, the Federal Reserve (the Fed) has managed short-term interest rates primarily through two activities. First, the Fed directly sets the *discount rate*, which is the interest rate charged to member banks by the Fed for overnight loans. Second, by engaging in open market buying and selling of U.S. government securities, the Fed indirectly targets the *federal funds rate*, which is the rate that banks charge each other for overnight reserves held by banks at the Fed. Through these two activities, the Fed moves short-term interest rates incrementally higher or lower usually in a series of small steps. Treasury bill returns therefore trend from lower levels to higher levels and from higher levels to lower levels. In the previous chapter, Exhibit 3.1 contains a column that specifies the serial correlations[1] of various investment alternatives. For Treasury bills, the serial correlation of 0.91 indicates a high degree of trending in the annual return data.

Because Treasury bill returns trend from year to year, the current year Treasury bill return is a reasonable base estimate for next year's return. Any difference will be due largely to incremental short-term interest rate changes initiated by the Fed. To forecast Treasury bill returns over a 10-year horizon, however, we first need an estimate of inflation for this period.

In Exhibit 3.1, we see that from 1926 through 2011 Treasury bills earned a 0.6 percent compound annual return over inflation. By adding this 0.6 percent premium to an estimate of future inflation, we can forecast the 10-year compound annual return for Treasury bills. Fortunately, the *TIPS spread* provides us with a market-consensus forecast of future inflation. The TIPS spread is equal to the difference between the yield to maturity of a conventional Treasury bond and the yield to maturity of a similar maturity Treasury Inflation Protected Security (TIPS). (See Chapter 9 for a fuller discussion of TIPS.) According to the Federal Reserve Bank of San Francisco:

> In principle, comparing the yields between conventional Treasury securities and TIPS can provide a useful measure of the market's expectation of future CPI inflation. At a basic level, the yield-to-maturity on a conventional Treasury bond that pays its holder a fixed nominal coupon and principal must compensate the investor for future inflation. Thus, this nominal yield includes two components: the real rate of interest and the inflation compensation over the maturity horizon of the bond. For TIPS, the coupons and principal rise and fall with the CPI, so the yield includes only the real rate of interest. Therefore, the difference, roughly speaking, between the two yields reflects the inflation compensation over that maturity horizon.

Below we compute a 10-year compound annual return forecast for Treasury bills using the TIPS spread for the January 2022 maturity Treasuries found in Exhibit 9.4 in Chapter 9:

1.62%	10-year Treasury bond yield to maturity
– (0.48)%	Minus 10-year TIPS yield to maturity (Note that the yield is negative.)
2.10%	10-year TIPS spread
+ 0.60%	Historical Treasury bill compound annual return premium over inflation
2.70%	10-year compound annual return forecast for Treasury bills

Will Treasury bill investors earn a return premium over inflation in the coming decade? Perhaps, as was the case in the 1940s, the Federal Reserve will hold short-term interest rates below the rate of annual inflation for some period. Recent Treasury bill returns in 2009, 2010, and 2011 failed to compensate investors for inflation. Should investors expect more of the same in the years to come?

Will the increasing level of U.S. government indebtedness present another issue? Investors had long thought of Treasury bills as a "risk-free" asset. On August 5, 2011, however, Standard & Poor's downgraded the U.S. government's AAA sovereign credit rating on long-term U.S. debt to AA+. If the creditworthiness of short-term U.S. debt were to deteriorate, Treasury bill investors might demand a larger premium over inflation than has been earned in the past.

The answers to these questions are important in estimating future long-term returns for Treasury bills, and yet they are unknowable. The uncertainty underscores the difficulty in forecasting future long-term returns and the imprecise nature of the exercise.

Long-Term Government Bonds

Throughout this section, "long-term government bonds" will be represented by a portfolio containing one government bond with a term of approximately 20 years. The data series is described by Ibbotson Associates in the *2012 Ibbotson® Stocks, Bonds, Bills, and Inflation®*

(*SBBI*®) *Classic Yearbook*.[2] In our discussion, therefore, long-term government bonds have a relatively constant 20-year maturity.

Unlike Treasury bills, year-to-year fluctuations in the principal value of long-term government bonds make the prior year's total return less helpful in forecasting the following year's total return. (The last column in the previous chapter's Exhibit 3.1 indicates that the serial correlation of annual total returns for long-term government bonds is −0.11.) However, whereas total returns fluctuate year to year, the yield to maturity for long-term government bonds trends over time.[3] This trending makes intuitive sense. The yield to maturity on a long-term government bond reflects consensus inflation expectations over the term of the bond. These inflation expectations change incrementally over time.

Exhibit 4.3 contrasts long-term government bonds' trending yield to maturity with the volatile annual total returns. As price volatility partially cancels out over long holding periods, interest payments and

Exhibit 4.3

Long-Term Government Bonds: Year-End Yields to Maturity Versus Annual Total Returns

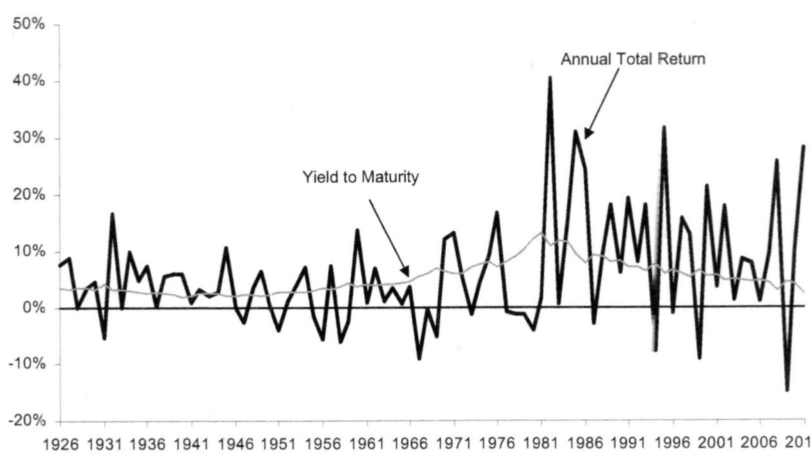

Data source: Calculated by Gibson Capital, LLC using data presented in *2012 Ibbotson® Stocks, Bonds, Bills, and Inflation® (SBBI®) Classic Yearbook*, © 2012 Morningstar. All rights reserved. Used with permission.

the cumulative appreciation or loss of principal value on the bonds become the primary sources of return.

Now we will consider the relationship between the yield to maturity on long-term government bonds and the subsequent 10-year compound annual return. Exhibit 4.4 is the scatterplot from a simple linear regression analysis, which examines the variation in a dependent variable (i.e., subsequent 10-year compound annual return) in terms of the variation in an independent variable (i.e., prior year-end yield to maturity).

Each diamond in Exhibit 4.4 represents a specific year in which an investor invested in long-term government bonds at the yield to maturity indicated on the horizontal axis and obtained the corresponding subsequent 10-year compound annual return

Exhibit 4.4

Long-Term Government Bonds: Yield to Maturity and Subsequent 10-Year Compound Annual Return (1926–2011)

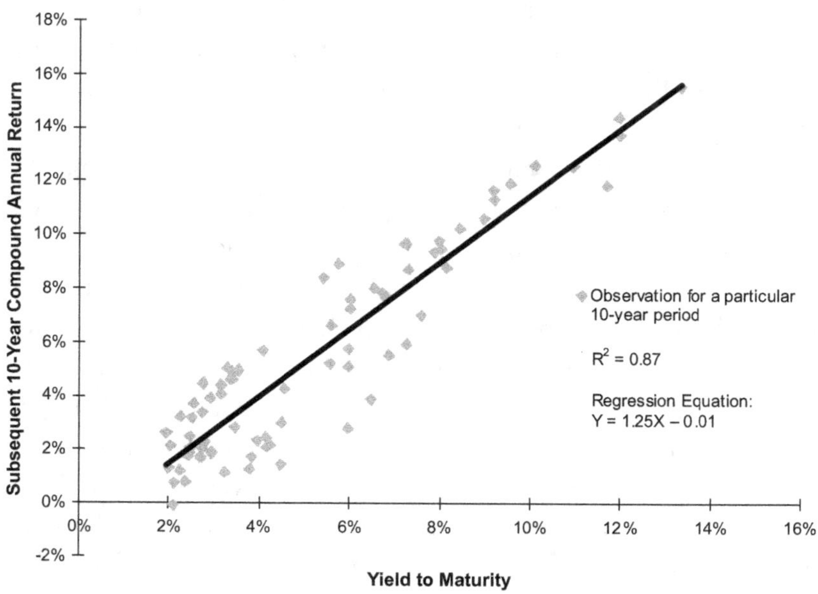

Data source: Calculated by Gibson Capital, LLC using data presented in *2012 Ibbotson® Stocks, Bonds, Bills, and Inflation® (SBBI®) Classic Yearbook*, © 2012 Morningstar. All rights reserved. Used with permission.

indicated on the vertical axis. The equation Y = 1.25X – 0.01 defines the regression line running through the diamonds and describes the relationship between the two variables. The strength of the relationship is measured by the statistic R^2, also known as the coefficient of determination.[4] In the case of this regression analysis, the R^2 of 0.87 represents an imperfect but still meaningful relationship. If each of the diamonds were to line up along the regression line, the R^2 would equal 1 and would indicate that the yield to maturity has been a perfect predictor of the subsequent 10-year compound annual return.

It appears from Exhibit 4.4 that the diamonds are more tightly clustered around the regression line at higher yields to maturity than at lower yields to maturity. In other words, it appears as though the yield to maturity is more predictive of the subsequent 10-year compound annual return when the yield to maturity is relatively high. We can test this observation by running two separate simple linear regression analyses: The first will contain only the above-median yields to maturity from 1926 through 2011, and the second will contain only the below-median yields to maturity. We present these two regression analyses in Exhibits 4.5 and 4.6, respectively.

These two exhibits confirm the observation that the yield to maturity is more predictive of the subsequent 10-year compound annual return when the long-term government bonds' yield to maturity is relatively high. For a particular coupon rate and maturity, government bond values are less sensitive to a given change in interest rates when yields to maturity are higher than when they are lower. Also, when a long-term government bond's coupon rate is higher, the bond's higher income component may dominate the cumulative change in the bond's principal value caused by interest rate movements. As a result, when the yields to maturity are above median, we find in Exhibit 4.5 a relatively high R^2 of 0.80, which indicates a stronger relationship between the yield to maturity and subsequent 10-year compound annual return.

Exhibit 4.5

Long-Term Government Bonds: Above-Median Yield to Maturity and Subsequent 10-Year Compound Annual Return (1926–2011)

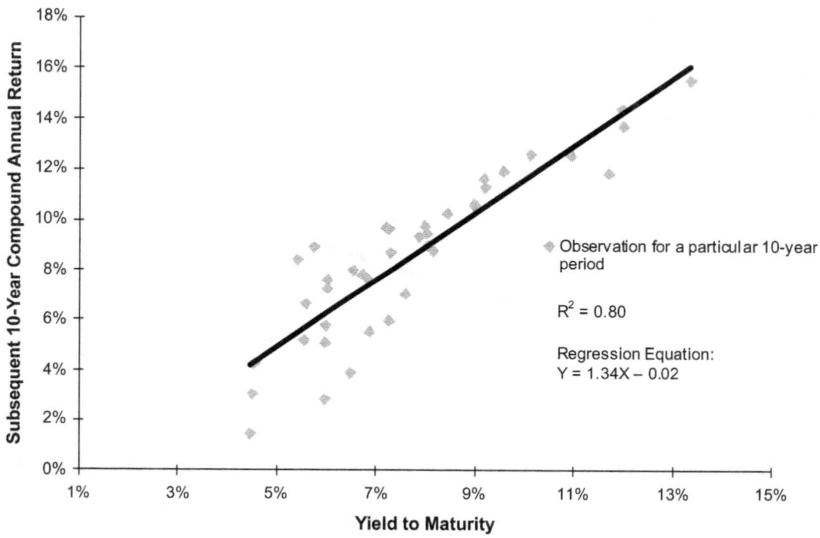

Data source: Calculated by Gibson Capital, LLC using data presented in *2012 Ibbotson® Stocks, Bonds, Bills, and Inflation® (SBBI®) Classic Yearbook*, © 2012 Morningstar. All rights reserved. Used with permission.

When the yields to maturity are below median, we find in Exhibit 4.6 a relatively low R^2 of only 0.13, which indicates a weak relationship and hence low predictive power. For a particular coupon rate and maturity, government bond values are more sensitive to a given change in interest rates when the yields to maturity are lower. At the same time, if the coupon rate on a long-term government bond is low, the bond's low income component is more easily dominated by the cumulative changes in the bond's principal value due to interest rate movements.

At the end of 2011, the yield to maturity on long-term government bonds was only 2.48 percent.[5] Based on that very low yield to maturity, the regression analysis in Exhibit 4.4 suggests that long-term government bond investors should anticipate a relatively low subsequent 10-year compound annual return. However, Exhibit 4.6 is a reminder that, at such a low yield to maturity, the subsequent 10-year return is less predictable based on the yield to maturity alone.

Exhibit 4.6
Long-Term Government Bonds: Below-Median Yield to Maturity and Subsequent 10-Year Compound Annual Return (1926–2011)

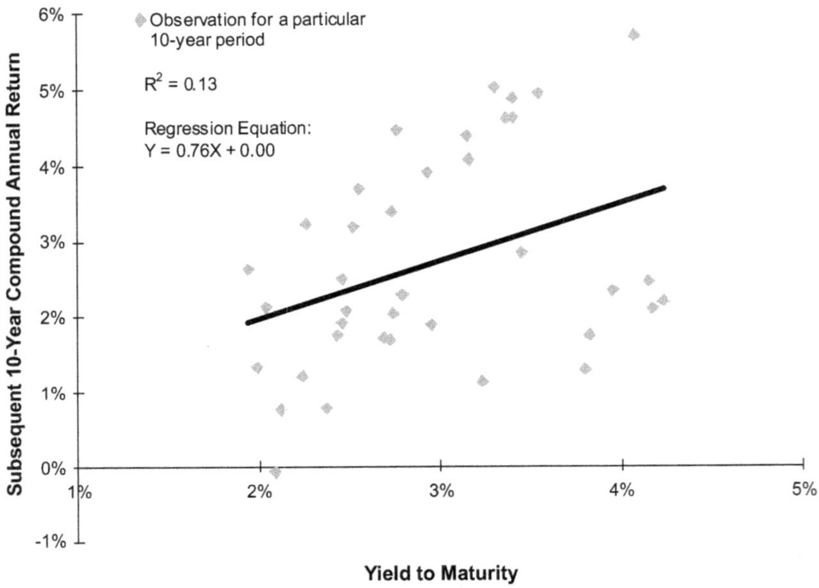

Data source: Calculated by Gibson Capital, LLC using data presented in *2012 Ibbotson® Stocks, Bonds, Bills, and Inflation® (SBBI®) Classic Yearbook*, © 2012 Morningstar. All rights reserved. Used with permission.

Large Company Stocks

To determine if future returns for large company stocks are likely to be higher or lower than the historical return, let us consider the price/earnings (P/E) ratio. The P/E ratio specifies the amount that investors must pay to acquire \$1 of corporate earnings. The lower the P/E ratio, all else being equal, the better the value for stock investors. As a result, we will refer to the P/E ratio as the *valuation* or *valuation level* of large company stocks.

P/E ratios can be calculated in a variety of ways depending on the context. For example, a P/E ratio might be calculated with the current price for large company stocks divided by the prior year's reported earnings. Another calculation method divides the current price for large company stocks by next year's earnings as forecasted by stock analysts. For our purposes, *price* for large company stocks is the inflation-adjusted index value for the S&P 500 index. The denominator, *earnings*, is the average of the previous 10 years of inflation-adjusted reported earnings for the same index. Averaging earnings over a multiple-year horizon reduces the impact of fluctuations in year-to-year earnings. This process is referred to as *normalization*, and we will refer to the P/E ratio used in our discussion as the *normalized P/E ratio*.[6]

Exhibit 4.7 depicts the normalized P/E ratio for large company stocks for the period 1926 through 2011. The normalized P/E ratio has varied considerably over time. The early 1930s and the late 1970s to early 1980s stand out as low points in terms of stock market valuation, while the late 1990s, coinciding with the technology bubble, mark the peak of investor optimism. The median normalized P/E ratio for the entire period is 16.45. If the normalized P/E ratio is to be helpful in terms of forecasting future long-term returns, periods of

Exhibit 4.7
Large Company Stocks 10-Year Normalized P/E Ratio*

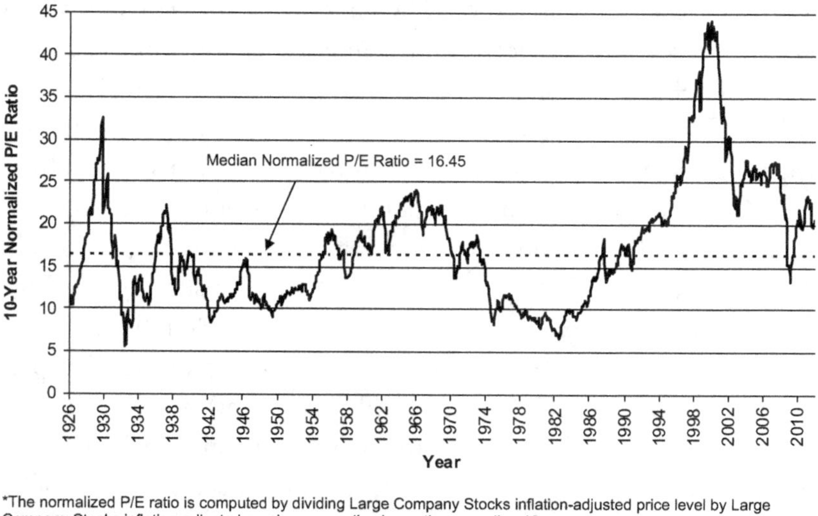

*The normalized P/E ratio is computed by dividing Large Company Stocks inflation-adjusted price level by Large Company Stocks inflation-adjusted earnings normalized over the preceding 10 years.

Source: © 2012 Compiled by Gibson Capital, LLC using data from Robert Shiller, http://www.econ.yale.edu/~shiller/data.htm.

Exhibit 4.8
Large Company Stocks 10-Year Normalized P/E Ratio and Subsequent 10-Year Compound Annual Return

10-Yr. Normalized P/E Ratio	Below 9	9 to 11	11 to 14	14 to 18	18 to 25	Above 25
Average 10-Yr. Compound Return	15.09%	15.40%	12.99%	10.90%	6.46%	3.07%
Range of Historical Outcomes:						
75th%	17.55%	17.09%	16.16%	15.63%	9.78%	6.54%
50th%	16.19%	15.26%	13.44%	9.18%	6.66%	2.17%
25th%	14.76%	14.33%	9.62%	7.95%	3.35%	-0.90%
Number of 10-Yr. Periods	5	13	17	16	18	8

Data from 1926 through 2011.

Data source: © Gibson Capital, LLC, 2012. Compiled using data from Robert Shiller, http://www.econ.yale.edu/~shiller/data.htm; and *2012 Ibbotson® Stocks, Bonds, Bills, and Inflation® (SBBI®) Classic Yearbook,* © 2012 Morningstar. All rights reserved. Used with permission.

high valuations should signal future periods of low returns, and vice versa.

In Exhibit 4.8 we sort the normalized P/E ratios into six categories, within which investors could acquire large company stocks at normalized P/E ratios of below 9, from 9 to 11, from 11 to 14, from 14 to 18, from 18 to 25, and above 25. We then indicate the average subsequent 10-year compound annual return for each of these acquisition ranges. The result is as we would expect: High prices in relation to normalized earnings have on average led to lower subsequent returns and vice versa.

Exhibit 4.8 also includes a range of historical outcomes. The 50th percentile is the median outcome, whereas the 25th percentile, for example, indicates that approximately three-fourths of historical observations exceeded the given compound annual return. Recall, for a moment, that the compound annual return for large company stocks from 1926 through 2011 was 9.8 percent. Two statistics in the range of historical outcomes are very close to 9.8 percent. Both the 25th percentile in the "11 to 14" column (9.62 percent) and the 75th percentile in the "18 to 25" column (9.78 percent) are close to the long-term compound annual return for large company stocks. In other words, acquiring large company stocks at normalized P/E ratios of 11 to 14 has led to *above-average* returns in approximately three-fourths of the subsequent 10-year periods. Acquiring stocks at normalized P/E ratios of 18 to 25 has resulted in *below-average* returns in approximately three-fourths of the subsequent 10-year periods.

We also can examine the relationship between the normalized P/E ratio and subsequent 10-year compound annual return with a simple linear regression analysis.[7] In Exhibit 4.9, the normalized P/E ratio is on the horizontal axis, and the subsequent 10-year compound annual return is on the vertical axis. Each diamond represents a year in which an investor purchased large company stocks at a particular normalized P/E ratio and earned the corresponding compound annual return over the subsequent 10-year period.

The downward-sloping regression line indicates that investing in large company stocks at higher multiples of normalized earnings has

Exhibit 4.9

Large Company Stocks 10-Year Normalized P/E Ratio and Subsequent 10-Year Compound Annual Return (1926–2011)

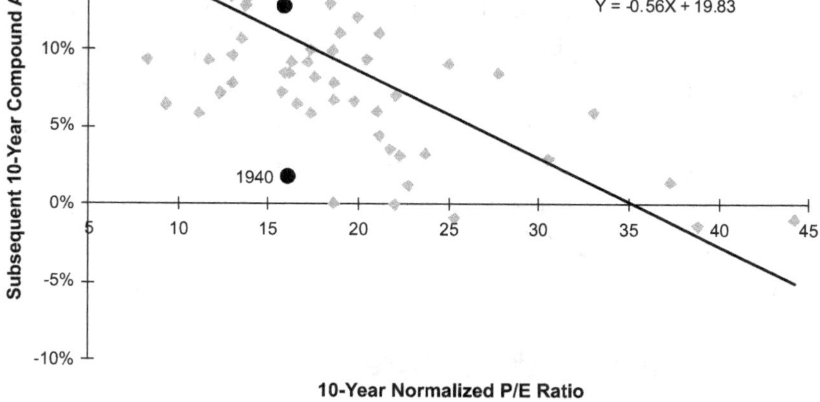

Data source: © Gibson Capital, LLC, 2012. Compiled using data from Robert Shiller, http://www.econ.yale.edu/~shiller/data.htm; and *2012 Ibbotson® Stocks, Bonds, Bills, and Inflation® (SBBI®) Classic Yearbook,* © 2012 Morningstar. All rights reserved. Used with permission.

generally led to lower subsequent returns. The R^2 of 0.51 indicates that approximately half the variation in subsequent 10-year compound annual returns is explained by the variation in the normalized P/E ratio. Given the dispersion of observations around the regression line, it is easy to identify specific instances in which observations with relatively similar normalized P/E ratios have resulted in very different subsequent return outcomes.

For example, in Exhibit 4.9, we have identified three such observations indicated by black circles. The 10-year periods ending in 1940, 1964, and 2000 all share a similar valuation starting point: near the median for the entire period of approximately 16 times normalized earnings. The outcomes, however, were very different. The 10-year period ending in 1940 resulted in a compound annual return of only 1.80 percent, while the 10-year period ending in 2000 resulted in a compound annual return of 17.46 percent. The 10-year period ending in 1964 had a compound annual return closer to what was predicted by the regression line.

With essentially equal starting points in terms of valuation, why were subsequent returns so different? One reason is that the end-of-period valuation levels were quite different. At the end of 1940, investors were willing to pay just under 14 times normalized earnings to acquire large company stocks. By the end of 2000, investors paid more than 37 times normalized earnings for an interest in large company stocks! Unfortunately, no metric provides insight into what P/E multiple investors will be willing to pay to acquire stocks a decade into the future. The normalized P/E ratio also can be thought of as a barometer of investor sentiment. High valuation levels indicate widespread investor optimism, and low valuation levels signal significant pessimism. The evidence presented in Exhibits 4.8 and 4.9 indicates that extreme investor sentiment in either direction has tended to moderate over time.

Implications for the Future

In this chapter, we presented approaches for estimating the future returns of three investment alternatives. In each case, the forecasting approach suggests a future return that is lower than the investment's historical compound annual return from 1926 through 2011. Treasury bills returned only 0.04 percent in 2011. Due to the trending nature of the annual returns, Treasury bill investors should expect very low returns in the near term and a longer-term compound annual return that on average provides a small incremental return over the expected rate of inflation. Note, however, the possibility of negative real returns for Treasury bills if the Fed maintains what Chairman Ben Bernanke has described as "exceptionally low levels of the federal funds rate."

At the conclusion of 2011, long-term government bonds offered a yield to maturity of only 2.48 percent. The last year in which the yield to maturity on long-term government bonds ended below 2.50 percent was 1950. Investors should expect a compound annual return over the 10-year period following 2011 that is below long-term government bonds' historical compound annual return of 5.7 percent. At such a low yield to maturity, the compound annual return over the following 10-year period is likely to be heavily influenced by the cumulative change in bond principal value triggered by changes in interest rates.

Likewise, advisors should guide clients toward an expectation of lower returns for large company stocks. The 2011 year-end normalized P/E ratio for large company stocks was 20.5.[8] Exhibits 4.8 and 4.9 argue that an above-average valuation level tends to lead to below-average returns. However, these exhibits also illustrate the wide range of subsequent outcomes at various valuation levels. Consequently, the development of a precise forecast of future returns is simply not possible.

Uses and Misuses of Forecasting Information

Investors want to know how much they need to invest in order to finance their children's college expenses or adequately fund their future retirements. The answers to these questions depend on the size of the investor's portfolio, its asset allocation, the size and timing of cash flows into and out of the portfolio, the time horizon over which the investor will be drawing on the portfolio, and finally the portfolio's future returns and the volatility of those returns. Given those factors,

Monte Carlo simulation techniques can model the likelihood that an investor will achieve his financial goals. Financial modeling outcomes, however, are particularly sensitive to the level of the portfolio's estimated return. The portfolio's estimated return is in turn dependent on asset class return forecasts, which often are not well estimated by long-term average returns. Although a detailed process for developing capital market assumptions is outside the scope of this chapter, the return forecasting approaches we have reviewed are helpful in estimating an approximate level of future asset class returns.

As we will discuss in the next chapter, however, advisors should exercise caution when using these forecasting approaches to engage in tactical trading strategies. For example, Exhibit 4.9 demonstrates that, while a relationship exists between large company stocks' normalized P/E ratio and the subsequent 10-year compound annual return, the relationship is far from perfect. Perhaps more importantly, the same factors that set the stage for periods of above-average or below-average stock returns may make it psychologically difficult for investors to execute a value-added trading strategy. For example, if investors' widespread "irrational exuberance" fueled the stock market's historically high valuation level of the late 1990s, how many investors had the conviction and guts to bet contrary to the exuberance? Answer: very, very few!

Chapter 5

Market Timing

The evidence on investment managers' success with market timing is impressive—and overwhelmingly negative.

—*Charles D. Ellis (1937–),* Investment Policy, *1985*

He that cannot abide a bad market, deserves not a good one.

—*John Ray (1627–1705),* English Proverbs, *1678*

Put all your eggs in one basket and—WATCH THAT BASKET.

—*Mark Twain (1835–1910),* Pudd'nhead Wilson, *1894*

The nightingale which cannot bear the thorn
It is best that it should never speak of the rose.

—*Anwar-i-Suhaili,* The Lights of Canopus

Common stocks have volatile returns. One consequence of this volatility is that investors historically have suffered negative annual returns approximately 28 percent of the time. Obviously, if there were a way to avoid the stock market's bad years, wealth would accumulate much more rapidly. Assume, for example, that it is December 31, 1925, and we are consulting a market timer who has made forecasts of 1926 security returns for Treasury bills, long-term corporate bonds, large company stocks, and small company stocks. Of these four investment alternatives, he correctly predicts that large company stocks will produce the best total return for 1926. We invest $1, which by the end of 1926 grows to be worth $1.12. Impressed with our market timer's predictive abilities, we again meet with him on December 31, 1926, for his advice on where to position our money for the following year. Year after year our market timer, with perfect predictive accuracy, advises us concerning which investment alternative is appropriate for our market-timed portfolio.

By compounding our wealth in this manner, our initial $1 investment would grow to be worth more than $224 million by the end of 2011. This result is impressive when compared with the best-performing investment alternative, small company stocks, with its ending value of $15,532, and with the more modest ending value of approximately $21 for Treasury bills. To contextualize this phenomenal result, consider the outcome had we initially invested $1 million with our market timer at the end of 1925: By the end of 2011, our portfolio would be valued at more than $224 trillion. Our portfolio would be worth nearly 2.5 times the world's total investable capital of $90.3 trillion shown in Exhibit 1.1.

Clearly, such market-timing ability does not exist. Why, then, is market timing so seductive? People want to believe it is possible. When we look at the long-term historical performance of large company stocks, the hope of market timing is reinforced by what appear to be predictive trends—sustained periods of either rising or falling prices. Despite these appearances to the contrary, large company stock returns do not follow a trend.[1] The problem is that a random series of numbers does not always look random. A simple experiment will verify this fact. Take a coin, flip it 100 times, and record the pattern of heads and tails produced. At the end of the experiment, you quite likely will notice occasional runs of heads or runs of tails. Are those runs predictive trends? No. Your knowledge that coin flipping is always a 50/50 proposition prevents you from inappropriately presuming the existence of predictive trends of either heads or tails. Each flip is independent of the preceding one.

When we examine the pattern of returns for large company stocks, a prolonged period of above-average returns is similar to a run of heads in our coin-flipping experiment, and a prolonged period of below-average returns is like a run of tails. With a prolonged bear market, such as occurred in 1973–1974 or 2000–2002, investors tend to berate themselves after the fact by concluding that they should have known that the bear market would continue once prices started falling. Investors can easily fall into this self-punishing attitude because they are continually bombarded by discouraging commentaries in the financial press and on the evening news concerning the magnitude of the stock market decline. If, however, the timing and magnitude of the market's decline are not predictable, there is no reason to add self-reproach to the pain of the market's reversal.

"Monday morning quarterbacking" also occurs with market advances. For example, stock prices bottomed out during the summer of 1982, prior to one of the biggest bull markets in history. With the benefit of retrospect, investors tend to conclude that everyone should have known that stocks were cheap during the summer of 1982 and poised for a big rise. The fact is that investors, in the aggregate, did not know stocks were a great bargain; otherwise, their prior buying activity would have prevented the stocks from becoming such bargains in the first place. As was the case with our coin-flipping experiment, the timing and duration of these bull and bear markets are not predictable; hindsight simply makes it seem so.

An efficient market incorporates into current security prices relevant known information, as well as consensus expectations regarding the unknown. Thus, when it comes to predicting short-term stock market movements, it is not of any value to know whether we are at war or peace, have a Republican or Democrat in the White House, or are in an economic expansion or contraction. What, then, moves the market in the short run? It is moved by investors' reactions to new information relevant to the pricing of securities. In essence, surprises trigger price movements in the markets. These surprises themselves are random events. More good than bad surprises result in above-average stock market returns. When the reverse is true, we have below-average stock market returns.[2] Bull markets and bear markets will always occur, but the evidence indicates that there is no consistent way to predict the turning points.

Before engaging in a review of several research studies on market timing, it is helpful to review some statistics on stock market cycles. Exhibit 5.1 shows the history of bear and bull markets over the past 100+ years.[3] If we eliminate the three worst and three mildest bear

Exhibit 5.1
Bear Markets and Bull Markets (1906–2011)

Bear Markets					Bull Markets				
Number	Peak Date	Peak Index	Number of Months	Percentage Decline*	Number	Trough Date	Trough Index	Number of Months	Percentage Advance*
1	09/1906	10.03	14	-37.69	1	11/1907	6.25	25	64.80
2	12/1909	10.30	60	-28.64	2	12/1914	7.35	23	38.91
3	11/1916	10.21	13	-33.40	3	12/1917	6.80	19	39.85
4	07/1919	9.51	25	-32.18	4	08/1921	6.45	96	394.88
5	09/07/1929	31.92	33	-86.22	5	06/01/1932	4.40	14	177.27
6	07/18/1933	12.20	20	-33.93	6	03/14/1935	8.06	24	131.76
7	03/06/1937	18.68	13	-54.50	7	03/31/1938	8.50	7	62.24
8	11/09/1938	13.79	5	-26.18	8	04/08/1939	10.18	9	25.44
9	01/03/1940	12.77	28	-41.50	9	04/28/1942	7.47	49	157.70
10	05/29/1946	19.25	12	-28.78	10	05/17/1947	13.71	13	24.43
11	06/15/1948	17.06	12	-20.57	11	06/13/1949	13.55	86	267.08
12	08/02/1956	49.74	15	-21.63	12	10/22/1957	38.98	50	86.35
13	12/12/1961	72.64	6	-27.97	13	06/26/1962	52.32	43	79.78
14	02/09/1966	94.06	8	-22.18	14	10/07/1966	73.20	26	48.05
15	11/29/1968	108.37	18	-36.06	15	05/26/1970	69.29	32	73.53
16	01/11/1973	120.24	21	-48.20	16	10/03/1974	62.28	24	73.14
17	09/21/1976	107.83	17	-19.41	17	03/06/1978	86.90	33	61.70
18	11/28/1980	140.52	20	-27.11	18	08/12/1982	102.42	60	228.81
19	08/25/1987	336.77	3	-33.51	19	12/04/1987	223.92	148	582.15
20	03/24/2000	1527.46	30	-49.15	20	10/09/2002	776.76	60	101.5
21	10/09/2007	1565.15	17	-56.78	21	3/09/2009	676.53		

*S&P 500 price only, without reinvestment of dividend income

markets, we identify a typical range of bear market declines of −22.18 to −49.15 percent. If we eliminate the three largest and three smallest bull markets, we identify a typical range of bull market advances of 39.85 to 228.81 percent. Note that the magnitude of price change varies much more widely for bull markets than for bear markets. Similarly, the typical duration varies more widely for bull markets than for bear markets.

Exhibit 5.2 provides summary statistics for these bear and bull markets. The simple average and median statistics are fairly similar for bear markets over both the last 106 years and the more recent post–World War II period. For bull markets, however, the simple averages are much higher than the median statistics for the duration (in months) as well as the percentage advance. The bull market simple average statistics are pulled higher by a few very large advances like the extraordinarily big bull market that began on December 4, 1987, and ended over 12 years later on March 24, 2000. The median statistics are not as sensitive to the impact of a few very big bull markets.[4] Both statistics are meaningful, but the median statistics are probably more representative

Exhibit 5.2
Summary Statistics for Bear Markets and Bull Markets

106 Years (1906 – 2011)				
	21 Bear Markets		20 Bull Markets	
	Number of Months	Percentage Decline*	Number of Months	Percentage Advance*
Simple Average	18.6	-36.46%	42.1	135.97%
Median	17	-33.40%	29	76.66%

Post World War II (1946 – 2011)				
	12 Bear Markets		11 Bull Markets	
	Number of Months	Percentage Decline*	Number of Months	Percentage Advance*
Simple Average	14.9	-32.61%	52.3	147.86%
Median	16	-28.38%	43	79.78%

*S&P 500 price only, without reinvestment of dividend income

of a typical bear or bull market. For example, over the 11 post–World War II market cycles:

1. The median bull market was up 79.78 percent versus the median bear market's decline of −28.38 percent.
2. The median bull market lasted more than 2.5 times as long as the median bear market—43 months for the up legs versus 16 months for the down legs.

Clearly, the typical advance in a bull market was more than sufficient to regain the ground lost during an average bear market. Even during bear markets, however, one-third of the months were up months, making it difficult to know that a bear market was occurring until after the fact. According to a research study by William F. Sharpe:

> ... a manager who attempts to time the market must be right roughly three times out of four, merely to match the overall performance of those competitors who don't. If he is right less often his relative performance will be inferior. There are two reasons for this. First, such a manager will often have his funds in cash equivalents in good market years, sacrificing the higher returns stocks provide in such years. Second, he will incur transaction costs in making switches, many of which will prove to be unprofitable.

Regarding the potential gains from market timing, Sharpe concludes:

> Barring truly devastating market declines similar to those of The Depression, it seems likely that gains of little more than four percent per year from timing should be expected from a manager whose forecasts are truly prophetic.[5]

A study by Robert H. Jeffrey concludes:

> No one can predict the market's ups and downs over a long period, and the risks of trying outweigh the rewards.

He goes on to comment:

> The rationale for being a full-time equity investor is not that there are more positive real return periods than negative ones in most time frames, but rather that most of the "positive action" is compressed into just a few periods, which (perversely but understandably) tend to follow particularly adverse times for stocks.[6]

Suppose that an investor missed the 8 best years for large company stocks during the 86-year period from 1926 through 2011. In each of those years he instead invested in Treasury bills. By being on the sidelines in Treasury bills during this critical time, $1 initially invested in stocks at the end of 1925 would grow to $202 by the end of 2011 compared with a value of $3,045 had he stayed fully invested in large company stocks for the entire 86-year period. An investor would have paid a terrible price for missing those 8 superlative stock return years.

The superior long-term returns available from stocks do not accrue in a uniform manner. Rather, they can be traced to a few periods of dramatic advances. Interestingly, these positive surges often occur when pessimism is running high. This makes sense: A market bottom is reached when pessimism reaches its maximum, and at that point any brightening of the outlook will move the market higher. Again, though, it is important to stress that these market turning points seem identifiable only in retrospect.

For example, at the end of 1990, both investors and investment managers were pessimistic. Large company stocks had just posted a negative total return of −3.10 percent—the first loss in nearly a decade. To make matters worse, recession was upon us, and we were on the brink of the Persian Gulf War. Many of my clients, including investment management firms for which I had consulted, argued that it had to be a good time to be out of the stock market with money parked safely in Treasury bills. I urged them to remain invested—not because I believed the market was poised for an advance, but rather because it is impossible to know when the particularly rewarding periods of stock investing will occur. As it turned out, 1991 was one such year, posting a total return of 30.47 percent for large company stocks, and a good portion of that return occurred quickly after the beginning of the Persian Gulf War.[7] Investors, who out of fear and pessimism tried to protect themselves by selling stocks and parking the proceeds in cash, missed a wonderful market advance.

Consider a market timer who has a 50/50 forecasting ability—that is, he is wrong in his predictions as often as he is right. Depending on which years he is wrong, his investment experience will vary widely. If he is in the wrong place at the wrong time when the spread in returns between Treasury bills and the S&P 500 is narrow, he will not suffer significantly from the error. If, however, his mistakes occur during periods when the spread is quite large, the results can be disastrous. Robert Jeffrey offers these conclusions based on the capital market experience from 1926 through 1982:

> ... if the theoreticians are correct about the inefficiency of market timing (that is, it will generally be accurate only 50 percent of the time), the probable outcome is a best-case real dollar return only about two times greater than what would come from continuous investment in the S&P, while the worst case produces about one hundred times less!
>
> The point of these ... statistics is simply to emphasize that a market-timing strategist has tremendous natural odds to overcome, and that these odds increase geometrically with the length of the time frame and with the frequency of the timing interval. There is probably no situation where caveat emptor is more apropos for the portfolio owner than in interviewing prospective timing managers.[8]

Much of the problem with market timing is that a disproportionate percentage of the total gain from a bull market tends to occur very rapidly at the beginning of a market recovery. If a market timer is on the sidelines in cash equivalents during this critical time, he is apt to miss too much of the action.

In another study, Jess S. Chua and Richard S. Woodward approach the subject from a different angle to ascertain whether the poor results achieved from market timing are due to an inability to avoid bear markets or the tendency to miss the early part of a market recovery. They conclude:

> Overall, the results show that it is more important to correctly forecast bull markets than bear markets. If the investor has only a 50 percent chance of correctly forecasting bull markets, then he should not practice market timing at all. His average return will be less than that of a buy-and-hold strategy even if he can forecast bear markets perfectly.

These researchers calculate that for market timing to pay:

> Investors require the forecast accuracies of at least:
> 80 percent bull and 50 percent bear;
> 70 percent bull and 80 percent bear; or
> 60 percent bull and 90 percent bear ...[9]

These conclusions are particularly interesting because professional market timers often stress capital preservation and the ability to avoid bear markets as the major benefits to be derived from their services.

The previous studies all point to the same conclusion: Attempts to time the market will most likely fail, and the downside risks are larger than the potential upside rewards. This conclusion is consistent with financial economic theory, which maintains that stock market returns should not be forecast easily using readily available information. A broader review of market-timing research studies conducted over the past several decades suggests that the empirical evidence generally supports economic theory.

In his wonderful book *Investment Policy*, Charles D. Ellis refers to an unpublished study of 100 large pension funds:

> … their experience with market timing found that while all the funds had engaged in at least some market timing, not one of the funds had improved its rate of return as a result of its efforts at timing. In fact, 89 of the 100 lost as a result of "timing"—and their losses averaged a daunting 4.5 percent over the five-year period.[10]

Is there evidence that mutual funds have had any better luck at timing the market? Wei Jiang, in a paper entitled "A Nonparametric Test of Market Timing," concludes:

> Overall, there is no evidence that mutual fund managers possess superior market timing abilities.[11]

John R. Graham and Campbell R. Harvey analyze the market-timing advice contained in a sample of 237 investment newsletters. Each of the newsletters recommended a mix of equity and cash. That is, rather than making specific security recommendations, the newsletters attempted to predict the direction of the market as a whole:

> Our paper investigates the ability of newsletters to predict the direction of the market. In analyzing over 15,000 asset allocation recommendations for the 1980–1992 period, we find little evidence that recommended equity weights increase before future positive market returns or decrease before negative market returns …. While some letters at certain times appear to have short-run insights, an investor cannot use a hot streak to identify a particular newsletter that will provide superior recommendations over the long term. Our Monte Carlo analysis indicates that the performance of investment newsletters is no better than, and potentially worse than, what would be expected from a set of letters that offer random recommendations.[12]

Despite the preponderance of evidence against market timing, some studies do suggest that it may be possible to time the market. For example, Pu Shen, an economist at the Federal Reserve Bank of Kansas City, argues for a market-timing strategy that sells stocks when the spread between the S&P 500 earnings/price ratio and the yield on the three-month Treasury bill falls below the 10th percentile value for the spread, that is, when the spread is extremely low compared with its historical range. Shen posits this explanation about why the strategy works:

> When the market is dominated by overly optimistic sentiment, the E/P ratio of the market index is more likely to be extremely low relative to yields of alternative investments, such as debt instruments. Therefore, extremely low values of the spreads may indicate that most stock prices are too high to be justified by the fundamentals, thus it may be a good time to alter the usual "buy-and-hold" strategy and exit the stock market temporarily.[13]

Shen's trading rule significantly outperformed a buy-and-hold strategy. For the entire sample period of 372 months (1970 through 2000), the monthly total returns of the stock market index averaged almost 1.1 percent. For the 300 months when the spread was not particularly low, the monthly total returns of the stock market index averaged 1.5 percent. By comparison, for the 72 low-spread months, the return averaged −0.4 percent per month. Shen concludes that this strategy "comfortably and robustly beat the market index even when transaction costs were incorporated."[14]

In a more recent study entitled "Timing Is Everything: A Comparison and Evaluation of Market Timing Strategies," Chris Brooks, Apostolos Katsaris, and Gita Persand test a variety of market-timing strategies that showed promising potential. The authors believe their study to be the first to compare different market-timing rules on a consistent basis using a very long single set of data, which consisted of monthly returns for the S&P 500 from January 1871 until

August 2003. Their research favors Shen's market-timing strategy discussed above. The authors conclude:

> In pure return terms, the best rule, based on the difference between the earnings-price ratio and short term Treasury yields, earns average returns of .96% per month (12.1% annualized), compared with .94% for buying and holding the equity index.[15]

Although the market-timing strategy worked, these researchers find it had an incremental compound annual return payoff of less than 0.3 percent compared to a buy-and-hold strategy with the S&P 500. This reward is much more modest than Shen found in his research.

We are left with an important question: Is market timing a game worth playing? Before using a market-timing strategy in an attempt to improve investment results, ask yourself these questions:

1. *Was the strategy discovered by "data mining"?* Data mining looks at a large variety of possible trading strategies, sifting for those that generate the best results. More attention is paid to dissecting the data than to thinking critically about why a particular strategy *should* work. Trading rules arrived at through data mining often do not work moving forward.
2. *Is there any economic reason for the market-timing strategy to work?* Empirical evidence of market-timing success should be supported by a sensible economic theory that explains why the strategy worked and why it will be successful in the future.
3. *How large and consistent was the market-timing payoff?* Some research papers show overall market-timing success for the entire study period, but widely varying results from good to bad over different subperiods. A small or inconsistent payoff calls for caution.

4. *Is the upside potential reward from the market-timing strategy as large as the downside risk if the strategy fails?* Empirical studies sometimes show a distribution of potential outcomes that is skewed toward poor performance. That is, even if the market-timing strategy works most of the time, it may underperform a buy-and-hold strategy if the reward when the strategy works is smaller than the loss that occurs when the strategy fails. For example, imagine dropping two white marbles and one black marble into an urn. Shake the urn. Now reach in and pull out a marble. If you draw a white marble, you win \$3. If you draw a black marble, you lose \$9. Return the ball to the urn and start again. Even though the odds are 2 to 1 that you will win money, the game is a losing proposition. The expected payoff from playing one round of this game is −\$1, calculated as the probability of drawing the white marble times the payoff for drawing the white marble plus the probability of drawing the black marble times the payoff for drawing the black marble: $(2/3)(\$3) + (1/3)(-\$9) = -\$1$. Even though you can reasonably expect to win twice as often as you lose, you will tend to lose more and more money the longer you play.
5. *Will the market-timing strategy add value net of transaction costs and associated taxes?* A buy-and-hold strategy using a low-cost index fund is inherently tax efficient. Any active market-timing strategy must first cover its transaction costs and associated taxes before it begins to add value.
6. *Is the strategy well known and widely used?* If so, the rewards will likely be arbitraged toward zero over time.
7. *Do I have the patience and discipline to follow the strategy?*

This last question raises an important behavioral issue. At a black-tie dinner for the American Enterprise Institute on December 5, 1996, Alan Greenspan posed his famous rhetorical question: "But how do we know when irrational exuberance has unduly escalated asset values, which then become subject to unexpected and prolonged contractions as they have in Japan over the past decade?" Toward the end of the 1990s, some smart investors believed the U.S. stock market was indeed "irrationally exuberant." How many of these investors, however, had the guts to get out early and stay out as they watched the market continue to move sharply higher before its eventual reversal?

Although long-term gains from market timing are unlikely, there will always be investors who have positive results from timing activities—particularly in the short run. This is because, over any given period, a wide dispersion of investor experiences will occur, with some investors doing very well and some doing very poorly. Statistically, this is what we expect. The danger is the leap of logic that presumes that the good market-timing result is caused by superior predictive ability. In the aggregate, market timing does not work, and most investor experiences have been and will be negative. Those market timers who have most recently made the right moves, however, are written up in financial publications and interviewed on television. This publicity fuels the hopes of those who wish a way existed to get the advantage of a bull market while avoiding the pain of a bear market. Meanwhile, unsuccessful market-timing firms fade away as their investors leave to reallocate what is left of their portfolios to the latest market-timing guru.

Many investors prefer to live with false hope rather than critically examine whether market timing is possible at all. As Aristotle observed, "A plausible impossibility is always preferable to an unconvincing possibility." To face the question of whether market timing is possible forces an investor to acknowledge that he may have to either periodically face the pain of a bear market or alternatively forgo investing in stocks altogether, thereby sacrificing the possibility of real capital growth. People have a pervasive tendency to interpret their experiences to fit their preconceptions. This is often the case with market timing, where hope springs eternal that somewhere, someone will somehow be able to consistently ride the bull while safely avoiding the bear.

An investor should not invest in stocks unless she has a sufficiently long investment time horizon. If she is truly investing for the long term, she will inevitably experience both bull and bear markets. The great value investor Benjamin Graham said, "Though the stock market functions as a voting machine in the short run, it acts as a weighing machine in the long run." In other words, in the short run, fear or greed may cause the stock market's price level to deviate significantly from its true value. This propensity should be of no concern to the long-term stock investor who knows that these excesses tend to reverse themselves. In the long run, the market's price level will gravitate toward its true value.

The alternative to market timing is to simply remain invested in the stock market. As William Sharpe points out:

> A manager who keeps assets in stocks at all times is like an optimistic market timer. His actions are consistent with a policy of predicting a good year every year. While such a manager may know that such predictions will be wrong roughly one year out of three, such an attitude is nonetheless likely to lead to results superior to those achieved by most market timers.[16]

DALBAR, Inc., in its study entitled "Quantitative Analysis of Investor Behavior," has similar words of wisdom for investors:

> Retention is critical to investment success for the obvious reason that you cannot benefit from the market if you are not *in* the market. While it is highly profitable to avoid market down turns, very few investors do this successfully. Unless you can predict when down turns will occur and for how long, the strategy of getting out to avoid a loss does not work. Consider that the market moved up 60% of the time and down only 40% for each month of the last 20 years. Remaining invested is betting with the odds.[17]

The Rise of Tactical Asset Allocation

Few investment advisors characterize their investment approaches as having a market-timing component. It makes for bad advertising. Decades of unfulfilled promises have left advisors and investors rightfully skeptical about market-timing strategies. Yet in a recent survey by Cerulli Associates, a research firm specializing in asset management and distribution trends, 61 percent of advisors who responded indicated that they now use either a pure tactical allocation or strategic allocation along with a tactical overlay. The percentage of advisors using tactical allocation was up 8.3 percent from 2010's survey results. To discuss tactical asset allocation, we must first describe *strategic asset allocation*. Strategic asset allocation:

1. Seeks to identify and maintain a portfolio asset allocation appropriate for an investor's financial goals, investment objective, time horizon, and volatility tolerance.
2. Makes no attempt to predict the direction or magnitude of short-term market volatility.
3. Is characterized by a fixed target allocation to each asset class in an investor's portfolio.
4. Requires periodic portfolio rebalancing in order to maintain the target allocation to each asset class. Strategic asset allocation is, therefore, not a buy-and-hold strategy.

Tactical asset allocation attempts to improve upon the performance of strategic asset allocation. With a tactical strategy, the investor periodically alters the allocation to various asset classes based upon forecasts of asset class returns. Critics of tactical asset allocation argue that tactical asset allocation is just a new name for market timing, which has a deservedly bad reputation. Proponents argue that tactical asset allocation is not market timing. Market timing makes dramatic shifts into and entirely out of asset classes, whereas tactical asset allocation is more nuanced. Tactical asset allocation retains the advantages of diversification by maintaining minimum commitments to all asset classes in a portfolio, while adding value by opportunistically over-weighting and underweighting the asset class commitments. But the scale of a tactical bet does not determine the likelihood of whether the bet pays off; it determines how much value is added *if* the bet pays off. That is, decreasing the size of tactical bets does not increase the likelihood of success. It only limits the rewards for success and the penalties for failure. The important question remains: Does tactical asset allocation work? Does it add value?

The research reviewed in this chapter suggests that most tactical approaches will not improve upon the performance of strategic asset allocation. The one possible exception cited was Pu Shen's strategy that sells stocks when the spread between the S&P 500 earnings/price ratio and the yield on the three-month Treasury bill falls below the 10th percentile value for the spread. Whereas many tactical trading strategies involve frequent changes in portfolio allocation in an attempt to improve shorter-term portfolio performance, Pu Shen's strategy involves infrequent allocation changes with payoffs that may take years to realize. Pu Shen's strategy differs from other tactical strategies in that it is based on the market's valuation level.

In Exhibit 4.8 we saw that, at various times, investors have been willing to pay a wide range of price/earnings (P/E) multiples to acquire U.S. large company stocks and that subsequent returns varied accordingly. One might conclude from this exhibit that market prices periodically diverge from underlying "true values." Why might this be the case? Perhaps, as posited by behavioral economists, investor decision making is influenced by human emotion. When investor greed prevails, markets can overshoot true value on the high side and set the stage for subsequent below-average returns. The "irrational exuberance" of the late 1990s is one such example. Similarly, when fear and panic rule, markets can overshoot true value on the downside and set the stage for future above-average returns.

The observation that investors are unlikely to ever drive emotion out of their decision-making process creates a paradox. On the one hand, patient investors pursuing a valuation-based tactical asset allocation strategy may be able to earn an above-average return by taking advantage of either an unusually expensive or inexpensive market condition caused by extreme market sentiment. On the other hand, if the majority of investors are either overly optimistic or overly pessimistic, only a small minority will have the courage and discipline to earn an above-average return by making the opposite bet. Incremental payoffs are possible but only by pursuing strategies that psychologically are exponentially harder to execute!

For example, during the euphoria of the late 1990s, P/E ratios reached historically high levels. An investor following a contrarian, valuation-based tactical asset allocation strategy would surely have seen this period as an opportunity to exit the stock market. Yet based on our experience at the time, if a client wanted to change his asset allocation, it was usually because he wanted *more* invested in stocks, not less. We steadfastly discouraged these clients from increasing their stock allocations and in some cases were fired as a result of our advice. The point is that the right course of action is often in direct opposition to what investors are most inclined to do.

Years later investors faced a very different market environment following the onset of the Global Financial Crisis of 2008. In March 2009, U.S. stocks reached their lowest valuation level in more than two decades. After patiently waiting for years for the right buying opportunity, tactical investors finally had their chance. How many investors were able to overcome their fear and *increase* their stock allocation at the depths of the bear market? In our experience, if a client wanted to alter his asset allocation at that time, he most likely was interested in *decreasing* his stock allocation. In both euphoric and fearful market environments, clients who stuck to their portfolios' target asset allocations eventually achieved better investment results than those who gave into their emotions and changed their allocations.

In this chapter, we presented seven questions for investors interested in pursuing a market-timing strategy. It is worth repeating the final question here: *Do I have the patience and discipline to follow the strategy?* When it comes to valuation-based tactical asset allocation strategies, the answer for most investors is decidedly no. The great irony is that widespread, extreme investor sentiment both creates the valuation-based tactical opportunity and simultaneously ensures that few will derive above-average returns by exploiting it.

This chapter opens with a quote from Charles D. Ellis, and the discussion will now close with another of his observations:

> In investment management, the real opportunity to achieve superior results is not in scrambling to outperform the market, but in establishing *and adhering to* appropriate investment policies over the long term—policies that position the portfolio to benefit from riding with the main long-term forces in the market.[18]

Chapter 6

Time Horizon

He who wishes to be rich in a day will be hanged in a year.
—*Leonardo da Vinci (1452–1519),* Notebooks, *c. 1500*

Money is of a prolific generating nature. Money can beget money, and its offspring can beget more.
—*Benjamin Franklin (1706–1790),*
Letters: To My Friend, A. B., *1748*

Time is Archimedes' lever in investing.
—*Charles D. Ellis (1937–),* Investment Policy, *1985*

If you were charged with the task of dividing all the investment alternatives we have reviewed thus far into two groups on the basis of their investment characteristics, how would you do it? One way would be to rank them on the basis of their historical returns and look for a natural dividing line. With reference to the information in Exhibit 3.1, we see that the biggest gap in historical returns is between long-term corporate bonds and large company stocks. Using this as our dividing line, we would find that one group of investments consists of Treasury bills, intermediate-term government bonds, long-term government bonds, and long-term corporate bonds—all the interest-generating alternatives. The second group consists of large company stocks and small company stocks—the equity alternatives with high historical returns.

If we instead approach the task by ranking the investment alternatives on the basis of volatility as measured by their historical standard deviations, we would draw the natural dividing line in exactly the same place: between interest-generating investments and equity investments. Let us now contrast the investment characteristics of these two broad groups.

An interest-generating investment is a loan that provides a return in the form of interest payments, with the promise that the principal will be returned at a stated maturity date. The primary advantage of this kind of investment is that the cash flows (interest payments and return of principal) are specified in advance. The major disadvantage is that these investments tend to be very susceptible to inflation. Historically, interest-generating alternatives have not been capable of simultaneously producing an income stream while maintaining purchasing power.[1]

By comparison, large company stocks and small company stocks are equity ownership interests in businesses. An equity investment provides a return in the form of dividends and/or capital appreciation. It does not have a stated maturity nor any promise that the principal will be returned some day. But it also has no upper limit on its return possibilities. The primary advantage of an equity investment is the prospect for real (i.e., inflation-adjusted), long-term capital growth. The major disadvantage of an equity investment is the high short-run volatility of principal value.

In essence, these two broad categories, interest-generating investments and equity investments, represent the two alternatives for putting money to work. The traditional distinction is between being a "loaner" or an "owner." A low return is the price paid by the loaner, who wants the advantage of a more predictable outcome. Short-run volatility of principal is the price paid by the owner, who wants the long-term capital growth that is possible with equities. These trade-offs simply acknowledge the volatility and return relationships among investment alternatives. We previously discussed a wide variety of risks. In my judgment, however, the two most important investment risks are:

1. Inflation, which is most damaging to interest-generating investments
2. Volatility, which is most pronounced with equity investments

To focus our discussion, let us use Treasury bills as a proxy for interest-generating investments and large company stocks as a proxy for equity investments. In summation:

	Treasury Bills	Large Company Stocks
Advantage	Stability of principal value	Long-term real capital growth
Disadvantage	Susceptibility to inflation	Volatile returns

Given the higher returns produced by equity investments, we could conclude that investors have a greater fear of stock market volatility than of inflation. The lower returns that they willingly accept from Treasury bills in order to have stable principal values support that conclusion. Many investors are overconcerned with the volatility of stock returns and underconcerned with the damaging effects of inflation for several reasons: First, inflation is insidious, taking its toll little by little. In the long run, however, the impact can be devastating, as demonstrated in Exhibit 6.1. If we assume a future inflation rate of 3 percent, the purchasing power of $1,000 declines to $744 by the end of 10 years, $554 by the end of 20 years, and $412 by the end of 30 years.[2]

Second, investors who are not aware of the impact of inflation over time tend to view their investment results in nominal terms and may prefer the less volatile nature of interest-generating alternatives. For example, during 1979 and 1980, when inflation reached a peak of 12 to 13 percent, Treasury bill returns were at a historical high of 10 to 11 percent. Treasury bill investors tended to look at the accumulation of interest, ignoring the fact that these high nominal returns were

Exhibit 6.1
Inflation Risk

Purchasing Power of $1,000					
	Inflation Rate				
	2%	3%	4%	5%	6%
10 Years	$ 820	$ 744	$ 676	$ 614	$ 558
20 Years	$ 673	$ 554	$ 456	$ 377	$ 312
30 Years	$ 552	$ 412	$ 308	$ 231	$ 174

Purchasing Power Loss					
	Inflation Rate				
	2%	3%	4%	5%	6%
10 Years	18%	26%	32%	39%	44%
20 Years	33%	45%	54%	62%	69%
30 Years	45%	59%	69%	77%	83%

insufficient to compensate for the impact of inflation. Many investors still look at 1979 and 1980 as the "good old days" of high money market returns and deplore the lower, single-digit returns available as interest rates fell through the 1980s. Yet these investors actually were much better off in the lower interest rate environment. Returns were much higher in *real* terms at that time than during the higher interest rate environment of 1979 and 1980. It would be interesting to see how perceptions would change if Treasury bill investors had their returns routinely reported to them in inflation-adjusted terms.

Third, stock volatility by comparison can do much more damage in the short run. For example, on October 19, 1987, large company stock prices dropped more than 20 percent *in one day*, compared with the highest *annual* inflation rate during the last half century of 13 percent in 1979. Unfortunately, many investors focus too narrowly on the short term and react as if stock market reversals are permanent losses of capital. Some investors who suffered through the 1973–1974 bear market sold their stocks near the bottom and later missed participating in a very generous market environment through the 1980s and 1990s. In their discouragement they said to themselves,

"Invest in stocks? Never again!" Likewise, the "lost decade" of the 2000s (during which U.S. large company stock investors with full reinvestment of income cumulatively lost 9 percent) undoubtedly drove some investors permanently out of the stock market despite the important role common stocks play as a component of a longer-term portfolio strategy.

In the short run, the possible negative consequences of stock market volatility will be much greater than the damage likely from inflation. Is this fear of stock volatility warranted? In some circumstances it is, and in other situations perhaps not. As we look into the future, we can count on two things. First, short-run stock returns will remain unpredictable and volatile. Second, people will prefer predictability over uncertainty. For example, consider a choice between the following two investment alternatives. Investment A has an expected return of 6 percent and a standard deviation of 2 percent. Investment B has an expected return of 6 percent and a standard deviation of 4 percent. Both investments offer the same expected return, but investment B has twice as much volatility as investment A. Rational investors are volatility averse. Given these alternatives, such investors will choose investment A. Investment B provides no incentive for bearing its higher volatility.

Economists refer to the "declining marginal utility of wealth" as the underlying explanation for this aversion to volatility. That is, each additional dollar that is acquired always increases one's well-being, but it does so at a declining rate. An extra $100 means more to you if your net worth is $1,000 than if you are a millionaire. In an investment context, the additional dollar you make with a good outcome is not as valuable as the dollar that you lose with a bad outcome. In the real world, investors would sell investment B to buy investment A. By their doing so, the price of A would rise and the price of B would fall. In equilibrium, investment B would have a higher expected return to compensate for its greater volatility.

The same pricing mechanism is at work in our comparison of Treasury bills and large company stocks. In a rational market, the buying and selling activities of investors cause large company stocks to be priced to provide higher expected returns than Treasury bills, as compensation for bearing the volatility of equities.

In the previous chapter, we presented evidence indicating that market timing does not work. Consider what would happen, however, if there were an easy way to time the stock market. Investors would buy stocks in advance of a market rise and sell them in advance of a foreseen decline. This buying and selling activity, however, would change the pattern of future stock price behavior by smoothing out the market's ups and downs. This scenario has only one problem: When stock volatility disappears, so does the reward for bearing it! I therefore *prefer* a world where stocks retain their short-run, unpredictable volatility. Stocks' long-term higher returns are built partially on the foundation of their high volatility. Implicit in the market timer's worldview is the notion that investors make money in stocks *despite* their volatility. In contrast, the worldview presented here rests on the notion that investors make money in stocks *because* of their volatility.

Now, the question becomes: Under what conditions is the volatility worth assuming? If we allocate the 5.8 percent equity risk premium across each of the 365 days in the year, we would find that the average daily performance advantage of large company stocks relative to Treasury bills practically disappears.[3] On any given day, the chances are basically 50/50 that large company stocks will outperform Treasury bills. The ever-present volatility of stock returns provides no incentive to assume equity risk on the basis of a one-day time horizon. The same is true for one-month and one-year investments in stocks. Over the past 86 years, the standard deviation of total returns for large company stocks has been 20.3 percent (refer to Exhibit 3.1). This standard deviation is much larger than the 5.8 percent equity risk premium that we expect to receive on average from holding large company stocks. In the short run, although we *expect* to have higher returns from large company stocks, their high volatility will swamp recognition of the equity risk premium. As a result, even though in most years stocks will beat Treasury bills, frequently the reverse will be true. This fact is particularly troublesome for unsophisticated investors who often misinterpret the nature of this uncertainty in short-term return as evidence of an irrational marketplace.

Time horizon is one of the most important dimensions of the investment management process. Unfortunately, investors often do not have a good understanding of the concept of time horizon. In assessing interest-generating investments versus equity investments, time horizon determines appropriateness. If an investor knows she will need $30,000 next month to buy a car, a money market fund is a reasonable investment in the interim. A pension plan with known future nominal obligations (i.e., with no provision for inflation-adjusted benefits) may decide to match the duration of those obligations with bonds of a similar duration or follow an immunization strategy.

Most long-term investment situations, however, do not involve objectives with specific future nominal needs. The direction and magnitude of inflation are simply too uncertain. More often the goal is the after-tax preservation and/or accumulation of wealth in real terms, which requires equity investing. Whereas in the short run we decided that the volatility of equities is too great relative to the expected reward, this conclusion changes as the time horizon lengthens. For example, from 1926 through 2011 large company stocks outperformed Treasury bills in 56 of the 86 years, or 65 percent of the time. If we compare the performance over longer holding periods of 5 years, 10 years, and 20 years, however, we find that large company stocks increasingly dominate Treasury bills 76 percent, 83 percent, and finally 100 percent of the time, respectively.

Assume for a moment that we have a stable inflation, interest rate, and equity risk premium environment. As the time horizon lengthens, the expected return from stocks will not change, but the variability of holding period compound annual returns will decline dramatically. The longer the holding period, the greater the opportunity for good years to offset bad years, resulting in a range of compound annual returns that converges toward the middle.

In Exhibit 6.2, for example, we compare compound annual returns for large company stocks, long-term corporate bonds, long-term government bonds, Treasury bills, and inflation for 1-, 5-, 10-, and 20-year holding periods. In examining the information for 1-year holding periods, we see that in 49 of the 86 years (57 percent of the time) large company stocks outperformed the other three investment alternatives. But the returns ranged from −43.3 to 54 percent. Hence, although we expect large company stocks to outperform the other three investment alternatives in any given year, the penalty for underperformance can be quite high. The ranges of returns for other investment alternatives are narrower, as expected given their lower standard deviations.

As we stretch the time horizon to 10 years, large company stocks now dominate the other investment alternatives in 57 out of 77 periods, or 74 percent of the time. Our confidence in being right with large company stocks increases, and the penalty for a bad outcome is considerably less. The worst 10-year large company stock experience produced a compound annual loss of −1.4 percent.[4] On that basis, a $10,000 investment with full reinvestment of income would have declined to $8,685. In 73 of the 77 ten-year holding periods, large company stocks had positive compound annual returns.

Finally, we see for 20-year holding periods that large company stocks outperformed the other three investment alternatives in 61 out of 67 periods, or 91 percent of the time. The 20-year periods beginning in 1928, 1929, and 1930 resulted in returns for long-term corporate bonds that were superior to those of large company stocks. The extreme market conditions accompanying the Great Depression caused this unusual result. More recently, the 20-year periods ending with 2008, 2009, and 2011 generated greater returns for long-term government bonds than for large company stocks. Investors in large company stocks will surely remember these periods as being marked by the significant price declines in 2000–2002 and in 2008.

The volatility of stocks is undoubtedly an enemy in the short run, but it is the basis for their higher expected returns. Time transforms this short-run enemy into a friend for the long-term investor.

Exhibit 6.2

Comparison of Investment Results for Various Holding Periods (1926–2011)

	Large Company Stocks	Long-Term Corporate Bonds	Long-Term Government Bonds	Treasury Bills	Inflation
86 One-Year Holding Periods					
Highest annual percent return	54.0%	42.6%	40.4%	14.7%	18.2%
Lowest annual percent return	-43.3%	-8.1%	-14.9%	-0.0%	-10.3%
Number of periods with negative returns	24	17	22	1	10
Number of periods with best of four returns	49	12	13	12	N/A
Percentage of periods with best of four returns	57%	14%	15%	14%	N/A
82 Five-Year Holding Periods					
Highest compound annual percent return	28.6%	22.5%	21.6%	11.1%	10.1%
Lowest compound annual percent return	-12.5%	-2.2%	-2.1%	0.1%	-5.4%
Number of periods with negative compound returns	12	3	6	0	7
Number of periods with best of four returns	56	15	7	4	N/A
Percentage of periods with best of four returns	68%	18%	9%	5%	N/A
77 Ten-Year Holding Periods					
Highest compound annual percent return	20.1%	16.3%	15.6%	9.2%	8.7%
Lowest compound annual percent return	-1.4%	1.0%	-0.1%	0.1%	-2.6%
Number of periods with negative compound returns	4	0	1	0	6
Number of periods with best of four returns	57	9	5	6	N/A
Percentage of periods with best of four returns	74%	12%	6%	8%	N/A
67 Twenty-Year Holding Periods					
Highest compound annual percent return	17.9%	12.1%	12.1%	7.7%	6.4%
Lowest compound annual percent return	3.1%	1.3%	0.7%	0.4%	0.1%
Number of periods with negative compound returns	0	0	0	0	0
Number of periods with best of four returns	61	3	3	0	N/A
Percentage of periods with best of four returns*	91%	4%	4%	0%	N/A

*Due to rounding, the numbers in this row do not sum to 100%.

Data source: Calculated by Gibson Capital, LLC using data presented in *2012 Ibbotson® Stocks, Bonds, Bills, and Inflation® (SBBI®) Classic Yearbook,* © 2012 Morningstar. All rights reserved. Used with permission.

In Exhibit 6.2 we noted that an investor's performance results will vary depending on the calendar year in which his holding period begins. Few investors, however, establish an investment position exactly at the beginning of a calendar year. The utilization of annual return data therefore understates the range of returns for various holding periods. By changing the beginning point for various holding periods to a monthly rather than a calendar-year basis, Exhibit 6.3 provides a more comprehensive comparison of the range of returns for Treasury bills versus large company stocks. The graph utilizes data from 1926 through 2011 and compares the range of returns for holding periods of 12 months (1 year) to 240 months (20 years). Observe the potentially high penalty for being in large company stocks for holding periods as short as 12 months to 60 months.

As the holding period lengthens, however, the range of compound annual returns converges dramatically. Note that *all* 240-month holding periods had positive compound annual returns. It is also quite interesting to observe that the median return for large company stocks was approximately the same across the 12-, 60-, 120-, and 240-month holding periods. The median return for Treasury bills was, of course, much lower than for large company stocks but was similarly relatively constant.

Exhibits 6.4A and 6.4B communicate the same message in a different form. Here we can directly compare relative returns in a contemporaneous way for various holding periods. Again, we see that, if stock market volatility is the disease, time is the cure.

The miracle of compound interest is also at work in the pattern of the increasing dominance of large company stocks over time. What seems like a modest equity risk premium produces huge differences in wealth accumulation over long holding periods. Assume Treasury bills now yield 3 percent, with the corresponding estimated compound annual return for large company stocks at 9 percent. In Exhibit 6.5,

Exhibit 6.3

Large Company Stocks Versus Treasury Bills: Range of Compound Annual Returns for Various Holding Periods (1926–2011)

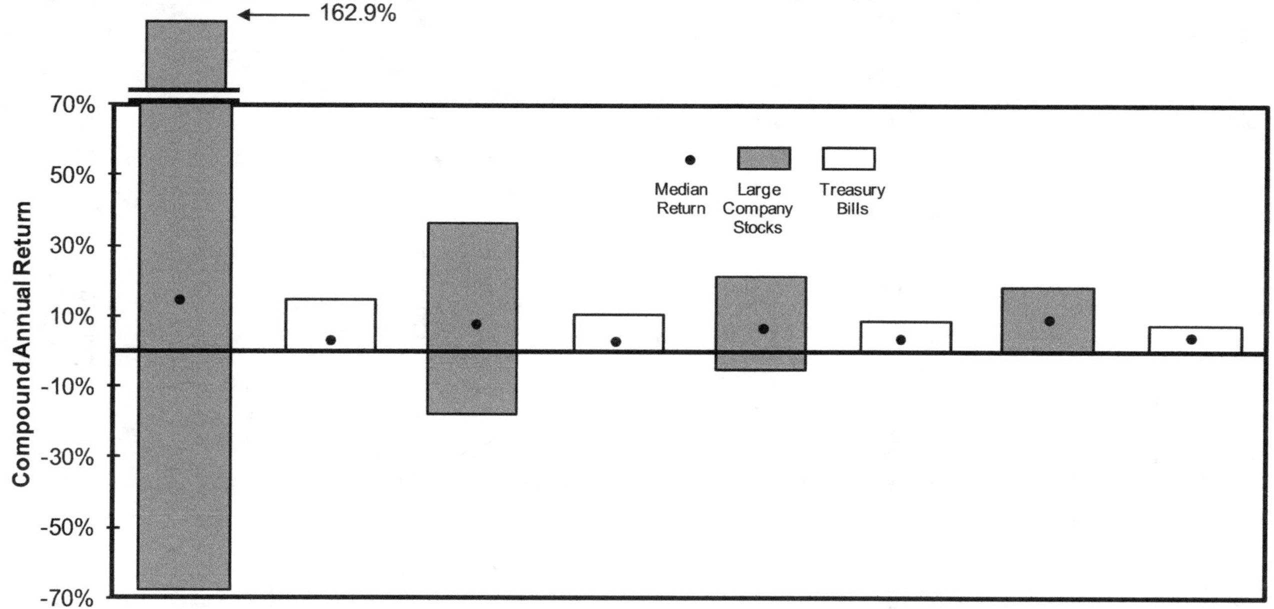

	12-Month Periods			60-Month Periods			120-Month Periods			240-Month Periods	
	Stocks	T-Bills		Stocks	T-Bills		Stocks	T-Bills		Stocks	T-Bills
High	+162.9%	+15.2%	H	+36.1%	+11.1%	H	+21.4%	+9.2%	H	+18.3%	+7.7%
Med	+12.6%	+3.2%	M	+10.7%	+3.0%	M	+10.7%	+3.6%	M	+11.7%	+4.2%
Low	-67.6%	0.0%	L	-17.4%	+0.1%	L	-4.9%	+0.1%	L	+1.9%	+0.4%

Data source: Calculated by Gibson Capital, LLC using data presented in *2012 Ibbotson® Stocks, Bonds, Bills, and Inflation® (SBBI®) Classic Yearbook*, © 2012 Morningstar. All rights reserved. Used with permission.

Exhibit 6.4A
Large Company Stocks Versus Treasury Bills: Compound Annual Returns for Various Holding Periods (1926–2011)

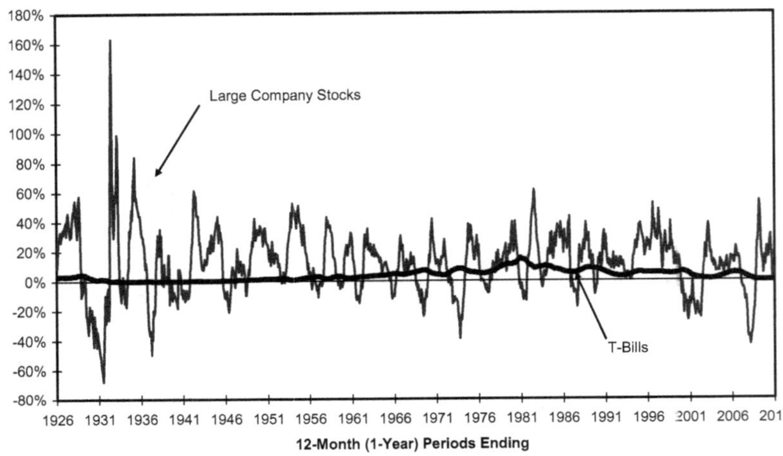

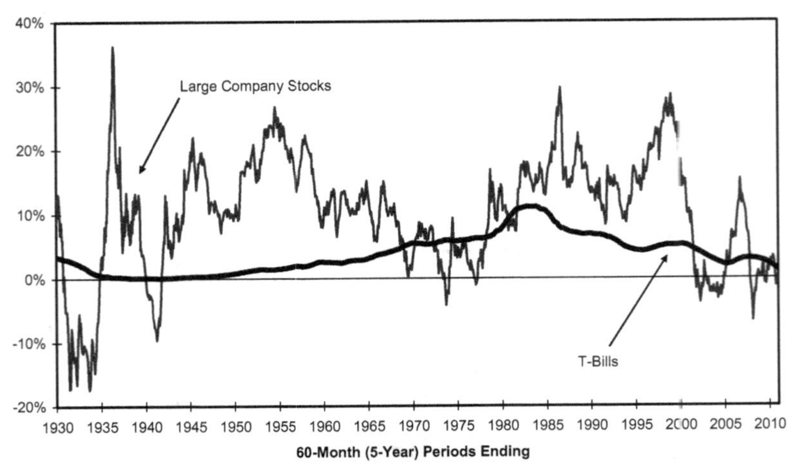

Data source: Calculated by Gibson Capital, LLC using data presented in *2012 Ibbotson® Stocks, Bonds, Bills, and Inflation® (SBBI®) Classic Yearbook*, © 2012 Morningstar. All rights reserved. Used with permission.

we see that, in only 13 years, the expected cumulative wealth from an investment in large company stocks would be double that of a corresponding investment in Treasury bills. By 20 years, large company stocks would be worth more than three times the value of an investment in Treasury bills.

Exhibit 6.4B

Large Company Stocks Versus Treasury Bills: Compound Annual Returns for Various Holding Periods (1926–2011)

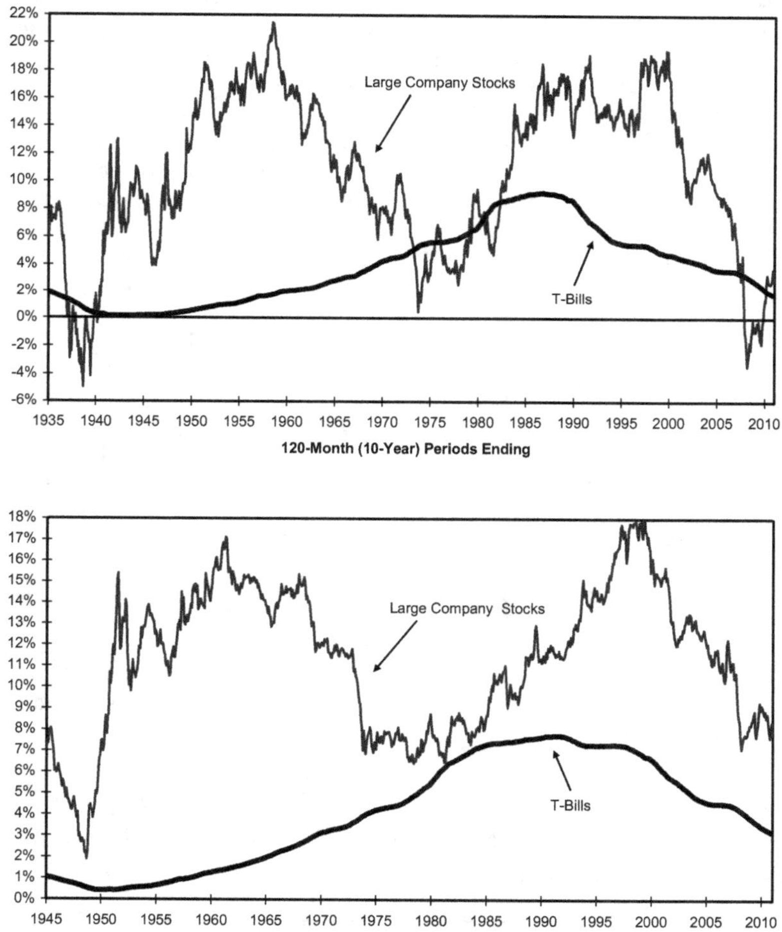

Data source: Calculated by Gibson Capital, LLC using data presented in *2012 Ibbotson® Stocks, Bonds, Bills, and Inflation® (SBBI®) Classic Yearbook*, © 2012 Morningstar. All rights reserved. Used with permission.

In summary, volatility swamps the expected payoff from stocks in the short run, making them a risk not worth taking. But in the long run, stocks emerge as the winner because of the convergence of average returns toward stocks' higher return growth path coupled with the miracle of compound interest.

Exhibit 6.5
Growth of $1 at Interest

Years	2%	3%	4%	5%	6%	7%	8%	9%	10%
1	1.02	1.03	1.04	1.05	1.06	1.07	1.08	1.09	1.10
2	1.04	1.06	1.08	1.10	1.12	1.14	1.17	1.19	1.21
3	1.06	1.09	1.12	1.16	1.19	1.23	1.26	1.30	1.33
4	1.08	1.13	1.17	1.22	1.26	1.31	1.36	1.41	1.46
5	1.10	1.16	1.22	1.28	1.34	1.40	1.47	1.54	1.61
6	1.13	1.19	1.27	1.34	1.42	1.50	1.59	1.68	1.77
7	1.15	1.23	1.32	1.41	1.50	1.61	1.71	1.83	1.95
8	1.17	1.27	1.37	1.48	1.59	1.72	1.85	1.99	2.14
9	1.20	1.30	1.42	1.55	1.69	1.84	2.00	2.17	2.36
10	1.22	1.34	1.48	1.63	1.79	1.97	2.16	2.37	2.59
11	1.24	1.38	1.54	1.71	1.90	2.10	2.33	2.58	2.85
12	1.27	1.43	1.60	1.80	2.01	2.25	2.52	2.81	3.14
13	1.29	1.47	1.67	1.89	2.13	2.41	2.72	3.07	3.45
14	1.32	1.51	1.73	1.98	2.26	2.58	2.94	3.34	3.80
15	1.35	1.56	1.80	2.08	2.40	2.76	3.17	3.64	4.18
16	1.37	1.60	1.87	2.18	2.54	2.95	3.43	3.97	4.59
17	1.40	1.65	1.95	2.29	2.69	3.16	3.70	4.33	5.05
18	1.43	1.70	2.03	2.41	2.85	3.38	4.00	4.72	5.56
19	1.46	1.75	2.11	2.53	3.03	3.62	4.32	5.14	6.12
20	1.49	1.81	2.19	2.65	3.21	3.87	4.66	5.60	6.73
21	1.52	1.86	2.28	2.79	3.40	4.14	5.03	6.11	7.40
22	1.55	1.92	2.37	2.93	3.60	4.43	5.44	6.66	8.14
23	1.58	1.97	2.46	3.07	3.82	4.74	5.87	7.26	8.95
24	1.61	2.03	2.56	3.23	4.05	5.07	6.34	7.91	9.85
25	1.64	2.09	2.67	3.39	4.29	5.43	6.85	8.62	10.83

Time horizon is the key variable in determining the appropriate balance of interest-generating investments versus equity investments in a portfolio, as summarized below:

	Interest-Generating Investments	Equity Investments
Advantage	Less volatility	Long-term real capital growth
Disadvantage	Inflation susceptibility	High volatility
Appropriate for	Short time horizons	Long time horizons

Investors generally tend to underestimate their relevant time horizons. For example, consider new clients, a husband and wife, both age 60. When discussing their time horizon, they comment, "We both work now but want to retire at age 65. Because we are only 5 years from retirement, our time horizon is very short. Equities were fine when we were young and building assets for retirement. Now that retirement is approaching, we should be cashing out of stocks to move into certificates of deposit and bonds so that we can use the interest for living expenses during retirement."

This couple has confused their retirement horizon with their investment portfolio time horizon. The latter is *much* longer. If they plan to rely on their portfolio to support them through retirement, their time horizon actually extends until the death of the survivor of the two. For a man and woman of average health, both 60 years old, the life expectancy of the survivor is more than 30 additional years. As we have seen, over long time horizons, the danger of inflation is greater than the risk of stock volatility. Accordingly, equities should be meaningfully represented in their portfolio.

The tendency for investors to underestimate their time horizons leads to portfolios that may be inappropriately underweighted in equities and therefore overexposed to inflation. This tendency is reinforced by the investor's desire to measure performance over quarterly and annual periods. Such measurement intervals are much too short to get a realistic assessment of progress toward the achievement of long-term objectives.

A proper understanding of time horizon can dramatically alter a person's volatility tolerance. The next chapter builds a simple model for guiding clients to make the most important decision impacting portfolio performance: the balance between interest-generating investments and equity investments.

Chapter 7

A Model for Determining Broad Portfolio Balance

Everything should be made as simple as possible, but not simpler.

—*Albert Einstein (1879–1955)*

You pays your money and you takes your choice.

—Punch, *1846*

The relationship between client and advisor begins with the data gathering session. The purpose of this process is to get to know the client. Much of the information solicited is factual in nature and can be determined objectively. For personal clients, this information includes the value of assets and liabilities, sources of income and expenditures, tax situation, family composition, employment information, and so on. For institutional clients, such as qualified retirement plans or endowments, this information includes a list of investment positions, anticipated contributions and withdrawals from the portfolio, and a description of legal or regulatory constraints.

Another area of data gathering is subjective in nature and requires a more qualitative approach. This area is the realm of client psychology, hopes and dreams, opinions and preferences regarding investments, and tolerance for various types of risk. Specifically, let us discuss the challenges involved in assessing the client's:

- Specific goals
- Investment objectives
- Investment knowledge
- Risks
- Volatility tolerance

Specific Goals

Examples of goals for an individual client include early retirement, college education for children, a vacation home purchase, or financial support for an aging parent. For institutional clients the goals might be to provide retirement benefits to participants in a qualified plan or to fund the charitable pursuits of an endowment fund.

When a client expresses these goals, they often lack specificity. The advisor needs to help the client flesh out the goals in more detail. For example, does early retirement mean age 50, 55, or 60? What lifestyle does the client want in retirement, and what level of income will be necessary to sustain it? If the client wants to send three children to college, will they attend high-priced private institutions or less expensive public universities? Will scholarships be likely? Will the children get jobs in order to contribute to their own expenses? If the children are young, at what rate will tuitions rise in the interim?

Is a vacation home purchase a short-term or long-term goal? Approximately what price range is the client considering? What would be the expenses associated with a vacation home? Does the client anticipate renting the vacation home when he is not using it? How much rental income could be generated?

In the situation of the aging parent, is support presently being provided by the client? What are the parent's sources of income, and does the parent have assets that can be sold to provide additional funds if needed? What kind of health insurance coverage does the parent have, and will he qualify for some form of government assistance for medical bills or income needs? Similarly, institutional clients need to specify the timing and size of future cash outflows.

Investment Objectives

Once the client's goals have been specified, the next step is to develop investment objectives that correspond to those goals. Subject to reasonable portfolio return and volatility assumptions, for example, we can calculate the annual investment necessary to accumulate a predetermined future sum of money.

Sometimes, however, client goals are more ambitious than they realistically can achieve. All too often, people procrastinate and only get serious about achieving financial independence a few years prior to retirement. They are ready to modify their lifestyles as necessary to free up funds for investment in order to be assured a comfortable retirement. By that point, however, the lifestyle supportable at retirement largely has been determined. If the lifestyle is found to be seriously inadequate, the client probably can do little to improve it materially.

Human desires tend to exceed the resources available to fund them. In developing investment objectives, therefore, goals must be prioritized and sometimes compromised in the process of determining what is realistically possible in any given situation. Sound investment objectives are built on realistic capital market assumptions and reflect the limitations of the client's available income and resources.

Investment Knowledge

The best clients understand the general principles of investment management and the performance characteristics of different investment alternatives. The long-term success of the investment management process depends to a large degree on the client's understanding of the reasoning underlying the structure of her portfolio and how it will behave. In the data gathering process, it is helpful to have clients describe their good and bad experiences with investments. From their comments the advisor can glean the breadth and depth of their knowledge. Often, advisors use questionnaires that exhaustively list many different types of investment alternatives. Clients are asked to indicate their familiarity with, preference for, and prior use of each investment alternative. I think it is important to recognize the primary purpose of such questionnaires and to be aware of their limitations.

A client who indicates familiarity with, preference for, and/or knowledge about common stocks on a questionnaire, for example, does not necessarily understand them sufficiently to make an informed decision about an appropriate allocation for her portfolio. At best, such questionnaires are a beginning point for an educational process that meaningfully involves the client. A significant danger exists in using the responses to such questions inappropriately as a basis for either inferring volatility tolerance or choosing building blocks for constructing a portfolio. A client who says she has never invested in bonds and prefers not to own them may only be expressing unfamiliarity with them. It would be inappropriate to develop a portfolio excluding bonds solely on the basis of such a response.

By analogy, consider a person who consults a physician because of an ache or pain. The physician will not recommend a course of treatment based on the patient's familiarity with various prescription drugs. Investment preferences often are based on incomplete or erroneous information and therefore should not be used as the basis of a portfolio strategy or assessment of volatility tolerance.

Risks

In investment management, risk is often equated with the uncertainty (variability or standard deviation) of possible returns around the expected return. Clients, however, do not typically think in terms of expected return and standard deviation. More often, clients think of risk as it is defined in the dictionary: the chance of loss. Many investment advisors agree that it is more accurate to describe investors as typically being loss averse rather than risk averse. For example, the variability of returns investors experience from one year to another may not be particularly troublesome so long as the returns are not *negative*. Beneath the psychology of loss aversion lurks a fear by some investors that negative returns may be permanent capital losses.

Another problem with loss-aversion psychology is that clients tend to think in terms of nominal rather than real returns. For example, many investors would feel better about earning 2 percent after taxes in a 6 percent inflationary environment than they would about losing 1 percent after taxes in a 2 percent inflationary environment. The positive nominal gain of 2 percent in this example creates the illusion of getting ahead although, adjusted for the 6 percent inflation, their real loss is 4 percent. In actuality they would be better off losing 1 percent in the 2 percent inflationary environment, resulting in a smaller real loss of 3 percent.

Many clients are fearful of equity investments. In working with them, the task is not to convert them from risk avoiders to risk takers. As we concluded earlier, it is very rational to be risk averse. Rather, the task is to sensitize clients to all the risks they face, then to prioritize the relative dangers of these risks *given the contexts of their situations*. This is why we explored in detail the impact that time horizon has on the portfolio design process.

We can determine whether volatility or inflation is the greater risk only in reference to the relevant investment time horizon. For the long-term investor, volatility is not the major risk; inflation is. Because risk is time horizon dependent, I will use the expression *volatility tolerance* when discussing the investor's ability to live with the ups and downs of investment markets. Although this distinction may seem subtle, it is an important one. Occasionally, traditional investment terminology contributes to investor confusion. Although it is true that people prefer stability over uncertainty and therefore are volatility averse, it is not necessarily true that volatility is the major risk confronting the investor. Hence, it is a mistake to use the words *risk* and *volatility* interchangeably. For example, it is wrong to label equity-oriented, long-term investors as risk takers. In my judgment, the equity-oriented investor with a long time horizon is following the *low-risk strategy* by holding a portfolio that offers protection from the biggest risk he faces—inflation!

Without guidance, many clients do not know how to realistically assess the risks they face. By default, they tend to assume that the familiar and comfortable path is the safe one, whereas anything unfamiliar or uncomfortable must be risky. For example, I have worked with a number of real estate professionals who consider themselves to be very risk averse and fearful of common stocks. Yet they are heavily invested in real estate (another equity investment) using high financial leverage. When the risk of such highly leveraged equity investing is pointed out to them, the response is often: "There's no risk there. I *understand* real estate and am *comfortable* with it."

Volatility Tolerance

Investment advisors use a variety of methods to assess a client's ability to tolerate volatility. Given the problems we have discussed regarding the use of the terms *risk* and *volatility* interchangeably, it obviously is not advisable to simply ask clients to describe themselves as being either risk avoiders or risk takers. Given that choice, rational investors should answer that they are risk avoiders. The real issue is the amount of volatility that the client can tolerate. Some investment advisors look for volatility tolerance cues based on the client's business and personal lifestyles. For example, a person who likes the security of working for one employer for a lifetime and prefers recreational horseshoes may be more volatility averse than a person who changes jobs relatively frequently to advance his career and likes to parachute on the weekends.

The problems with these approaches are that they are highly subjective and difficult to translate into a quantitative measurement of volatility tolerance. An examination of the client's current investment portfolio provides some clues, but, again, the danger is that his current holdings may reflect his familiarity and comfort with various investments rather than indicate his informed volatility tolerance.

Whatever approach an advisor uses to assess volatility tolerance, it is important to remember that it is not a fixed, inherited characteristic, like blue eyes that stay blue for the rest of one's life. Accordingly, it is dangerous to develop an investment strategy on the basis of an initial assessment of volatility tolerance, regardless of how accurate the reading may be. To do so inappropriately presumes that clients already know what is in their best interests. If clients' risk perceptions are inaccurate, they cannot make wise decisions. The investment advisor's task is to provide a frame of reference that enables clients to correctly perceive risks within the contexts of their situations. Surprisingly, a client's volatility tolerance can shift within a rather broad range, based on an improved understanding of the pros and cons of different investment alternatives and the general principles of portfolio design.

The informed modification of volatility tolerance is one of the investment advisor's major responsibilities to her clients and represents a great opportunity to add value. The modification of volatility tolerance may increase the client's comfort with equity investments if the investment time horizon is long. On the other hand, if the time horizon is short, a client may realize that the incremental return expected from equity investments is not sufficient compensation for the high level of return volatility. In this situation, volatility tolerance is appropriately lowered with a corresponding reduction in equity investments as the client's perceptions become more realistic.

The euphoria of the U.S. stock market's spectacular gains toward the end of the 1990s convinced many investors that, in the "new economy," great returns were achievable with relatively little risk. As a result of their misperceptions regarding risk, they overallocated to stocks and exposed themselves to subsequent portfolio declines that were more severe than they could tolerate either financially or psychologically. Had they fully understood the risks they were taking, they might have had more reasonable stock allocations prior to the onset of the bear market, thereby limiting both their portfolio losses and their stress.

Exhibit 7.1 is an effective visual aid for contrasting the return and volatility characteristics of Treasury bills versus large company stocks. The stable pattern of positive annual total returns for Treasury bills looks like the skyline of a large city. Superimposed on this skyline is the wildly fluctuating pattern of annual total returns for large company stocks. A solid horizontal line drawn across the graph corresponds to large company stocks' 11.8 percent simple average return. It is interesting to note that over the entire 86-year period, 1981 was the only year when Treasury bills had a return in excess of large company

Exhibit 7.1
Volatility Risk (1926–2011)

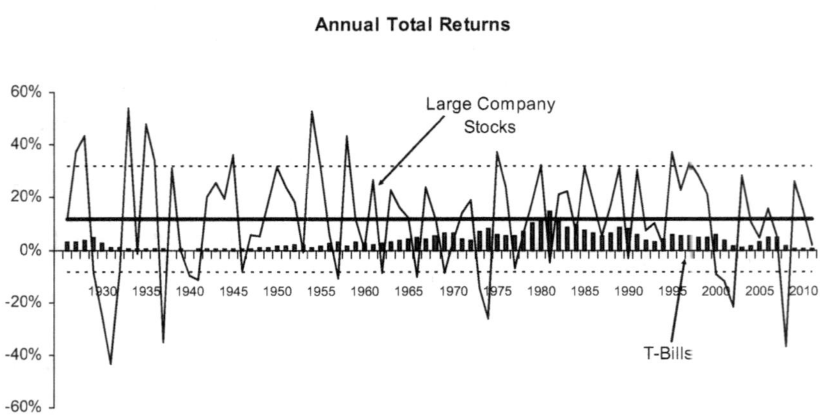

Source: © Roger C. Gibson, "Asset Allocation and the Rewards of Multiple-Asset-Class Investing," 1998. Updated by author. Data source: *2012 Ibbotson® Stocks, Bonds, Bills, and Inflation® (SBBI®) Classic Yearbook,* © 2012 Morningstar. All rights reserved. Used with permission.

stocks' simple average return of 11.8 percent. That does not, however, justify common stock investing for short time horizons. Over one-third of the time, large company stock annual total returns lagged behind those of Treasury bills, often by a significant margin.

On Exhibit 7.1, it is easy to identify the particularly bad years for large company stocks. It is also fairly easy to spot the bad 2- and 3-year periods. It is more difficult to identify bad 5- and 10-year periods since good years invariably become averaged in with the bad years. The passage of time therefore mitigates the risk posed by volatility while giving an opportunity for the equity risk premium to compound its advantage.

The standard deviation statistic of 20.3 shown in Exhibit 3.1 quantifies the high level of large company stock return volatility. With the simplifying assumption that large company stock returns are normally distributed, roughly two-thirds of the yearly return observations should fall within plus or minus 20.3 percent of the simple average return of 11.8 percent. Dashed horizontal lines are drawn on Exhibit 7.1 one standard deviation below and one standard deviation above large company stocks' simple average return of 11.8 percent at −8.5 percent and 32.1 percent, respectively. These upper and lower dashed horizontal lines form an envelope that contains approximately two-thirds of the annual total return observations. The remaining one-third of the annual total return observations falls outside the envelope.[1] The relative range defined by one standard deviation is 40.6 percentage points wide. Historically, the reward for bearing this volatility has been an incremental compound return of 5.8 percent above that available from stable principal value Treasury bills.[2] Now, which number is bigger: the 40.6 percentage points of relative volatility or the 5.8 percentage points of reward?

The relationship between these two numbers is very important in effectively managing client expectations. The expected reward for bearing volatility risk is small relative to the high level of volatility. Therefore, it always will be impossible for the client to have any short-run recognition of the higher average return she expects to receive from making equity investments. The high volatility of common stock returns will simply swamp the short-term expected reward. A corollary of this observation is that short-term common stock performance is meaningless for a truly long-term investor. A quarterly or annual performance report does not measure return as much as it measures volatility around a long-term growth path completely obscured by that volatility. This growth path will become clear only in retrospect as the holding period becomes very long.

The Portfolio Balance Model

Admittedly, a gap separates the investment manager's world of "expected returns and standard deviations" from the client's world of "wanting to make lots of money without taking risks!" The first part of this book discussed the long-term historical performance of various U.S. capital market investment alternatives. On the basis of this information, we developed simple models to estimate the long-term compound annual returns and risks associated with these investment alternatives. As we guide clients through this capital market review, their perceptions and expectations become more realistic, and they develop the capacity to make better investment decisions. Without this education, few clients are equipped to make the best decisions for themselves.

The portfolio balance chosen between interest-generating investments and equity investments is one of the most important decisions that the client makes. This decision determines the basic volatility and return characteristics of the portfolio. We need a methodology that forces the client to deal realistically with the trade-off between volatility and return. The model we will develop uses simplistic assumptions. Although some rigor may be lost in this simplicity, we ultimately should judge the value of the model by whether it effectively helps the client understand the volatility versus return trade-off. If the client makes better decisions and adheres more confidently to an appropriate long-term strategy, the model accomplishes its purpose.

In Chapter 6, we divided the investment world into two categories—interest-generating investments and equity investments. We concluded that each category has a primary advantage and disadvantage. Interest-generating investments provide promises regarding payment of interest and principal but are susceptible to purchasing power erosion as a consequence of inflation. By contrast, equity investments historically have been able to build purchasing power through capital growth but have the disadvantage of high volatility.

To highlight these differences, we chose Treasury bills as a proxy for interest-generating investments in general and large company stocks as a proxy for the wide variety of equity investments. We concluded that the appropriateness of Treasury bills versus large company stocks is determined primarily in reference to the investment time horizon. For a long time horizon, inflation poses a larger risk than stock market volatility, and accordingly we should orient the portfolio more heavily toward common stocks and other forms of equity investments. For a short time horizon, stock market volatility is more dangerous than inflation, and so we should weight the portfolio more heavily in Treasury bills and other interest-generating investments that have more predictable returns.

Let us review the steps involved in guiding clients to make this most important broad portfolio balance decision:

Step 1. Verify that the client fully understands the return characteristics of Treasury bills and large company stocks:

- A. Refer to Exhibit 2.1, "Wealth Indices of Investments in the U.S. Capital Markets."
- B. Refer to Exhibit 3.1, "Summary Statistics of Annual Total Returns."

Step 2. Verify that the client fully understands the volatility characteristics of Treasury bills and large company stocks. Refer to Exhibit 7.1, "Volatility Risk."

Step 3. Review with the client the importance of time horizon in assessing risks and evaluating the appropriateness of interest-generating investments versus equity investments. Refer to Chapter 6.

Step 4. Determine the current value of the client's total investment portfolio. This includes:

A. The value of all liquid and nonliquid investments (e.g., investment real estate) even though the latter cannot be converted easily to cash.

B. The value of employer-sponsored retirement plans, even though the client may not have investment discretion of the funds.

C. The present value of annuitized streams of income. Although these are not normally thought of as investment assets and are seldom reflected on the client's balance sheet, they are nevertheless important economic assets that should be considered in structuring portfolios.

This fourth step helps the client think of his portfolio in the broadest terms and focuses his attention on the big picture.

Step 5. Instruct the client to hypothetically convert his entire investment portfolio to cash. This conversion overcomes inertia by freeing the client from the ghosts of past investment decisions.

Step 6. Describe a hypothetical investment world with only two investment alternatives—Treasury bills and large company stocks. In this world we will assume:

A. Modeled returns of 3 percent for Treasury bills and 9 percent for large company stocks. (Each return is below its long-term historical average.)

B. Standard deviations of 0 percent for Treasury bills and 20 percent for large company stocks. (The Treasury bill standard deviation is assumed to be 0 percent because over a one-year horizon, a Treasury bill return can be locked in with no uncertainty.)

Step 7. Ask the client to allocate the cash from his liquidated investment portfolio between these two investment alternatives. In doing so, the client should keep in mind the volatility and return characteristics of each investment and his relevant investment time horizon.

As you review the range of choices available to the client, consider a portfolio composed entirely of Treasury bills. Of all possible alternatives, this portfolio has the lowest modeled return. This is the price paid for the elimination of short-run volatility. As we begin to allocate money to large company stocks, the portfolio volatility will increase in direct proportion to the percentage invested in stocks. Exhibit 7.2 shows the volatility and return characteristics of five portfolios ranging from 100 percent Treasury bills through 50 percent Treasury bills/50 percent large company stocks to 100 percent large company stocks.

Exhibit 7.2
Example Portfolio Choices

	Portfolio Balance		Modeled Portfolio Performance				
	Treasury Bills	Large Company Stocks	Modeled Return*	Volatility*	Typical Range of Results**		
1	100%	0%	3.0%	± 0.0%	3.0%		
2	70%	30%	4.8%	± 6.0%	-1.2%	to	10.8%
3	50%	50%	6.0%	±10.0%	-4.0%	to	16.0%
4	30%	70%	7.2%	±14.0%	-6.8%	to	21.2%
5	0%	100%	9.0%	±20.0%	-11.0%	to	29.0%

*Calculated as the weighted average of the modeled returns and volatilities of Treasury bills and large company stocks. For example, for Portfolio 4 above, which is made up of 30% Treasury bills and 70% large company stocks:

Portfolio Modeled Return = 0.30 (3%) + 0.70 (90%) = 7.2%
Portfolio Volatility = 0.30 (0%) + 0.70 (20%) = 14.0%

**The odds are approximately two out of three that a single year's total return will be in a range defined by the modeled return plus or minus the volatility.

Note: As the percentage allocated to large company stocks increases, the portfolio volatility increases much more rapidly than the incremental increase in modeled return. The longer the time horizon, the more worthwhile it is to bear higher levels of short-run volatility. In deciding how they would divide their investment funds between Treasury bills and large company stocks, investors are forced to acknowledge and deal with the volatility/return trade-off issue.

Investment decisions are made under terms of uncertainty. For this reason, it is better to forecast portfolio results in terms of typical ranges around modeled returns. For example, rather than simply saying that portfolio 2 has a modeled return of 4.8 percent, it is much more meaningful to indicate that the odds are approximately 2 out of 3 that the actual return will be within plus or minus 6 percent of the modeled return of 4.8 percent. This implies a typical annual range of results from −1.2 to 10.8 percent.

Clients bring to the client-advisor relationship their own expectations regarding the returns and volatility levels associated with various investment alternatives. Often, clients believe that returns are achieved more easily with less volatility than indicated here. Such clients struggle with the portfolio choices presented in Exhibit 7.2. If so, that is good. If a struggle is going to occur over the nature of the volatility versus return trade-off, it is best to deal with it at this point in the portfolio design process.[3]

By dividing the 20 percent standard deviation of large company stocks by the 6 percent difference between the modeled returns of 9 percent for large company stocks and 3 percent for Treasury bills, we see that for every 1 percent increase in the portfolio's modeled return, portfolio volatility will increase by approximately plus or minus 3.3 percent. For example, portfolio 1 has 100 percent of its assets in Treasury bills and has a modeled return of 3 percent. In order to increase the modeled return by only 1.8 percent, we need to shift 30 percent of the portfolio out of Treasury bills into large company stocks. Doing so, however, increases portfolio volatility by an additional plus or minus 6 percent—a large increase in short-run uncertainty.

Awareness of this trade-off forces the client to focus more attention on her ability to tolerate short-run portfolio volatility. This process is healthy, because in determining broad portfolio balance, it is more important to concentrate on volatility tolerance than on the return requirement. Some clients require unusually high rates of return to achieve all their goals. These high rates of return may not be realistically possible given reasonable capital market assumptions. Even if they are possible, they should not be pursued unless the client has both the financial and psychological capacity to tolerate the associated volatility.

Having reviewed the historical performance of the capital markets, clients should understand that the higher returns from equity investments are the compensation they expect to receive in exchange for the volatility they assume. A client's volatility tolerance, in this framework, is simply the added volatility she is willing to accept in exchange for an extra unit of modeled return. If the return associated with a client's maximum volatility tolerance is insufficient to realize her goals, she either should modify her goals or acknowledge that she most likely will not realize them. If the return associated with the upper limit of her volatility tolerance is more than is needed to accomplish her goals, it is easy to move down the volatility scale to a more stable portfolio, should that be her preference.

Psychologically, it is easier to tolerate volatility if the final outcome occurs in the distant future. A proper understanding of time horizon, therefore, increases volatility tolerance for the long-time-horizon investor. Unfortunately, however, the liquidity of the capital markets provides constant revision of security prices and a heightened awareness of short-run performance. The trick is to avoid attaching too much significance to short-run performance numbers if the relevant outcome is truly associated with a long-term investment time horizon.

Exhibit 7.2 by itself may be sufficient for those clients who have a good intuitive grasp of the impact that the passage of time has on narrowing the range of portfolio compound annual returns. Other clients may need to have the range of returns over time for each portfolio specified in more detail. For them, Exhibits 7.3 through 7.7 can be used in conjunction with Exhibit 7.2 to communicate the impact of time on the choice of broad portfolio balance. For those who like graphs, Exhibits 7.4A through 7.7A show the distribution of returns for a one-year time horizon for portfolios 2 through 5. No such distribution is shown for portfolio 1 because it has a fixed annual return of 3 percent. Exhibits 7.4B through 7.7B show in tabular form the

Exhibit 7.3
Portfolio 1

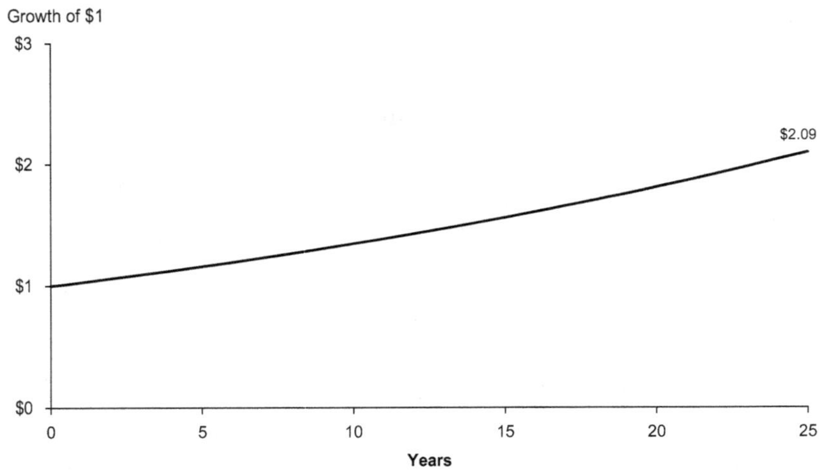

Source: Illustrations produced using Vestek Systems, Inc. software.

distributions of portfolio annualized returns, which describe the likelihood of achieving various returns over 1-, 3-, 5-, 10-, 15-, and 25-year time horizons. Finally, Exhibit 7.3 and Exhibits 7.4C through 7.7C show the path of wealth accumulation over time for each of the five portfolios for the 10th, 50th, and 90th percentile compound annual return probabilities.

As we review the distribution of portfolio annualized returns for portfolio 3 in Exhibit 7.5B, we see a return of −5.97 percent shown at the 10th percentile for a 1-year time horizon. This means that there is a 90 percent likelihood that the actual return will be higher than −5.97 percent and a 10 percent likelihood that it will be lower. Under the 10th percentile column for a 5-year time horizon, however, we see a value of 0.49 percent. That is, the likelihood is 90 percent that, for a 5-year holding period, this portfolio will have a compound annual return in excess of 0.49 percent. For a 25-year horizon, the likelihood is 90 percent that the compound annual return will be greater than

Exhibit 7.4
Portfolio 2

A. Distribution of Returns: One-Year Time Horizon

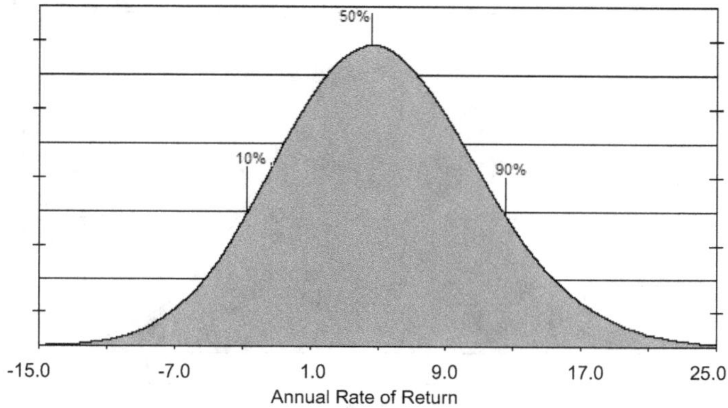

B. Distribution of Portfolio Annualized Returns

Year	10th %	25th %	50th %	75th %	90th %
1	-2.62	0.82	4.78	8.89	12.74
3	0.44	2.48	4.78	7.13	9.30
5	1.40	2.99	4.78	6.60	8.27
10	2.38	3.51	4.78	6.06	7.23
15	2.82	3.74	4.78	5.83	6.78
25	3.26	3.98	4.78	5.59	6.32

C. Growth of $1

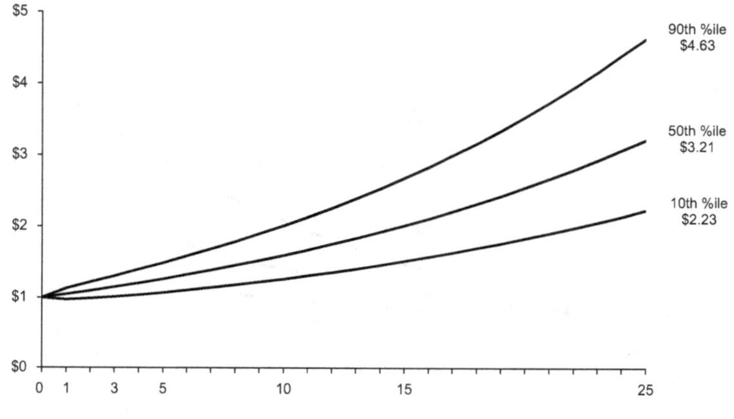

Source: Illustrations produced using Vestek Systems, Inc. software.

Exhibit 7.5
Portfolio 3

A. Distribution of Returns: One-Year Time Horizon

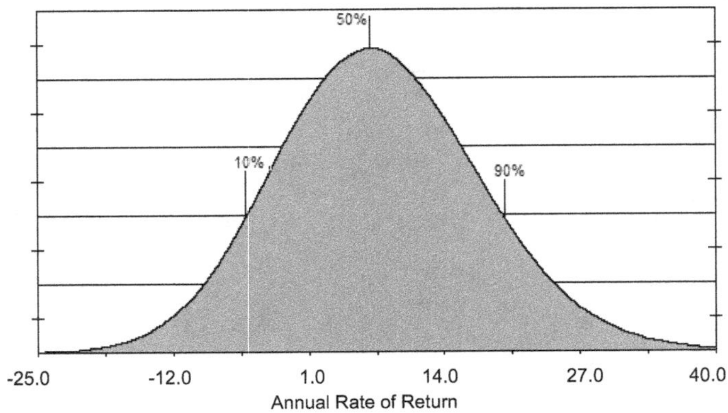

B. Distribution of Portfolio Annualized Returns

Year	10th %	25th %	50th %	75th %	90th %
1	-5.97	-0.46	6.03	12.95	19.57
3	-1.07	2.24	6.03	9.97	13.65
5	0.49	3.08	6.03	9.07	11.88
10	2.08	3.94	6.03	8.17	10.14
15	2.80	4.32	6.03	7.78	9.37
25	3.52	4.70	6.03	7.38	8.61

C. Growth of $1

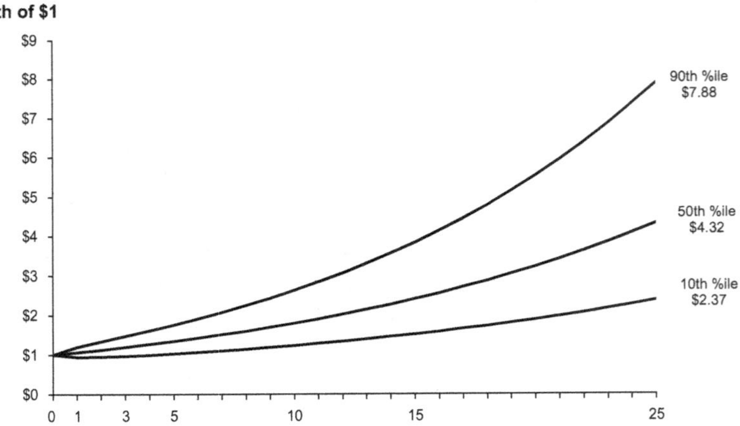

Source: Illustrations produced using Vestek Systems, Inc. software.

Exhibit 7.6
Portfolio 4

A. Distribution of Returns: One-Year Time Horizon

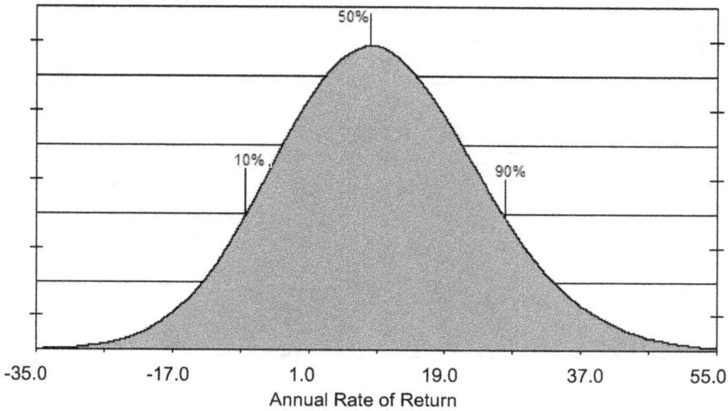

B. Distribution of Portfolio Annualized Returns

Year	10th %	25th %	50th %	75th %	90th %
1	-9.12	-1.71	7.21	16.95	26.49
3	-2.55	1.97	7.21	12.73	17.95
5	-0.43	3.13	7.21	11.46	15.44
10	1.75	4.31	7.21	10.20	12.97
15	2.73	4.84	7.21	9.65	11.89
25	3.73	5.37	7.21	9.09	10.82

C. Growth of $1

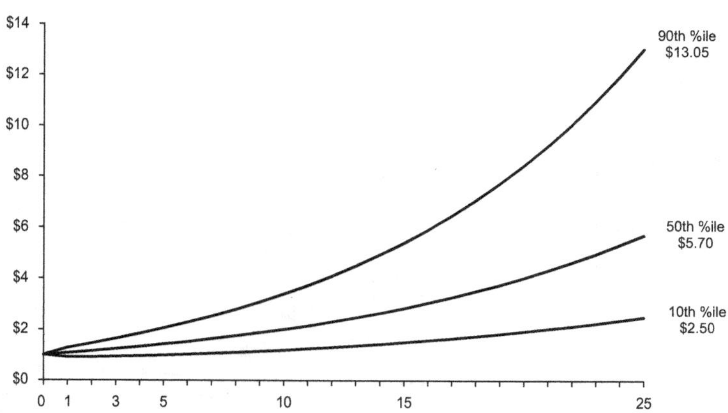

Source: Illustrations produced using Vestek Systems, Inc. software.

Exhibit 7.7
Portfolio 5

A. Distribution of Returns: One-Year Time Horizon

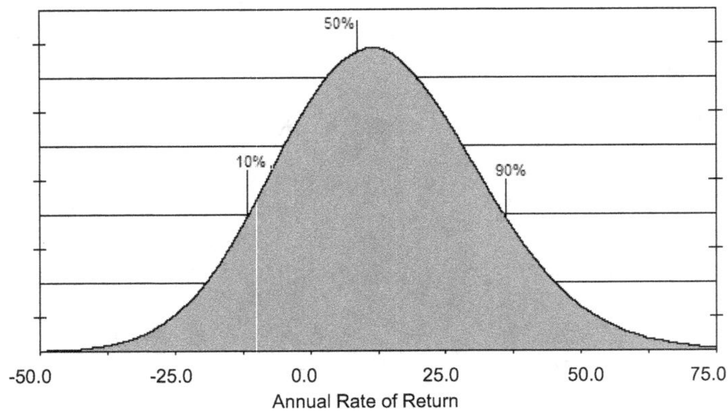

B. Distribution of Portfolio Annualized Returns

Year	10th %	25th %	50th %	75th %	90th %
1	-13.13	-3.16	9.24	23.23	37.37
3	-4.30	1.90	9.24	17.11	24.69
5	-1.40	3.51	9.24	15.29	21.03
10	1.60	5.16	9.24	13.48	17.45
15	2.97	5.90	9.24	12.69	15.90
25	4.35	6.64	9.24	11.90	14.36

C. Growth of $1

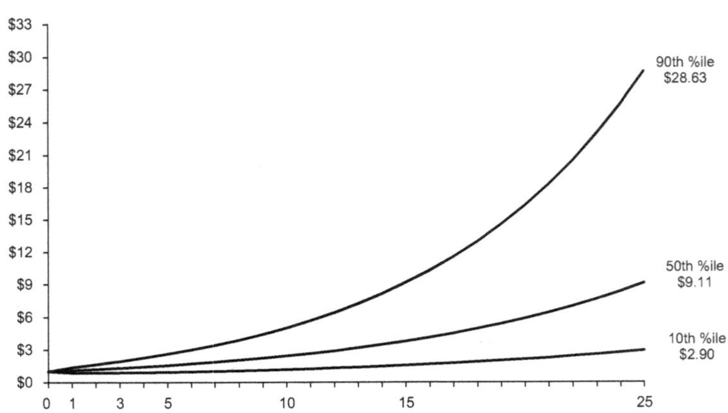

Source: Illustrations produced using Vestek Systems, Inc. software.

3.52 percent—an interesting outcome when one considers that Treasury bills have a modeled return of 3 percent. In other words, given our modeling assumptions, over a 25-year investment horizon the chances are 9 out of 10 that a 50/50 mix of Treasury bills and large company stocks will outperform an all-Treasury bill portfolio. As expected, with longer time horizons, more opportunities exist for good and bad years to offset each other and thereby narrow the range of outcomes and mitigate the downside risk posed by volatility.

The 25th percentile column provides a less severe and more likely picture of the downside risk of the portfolio. For example, under the 25th percentile column we find a value of −0.46 percent for a 1-year time horizon. That indicates that the chances are 3 out of 4 that the portfolio return will exceed −0.46 percent over a 1-year time horizon, and so forth.

If we compare portfolio 2 with portfolio 3, we will find that the median (50th percentile) return is lower and that the range of possible outcomes for any comparative period is correspondingly smaller for portfolio 2. By contrast, portfolio 4 will have a wider range of possible outcomes with a correspondingly higher median (50th percentile) return.

A comparison of these exhibits shows the variation in short-run volatility based on the percentage of the portfolio allocated to large company stocks. It also clearly demonstrates that the passage of time dramatically narrows the range of compound annual returns for each portfolio. This conclusion is consistent with the ones that we reached in Chapter 6, which dealt with the importance of time horizon.

Investment objectives usually are solicited from clients during the initial data gathering session. Occasionally, a client will express an objective like "a 12 percent compound annual return with little or no risk," which qualitatively translates to "very high returns with stable principal values." This is not one investment objective; it is two competing objectives, and to the extent that the one objective is pursued, the other must be sacrificed. The portfolio choices in Exhibit 7.2 clarify this unavoidable volatility versus return trade-off.

We now have an appreciation of the necessity to educate clients and provide them with a context for making good decisions. According to Charles D. Ellis, the broad portfolio balance decision is an investment policy decision, which is the nondelegatable responsibility of the *client*. Within the framework developed, the client's choice of a portfolio from Exhibit 7.2 is an indirect measure of the client's *informed* volatility tolerance.

This model is not without its drawbacks. The notion of standard deviation is not well understood by most clients. For this reason, the model has been designed to be as simple and straightforward as possible. Another risk is that the choices are too hypothetical and therefore not realistic to clients. You can help the client to overcome this risk by incorporating discussions of historical capital market experiences like the bear market of 2000–2002 and the bear market during the Global Financial Crisis, when large company stocks lost approximately half their value. Although such severe market declines are unusual, they have occurred in the past and likely will occur again in the future. We need to educate clients to expect it.[4]

Periodically, advisors should re-engage their clients in this exercise for determining broad portfolio balance. Over time, clients' experiences with investments will change, and their reactions may differ from what they initially expected. For example, some clients who thought they thoroughly understood stock volatility and could live with it may temper their opinions following the steep price declines during the Global Financial Crisis or the prolonged 2000–2002 bear market. Various life events also can occur that will alter a client's volatility tolerance, such as changes in family composition, job or career changes, or health problems.

Through these changes, this decision-making model will continue to emphasize the fact that the client must willingly accept increased volatility to increase the portfolio's modeled return. The balance chosen between interest-generating investments, as represented by Treasury bills, and equity investments, as represented by large company stocks, is one of the most important investment decisions the client will make. It simultaneously determines the portfolio's general volatility level and its long-term growth path. Subject to this broad portfolio balance decision, the advisor can proceed to design a more diversified portfolio, utilizing multiple asset classes. This brings us to the next chapter, which discusses diversification.

Chapter 8

Diversification: The Third Dimension

Better a steady dime than a rare dollar.

—*Anonymous*

Diversification in the naive sense is simply avoiding putting all your eggs in one basket. Certainly, spreading your risks across a number of different investments has value, but diversification is both more powerful and more subtle than this. In this chapter we explore the concept of diversification and find that describing an investment only in terms of a two-dimensional world of return and volatility is not sufficient. We also need to describe an investment along a third dimension called the *diversification effect.* The diversification effect is a beneficial reduction of portfolio volatility below the weighted average of the volatilities of the investments in the portfolio. The following three examples illustrate the conditions that create this advantageous diversification effect. Each example describes the portfolio performance produced by combining two hypothetical investments, each of which has a continually repeating pattern of returns.

Exhibit 8.1A shows the annual patterns of returns for two investments, A and B, and for the portfolio AB. Portfolio AB is composed of an equally allocated, annually rebalanced combination of these two investments. Investments A and B move in lockstep with each other. An above-average return from investment A is always associated with an above-average return from investment B. Likewise, when investment A generates a below-average return, so does investment B. A statistician would say that the returns of investments A and B are *perfectly positively correlated.*

Investment A generates alternating annual returns of −5 percent and 25 percent. Exhibit 8.1B shows that investment A has a simple average return of 10 percent with a standard deviation of 15.81 percent. Investment B has alternating annual returns of −20 percent and 40 percent. Investment B also has a simple average return of 10 percent, but its standard deviation of 31.62 percent is twice that of investment A. Portfolio AB has the same simple average return of 10 percent. The standard deviation of portfolio AB is 23.72 percent and is equal to the average of the standard deviations of investments A and B.

For any series of returns, the larger the standard deviation, the more the compound annual return drops below the simple average return. Only when an investment's returns are the same every year (i.e., the standard deviation equals zero) will its compound annual return equal its simple average return. In every other situation, the compound annual return will be less than the simple average return. *Volatility therefore impairs the compounding of returns.* For example, despite the fact that investment A, investment B, and portfolio AB each generates a simple average return of 10 percent, investment A, with its lower standard deviation, has the highest compound annual return of 8.97 percent, whereas investment B, with its higher standard deviation, has the lowest compound annual return of 5.83 percent. Portfolio AB's compound annual return of 7.67 percent is between those of investments A and B. These differences in compound annual returns

Exhibit 8.1

Perfect Positive Correlation: +1.0

A. Annual Returns

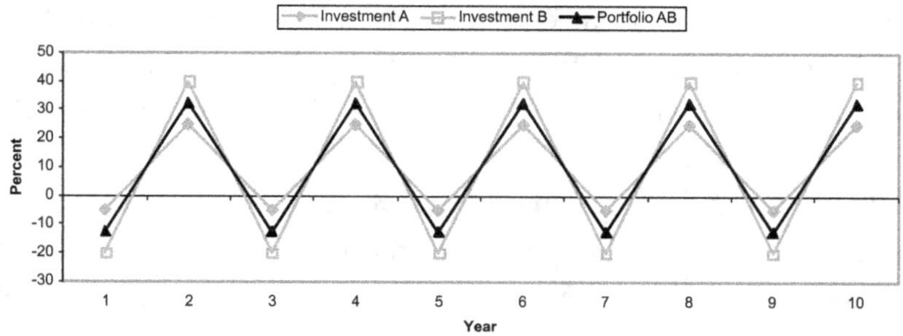

B. Annual Returns, Growth of $1, and Summary Statistics

	Investment A		Investment B		Portfolio AB	
Year	Return in Percent	Growth of $1.00	Return in Percent	Growth of $1.00	Return in Percent	Growth of $1.00
1	-5%	$ .95	-20%	$ .80	-12.5%	$ .88
2	25	1.19	40	1.12	32.5	1.16
3	-5	1.13	-20	.90	-12.5	1.01
4	25	1.41	40	1.25	32.5	1.34
5	-5	1.34	-20	1.00	-12.5	1.18
6	25	1.67	40	1.40	32.5	1.56
7	-5	1.59	-20	1.12	-12.5	1.36
8	25	1.99	40	1.57	32.5	1.81
9	-5	1.89	-20	1.26	-12.5	1.58
10	25	2.36	40	1.76	32.5	2.09
Simple Average Return		10.00%		10.00%		10.00%
Standard Deviation		15.81%		31.62%		23.72%
Compound Annual Return		8.97%		5.83%		7.67%

C. Growth of $1

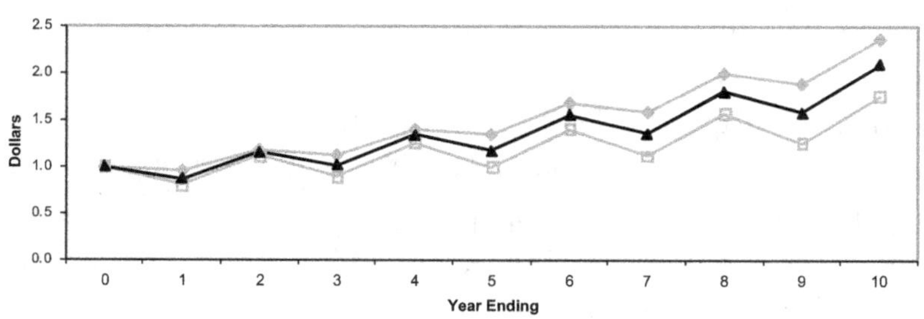

are attributable to the differences in the volatilities of investment A, investment B, and portfolio AB.

Because investments A and B move in lockstep with each other, the volatility of portfolio AB is an average of the volatilities of investments A and B. In this example we have only an averaging of volatilities—we have put our eggs into two baskets rather than one. As we defined the term, we achieve no diversification effect when we combine these two investments to form a portfolio. Exhibit 8.1C traces the growth of $1 for investments A and B and portfolio AB. In this example, portfolio AB's growth path falls between those of investments A and B.

In Exhibit 8.2 we again have two investments, C and D, and portfolio CD, which is composed of an equally allocated, annually rebalanced combination of these two investments. Investments C and D each has the same simple average return of 10 percent and standard deviation of 31.62 percent. However, unlike the example in Exhibit 8.1, investments C and D move in opposite cycles. Each time investment C generates an above-average return, investment D delivers a below-average return and vice versa. This is an example of *perfectly negative correlation*. The countercyclical patterns of returns for investments C and D produce a marvelous result for portfolio CD—the complete elimination of portfolio volatility. Since portfolio CD has a standard deviation of returns equal to zero, its compound annual return is equal to its simple average return of 10 percent. By comparison, investments C and D each has a much lower compound annual return of 5.83 percent. Strange as it may seem, portfolio CD grows much more quickly than either investment C or investment D. Exhibit 8.2C traces the growth of $1 for investments C and D as compared with that for portfolio CD. Due to portfolio CD's higher compound annual return, by year 8, portfolio CD permanently pulls ahead of both its components, investments C and D. As investments C and D combine to build portfolio CD, diversification effect is at its maximum. Such perfectly negatively correlated investments generally do not exist in the real world. If they did, no one would buy low yielding Treasury bills or certificates of deposit when they could buy two volatile investments, like C and D, and combine them in such a manner as to produce a constant annual return of 10 percent.

Exhibit 8.2
Perfect Negative Correlation: −1.0

A. Annual Returns

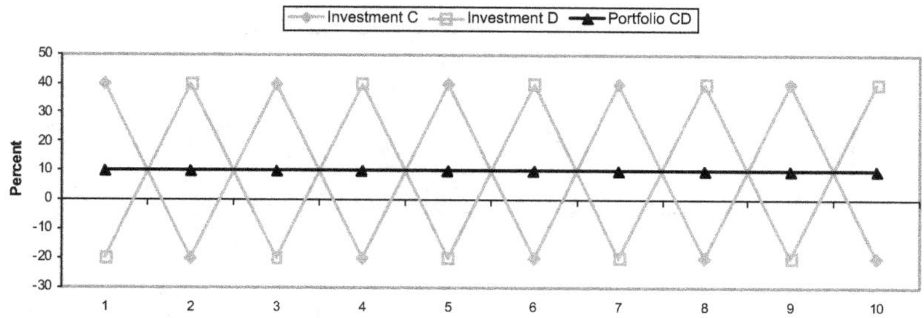

B. Annual Returns, Growth of $1, and Summary Statistics

	Investment C		Investment D		Portfolio CD	
Year	Return in Percent	Growth of $1.00	Return in Percent	Growth of $1.00	Return in Percent	Growth of $1.00
1	40%	$ 1.40	-20%	$ .80	10%	$ 1.10
2	-20	1.12	40	1.12	10	1.21
3	40	1.57	-20	.90	10	1.33
4	-20	1.25	40	1.25	10	1.46
5	40	1.76	-20	1.00	10	1.61
6	-20	1.40	40	1.40	10	1.77
7	40	1.97	-20	1.12	10	1.95
8	-20	1.57	40	1.57	10	2.14
9	40	2.20	-20	1.26	10	2.36
10	-20	1.76	40	1.76	10	2.59
Simple Average Return		10.00%		10.00%		10.00%
Standard Deviation		31.62%		31.62%		0.00%
Compound Annual Return		5.83%		5.83%		10.00%

C. Growth of $1

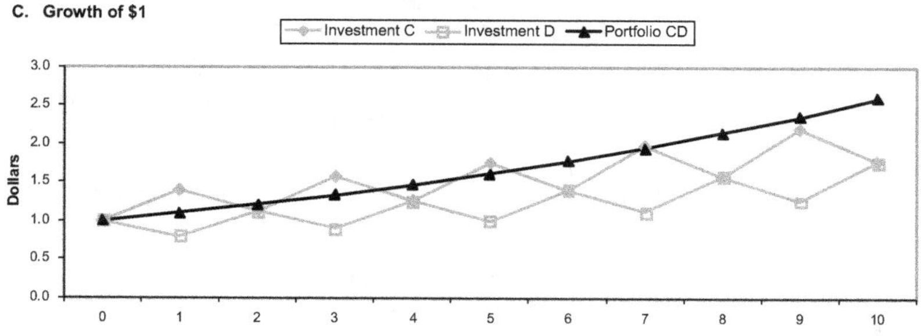

Exhibit 8.3A shows the annual patterns of returns for two investments, E and F, and for the portfolio EF. Portfolio EF is composed of an equally allocated, annually rebalanced combination of investments E and F. Investments E and F each has a simple average return of 10 percent, standard deviation of 19.70 percent, and

Exhibit 8.3
Correlation: +0.45

A. Annual Returns

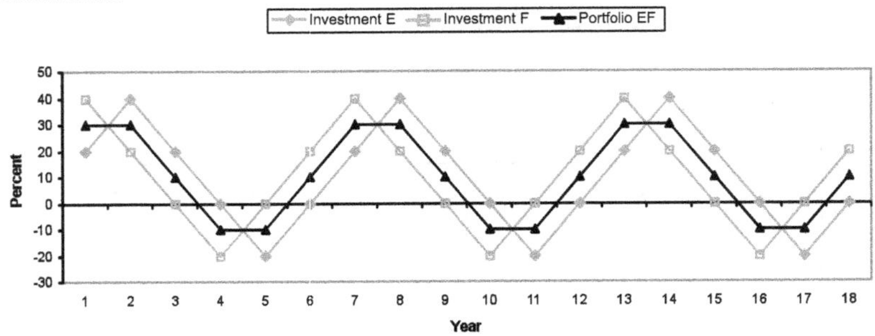

B. Annual Returns, Growth of $1, and Summary Statistics

	Investment E		Investment F		Portfolio EF	
Year	Return in Percent	Growth of $1.00	Return in Percent	Growth of $1.00	Return in Percent	Growth of $1.00
1	20 %	$ 1.20	40 %	$ 1.40	30 %	$ 1.30
2	40	1.68	20	1.68	30	1.69
3	20	2.02	0	1.68	10	1.86
4	0	2.02	-20	1.34	-10	1.67
5	-20	1.61	0	1.34	-10	1.51
6	0	1.61	20	1.61	10	1.66
7	20	1.94	40	2.26	30	2.15
8	40	2.71	20	2.71	30	2.80
9	20	3.25	0	2.71	10	3.08
10	0	3.25	-20	2.17	-10	2.77
11	-20	2.60	0	2.17	-10	2.49
12	0	2.60	20	2.60	10	2.74
13	20	3.12	40	3.64	30	3.57
14	40	4.37	20	4.37	30	4.64
15	20	5.24	0	4.37	10	5.10
16	0	5.24	-20	3.50	-10	4.59
17	-20	4.20	0	3.50	-10	4.13
18	0	4.20	20	4.20	10	4.54
Simple Average Return		10.00%		10.00%		10.00%
Standard Deviation		19.70%		19.70%		16.80%
Compound Annual Return		8.29%		8.29%		8.77%

C. Growth of $1

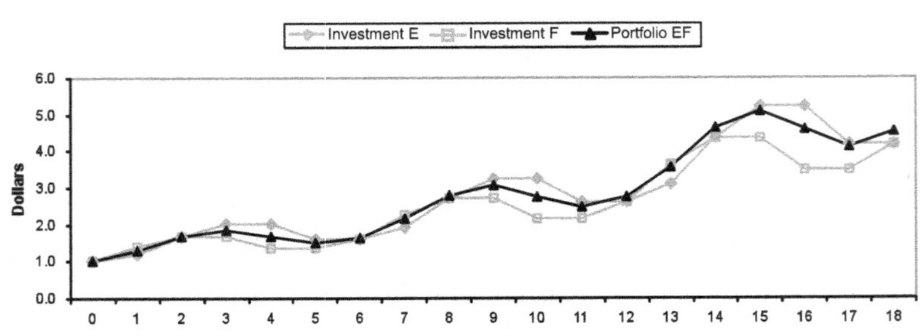

compound annual return of 8.29 percent. The patterns of returns for investments E and F are slightly out of phase with each other. This example is a middle-ground illustration of investments that are neither perfectly positively nor perfectly negatively correlated. Even though, more often than not, an above-average return from investment E is associated with an above-average return from investment F and vice versa, there are times when one of these investments is generating an above-average return while the other is producing a below-average return. Investments E and F are therefore positively correlated, but less than perfectly so. This level of correlation is more representative of real-world investment situations. Although differing in degree, most financial asset classes are positively correlated to one another.

The diversification effect produced by the dissimilarity in patterns of returns for investments E and F results in a volatility level for portfolio EF that is below the weighted average of the volatilities of investments E and F. For example, Exhibit 8.3B shows a standard deviation of 16.8 percent for portfolio EF, which is less than the standard deviation of 19.7 percent for investments E and F. Investments E and F and portfolio EF each has a simple average return of 10 percent. Due to its lower standard deviation, however, portfolio EF has a higher compound annual return than either investment E or F.

Exhibit 8.3C shows the growth of $1 for investments E and F and portfolio EF. In this example, it takes 6 years to cycle through a full rotation of annual returns for investments E and F and portfolio EF. At the end of each 6-year cycle, the growth paths of investments E and F coincide. Note, however, that at the end of each 6-year cycle, portfolio EF outperforms both investments E and F, and the margin of outperformance increases with each successive cycle. For example, in Exhibit 8.3B, I have highlighted the growth of $1 for investments E and F and portfolio EF at the end of years 6, 12, and 18. With the

Exhibit 8.4
Portfolio EF Dominates Investments E and F

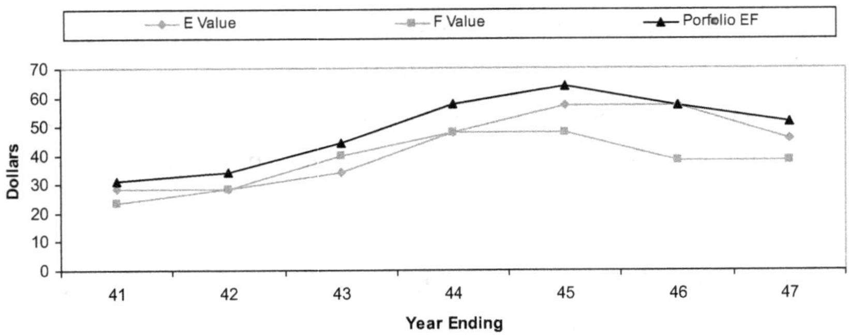

passage of time, the initially small incremental performance advantage of portfolio EF compounds to an increasingly larger diversification payoff. In Exhibit 8.3C we see that, with each cycle, the growth path of portfolio EF moves progressively higher than the average of the growth paths of investments E and F. Given sufficient time, every point on portfolio EF's growth path will eventually move permanently above the growth path of either investment E or F. In this example, it occurs after year 40, as illustrated in Exhibit 8.4.

The *cross-correlation coefficient* (or simply correlation) of returns between two investments indicates the extent to which knowledge of the return of one investment provides information regarding the behavior of the other. For example, a correlation of +1.0 describes the perfectly positive correlation between the returns of investments A and B in Exhibit 8.1. A correlation of −1.0 describes the perfectly negative correlation between the returns of investments C and D in Exhibit 8.2. All correlation measures are bound by these two extremes. Patterns of returns that are unrelated to one another (i.e., neither positively nor negatively correlated) have correlations near zero.[1]

In each of the examples above, the portfolio's simple average return is simply a weighted average of the simple average returns of the investments that compose the portfolio. This will always be true, regardless of the volatilities and patterns of returns among the investments. The portfolio volatility, however, will be *less* than the weighted average of the volatility levels of the investments in the portfolio in all cases except the rare situation of perfectly positive correlations among the investments. The diversification effect, caused by investments whose patterns of returns partially offset one another, thereby dampens portfolio volatility. The dampening of portfolio volatility in turn has a beneficial impact on the compound return of the portfolio relative to its components.

Diversification is much more than simply putting all your eggs into more than one basket. We now also see why we cannot predict the compound annual return and volatility of a portfolio using only measurements of the returns and volatilities of the investments within the portfolio. Diversification effect, as measured by the correlation of returns for each possible pairing of investments within the portfolio, provides the third measurement dimension needed to describe a portfolio's return and volatility characteristics.

How do these concepts apply in the real world? Consider the portfolio possibilities created by various combinations of large company stocks and long-term corporate bonds. To map out the volatility and return characteristics of different portfolio allocations of stocks and bonds, we need estimates of the expected return and standard deviation for both large company stocks and long-term corporate bonds, as well as the correlation statistic that measures the degree of dissimilarity in the patterns of returns between the two. In Chapter 3 we learned that, from 1926 through 2011, large company stocks had a simple average annual return of 11.8 percent with a standard deviation of 20.3 percent, whereas long-term corporate bonds had a simple average annual return of 6.4 percent with a standard deviation of 8.4 percent. The correlation between bond and stock returns over this period was +0.16. If we assume that the future will be like the past (a big assumption, as we will see), the curved solid line in Exhibit 8.5 describes the range of portfolio possibilities using large

Exhibit 8.5
Large Company Stocks/Long-Term Corporate Bonds

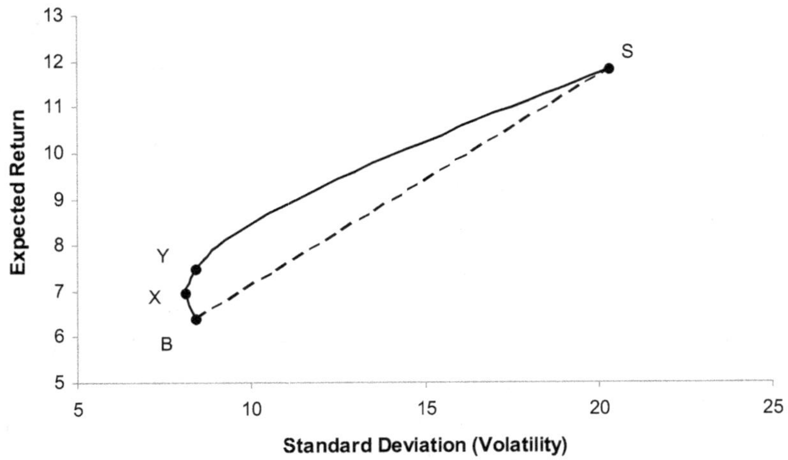

Data source: Calculated by Gibson Capital, LLC using data presented in *2012 Ibbotson® Stocks, Bonds, Bills, and Inflation® (SBBI®) Classic Yearbook,* © 2012 Morningstar. All rights reserved. Used with permission.

company stocks and long-term corporate bonds. Point B represents an all-bond portfolio, and point S represents an all-stock portfolio. The straight dashed line connecting B and S shows the performance of the portfolio possibilities if stocks and bonds are perfectly positively correlated. If this is true, no diversification effect will occur, and the portfolio's volatility will be equal to the weighted average of the stock and bond volatilities.

Because stocks and bonds are *not* perfectly positively correlated, however, each stock and bond portfolio allocation has less volatility than the weighted-average volatility of its components. As a result, the bowed solid line describes the set of portfolio possibilities. The horizontal distance between the dotted and solid lines measures the beneficial diversification effect for any stock and bond portfolio allocation. The relatively low stock and bond correlation of +0.16 drives this diversification effect.

Somewhat surprisingly, the minimum-volatility portfolio is not composed entirely of long-term corporate bonds. Point X on the graph corresponds to the minimum-volatility portfolio, which is allocated 89.8 percent to bonds and 10.2 percent to stocks. This portfolio has a standard deviation of 8.1 percent, which is lower than the 8.4 percent standard deviation of long-term corporate bonds, and its expected return of 6.9 percent is one-half percentage point higher. An ultraconservative investor, lacking an understanding of the power of diversification, may hold a portfolio allocated entirely to bonds. This illustration demonstrates that such an investor has an opportunity to simultaneously improve his portfolio's expected return while lowering the volatility risk through modest diversification into equity investments. If the ultraconservative investor is already comfortable with the volatility level of an all-bond portfolio, he can choose portfolio Y, allocated 79.8 percent to bonds and 20.2 percent to stocks. Portfolio Y has a standard deviation of 8.4 percent, which is equal to that of an all-bond portfolio, but its expected return is 7.5 percent, which is 1.1 percent higher than that of bonds. This example demonstrates the power of diversification.

The volatility and return characteristics of and correlation between stocks and bonds as described in the preceding paragraph are based on the entire 86-year period from 1926 through 2011. It is important to keep in mind, however, that there has been and will continue to be considerable variability in these relative performance numbers. For example, Exhibit 8.6 compares the 60-month (5-year) compound annual returns of large company stocks versus long-term corporate bonds on a rolling monthly basis. The dominance of stock returns over bond returns is apparent, but we also see over periods as short as 5 years that the higher volatility associated with stocks results in many instances when their returns lag those available from bonds.

This comparison in Exhibit 8.6 highlights the danger of paying too much attention to the long-term relationships among returns from various investment alternatives, without simultaneously considering the variability in these relationships. This is true particularly in the short run,

Exhibit 8.6
Large Company Stocks Versus Long-Term Corporate Bonds: Compound Annual Returns (1926–2011)

Data source: Calculated by Gibson Capital, LLC using data presented in *2012 Ibbotson® Stocks, Bonds, Bills, and Inflation® (SBBI®) Classic Yearbook*, © 2012 Morningstar. All rights reserved. Used with permission.

when high standard deviations produce short-term and intermediate-term experiences that differ considerably from long-term experience. Advisors must therefore guide their clients through the exercise of developing models of long-term performance relationships among investment alternatives, while stressing that short-term experiences will vary widely.

Exhibit 8.7 graphs on a rolling monthly basis the 60-month (5-year) standard deviations of returns for large company stocks versus long-term corporate bonds. Exhibit 3.1 previously indicated that, based on the entire period from 1926 through 2011, the standard deviation of returns was 20.3 percent for large company stocks and 8.4 percent for long-term corporate bonds. We see from Exhibit 8.7, however, that the return volatilities of both stocks and bonds have varied widely over time. Stock returns had their highest volatility during the period preceding World War II. On the other hand, bond returns had low volatility until the mid-1960s, when volatility began to increase dramatically through the 1980s as a result of a rapidly changing interest rate environment. The Financial Crisis of 2008 triggered an increase in both bond and stock volatilities.

Exhibit 8.7

Large Company Stocks Versus Long-Term Corporate Bonds: Standard Deviation of Returns (1926–2011)

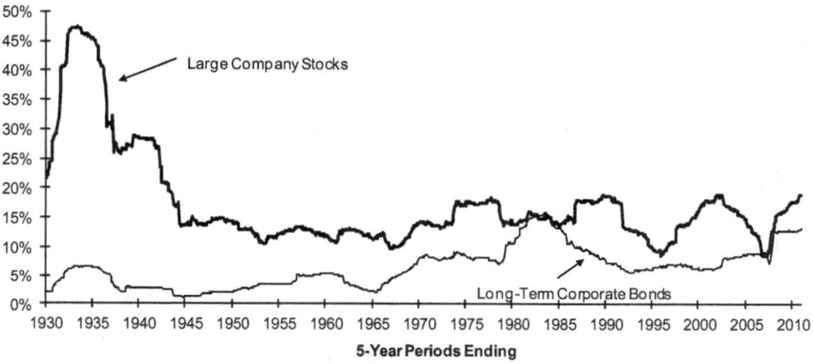

Data source: Calculated by Gibson Capital, LLC using data presented in *2012 Ibbotson® Stocks, Bonds, Bills, and Inflation® (SBBI®) Classic Yearbook,* © 2012 Morningstar. All rights reserved. Used with permission.

Exhibit 8.8 graphs on a rolling monthly basis the 60-month (5-year) correlation of returns between large company stocks and long-term corporate bonds. For this entire 86-year period, the correlation was +0.16. The correlation, however, has actually varied widely from a high of +0.62 to a low of −0.28. The diversification effect is strongest during the periods of negative correlation, offering investors an opportunity for significant reductions in portfolio volatility by simultaneously investing in both asset classes.

In Chapter 11, we will discuss the mathematics of portfolio optimization, which identifies ideal asset allocations *based on the inputs* to a computer program. The output from such programs is highly sensitive to the inputs. One purpose in reviewing Exhibits 8.6 through 8.8 is to increase our awareness of the uncertainty inherent in the inputs upon which these computer programs rely. At best, historical data are *helpful* in understanding asset class volatility and return characteristics and relationships. The data cannot, however, be massaged in such a way as to extract "the truth" from constantly changing markets. Precise answers simply are not possible.

Exhibit 8.8
Large Company Stocks Versus Long-Term Corporate Bonds: Cross-Correlation of Returns (1926–2011)

Data source: Calculated by Gibson Capital, LLC using data presented in *2012 Ibbotson® Stocks, Bonds, Bills, and Inflation® (SBBI®) Classic Yearbook*,

When we examine the range of portfolio possibilities utilizing only two investment alternatives, each level of portfolio expected return has a unique asset allocation associated with it. This is not true when we consider the range of portfolio possibilities utilizing three or more investment alternatives. We may identify a wide range of asset allocations, all of which produce the same portfolio expected return but with different levels of portfolio volatility. Obviously, the optimal asset allocation for a particular portfolio expected return is that unique allocation that minimizes portfolio volatility. Other asset allocations are undesirable because of their unnecessarily high levels of volatility. By definition, a portfolio that minimizes portfolio volatility for a given expected return (or equivalently maximizes portfolio expected return for a given level of volatility) is said to be *efficient*. If we join together all the efficient portfolios for a given set of investment alternatives, we form what is called the *efficient frontier*.

We intuitively understand the wisdom of not putting all our eggs in one basket, and we know that it is important to understand the volatility and return characteristics of each basket we use. Earlier in this chapter we gained an appreciation of the importance of the diversification effect, which considers how the various baskets we use behave relative to one another and thereby reduce portfolio volatility. Now we have gone an additional step to emphasize the importance of determining the *right amount* to place in each of our baskets in order to construct an efficient portfolio.

The implications of this last step are important. There are good and bad portfolio asset allocations, and the objective is to allocate assets in such a way as to own a portfolio that lies on the efficient frontier. A portfolio that lies on the efficient frontier has less volatility than any other portfolio with an equivalent expected return, or it alternatively has more expected return than any other portfolio with equivalent volatility.

We should avoid inefficient portfolios because they have levels of volatility that could be reduced through proper reallocation. The idea of an inefficient portfolio may sound like evidence against the notion of the volatility versus return trade-off we worked so hard to establish in Chapter 7. In that chapter, we concluded that the only way to increase expected return is to assume a higher level of portfolio volatility. Now we are told that we can improve the expected return of an inefficient portfolio without increasing volatility. Isn't this a contradiction? No. The volatility versus return trade-off is alive and well, living on the efficient frontier! That is, presuming that you now have an efficient portfolio, the only way to increase the expected return (if constrained to a given set of investment alternatives) is to increase portfolio volatility.

The notion of inefficient portfolios may also suggest the apparent existence of an economic "free lunch," where it is possible to pick up incremental return without an increase in portfolio volatility. But in an efficient market there are no free lunches. Rather than thinking of this situation as a free lunch, we can more appropriately describe an inefficient portfolio as one where volatility is needlessly incurred without compensation or, alternatively, incremental returns are unnecessarily sacrificed.

Let's extend our diversification example by adding a fourth investment alternative with different return, volatility, and correlation characteristics from those of the other three. We now have even more options to consider when building our portfolios. The new investment alternative provides the *possibility* of further portfolio volatility reduction at various levels of expected return. I emphasize the word *possibility* because sometimes a new investment alternative is valuable as a portfolio building block and sometimes it is not. This fourth investment alternative is valuable as a portfolio building block if its return, volatility, and correlation characteristics create less volatile ways of building portfolios for various levels of expected return. If this occurs, a new efficient frontier forms above the old one, as shown in Exhibit 8.9.

Exhibit 8.9
Three Versus Four Investment Alternative Efficient Frontiers

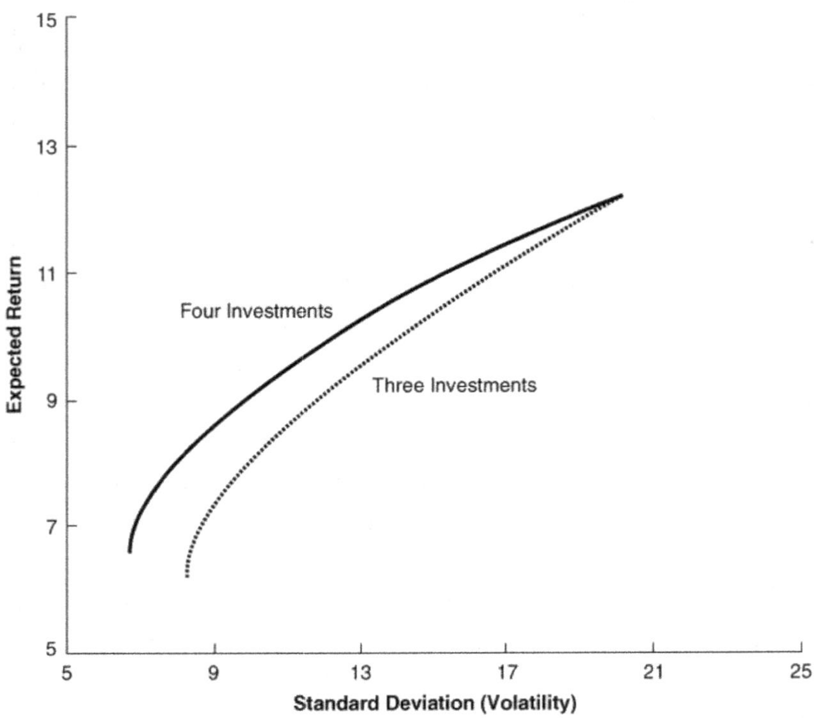

Expanding the menu of investment alternatives that can be used as possible building blocks for the portfolio adds more possibilities to earn increasingly higher expected returns at whatever level of volatility the investor can tolerate. We can likewise view the increasing number of investment alternatives as providing more possibilities to reduce volatility at whatever level of expected return we seek. The message is clear: Although it is not always advisable to utilize all the investment alternatives available in a given situation, it is always preferable to have more, rather than fewer, investment alternatives from which to choose. Any time the investment opportunity set is arbitrarily restricted, the investor bears the risk of being confined to a portfolio choice along a lower efficient frontier than would otherwise be possible.

The diversification payoff can be taken one of two ways: as less portfolio volatility for the same expected return or as more portfolio expected return for the same volatility. Understanding this payoff is important for aggressive investors, who often are not interested in discussing diversification strategies because they incorrectly believe that diversification impairs returns. This is not necessarily so. In essence, the diversification effect enables the more aggressive investor to improve his portfolio's expected return by committing an even greater percentage of his portfolio to equity investments than he otherwise would choose to do, were it not for the smoothing effect of dissimilar patterns of returns among different asset classes.

If we want to eliminate as much volatility as possible from our portfolio, we might consider taking diversification to its logical conclusion by representing all major asset classes in our portfolio. This approach would provide the greatest opportunity for dissimilar patterns of returns among investments to partially offset one another. Would this strategy, however, eliminate all portfolio volatility? No. The remaining volatility exists despite diversification; we will call it *nondiversifiable volatility*. When we think about bearing unavoidable volatility, we expect to be commensurably rewarded. For example, in Chapter 7 we devised a hypothetical world composed of only two investment alternatives—Treasury bills and large company stocks. In that world, the only route to a higher modeled portfolio return is by increasing our stock allocation and living with the accompanying increase in portfolio volatility. Therefore, we expect to be rewarded for bearing this unavoidable volatility.

But what about the kind of volatility that diversification easily eliminates? We will call this *diversifiable volatility*. Should we be rewarded for bearing it? By analogy, consider a firefighter who deserves to be well compensated because of the risks inherent in his occupation. One day he heroically enters a burning building to successfully save a child from the flames. For this and other similar acts of courage and skill, he receives a promotion with a pay raise. During a subsequent fire, he hears the screams of another young child. This time, before entering the burning building, he takes off his protective suit and, wearing only his underwear, rescues the child from the flames. The next day he approaches the fire chief and asks for an additional pay raise because of the increased risks he took rescuing the child. How do you imagine the fire chief will respond?

One big lesson of modern portfolio theory is that an efficient market does not compensate investors for bearing volatility that they can easily eliminate. Diversifiable volatility therefore deserves and receives no compensation. For example, Exhibit 8.10 describes the volatility characteristics of two stocks, A and B. Initially, one might naively conclude that stock A, with its greater total volatility, will be priced to provide for a greater expected return than that of stock B. But in this example we see that stock B has more nondiversifiable volatility than stock A and, accordingly, will be priced by the marketplace to have a higher expected return than stock A.

Consider an investor who has 90 percent of her portfolio allocated to the stock of one large publicly traded corporation. She obviously retains considerable diversifiable volatility, *which is not priced by the marketplace to reward her or anyone else*. We can liken this situation to the firefighter who takes off his protective suit before running into

Exhibit 8.10
Diversifiable Versus Nondiversifiable Volatility

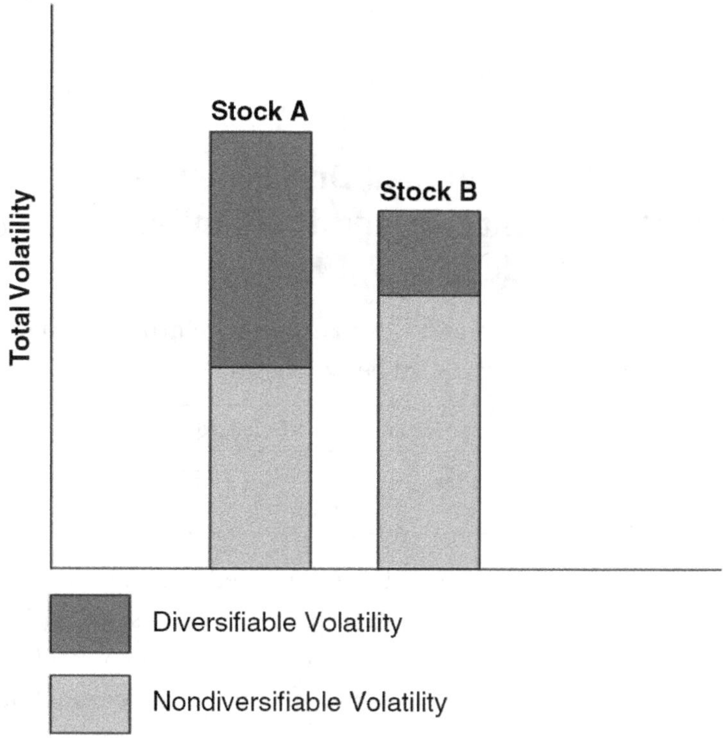

a burning building. The pricing mechanism of an efficient market in effect assumes that investors are smart enough to eliminate diversifiable volatility through broad diversification. Those who do not diversify pay the price by assuming an unnecessarily high level of volatility. And as we have demonstrated, not only is volatility hard to live with, but it also impairs the rate at which money compounds. The argument for diversifying an investor's portfolio away from overconcentration in one stock is more than the notion of simply not putting all your eggs in one basket.

The following Appendix is for readers who are interested in a deeper discussion of the concepts developed in this chapter. We begin with several additional diversification examples and then explore the relationship of this material to the capital asset pricing model (CAPM). Those who are not interested in further elaboration can safely proceed to the next chapter.

Appendix: A More Detailed Discussion of Diversification Concepts and the Capital Asset Pricing Model

Consider two investments, X and Y, with expected returns and volatilities, as measured by their standard deviations, of:

Investment	Expected Return	Standard Deviation
X	10%	18%
Y	8%	10%

Exhibit 8.11 shows both investments plotted in volatility and return space. Initially, one might presume that portfolios built using these two investments will plot along the straight line connecting points X and Y. This will be true, however, only if the correlation of returns between X and Y is perfectly positive, as it was for the two investments in Exhibit 8.1. To get an expected return of 9 percent with perfectly positive correlation, one must be willing to accept a volatility level of 14 percent. (Note the distance on the horizontal axis that corresponds to the point where a horizontal line drawn from an expected return of 9 percent intercepts the straight line connecting points X and Y.)

The opposite extreme occurs when X and Y are perfectly negatively correlated in a fashion similar to the two investments in Exhibit 8.2. Let us start at point Y with 100 percent of the portfolio committed to investment Y. As we begin to reallocate some money to investment X, we begin moving the portfolio along the line connecting point Y to point W. At point W, we have approximately

Exhibit 8.11
Perfectly Positive Versus Perfectly Negative Correlation

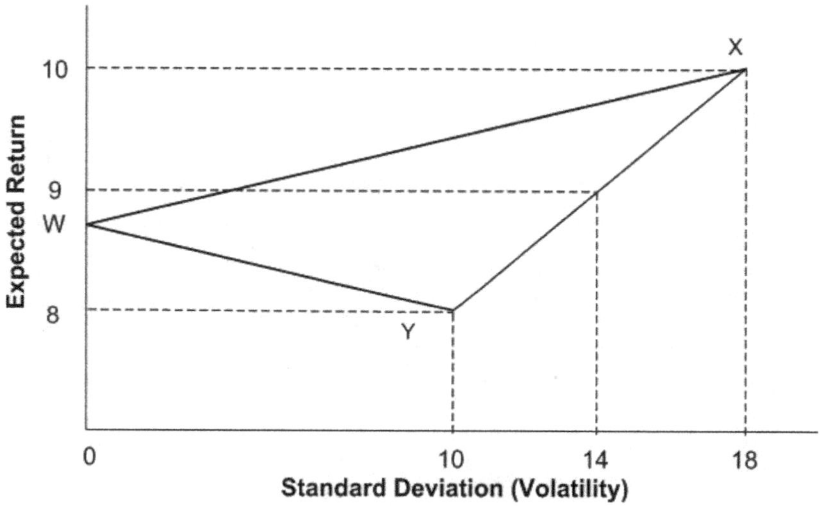

64 percent of our money in investment Y, with the remainder in investment X. With this asset allocation, the perfectly countercyclical patterns of returns have completely eliminated volatility on a portfolio level: Portfolio W has an expected return of 8.7 percent with no volatility. As we further increase the percentage of the portfolio allocated to investment X, the portfolio moves along the line connecting point W to point X, until we reach the point where 100 percent of the portfolio is committed to investment X.

The curved line of Exhibit 8.12 that connects points Y and X describes the more typical situation of neither perfectly positive nor perfectly negative correlation. Assume, for example, that we want to achieve a 9 percent expected return from a portfolio composed of investments X and Y. A horizontal line drawn from the 9 percent point on the vertical axis intercepts the curved line at a point corresponding to a volatility level of 11 percent. Note that this horizontal line intercepts a straight line that connects points Y and X

Exhibit 8.12
Neither Perfectly Positive nor Perfectly Negative Correlation

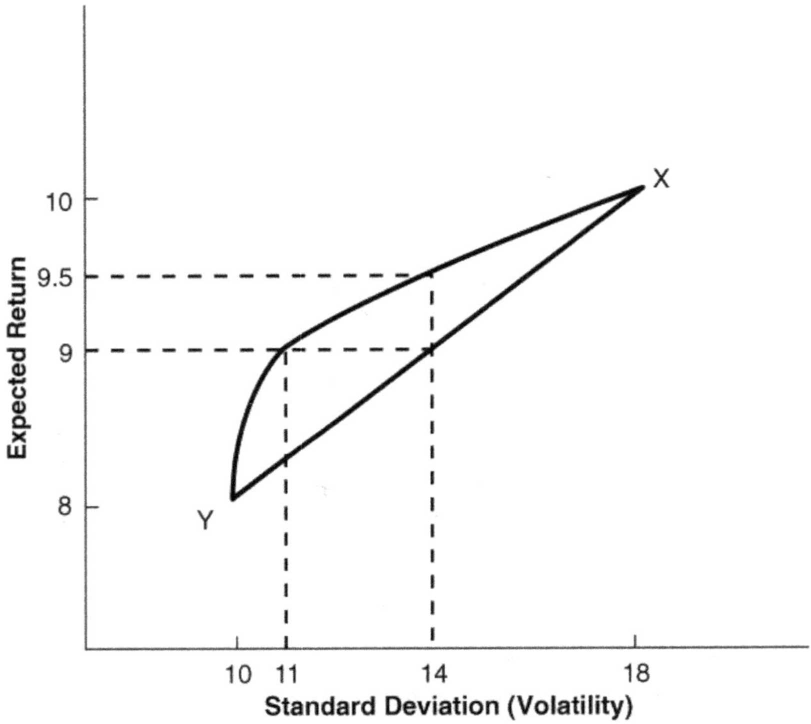

at a volatility level of 14 percent. In essence, the difference between this 14 percent volatility level (which assumes perfectly positive correlation and, hence, no diversification effect) and the 11 percent volatility level implied by the curved line represents the reduction in portfolio volatility associated with the diversification effect.

If X and Y are perfectly positively correlated and we are willing to live with a volatility level of 14 percent, we must accept a portfolio expected return of 9 percent. Because they are not perfectly positively correlated, we can obtain a portfolio expected return of 9.5 percent. This 9.5 percent return corresponds to a point where a vertical line drawn from a volatility level of 14 percent intercepts the curved line.

We can equally attribute this extra 0.5 percent in portfolio expected return to the diversification effect.

Thus far, we have discussed diversification in the context of two investment alternatives, where each unique combination of the two investments is associated with a particular portfolio expected return. For example, in Exhibit 8.12, an expected return of 9 percent is associated with only one specific combination of investments X and Y. Lowering the percentage allocated to X produces a lower expected return for the portfolio, while increasing the percentage allocated to X increases the expected return.

Let us now consider diversification in a situation involving three investment alternatives, X, Y, and Z, with the following volatility and return characteristics:

Investment	Expected Return	Standard Deviation
X	10%	18%
Y	8%	10%
Z	6%	2%

With three investment alternatives, we need to specify three correlations. This is usually done in the form of a correlation matrix. The matrix has a row and a column for each investment. The correlation between any two investments is found at the intersection of one investment's row with the other investment's column:

Investment	X	Y	Z
X	1.00		
Y	0.50	1.00	
Z	0.10	0.30	1.00

With three or more investment alternatives, we no longer have unique solutions associated with various portfolio expected returns. For example, we can build any number of different portfolios to obtain a portfolio expected return of 8 percent. Some examples are:

Portfolio	Percentage Allocation to Investment: X	Y	Z	Portfolio Expected Return	Portfolio Standard Deviation
1	0	100	0	8	10.0
2	50	0	50	8	9.2
3	30	40	30	8	8.3
4	25	50	25	8	8.4

Of the four choices listed, portfolio 3 is the best option because it produces the expected return of 8 percent with the least volatility, as measured by the portfolio's standard deviation. Can we improve this portfolio? Would some other asset allocation produce the same expected return of 8 percent with even less portfolio volatility? Although an infinite number of different portfolio allocations would produce the desired expected return of 8 percent, only one specific allocation pushes portfolio volatility to its minimum possible value. The same is true for any specific expected return between the maximum return of 10 percent associated with investment X and the expected return associated with the lowest-volatility portfolio that can be constructed using investments X, Y, and Z as possible building blocks.[2] With respect to *any* specific expected return within that range, many different portfolio allocations can produce the specific expected return, but only one allocation optimally produces the specific expected return with a minimum of portfolio volatility.

The specific allocation that minimizes portfolio volatility for a given expected return is said to be *efficient*. Other portfolios that produce the same expected return but with greater volatility are *inefficient*. If we connect each of the efficient portfolios associated with each possible level of expected return, we form the *efficient frontier*.

The Capital Asset Pricing Model (CAPM)

Let us now approach the subject of diversification from yet another direction. Assume we have a large collection of volatile investments.

Exhibit 8.13
Scatterplot of Volatile Investments

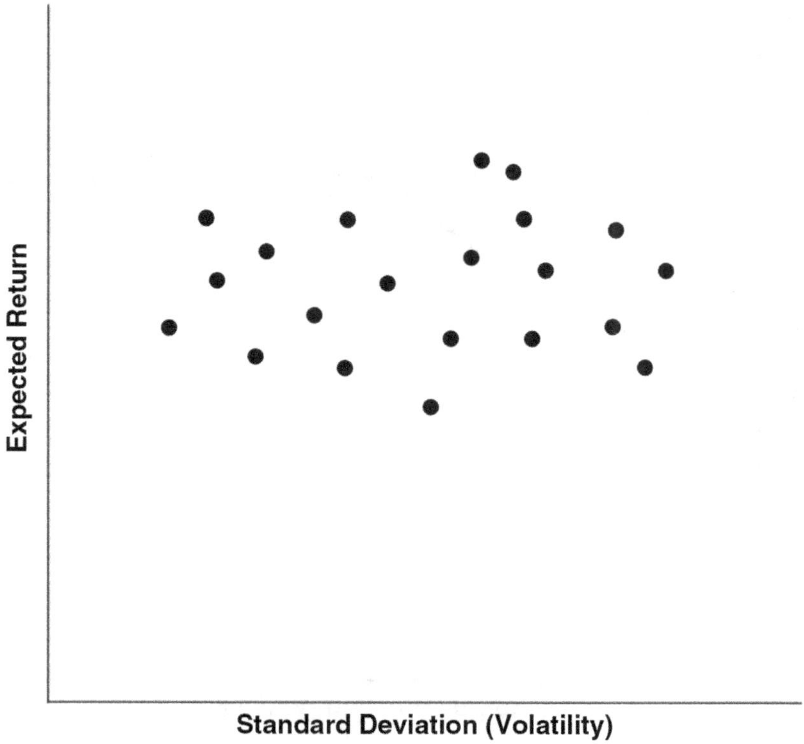

Exhibit 8.13 shows each investment plotted in terms of its volatility and return characteristics. As we consider the nature of the volatility versus return trade-off, we perhaps expect to see these investments form a pattern that slopes upward to the right, such that more volatile investments have higher expected returns. Yet we see no such pattern. The reason will become clear later.

Now consider the portfolio possibilities based on the various combinations and weightings of these volatile investments. Exhibit 8.14 shows this set of possible portfolios as the shaded area bound on the upper left by the efficient frontier connecting points A and B. We again see that, for any given expected return, there are good (efficient) and bad (inefficient) ways to combine investments to build

Exhibit 8.14
Efficient Frontier

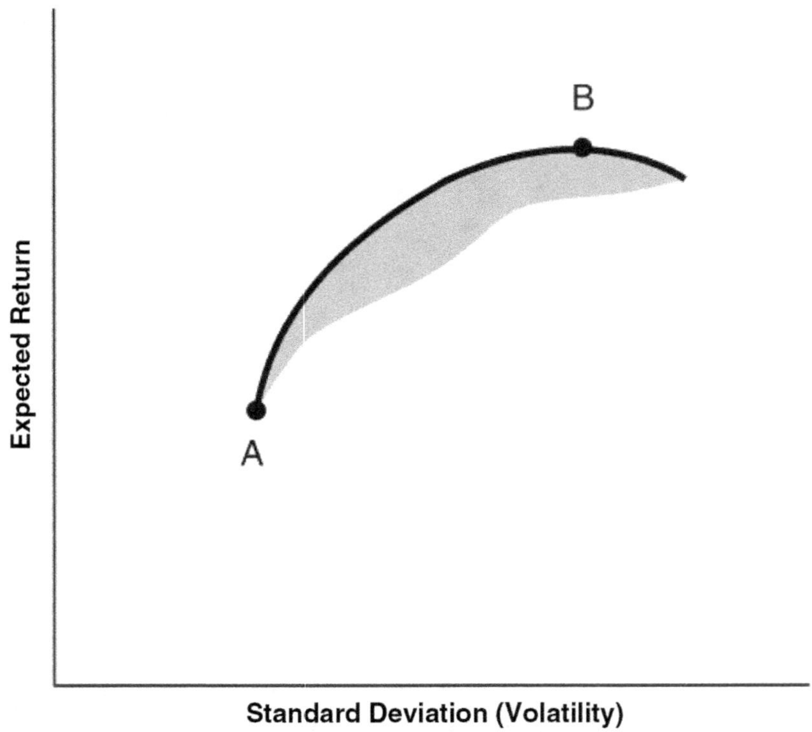

portfolios. If we are limited to choosing from only these volatile investments in building our portfolios, we should choose a portfolio lying somewhere along the curved efficient frontier connecting point A with point B.

What happens if we change the example by permitting investors to either borrow money or invest it at some volatility-free rate of interest, R_f? Exhibit 8.15 shows a line drawn from point C corresponding to R_f on the vertical axis to the point of tangency M on the efficient frontier. In this situation, it is advantageous for *all* investors to hold the same optimal volatile portfolio M, in combination with either borrowing or

Exhibit 8.15
Efficient Frontier with Borrowing and Lending

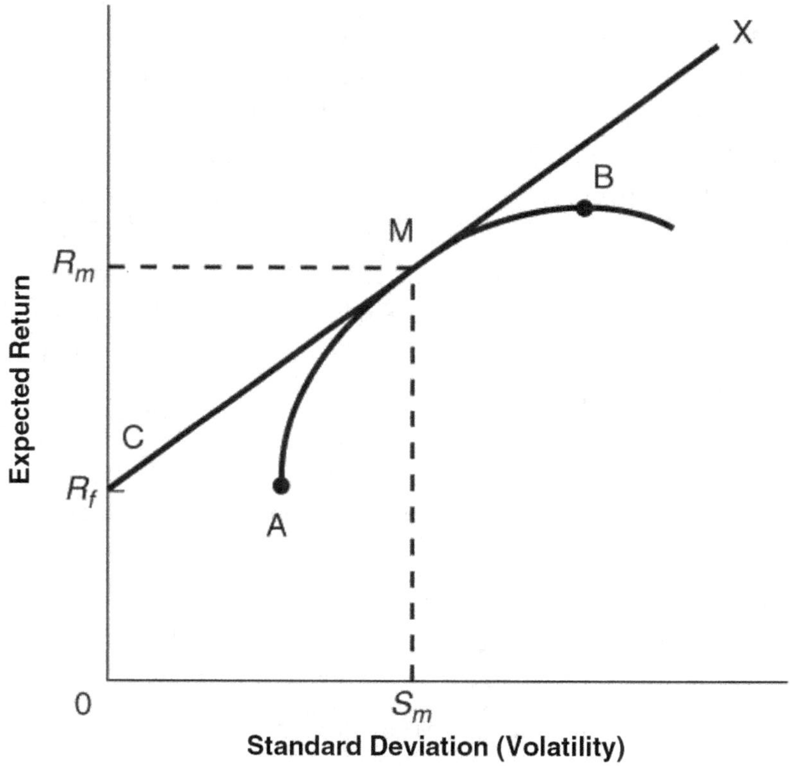

investing at the volatility-free rate of interest in accordance with their volatility tolerance.

Investors who are more volatility averse would invest part of their money at the volatility-free rate of interest and hold the balance in the volatile portfolio M. Depending on the percentage invested at the volatility-free rate of interest, their portfolio would lie somewhere on the straight line connecting point C, corresponding to the volatility-free rate of interest, and point M, the optimal volatile portfolio. Investors with greater volatility tolerance could hold portfolios lying along line MX by borrowing money at the volatility-free rate of interest in order to provide additional funds for making larger investments in the optimal volatile portfolio M. Note that, with the added possibility of borrowing or lending, the portfolio possibilities on line CMX lie above, and are therefore superior to, those lying on the prior efficient frontier connecting points A and B, where borrowing or lending is not possible.

This leads to the CAPM, which was developed in the mid-1960s by William F. Sharpe in conjunction with other researchers.[3] It provides a powerful description of the relationship between volatility and expected return in an efficient capital market. As is the case with most models, simplifying assumptions are made to abstract the essence of the relationship being modeled. With the CAPM, several such assumptions are made:

1. All investors are assumed to have the same investment information and to hold identical expectations regarding the future.
2. The market is perfectly competitive.
3. There are no transaction costs for buying and selling securities.
4. Investors live in a tax-free world.
5. Investors can either invest or borrow at the same volatility-free rate of interest.
6. Investors are volatility averse.

In such a world, all investors would create and hold the same efficient portfolio of volatile investments. This portfolio is called the *market portfolio* and is composed of all volatile investments, each weighted in terms of its outstanding market value. Let us now define point M in Exhibit 8.15 to be the market portfolio. In order to accommodate individual differences in volatility tolerance, investors can either borrow or invest at the volatility-free rate of interest in combination with holding the market portfolio. The volatility associated with the market portfolio is the nondiversifiable volatility inherent in the market as a whole. This volatility is quantified by the distance $0S_m$ on the horizontal axis. On the vertical axis, R_m corresponds to the expected return on the market portfolio. Line CMX is known as the *capital market line*. The capital market line reflects the upward-sloping relationship between volatility and expected return among the efficient investment strategies that lie on this line. Think of the slope of the capital market line as the reward one expects to receive per unit of volatility borne.

Each volatile investment in the market portfolio can have its total volatility (standard deviation) broken down into diversifiable and nondiversifiable components. One conclusion of the CAPM is that only the latter, nondiversifiable component of total volatility justifies extra compensation. Beta, β, is the measure of an investment's nondiversifiable volatility relative to the market portfolio. It is computed by a statistical comparison of the investment's pattern of returns relative to the returns of the market portfolio.

We can now explain why the volatile investments in Exhibit 8.13 do not form a pattern that slopes upward to the right. If diversifiable volatility is not rewarded by the marketplace, then we should plot expected return against nondiversifiable volatility (i.e., β) rather than against total volatility, as we did in Exhibit 8.13. A plot of this new relationship forms what is called the *security market line* shown in Exhibit 8.16. The security market line begins at R_f and passes through point M, which corresponds to the market portfolio. In equilibrium, the buying and selling activities of investors in an efficient capital market will price securities such that they fall on the security market line. In other words, according to the CAPM, a security's expected return is a function of the volatility-free rate of interest, the expected return on the market, and its nondiversifiable volatility as measured by β. This is mathematically expressed by:

$$R_i = R_f + (R_m - R_f)\,\beta_i$$

Exhibit 8.16
CAPM

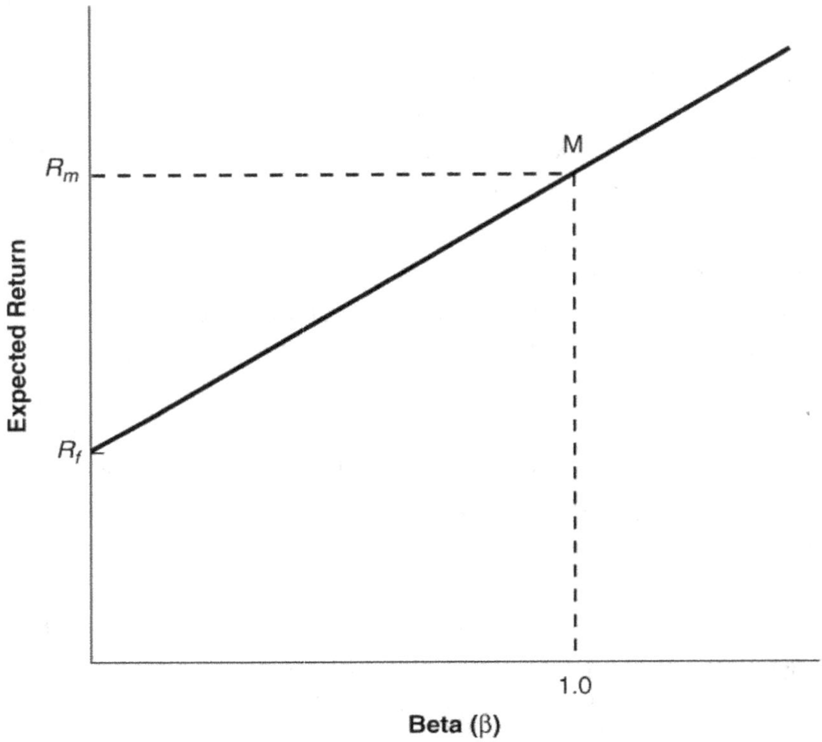

where:

R_i = expected return on security I
R_f = volatility-free rate of interest
R_m = expected return on the market portfolio
β_i = beta value for security I

Most often, a broad-based stock index such as the S&P 500 is used as a proxy for the market portfolio. In this context, β is a measure of how an individual stock's returns co-vary with the returns of the S&P 500. Arguably, however, the S&P 500 is much too narrow a proxy for the market portfolio. By definition, the market portfolio should contain all volatile investments, each weighted in terms of its outstanding market value. Hence, it is more appropriate to describe the market portfolio in global terms, including both U.S. and non-U.S. stocks and bonds, real estate, and all other major investment asset classes. Such a market portfolio is better approximated by the allocation of the total investable capital market shown in Exhibit 1.1. In this more comprehensive context, β is a measurement of each investment's pattern of returns relative to the returns of this world market portfolio. By implication, all investors should hold the same world market portfolio and adjust for volatility-tolerance differences by either investing or borrowing at the volatility-free rate of interest.

Various extended models of the original CAPM have been developed since the mid-1960s, as well as other models concerning security pricing. For example, arbitrage pricing theory asserts that multiple factors, in addition to market volatility, are involved in security pricing. The CAPM has been criticized on the basis of its unrealistic assumptions and as not providing a completely accurate description of real-world security pricing. It nevertheless remains a powerful model that highlights the importance of diversification and the relationship between nondiversifiable volatility and security expected returns.

Chapter 9

Expanding the Efficient Frontier

My ventures are not in one bottom trusted,
Nor to one place; nor is my whole estate
Upon the fortune of this present year;
Therefore, my merchandise makes me not sad.

—*William Shakespeare (1564–1616),*
Merchant of Venice, *Act I, Scene 1*

Over 30 years ago, U.S. stocks and bonds constituted most of the world's liquid investable capital market. Our capital markets were not only the largest but also the most liquid and efficient. Our economy was broadly diversified, dynamic, and resilient. It is not surprising, therefore, that U.S. investors traditionally have held portfolios composed predominantly of U.S. stocks and bonds. Would investors be better off in the long run if they followed a more broadly diversified asset allocation strategy?

Imagine for a moment that we have two competing investment organizations, alike in every aspect—each firm is well staffed by highly qualified, talented professionals with ready access to quality research services—except that one firm can invest globally, whereas the other is restricted to U.S. stocks and bonds. Which firm is likely to deliver the better risk-adjusted performance results? All other things being equal, the global firm with its broader set of investment possibilities has a greater chance for superior performance. The worst case for the global firm is that it will find no attractive investment opportunities outside the United States. In this unlikely situation, the global firm still has a 50/50 chance of outperforming the investment firm that is restricted to U.S. stocks and bonds. If, however, the global firm finds attractive investment opportunities not available to the U.S. investment firm, the expectation is that the global firm's performance will be superior.

Exhibit 1.1 showed the estimated allocation of the world's total investable capital as of the end of 2011. The non-U.S. capital markets are as large, and therefore as important, as the U.S. capital markets. Why not design portfolios that utilize all these major world asset classes? Doing so would create more opportunities for the ups and downs of one asset class to partially offset the ups and downs of another. Globally diversified portfolios should give investors a better relationship between the returns they want and the volatility they wish to mitigate.

Non-U.S. Bonds

Let's begin with interest-generating investments and examine the impact of diversifying a U.S. bond portfolio with non-U.S. bonds. Exhibit 9.1 graphs the comparative performance over rolling 25-year periods of a 100 percent U.S. long-term corporate bond portfolio versus portfolios with 10 percent, 20 percent, and 30 percent non-U.S. bond allocations. The chart has 15 lines, 1 for each 25-year rolling period ending with 1997 through 2011. Depending on the particular 25-year period, international diversification of the U.S. bond portfolio sometimes slightly increased and other times slightly decreased the compound annual return relative to a 100 percent U.S. long-term corporate bond portfolio. In every case, however, bond portfolio volatility decreased as the allocation to non-U.S. bonds increased from

Exhibit 9.1
International Diversification of a U.S. Bond Portfolio

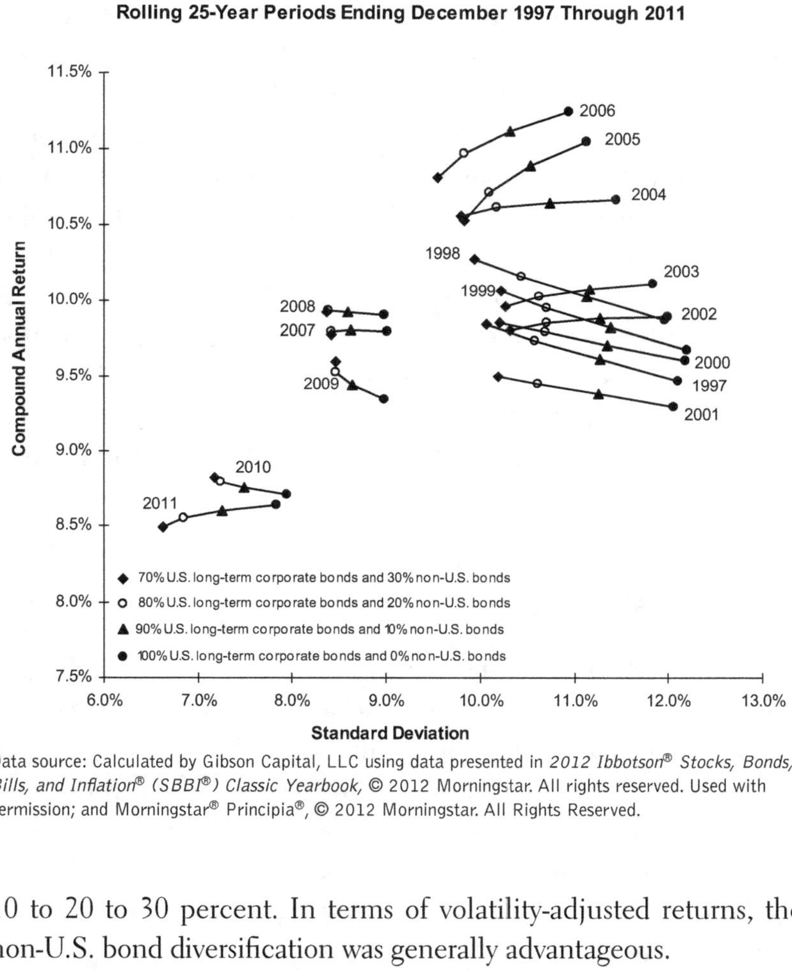

Data source: Calculated by Gibson Capital, LLC using data presented in *2012 Ibbotson® Stocks, Bonds, Bills, and Inflation® (SBBI®) Classic Yearbook,* © 2012 Morningstar. All rights reserved. Used with permission; and Morningstar® Principia®, © 2012 Morningstar. All Rights Reserved.

10 to 20 to 30 percent. In terms of volatility-adjusted returns, the non-U.S. bond diversification was generally advantageous.

Over the past 25 years, emerging market economies have expanded significantly in number and size. In many of these countries, the credit quality of their bond markets has improved markedly. Emerging market bonds provide investors with another opportunity to broaden portfolio diversification. Investing in non-U.S. capital markets entails risks that we will review briefly in the next section on non-U.S. stock investing. These risks make it important to diversify geographically across a number of countries and adequately across securities within countries.

Historically, non-U.S. bonds have provided returns that are competitive with those of U.S. bonds, but it is important to realize that the higher coupon returns from some non-U.S. bonds are not fully realizable by U.S. investors. The *theory of interest rate parity* explains why. This theory suggests that a higher foreign interest rate is often associated with a higher foreign inflation rate. The higher inflation rate triggers depreciation in the foreign currency relative to the U.S. dollar, thus diminishing the realizable returns to a U.S. investor. In the end, some non-U.S. bonds' dollar-adjusted interest rates may not be as advantageous for U.S. investors as their high coupons would indicate. The evidence suggests, however, that non-U.S. diversification of a U.S. bond portfolio likely will improve long-term volatility-adjusted returns.

Non-U.S. Stocks

Non-U.S. stock investing has gained wider acceptance over the past couple of decades. A variety of factors have contributed to this warming of U.S. investor attitudes toward international investing. First, non-U.S. markets account for a significant percentage of world gross domestic product and world market capitalization. Second, many of the world's major corporations are headquartered outside the United States. For example, according to Morningstar's stock database, in non-U.S. markets you will find, by market capitalization:

8 of the 10 largest auto manufacturers
7 of the 10 largest banks
6 of the 10 largest drug manufacturers
7 of the 10 largest household products companies
7 of the 10 largest integrated oil and gas companies
8 of the 10 largest telecommunication services companies

Many countries have higher rates of savings, capital formation, and economic growth than the United States. The work ethic is also stronger in some countries, particularly in the Pacific Basin. Finally, during some periods, non-U.S. stock markets outperform the U.S. stock market, and the dissimilarity in patterns of returns between the U.S. and non-U.S. stock markets creates an opportunity to improve portfolio volatility-adjusted returns through the diversification effect.

Over long holding periods, U.S. large company stock investors have benefited from non-U.S. large company stock diversification, though the benefits seem fairly small. Despite the fact that non-U.S. large company stock returns historically have been more volatile than U.S. large company stock returns, modest diversification into non-U.S. stocks often has resulted in a *reduction* of stock portfolio volatility.[1] The impact of non-U.S. large stock diversification on portfolio return has been mixed—in some periods increasing and in other periods decreasing the portfolio compound annual return.

Exhibit 9.2 shows the rolling 5-year (20-quarter) correlations of U.S. large company stocks with both non-U.S. large company stocks and non-U.S. small company stocks. Note how the correlation between U.S. large company stocks and non-U.S. large company stocks started moving higher during the 1990s and remained above 0.8 for the 5-year periods ending with December 1998 through December 2011. The rise of large multinational companies may partially explain the increased correlation between U.S. large company stocks and non-U.S. large company stocks. The worldwide speculative boom in technology and Internet stocks toward the end of the 1990s, followed by their demise during the 2000–2002 bear market, also fueled the high correlation. Similarly, during and after the Global Financial Crisis of 2008, a "risk-on, risk-off" trading pattern resulted in high correlations among most equity asset classes. During risk-off periods, negative market sentiment caused investors to sell not just U.S. and non-U.S. stocks but all risky asset classes. Conversely, during risk-on periods, investors bought risky asset classes across the board.

Exhibit 9.2
Correlations with U.S. Large Company Stocks

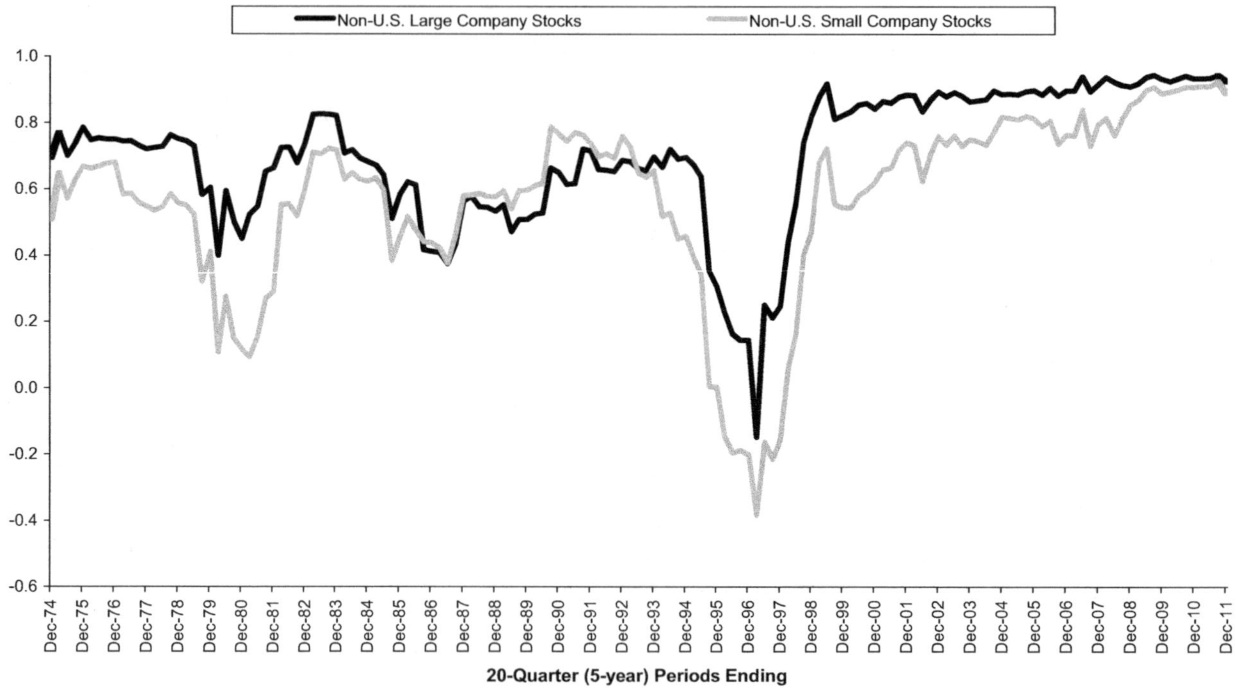

U.S. large company stocks: S&P 500 Index

Non-U.S. large company stocks: MSCI EAFE Index

Non-U.S. small company stocks: DFA International Small Company Simulated Index (Dimensional Fund Advisors)

Data source: Morningstar® Principia®, © 2012 Morningstar. All Rights Reserved.

Exhibit 9.3
Performance Comparison, 25 Years Ending 2011

	Non-U.S. Large Company Stocks	Non-U.S. Small Company Stocks
Compound Annual Return	5.74	7.54
Standard Deviation	20.75	25.15
Correlation with U.S. Large Company Stocks	.71	.54

U.S. large company stocks: S&P 500 Index
Non-U.S. large company stocks: MSCI EAFE Index
Non-U.S. small company stocks: DFA International Small Company Simulated Index (Dimensional Fund Advisors)

Data source: Morningstar® Principia®, © 2012 Morningstar. All Rights Reserved.

By comparison, Exhibit 9.2 illustrates that the correlation between U.S. large company stocks and non-U.S. small company stocks usually has been lower. The lower correlation results from the fact that non-U.S. small company stocks are more likely to be affected by economic conditions in the country in which the companies are domiciled. Exhibit 9.3 shows that although non-U.S. small company stocks have been more volatile than non-U.S. large company stocks, they have generated higher returns. Over long holding periods, the higher returns and lower correlations of non-U.S. small company stocks combined to give U.S. stock investors better diversification benefits than from investing in non-U.S. large company stocks.

Non-U.S. stock and bond investing is not without its special problems. Accounting practices in other countries differ from those in the United States and often provide less complete disclosure to investors. Many non-U.S. stock and bond markets are not as liquid or as well regulated as the U.S. capital markets. These differences may result in higher transaction costs and possible delays in the settlement of security transactions. Some nations suffer from political instability, adding another dimension of risk to the investment management process. International governments may also tax and/or restrict the flow of investment capital in various ways. Finally, for U.S. investors, the currency risk of a rising dollar can result in a poor dollar-denominated return, even though the securities perform well in terms of their native currency. Unless the currency exposure is hedged, every non-U.S. investment is essentially two investments—one in the security itself, the other in the currency of the country where the company is headquartered.

The risks mentioned above are even more pronounced with investments in the emerging markets of developing third world economies. Nevertheless, investing in emerging markets can offer significant long-term rewards.

Early in my career, clients often resisted my recommendations to invest in non-U.S. stock and bond markets. In more ways than one, it was a foreign concept to them. Things have changed. For most clients today the question is no longer, "Should I invest internationally?" but, rather, "How much of my portfolio should I allocate to non-U.S. stocks and bonds?"

Real Estate

Real estate is quite different from the other investment alternatives we have discussed. Each real estate property is unique in its geographic location, physical structure, and tenant mix and in a variety of other attributes. The purchase and sale of real estate properties are negotiated transactions, which can become very complex. Because the real estate market is composed of noninterchangeable, unique, nonliquid properties, it is probably less efficient than the stock and bond markets. This inefficiency may give rise to exploitable opportunities for skilled investors to secure superior investment results. At the same time, however, the search and transaction costs involved with real estate investments are often high relative to the costs of other investment alternatives.

As an equity investment, real estate's capital appreciation generally has served as an effective hedge against inflation over long time horizons. Well-purchased real estate also often produces generous current cash flow. Many investors prefer to leverage their real estate investments with borrowed money. Although this increases the risk of the investment and diverts cash flow for debt service, it may magnify the potential gains on the upside. Real estate is a major asset class that should have a meaningful allocation in a well-diversified portfolio. Because each real estate investment is unique and nonliquid, it is very important that real estate investments be adequately diversified. Investors can accomplish this by having ownership interests in different types of real estate investments, such as office buildings, residential apartment complexes, and shopping centers in a variety of geographic locations.

Equity real estate investment trusts (REITs) provide an alternative method of real estate diversification. Equity REITs are publicly traded operating companies that own and manage real estate properties. Like mutual funds, equity REITs serve as a conduit for earnings on investments and avoid corporate taxation by meeting certain investment and income distribution requirements. Shares of equity REITs are traded on major stock exchanges. This liquidity and trading activity provides continuous market-consensus pricing of these investments.

Because equity REITs are an indirect form of ownership, some argue that they therefore are not actually real estate investments. Joseph L. Pagliari, Jr., Kevin A. Scherer, and Richard T. Monopoli address this question in their article "Public versus Private Real Estate Equities."[2] The authors examined the performance of two real estate indices over the 24-year period ending with 2001. The first index was the NAREIT (National Association of Real Estate Investment Trusts) Equity Index, which measures the performance of the publicly traded equity REIT market. The second index was the NCREIF (National Council of Real Estate Investment Fiduciaries) Property Index, which measures the performance of private, nonliquid, institutionally held real estate. After adjusting the two indices for differences in allocation across property types, leverage, and the effects of "appraisal smoothing," publicly traded equity REITs had modestly higher returns than the private, nonliquid form of real estate ownership, but not by a statistically significant margin. After adjustments for property type, leverage, and appraisal smoothing, the volatilities of the two indices were also comparable. In other words, equity REITs are real estate. Investors seeking real estate diversification for their portfolios have two relatively interchangeable ways to access the asset class: private, nonliquid real estate investments or equity REITs.

When I published the first edition of this book in 1990, U.S. equity REITs had a market capitalization of less than $7 billion. At the time, equity REITs were considered something of a "no man's land" in the investment world. Real estate professionals disregarded them because they traded like stocks, and many stock portfolio managers ignored them because they considered equity REITs to be real estate investments rather than stocks! The increasing securitization of real estate and wider acceptance of REITs as a viable form of real estate ownership would soon change this thinking.

By the end of 2011, U.S. equity REIT market capitalization exceeded $400 billion. Ironically, the savings and loan (S&L) crisis of the 1980s spawned the explosive growth of equity REITs. Charged with the task of cleaning up the S&L mess, the Resolution Trust Company liquidated the real estate holdings of insolvent S&L associations, often at bargain prices to the purchasers. With conventional forms of financing drying up, equity REITs provided an alternative means of raising money for real estate acquisition via the capital markets. Beginning in 1992, many of the best real estate companies launched REIT initial public offerings, leading to the birth of what is called the "modern REIT era." These newer equity REITs often held higher quality real estate properties managed by seasoned, integrated real estate operating companies. Equity REITs had come of age, permanently changing the landscape of real estate investing.

The diversification achievable with equity REITs is particularly valuable to noninstitutional investors. Unlike direct real estate ownership, an equity REIT investor can easily diversify a relatively small sum of money both geographically and across different types of real estate investments, such as office buildings, apartments, regional malls, shopping centers, and industrial facilities.[3] Compared with direct real estate investments, equity REITs also have the advantages of lower transaction costs and a corporate structure that provides transparency and governance.

Over the long term, equity REITs have had total returns that are competitive with those of U.S. stocks. Dividend income has been the major portion of total return, with price appreciation generally outpacing inflation. The volatility of equity REIT returns has been similar to that of U.S. large company stocks. Equity REITs also have had a relatively low correlation with both U.S. bond and stock markets, which made them an attractive portfolio diversifier. For example, during the 2000–2002 global stock bear market, equity REITs advanced each year, generating a three-year compound annual return of 14.3 percent.[4] Against the backdrop of evaporating promises regarding the future earnings from technology and Internet stocks, the generous distributable cash flow from equity REITs suddenly looked great to investors. Prior to the bear market, though, most investors were simply not interested. At the time, I had many long conversations with some clients, urging them to remain committed to their real estate security allocations. Those who followed the advice were later very glad that they did.

By stock market standards, equity REITs tend to generate above-average yields and to have smaller capitalizations. As a result, changes in interest rates and the relative performance of small company stocks will also impact the short-term performance of equity REITs.

Just as it makes good sense to invest in both U.S. and non-U.S. bonds and stocks, it is also advisable to diversify into both U.S. and non-U.S. real estate securities. The market capitalization of non-U.S. real estate securities represents a significant portion of the opportunity set for global listed real estate securities. U.S. stock and bond markets have lower correlations with non-U.S. real estate securities than with U.S. real estate securities. Non-U.S. real estate securities therefore offer more potential diversification benefits to U.S.-based investors, who typically have their largest portfolio allocations in U.S. stocks and bonds.[5]

1997 Was a Very Good Year ...

Investors were having a great time with the increasingly speculative U.S. stock market boom, but that is not why 1997 was a very good year. Quietly, a new asset class was being born—Treasury Inflation Protected Securities (TIPS). Most investors greeted the arrival of TIPS with a yawn. The excitement was elsewhere. The year 1997 was also a very good year because Oppenheimer & Co., Inc., launched the Real Asset Fund (now called the Oppenheimer Commodity Strategy Total Return Fund), the first mutual fund offering an investment benchmarked to a recognized commodities index. Although this new fund was largely ignored for the first several years of its existence, it was a significant investment product development because it created easy access to a very interesting asset class—commodity-linked securities. In the next two sections, we will discuss these two innovative asset classes.

Treasury Inflation Protected Securities (TIPS)

TIPS are a special kind of bond that was first issued by the U.S. Department of the Treasury in January 1997. When investors want long-term inflation protection, they typically think of equity investments, not bonds. TIPS, however, are unlike either conventional bonds or equities. Whereas conventional Treasury bonds have known nominal returns if held to maturity but unknown real (i.e., inflation-adjusted) returns, TIPS have known real returns but unknown nominal returns. TIPS are designed to eliminate inflation risk by adjusting both the redemption value and coupon payments to keep up with inflation over the life of the bond. The inflation adjustments are made every six months, based on changes in the Consumer Price Index for All Urban Consumers (CPI-U). TIPS total returns are thus positively correlated with inflation. In the unlikely event of deflation, the inflation adjustments will result in lower interest and redemption payments. A deflation floor option value, however, guarantees that the Treasury will at minimum pay the original par value at maturity.

TIPS are a true buy-and-hold hedge against inflation. An unexpected spike in inflation will affect both stocks and conventional bonds negatively. TIPS, however, will be impacted positively. Due to their unusual return, volatility, and correlation attributes, TIPS are arguably a separate asset class that offers portfolios unique diversification benefits. In unconstrained portfolio optimization studies with traditional asset classes, TIPS expand the efficient frontier.

Exhibit 9.4 compares the yields to maturity of conventional Treasury bonds versus TIPS for a variety of maturities as of June 30, 2012. As expected, the TIPS yields to maturity were lower than the Treasury bond yields to maturity because the TIPS yields to maturity were real, i.e., inflation adjusted. When yields on Treasury securities are extremely low, the yields to maturity on TIPS can easily be negative if TIPS trade at a premium to their par values. This was the case in June 2012 as indicated by the negative yields to maturity for many of the TIPS maturities listed in Exhibit 9.4. For example, an investor in TIPS maturing July 2017 will earn a compound annualized return of inflation minus 1.02 percent if held to maturity. The spread between the Treasury bond yield to maturity and the TIPS yield to maturity is often interpreted as an approximate market-consensus forecast of future inflation rates.[6] For a given

Exhibit 9.4

Treasury Bond Yields to Maturity Versus TIPS Yields to Maturity (June 30, 2012)

Maturity	Treasury Bond Yields-to-Maturity	TIPS Yields-to-Maturity	TIPS Spread
Jul-2013	0.25%	-0.46%	0.71%
Jul-2014	0.34%	-0.92%	1.26%
Jul-2015	0.45%	-0.99%	1.43%
Jul-2016	0.60%	-1.02%	1.62%
Jul-2017	0.77%	-1.02%	1.78%
Jan-2019	1.03%	-0.82%	1.85%
Jan-2022	1.62%	-0.48%	2.10%
Jan-2029	2.27%	0.11%	2.15%
Feb-2042	2.75%	0.55%	2.21%

Source: Data from Wall Street Journal Market Data Center, online.wsj.com/mdc/public/page/marketsdata.html.

maturity, if the future inflation rate is equal to the spread, the realized returns from Treasury bonds and TIPS will be equal. If the future inflation rate is higher than the spread, TIPS will outperform Treasury bonds. If the future inflation rate is lower than the spread, Treasury bonds will outperform TIPS.

Both the interest payments and the inflation adjustments to the redemption value of the TIPS are taxed as ordinary income for federal income tax purposes. This tax treatment is designed to prevent a tax advantage with TIPS relative to conventional Treasury bonds. The phantom income associated with the inflation adjustment of the redemption value, however, creates the possibility that income tax liabilities may exceed the interest payments.

Commodity-Linked Securities

Commodities are sometimes called *real assets* to distinguish them from financial assets like stocks and bonds. There are five major commodity sectors:

1. Energy: crude oil, natural gas, gasoline, and heating oil
2. Agriculture: wheat, corn, soybeans, cotton, sugar, coffee, and cocoa
3. Industrial metals: aluminum, copper, nickel, lead, and zinc
4. Livestock: live cattle, feeder cattle, and lean hogs
5. Precious metals: gold and silver

The global production of these commodities is measured in the trillions of dollars annually, and they constitute an important part of the world economic system. When we discuss investing in commodities as an asset class, I am not suggesting that an investor buy actual barrels of crude oil, bushels of wheat and corn, and ingots of silver and gold. Rather, I recommend an investment that is benchmarked to either the S&P Goldman Sachs Commodity Index (S&P GSCI) or the Dow Jones-UBS Commodity Index (DJ-UBSCI). These indices provide investment exposure to changes in the expected future prices of a diversified basket of commodities selected from the five major commodity sectors listed above.[7] Investors cannot get this kind of investment exposure by owning shares of stock in commodity producers. For example, many things other than the price of crude oil impact the price of a share of Exxon stock. Actively managed commodity partnerships also may fail to give investors the kind of investment exposure provided by either the S&P GSCI or DJ-UBSCI. Due to the active bets made by a commodity partnership's investment manager and an often high level of fees and expenses, an investor in an actively managed commodity partnership may not have results that reflect broad commodity market returns.

Let's take a closer look at both of these commodity indices. Each commodity in the S&P GSCI is weighted according to worldwide production over the most recent five years of available data. This weighting scheme typically results in a large allocation to the energy commodity sector. For example, in 2012, energy commodities represented 70.5 percent of the S&P GSCI. (See Exhibit 9.5.) The creators of the S&P GSCI argue that worldwide production is the appropriate

Exhibit 9.5
2012 Index Component Weights

	S&P Goldman Sachs Commodity Index (S&P GSCI)	Dow Jones – UBS Commodity Index (DJ-UBSCI)*
Energy	70.5%	32.6%
Agriculture	14.7%	30.4%
Industrial Metals	6.6%	18.6%
Livestock	4.7%	5.7%
Precious Metals	3.5%	12.6%
Totals	100.0%	99.9%*

*Due to rounding, the numbers in this column do not sum to 100%.

measure of economic importance. For example, a doubling in the price of energy commodities will have a larger impact on inflation and world economic growth than a doubling in the price of livestock or precious metals. By contrast, the DJ-UBSCI primarily uses a liquidity weighting scheme that considers the amount of trading activity for each commodity in the index and secondarily considers worldwide production. The creators of the DJ-UBSCI argue that liquidity is often a better measure of economic significance, particularly for nonperishable commodities like precious metals, whose trading volume exceeds average worldwide production. The DJ-UBSCI also has diversification rules to prevent any commodity or commodity sector from dominating the index. One rule requires that each commodity constitute at least 2 percent of the index. Another rule limits the weight of any commodity sector to no more than 33 percent of the index. The energy sector is therefore capped at 33 percent in the DJ-UBSCI, resulting in higher weights given to agriculture, industrial metals, livestock, and precious metals when compared with the S&P GSCI commodity sector weights. Energy commodities are among the most volatile of all commodities. As a result, the S&P GSCI, with its high energy sector allocation, is a more volatile index than the DJ-UBSCI.

Both the S&P GSCI and the DJ-UBSCI measure the performance of unleveraged, long-only investments in commodity futures that are diversified across the energy, agriculture, industrial metals, livestock, and precious metals commodity sectors. The index return calculations presume that the futures contracts are fully collateralized by Treasury bills. For example, consider a long-only investor who owns a crude oil futures contract that gives her the right to buy 1,000 barrels of crude oil at its current market price of $60 per barrel with an expiration date three months in the future. Futures contracts are highly leveraged. That is, an investor can purchase a futures contract for only a fraction of the $60,000 value of the crude oil that the contract controls. The leverage magnifies profits for the futures contract investor when crude oil's expected future price rises. The leverage that works for an investor on the upside, however, works against her on the downside. Even a modest decline in the expected future price of crude oil can cause the value of the futures contract to drop precipitously. The investor can guarantee a continuing right to purchase the 1,000 barrels at $60 per share by fully collateralizing the contract with $60,000 of Treasury bills. In essence, the fully collateralized futures position creates unleveraged exposure to changes in the expected future price of crude oil while guaranteeing the availability of funds that could be used to exercise the contract and take delivery of the 1,000 barrels of crude oil. In this example, the investor's return will be the interest earned on the Treasury bill pledged as collateral plus (or minus) increases (or decreases) in the expected future price of crude oil. In a similar way, the S&P GSCI and DJ-UBSCI presume that the futures are fully collateralized for all the commodities represented in each index. In order to maintain continuous exposure to each of the commodities, both indices presume that near-term futures contracts are sold prior to maturity, with the proceeds rolled into contracts with longer maturities.

In 1930, John Maynard Keynes articulated his theory of *normal backwardation,* which postulates that buyers of commodity futures should earn a risk premium for bearing commodity price volatility.[8] The source of this risk premium is the commodity producer's desire to hedge the price risk of his output. For example, a farmer plants corn not knowing what the price of a bushel of corn will be when he is ready to take it to the market. He may, however, choose to sell some of his anticipated harvest in the futures market today at a predetermined price and thereby insure against the possibility of experiencing a severe financial hardship due to a large, unanticipated drop in the price of corn. The farmer willingly accepts a lower price than the expected price at harvest time in order to entice the purchaser of the futures contract to bear the risk of lower corn prices.

An investor with long-only investments in a variety of commodity futures subjects himself to volatilities in the expected future prices of those commodities. According to Keynes's theory of normal backwardation, the investor deserves a risk premium for bearing those price risks. The S&P GSCI therefore has two sources of expected return: the return on the Treasury bill, which serves as collateral for the commodity futures, plus a risk premium for bearing the volatilities of the expected future prices of the commodities. The DJ-UBSCI also has these two sources of expected return, plus a third source. As a result of its different methodology for annually reweighting the major commodity sectors and specific commodities, the DJ-UBSCI tends to rebalance funds from outperforming commodities that have appreciated in value to commodities that have underperformed. The various commodities have dissimilar patterns of returns, many of which tend to revert toward their means. This dissimilarity in patterns of returns occurs because different commodities face different economic risks. For example, weather conditions that may impact corn prices will likely have no effect on either crude oil prices or copper prices. The periodic rebalancing among mean-reverting commodities with dissimilar patterns of returns creates DJ-UBSCI's third source of potential return.

An indexed commodity investment like the S&P GSCI or the DJ-UBSCI is very different from financial assets like stocks and bonds. The value of a stock or bond is simply the discounted present value of its anticipated cash flows that may extend many years into the future. Returns from long-only investments in commodity futures, on the other hand, are determined by short-term supply and demand and by short-term risks that can limit the production or distribution of the commodities. The events that trigger an unexpected rise in the S&P GSCI often take a negative toll on stock and bond markets. Consider a sudden 25 percent run-up in the price of crude oil: great news for an investment benchmarked to the S&P GSCI, bad news for stocks and bonds. More generally, rising commodity prices are one source of fuel for the inflation that is anathema to stock and bond markets. Historically, the S&P GSCI has delivered highly volatile, equity-like returns that are usually either negatively correlated or relatively uncorrelated with many financial asset classes. The DJ-UBSCI has a shorter history than the S&P GSCI. It is less volatile than the S&P GSCI, but it is still usually negatively correlated or relatively uncorrelated with many financial asset classes. The return, volatility, and correlation attributes of commodity-linked securities make this asset class a potentially powerful portfolio diversifier.

Commodity-linked securities are growing in popularity as a viable asset class for portfolio diversification. Not everyone agrees, however. John Maynard Keynes's theory of normal backwardation has engendered controversy over the years. If commodity futures are not priced on the basis of the producer's incentive to hedge the price risk of their output, what determines the price of commodity futures? Some argue that the marketplace should price commodity-linked securities such that the producers of commodities receive the price risk premium. Commodity producers deserve to receive this price risk premium for having contributed to a very valuable asset class that is negatively correlated (or at other times relatively uncorrelated) with many financial asset classes in investors' opportunity sets. The essence of this argument is that commodity-linked securities generate returns that act like an (admittedly imperfect) insurance policy against poor returns from financial asset classes. The premium paid by the investor for this insurance is the risk premium priced by the marketplace to reward the producer, not the investor.

The pricing mechanism for commodity futures is both a theoretical and empirical question. Even if we assume that the question will remain unresolved for the time being, we can nevertheless model the capital market assumptions under which commodity-linked securities are attractive as a portfolio building block. If we assume that commodity-linked securities will have a level of future volatility similar to that of the past and will remain negatively correlated (or relatively uncorrelated) with traditional asset classes, we can use unconstrained mean-variance optimization techniques to solve for the minimum rate of return needed to justify a portfolio allocation to commodity-linked securities. With this approach, I have calculated that commodity-linked securities can have lower returns in the future than they have had historically and still justify their inclusion in a portfolio. This gives me an extra measure of confidence in recommending the asset class while the debate continues.

Chapter 10

The Rewards of Multiple-Asset-Class Investing

> The Perfect Way is only difficult for those who pick and choose;
> Do not like, do not dislike; all will then be clear.
> Make a hairbreadth difference, and Heaven and Earth are set apart;
> If you want the truth to stand clear before you, never be for or against.
> The struggle between "for" and "against" is the mind's worst disease;
> When the deep meaning of things is not understood,
> The mind's essential peace is disturbed to no avail.
>
> —*Jianzhi Sengcan, Third Chinese Patriarch of Zen (?–606),* Hsin Hsin Ming

People have preferences. It is natural. Investors have asset classes that they like and others that they don't like. When an asset class underperforms, particularly if for a long period, investors often eject it from their portfolios. What would happen if investors set aside their impulse to "pick and choose" and instead embraced a more broadly diversified asset allocation strategy?

Interest-generating investments play an important role in most investors' portfolios: They help to mitigate portfolio volatility but usually at the price of lower portfolio returns. Equity investments usually are responsible for great portfolio returns when they occur, but they also are most often responsible for significant losses. Will broadening the asset class diversification of the equity side of investors' portfolios mitigate volatility without sacrificing portfolio returns? This chapter seeks to answer that question.

Exhibit 10.1 shows the performance of 15 different equity portfolios over the period from 1972 through 2011. The portfolios are intentionally unlabeled in order to conduct a blindfolded preference test. Of these 15 portfolios, 4 are represented by squares, 6 by triangles, 4 by diamonds, and 1 by a circle. As you move to the right along the chart, portfolio volatility increases. Returns increase as you move from bottom to top. Assume that you have a reliable crystal ball and know with certainty that each one of these portfolios will perform the same way over the next 40 years as it did over the period from 1972 through 2011. Based on that assumption, answer these questions:

- If you had to choose between owning either a randomly chosen square portfolio or a randomly chosen triangle portfolio, which would you choose: square or triangle?
- If you had to choose between owning either a randomly chosen triangle portfolio or a randomly chosen diamond portfolio, which would you choose: triangle or diamond?
- If you had to choose between owning either a randomly chosen diamond portfolio or simply owning the circle portfolio, which would you choose: diamond or circle?

I have posed this series of questions to my clients and to audiences at speaking engagements. Their answers are consistent. People prefer

Exhibit 10.1

Blindfolded Preference Test: Fifteen Equity Portfolios (1972–2011)

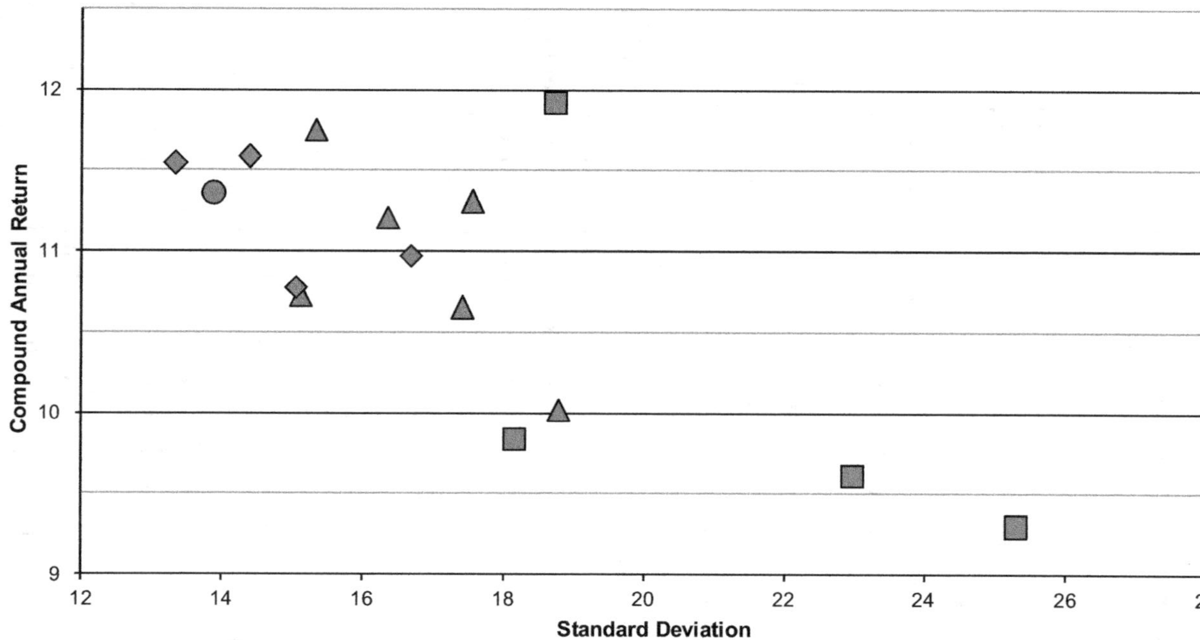

Source: © Roger C. Gibson, "Asset Allocation and the Rewards of Multiple-Asset-Class Investing," 1998. Updated by author. Data source: Morningstar® Principia®,

the triangles over the squares, the diamonds over the triangles, and the circle over the diamonds.

Now let's take off the blindfold and look at Exhibit 10.2. Each square is a single-asset-class portfolio:

- "A (U.S. Stocks)" is the S&P 500, a capitalization-weighted total return index of 500 widely held U.S. large company stocks.
- "B (Non-U.S. Stocks)" is the MSCI EAFE Index, a total return index of non-U.S. large company stocks from 22 countries that represent many of the major markets of the world.
- "C (Real Estate Securities)" is the FTSE NAREIT Equity REITs Index, a capitalization-weighted total return index of U.S. equity real estate investment trusts (REITs). This index is a good proxy for the real estate asset class.
- "D (Commodity-Linked Securities)" is the S&P GSCI Index, a composite index of commodity sector total returns representing an unleveraged, long-only investment in commodity futures that is broadly diversified across the energy, agriculture, industrial metals, livestock, and precious metals commodity sectors.

The triangles represent every possible two-asset-class portfolio that investors can construct using the four individual asset classes (portfolios A, B, C, and D) as building blocks. Each portfolio is rebalanced annually to maintain an equally weighted allocation among the asset classes. For example, the triangle AB represents the performance of an annually rebalanced portfolio weighted equally between U.S. stocks and non-U.S. stocks.

The diamonds represent every possible three-asset-class portfolio that investors can construct with the four individual asset classes. The circle is an equally allocated, annually rebalanced portfolio using all four asset classes.

Exhibit 10.2

Fifteen Equity Portfolios (1972–2011)

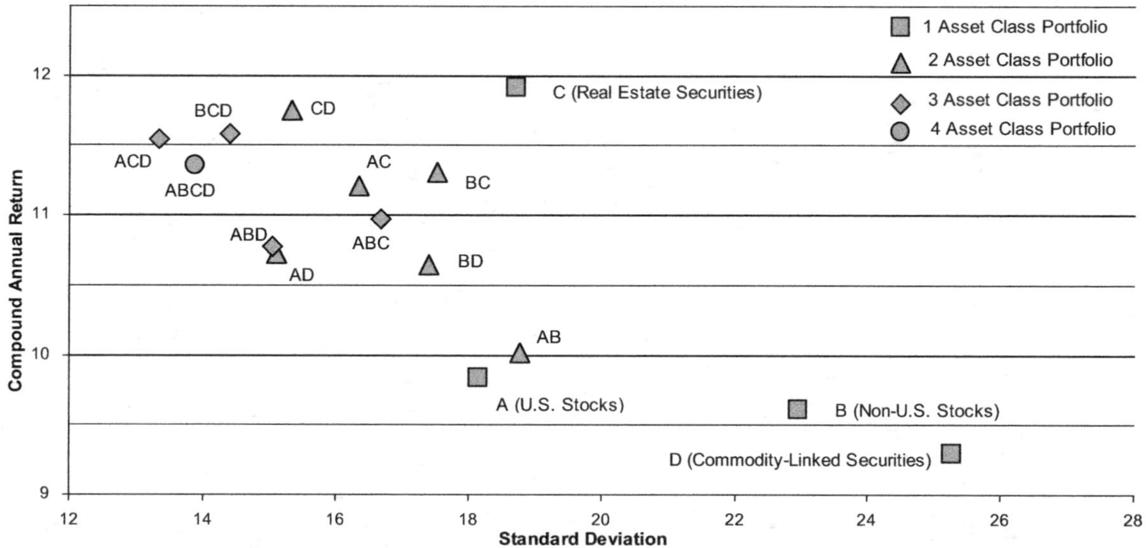

<u>Single-Asset-Class Portfolios</u>

A – U.S. Stocks (S&P 500 Index)

B – Non-U.S. Stocks (MSCI EAFE Index)

C – Real Estate Securities (FTSE NAREIT Equity REITs Index)

D – Commodity-Linked Securities (S&P GSCI Index)

<u>Two-Asset-Class Portfolios: Equally Allocated, Annually Rebalanced</u>

AB – U.S. Stocks, Non-U.S. Stocks

AC – U.S. Stocks, Real Estate Securities

AD – U.S. Stocks, Commodity-Linked Securities

BC – Non-U.S. Stocks, Real Estate Securities

BD – Non-U.S. Stocks, Commodity-Linked Securities

CD – Real Estate Securities, Commodity-Linked Securities

<u>Three-Asset-Class Portfolios: Equally Allocated, Annually Rebalanced</u>

ABC – U.S. Stocks, Non-U.S. Stocks, Real Estate Securities

ABD – U.S. Stocks, Non-U.S. Stocks, Commodity-Linked Securities

ACD – U.S. Stocks, Real Estate Securities, Commodity-Linked Securities

BCD – Non-U.S. Stocks, Real Estate Securities, Commodity-Linked Securities

<u>Four-Asset-Class Portfolio: Equally Allocated, Annually Rebalanced</u>

ABCD – U.S. Stocks, Non-U.S. Stocks, Real Estate Securities, Commodity-Linked Securities

Source: © Roger C. Gibson, "Asset Allocation and the Rewards of Multiple-Asset-Class Investing," 1998. Updated by author. Data source: Morningstar® Principia®, © 2012 Morningstar. All Rights Reserved.

An investor who chooses a triangle portfolio over a square is indicating a preference for a two-asset-class portfolio over a single-asset-class portfolio. This decision is a rational one, since two-asset-class portfolios, in general, have lower volatilities and higher returns than single-asset-class portfolios. Likewise, the three-asset-class portfolios (diamonds) have better volatility and return characteristics than do the two-asset-class portfolios (triangles). The four-asset-class portfolio (circle) is a better choice than a random placement in one of the three-asset-class portfolios (diamonds). The order of preference moves to the left, in the direction of less volatility, and upward, toward higher returns.

The best-performing portfolios occupy the upper left portion of the graph. These portfolios generated the highest returns with the least volatility. Multiple-asset-class portfolios dominate this space. The worst-performing portfolios are in the lower right portion of the graph. Four portfolios occupy this space. Three are single-asset-class portfolios (U.S. stocks, non-U.S. stocks, and commodity-linked securities), and one is a two-asset-class portfolio (U.S. stocks plus non-U.S. stocks).

When comparing only the returns of these 15 equity portfolios, single-asset-class portfolios generated the three lowest returns, whereas the portfolios with the highest returns were mostly multiple-asset-class structures. When we compare just the volatility levels of these portfolios, we find that 4 out of the 5 most volatile portfolios were single-asset-class structures. The low-volatility alternatives were all multiple-asset-class portfolios.

The reduction in volatility observed as we progress from one- to four-asset-class portfolios is not surprising. We expect it because of the dissimilarity in returns among the portfolio components. The generally rising pattern of returns, however, is surprising. Portfolio D (commodity-linked securities), for example, had lower returns with considerably more volatility than portfolio A (U.S. stocks); yet an annually rebalanced portfolio allocated equally between the two (portfolio AD) had a higher return with much less volatility than either of its asset class components.

Return for a moment to the four single-asset-class portfolios A, B, C, and D in Exhibit 10.2. If we offer investors the opportunity to choose how they would invest their money, given complete certainty that each asset class will perform in the future as indicated on the graph, they will likely pick portfolio C, real estate securities. The choice seems obvious: The real estate securities asset class has a higher compound annual return than any of the other asset classes and has the second lowest level of volatility. Yet by comparing the position of the broadly diversified portfolio ABCD with portfolio C in Exhibit 10.2, we see that a portfolio allocated equally among all four asset classes generates a compound annual return that is only slightly less than that of real estate securities, but it does so with 26 percent less volatility. This amazing result occurs even though each of the other three asset classes has a much lower return, and two of the other three asset classes are much more volatile than real estate securities! For investors concerned simultaneously with both volatility and return—and this is almost everybody—portfolio ABCD is superior to portfolio C.

If we ask a volatility-averse investor to eliminate one of the four asset classes as a building block for the multiple-asset-class portfolios, she will probably choose portfolio D, commodity-linked securities. Of all 15 portfolios in Exhibit 10.2, the commodity-linked securities asset class is the most volatile. Yet the 6 *least* volatile portfolios have portfolio D as an equal component—portfolios ACD, ABCD, BCD, ABD, AD, and CD.

Obviously, the return and volatility dimensions of Exhibit 10.2 do not capture everything that is going on here. We are missing the crucial information about how each asset class's pattern of returns correlates with the others'. The commodity-linked securities asset class, for example, has the pattern of returns that is the most dissimilar to the other asset classes' patterns of returns. It accordingly produces the strongest diversification effect when combined with the other asset classes.

Most financial asset classes are positively correlated. An uncorrelated asset class is unusual. A negatively correlated asset class is rare. Exhibit 10.3 shows a correlation matrix for U.S. stocks,

Exhibit 10.3
Correlation Matrix (1972–2011)

	Asset Class	(1)	(2)	(3)	(4)
(1)	U.S. Stocks	1.00			
(2)	Non-U.S. Stocks	0.66	1.00		
(3)	Real Estate Securities	0.57	0.41	1.00	
(4)	Commodity-Linked Securities	-0.06	-0.04	-0.05	1.00

U.S. Stocks: S&P 500 Index
Non-U.S. Stocks: MSCI EAFE Index
Real Estate Securities: FTSE NAREIT Equity REITs Index
Commodity-Linked Securities: S&P GSCI Index

Data source: Morningstar® Principia®, © 2012 Morningstar. All Rights Reserved.

non-U.S. stocks, real estate securities, and commodity-linked securities for the same period covered by the 15-equity portfolio illustration of Exhibit 10.2. Note that the commodity-linked securities asset class was slightly negatively correlated with each of the other three asset classes.

Exhibit 10.4 shows the 20-quarter (5-year) rolling correlations of U.S. stocks with non-U.S. stocks, real estate securities, and commodity-linked securities. Before the 1990s, U.S. stocks had a lower correlation with non-U.S. stocks than with real estate securities. This correlation changed beginning in the 1990s. U.S. stocks and non-U.S. stocks became highly correlated, while the correlation between U.S. stocks and real estate securities dropped. This shift partially explains why, during the 2000–2002 bear market, real estate securities diversification offered U.S. stock investors more protection than non-U.S. stock diversification. The most interesting line on the chart, however, is the correlation between U.S. stocks and commodity-linked securities. Although this correlation occasionally rose to positive levels, most of the time these two asset classes were either negatively correlated or noncorrelated. This low-to-negative correlation, coupled with a competitive long-term return, made commodity-linked securities a powerful portfolio diversifier. As mentioned in the last chapter, during and after the Global Financial Crisis

Exhibit 10.4

Correlations with U.S. Stocks

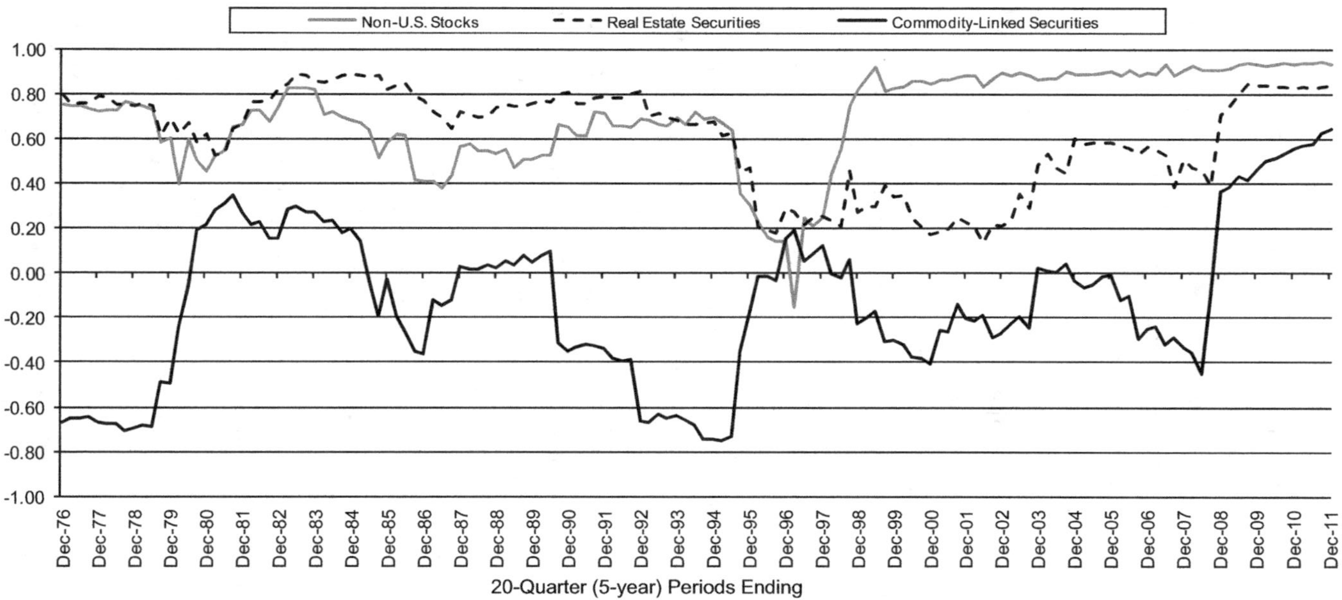

U.S. Stocks: S&P 500 Index

Non-U.S. Stocks: MSCI EAFE Index

Real Estate Securities: FTSE NAREIT Equity REITs Index

Commodity-Linked Securities: S&P GSCI Index

Data source: Morningstar® Principia®, © 2012 Morningstar. All Rights Reserved.

of 2008, a "risk-on, risk-off" trading pattern pushed correlations higher among most equity asset classes, as evidenced by the rising correlations toward the end of the timeline in Exhibit 10.4.

People are often puzzled by the seemingly impossible positioning of the multiple-asset-class portfolios relative to the single-asset-class portfolios A, B, C, and D in Exhibit 10.2. For example, how can you combine portfolio A with portfolio D, which has a much higher standard deviation than portfolio A, and obtain portfolio AD, which has much *less* volatility than either portfolio A or portfolio D? And how can portfolio AD have a higher compound annual return than either portfolio A or portfolio D? Let's explore this question with a few graphs. Exhibit 10.5 shows the pattern of returns for U.S. stocks (portfolio A) from 1972 through 2011. Compare the volatility of U.S. stock returns with that of commodity-linked securities (portfolio D), shown in Exhibit 10.6. The volatility of returns of commodity-linked securities is much higher. If you want to reduce the volatility of a U.S. stock portfolio, does diversification into commodity-linked securities look like a good idea? No, it doesn't. But Exhibit 10.7 shows the surprising pattern of annual returns of portfolio AD—an equally allocated, annually rebalanced allocation of U.S. stocks and commodity-linked securities. Portfolio AD has much less volatility on average than either portfolio A or portfolio D.

Exhibit 10.8 solves the mystery. On average, U.S. stocks and commodity-linked securities had relatively uncorrelated patterns of returns. The degree of dissimilarity in patterns of returns, however, varied considerably over time. During the 1970s, U.S. stocks and commodity-linked securities moved in countercyclical patterns and thereby delivered significant volatility reduction to the 50/50 allocation portfolio. Note also that at other times the two asset classes were moving up and down together. Remember, the correlation is not a static, unchanging number. The correlation changed through time, and, periodically, it turned positive. Commodity-linked securities have been a powerful, but not a perfect, portfolio diversifier. Exhibit 10.9 shows the growth of $1 for investments in U.S. stocks, commodity-linked

Exhibit 10.5

U.S. Stocks (1972–2011)

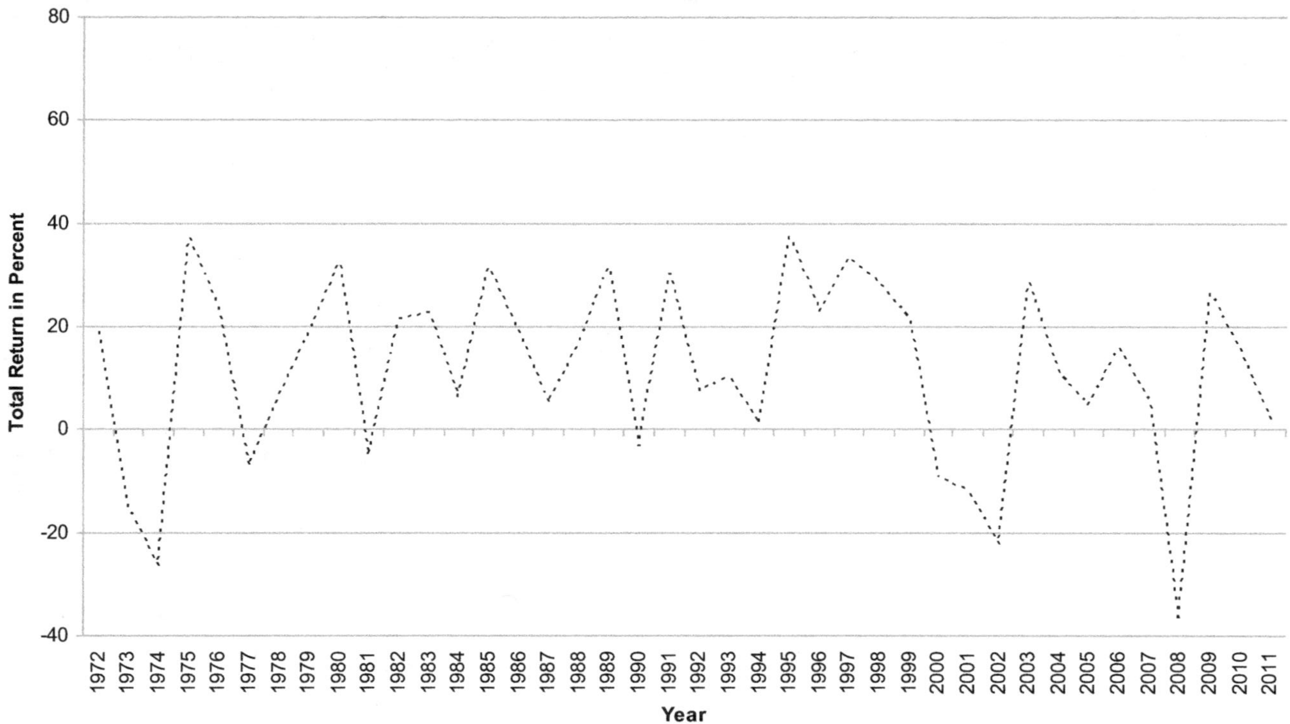

U.S. Stocks: S&P 500 Index

Data source: Morningstar® Principia®,

Exhibit 10.6
Commodity-Linked Securities (1972–2011)

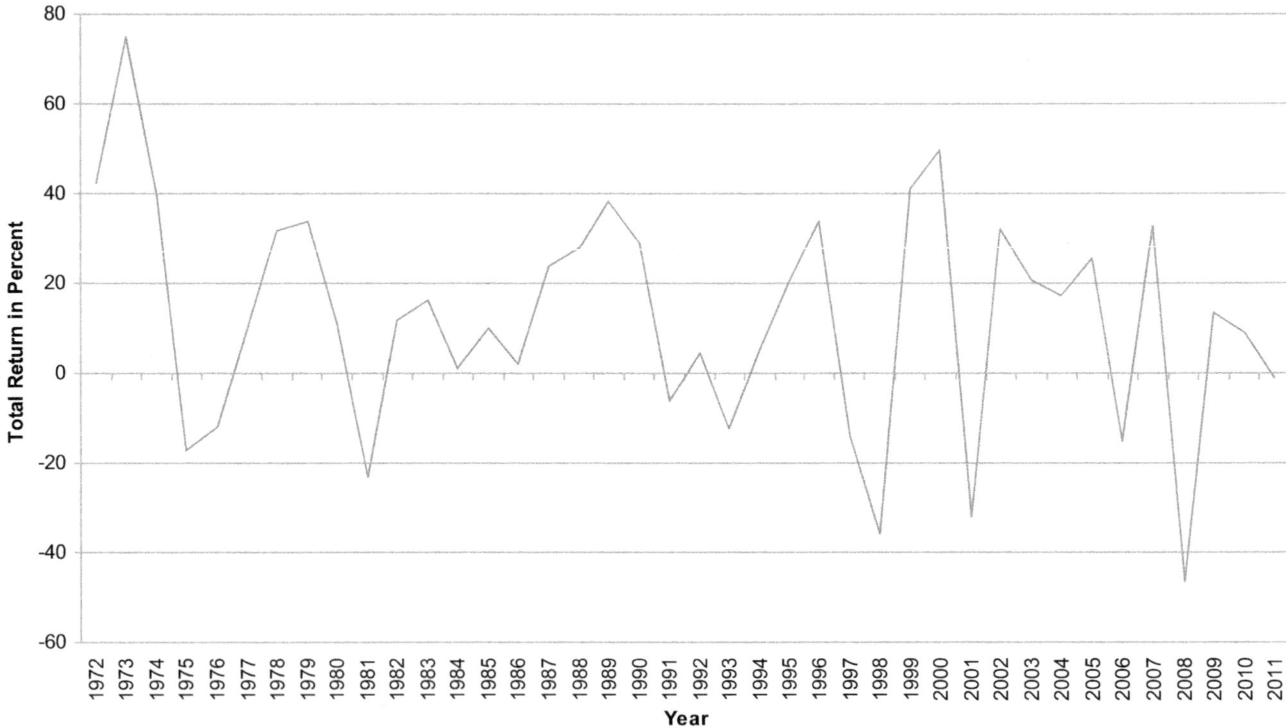

Commodity-Linked Securities: S&P GSCI Index

Data source: Morningstar® Principia®, © 2012 Morningstar. All Rights Reserved.

Exhibit 10.7

50/50 Allocation: U.S. Stocks and Commodity-Linked Securities (1972–2011)

U.S. Stocks: S&P 500 Index

Commodity-Linked Securities: S&P GSCI Index

Data source: Morningstar® Principia®, © 2012 Morningstar. All Rights Reserved.

Exhibit 10.8

U.S. Stocks Versus Commodity-Linked Securities Versus 50/50 Allocation (1972–2011)

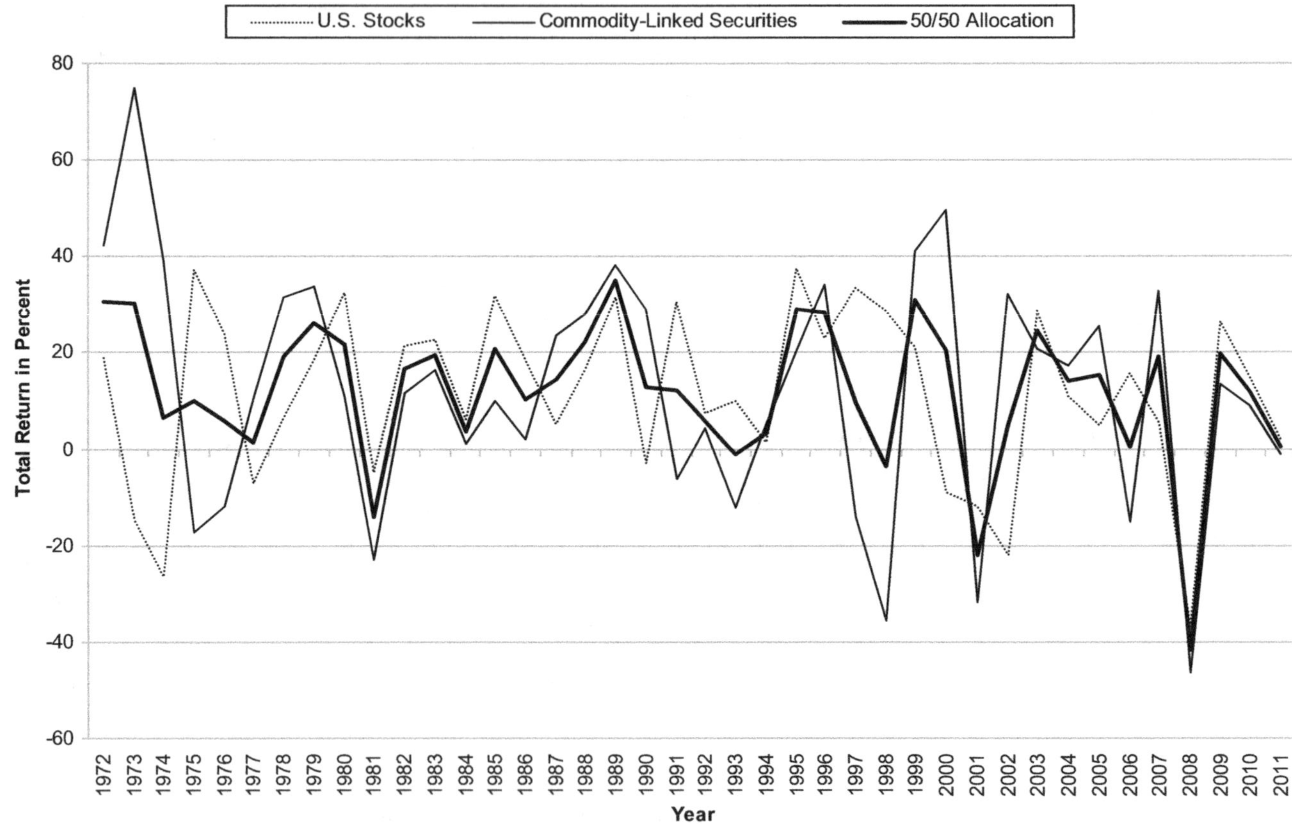

U.S. Stocks: S&P 500 Index

Commodity-Linked Securities: S&P GSCI Index

Data source: Morningstar® Principia®, © 2012 Morningstar. All Rights Reserved.

Exhibit 10.9

Growth of $1: U.S. Stocks Versus Commodity-Linked Securities Versus 50/50 Allocation (1972–2011)

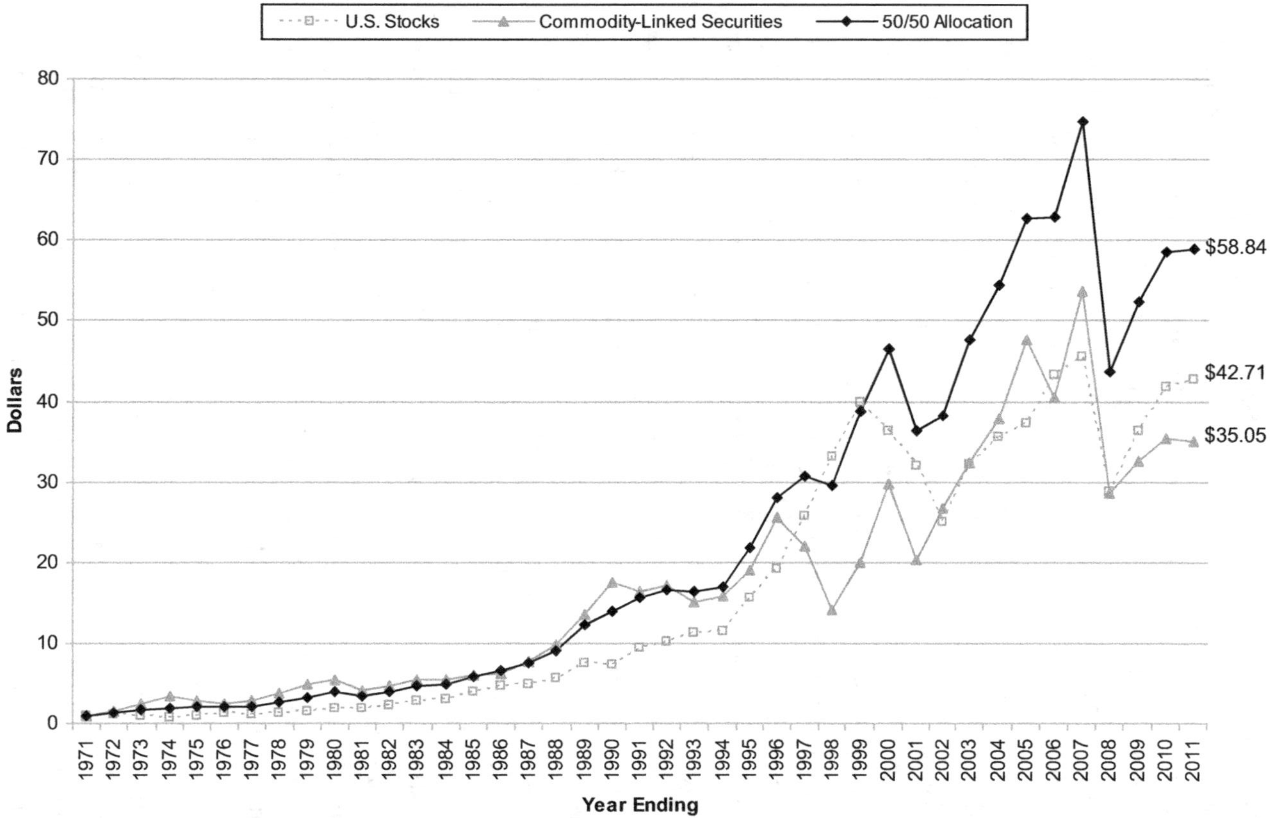

U.S. Stocks: S&P 500 Index

Commodity-Linked Securities: S&P GSCI Index

Data source: Morningstar® Principia®, © 2012 Morningstar. All Rights Reserved.

securities, and the equally allocated, annually rebalanced portfolio of U.S. stocks and commodity-linked securities. An investment of $1 grew to be worth $42.71 in U.S. stocks, $35.05 in commodity-linked securities, and $58.84 in the equally allocated, annually rebalanced portfolio of both asset classes. As we discussed in Chapter 8, diversification among asset classes with dissimilar patterns of returns can not only reduce portfolio volatility but also increase the portfolio compound annual return to a level above that of its component asset classes. We now have real-world examples that back up the theory.

Exhibit 10.10A shows in tabular form the performance statistics for the 15 equity portfolios from Exhibit 10.2. The data in this exhibit make a very strong case for multiple-asset-class investing. For investors concerned primarily with maximizing portfolio returns, multiple-asset-class strategies have dominated single-asset-class strategies. For investors who are more concerned about mitigating volatility, multiple-asset-class strategies again proved superior. The Sharpe ratios displayed provide a volatility-adjusted performance measurement for each portfolio.[1] Again, we find that multiple-asset-class strategies delivered much higher rates of volatility-adjusted returns than did single-asset-class strategies.

Exhibit 10.10B shows summary comparisons for four-, three-, two-, and one-asset-class approaches. This summary provides perhaps the most compelling argument for multiple-asset-class investing. As we move toward broader diversification, rates of return increase, volatility levels decrease, and Sharpe ratios improve. The four-asset-class portfolio ABCD has a compound annual rate of return that is 1.19 percentage points higher than the average compound annual return of its components. That is, a $1 investment in an equally allocated, annually rebalanced portfolio of all four asset classes had a future value of $73.97 compared with an average future value of $51.86 for the four asset classes standing alone. The four-asset-class portfolio had 35 percent less volatility than the average volatility levels of its components. And the Sharpe ratio of the four-asset-class portfolio ABCD shows that it generated a volatility-adjusted return that was more than 50 percent higher than the average of its components.

Exhibit 10.10A

Fifteen Equity Portfolios: Performance Statistics (1972–2011)

Compound Annual Returns & Future Values of $1.00 Ranked High to Low			Standard Deviations (Volatility) Ranked Low to High		Sharpe Ratios Ranked High to Low	
Portfolio	**%**	**$**	**Portfolio**	**%**	**Portfolio**	**Ratio**
C	11.92	90.42	ACD	13.34	ACD	0.49
CD	11.75	85.20	ABCD	13.88	BCD	0.47
BCD	11.58	80.10	BCD	14.40	ABCD	0.47
ACD	11.54	78.94	ABD	15.06	CD	0.46
ABCD	11.36	73.97	AD	15.12	C	0.41
BC	11.31	72.59	CD	15.33	AC	0.41
AC	11.21	70.13	AC	16.34	ABD	0.41
ABC	10.98	64.43	ABC	16.68	AD	0.40
ABD	10.78	59.96	BD	17.41	BC	0.40
AD	10.72	58.84	BC	17.54	ABC	0.39
BD	10.65	57.28	A	18.16	BD	0.37
AB	10.02	45.54	C	18.72	AB	0.32
A	9.84	42.71	AB	18.78	A	0.31
B	9.61	39.28	B	22.96	B	0.27
D	9.30	35.05	D	25.30	D	0.26

Single-Asset-Class Portfolios
A – U.S. Stocks (S&P 500 Index)
B – Non-U.S. Stocks (MSCI EAFE Index)
C – Real Estate Securities (FTSE NAREIT Equity REITs Index)
D – Commodity-Linked Securities (S&P GSCI Index)

Two-Asset-Class Portfolios: Equally Allocated, Annually Rebalanced
AB – U.S. Stocks, Non-U.S. Stocks
AC – U.S. Stocks, Real Estate Securities
AD – U.S. Stocks, Commodity-Linked Securities
BC – Non-U.S. Stocks, Real Estate Securities
BD – Non-U.S. Stocks, Commodity-Linked Securities
CD – Real Estate Securities, Commodity-Linked Securities

Three-Asset-Class Portfolios: Equally Allocated, Annually Rebalanced
ABC – U.S. Stocks, Non-U.S. Stocks, Real Estate Securities
ABD – U.S. Stocks, Non-U.S. Stocks, Commodity-Linked Securities
ACD – U.S. Stocks, Real Estate Securities, Commodity-Linked Securities
BCD – Non-U.S. Stocks, Real Estate Securities, Commodity-Linked Securities

Four-Asset-Class Portfolio: Equally Allocated, Annually Rebalanced
ABCD – U.S. Stocks, Non-U.S. Stocks, Real Estate Securities, Commodity-Linked Securities

Source: © Roger C. Gibson, "Asset Allocation and the Rewards of Multiple-Asset-Class Investing," 1998. Updated by author. Data source: Morningstar® Principia®, © 2012 Morningstar. All Rights Reserved.

Exhibit 10.11 shows yet another picture of the risk reduction achieved by multiple-asset-class investing. Here we list the five worst years, from 1972 through 2011, generated by each of the single asset classes and by the four-asset-class portfolio ABCD. The year 2008

Exhibit 10.10B
Fifteen Equity Portfolios: Performance Statistics (1972–2011)

Average Performance Statistics: Four-, Three-, Two-, & One-Asset-Class Portfolios						
Compound Annual Returns & Future Values of $1.00 Ranked High to Low			Standard Deviations (Volatility) Ranked Low to High		Sharpe Ratios Ranked High to Low	
Four	11.36%	$73.97	Four	13.88%	Four	0.47
Three	11.22%	$70.86	Three	14.87%	Three	0.44
Two	10.94%	$64.93	Two	16.75%	Two	0.39
One	10.17%	$51.86	One	21.28%	One	0.31

Source: © Roger C. Gibson, "Asset Allocation and the Rewards of Multiple-Asset-Class Investing," 1998. Updated by author. Data source: Morningstar® Principia®,

stands out not only because it is shared by all portfolios as the single worst year but because of the sheer magnitude of the declines. Yet the next four worst annual outcomes for portfolio ABCD are much less severe than the worst outcomes of the single-asset-class portfolios. Much of the improvement in downside risk with portfolio ABCD is due to the greater dissimilarity in patterns of returns of either real estate securities or commodity-linked securities as compared with those of either U.S. stocks or non-U.S. stocks. These dissimilarities were particularly valuable in mitigating risk during the bear markets of 1973–1974 and 2000–2002. As 2008 reminds us, however, multiple-asset-class investing does not guarantee protection against short-term losses.

Diversification illustrations often obscure the beneficial impact on return that broader diversification creates because the illustrations tend to mix interest-generating investments with equity investments. In such illustrations, the large differences between the returns of interest-generating investments and equity investments obscure the increase in portfolio return attributable to the diversification effect. Because the longer-term rates of return of the four equity asset classes used in the illustrations were fairly similar, we can see the positive impact that diversification had on both dampening volatility and increasing return.[2]

Exhibit 10.11

The Five Worst Years (1972–2011)

Portfolio Structures									
A U.S. Stocks		B Non-U.S. Stocks		C Real Estate Securities		D Commodity-Linked Securities		ABCD Equal Allocation	
Year	Return	Year	Return	Year	Return	Year	Return	Year	Return
2008	-37.00	2008	-43.06	2008	-37.73	2008	-46.49	2008	-41.07
1974	-26.47	1990	-23.20	1974	-21.40	1998	-35.75	2001	-12.78
2002	-22.10	1974	-22.15	1998	-17.50	2001	-31.93	1974	-7.63
1973	-14.69	2001	-21.21	2007	-15.69	1981	-23.01	1981	-5.74
2001	-11.89	2002	-15.66	1973	-15.52	1975	-17.22	1990	-3.14

A – U.S. Stocks (S&P 500 Index)

B – Non-U.S. Stocks (MSCI EAFE Index)

C – Real Estate Securities (FTSE NAREIT Equity REITs Index)

D – Commodity-Linked Securities (S&P GSCI Index)

ABCD – U.S. Stocks, Non-U.S. Stocks, Real Estate Securities, Commodity-Linked Securities

Data source: Morningstar® Principia®,

Why Isn't Everyone Doing Multiple-Asset-Class Investing?

If multiple-asset-class investing is so wonderful, why isn't everyone doing it? There are three primary reasons. First, investors lack an awareness of the power of diversification. The typical investor understands that diversification may reduce volatility but suspects that it simultaneously impairs returns. But as we have demonstrated, diversification tends to improve returns, not diminish them. Investors need to be educated about this dual benefit.

Second, the question of market timing arises. Investors naturally want to believe that some way exists to predict which asset class will come in first place, and some investment managers suggest that they in fact can make such market-timing predictions accurately. Let's assume that we have a market timer whom we consult annually for his prediction of the upcoming year's best-performing asset class among U.S. stocks, non-U.S. stocks, real estate securities, and commodity-linked securities. Had he successfully predicted the winning asset class over the 15-year period from 1997 through 2011, an investor following his recommendations would have earned a compound rate of return of 24.24 percent. If such market-timing skill exists, we should find evidence that investment managers have earned these rates of return. A check of Morningstar's database reveals a universe of 2,462 mutual funds with at least 15 years of performance history. This universe includes the full variety of professionally managed U.S. and non-U.S. funds, equity and fixed-income funds, and various specialty funds. How many of these funds had compound rates of return in excess of 24.24 percent? None. Not one got remotely close.

Maybe we are asking for too much proficiency from our market timer. Let's assume that his predicted winning asset class each year never finished first but instead came in second among the four asset classes. This does not seem like a particularly impressive achievement; yet it would have generated a 15-year compound annual return of 11.80 percent. Another search through Morningstar's database reveals that less than 1 percent of the 2,462 professionally managed mutual funds had better investment performance.

What if we asked our market timer to simply recognize the long periods of dominance of one asset class over another, commonly referred to as "seeing the fat pitch"? For example, our market timer might have instructed us to invest our funds in U.S. stocks during the portion of the 15-year period that fell in the late 1990s and then switch to real estate securities for the 2000s. This strategy would have generated a compound annual return of 14.77 percent. Only two mutual funds out of the universe of 2,462 funds exceeded that rate of return, and neither employed market timing as part of its strategy. Apparently, it is difficult to successfully predict the relative performance of asset classes.

The third reason that not everyone is embracing multiple-asset-class investing involves investor psychology. Investors use their domestic market as a frame of reference for evaluating their investment results. For example, a U.S.-based investor will compare her equity returns with those of a market index like the S&P 500. This frame-of-reference issue is not a problem in years when the U.S. stock market underperforms other asset classes, since diversification into better-performing markets rewards the multiple-asset-class investor. When the U.S. stock market comes out on top, however, the investor perceives that diversification has impaired her returns. This sense of winning or losing arises primarily from the investor's immediate frame of reference. For example, the four-asset-class portfolio we have been discussing had a 10.40 percent return in 1997. Given either a non-U.S. stock or commodity-linked securities frame of reference, investors would have perceived this as a winning return, since these asset classes had returns in 1997 of 2.06 and –14.07 percent, respectively. But this return was lousy from either a U.S. stocks or real estate securities perspective, since these asset classes had returns of 33.36 and 20.26 percent, respectively.

Each year, the multiple-asset-class strategy loses relative to some of its component asset classes and wins relative to others. That is the nature of diversification. The frame-of-reference problem, however, is particularly acute during a prolonged period of superior performance by U.S. stocks, such as the second half of the 1990s. At that time, the seemingly unending dominance of U.S. stocks relative to other asset classes fueled investors' dissatisfaction with the lower returns generated over the same period by a multiple-asset-class strategy. As a friend in the business observed, the problem with diversification is that it works whether you want it to or not.

We should not underestimate this frame-of-reference problem. Investors compare their investment results with their friends' results while playing golf or at cocktail parties. The true multiple-asset-class investor is still in the minority. During periods when the U.S. market prevails, this person will feel particularly vulnerable talking with friends who own a more traditional U.S. stock and bond portfolio. Years ago, a client told me that he would rather follow an inferior strategy that wins when his friends are winning and loses when his friends are losing than follow a superior long-term strategy that at times results in him losing when his friends are winning. Being different is painful.

Equity investing is a long-term endeavor, and investors should devise and implement strategies with the long term in mind. Investors naturally attach more significance to recent investment experience than to longer-term performance, but they should resist the temptation to abandon more diversified strategies in favor of chasing yesterday's winner.

The analysis of multiple-asset-class investing presented in this chapter is a pedagogical illustration that, for simplicity, utilizes various equally weighted combinations of U.S. stocks, non-U.S. stocks, real estate securities, and commodity-linked securities. As a teaching example, my goal is to demonstrate the power of diversification. Although I am a strong proponent of multiple-asset-class investing, I do not recommend an equally weighted equity strategy for my clients. My reasoning is partially rooted in the psychological concerns related to this frame-of-reference issue. For clients domiciled in the United States, I recommend equity structures that are allocated more heavily to U.S. stocks, with smaller commitments to non-U.S. stocks, real estate securities, and commodity-linked securities. Although such portfolios may be mathematically suboptimal, these allocations still capture much of the advantage of multiple-asset-class diversification.[3] Most importantly, an investor will likely have an easier time living with the portfolio's pattern of returns. In other words, a client will likely have better long-term investment results by consistently following a strategy that accommodates his need to sleep well at night, even if the strategy is mathematically suboptimal. By comparison, a mathematically optimal strategy obviously will not work if the client abandons it.

I want to reiterate that this teaching illustration focuses solely on the equity side of an investor's portfolio in order to illustrate the power of diversification in both improving returns and mitigating volatility. Had I included interest-generating investments in the analysis, the significant differences in growth paths between interest-generating asset classes and equity asset classes would have obscured the diversification benefits. My choice to exclude interest-generating investments from the analysis does not imply that I advocate portfolios that are allocated 100 percent to equity investments. In the majority of client situations, I recommend diversification into interest-generating asset classes.

Occasionally, a client questions the merit of this teaching illustration because it relies on historical data that may be irrelevant when looking to the future. Her argument rests on the notion that the world is very different today than it was during the period covered by my multiple-asset-class investing analysis; risks and opportunities exist now that have no historical precedent. Although that may be true, some things do not change: Investors prefer predictability to uncertainty, and they face a menu of investment alternatives differentiated according to their levels of volatility. The buying and selling activity of investors establishes security prices that bring supply and demand into equilibrium. For this to occur, more volatile asset classes generally will have higher expected returns than less volatile asset classes, ultimately leading to competitive, volatility-adjusted returns across asset classes.

The diversification benefits of a multiple-asset-class approach rest on the dissimilarities in patterns of returns across asset classes in the short run and competitive asset class pricing in the long run. These conditions will likely hold true in the future, even in the face of risks and opportunities that are unique to the times. The wisest investment strategy is to diversify portfolios broadly in order to mitigate the risks of an unknowable future.

Summary

Asset allocation is vitally important. The benefits of diversification are powerful and robust, not just in terms of volatility reduction but also for return enhancement. To evaluate the desirability of an asset class as a portfolio building block, it is not enough to know only its return and volatility characteristics. One must also know how its pattern of returns correlates to the patterns of returns of the other portfolio components. All other things being equal, the more dissimilarity there is among the patterns of returns of the asset classes within a portfolio, the stronger the diversification effect that provides investors with not only less volatility but also greater returns in the long run.

The beauty of diversification lies in the fact that its benefits are not dependent on the exercise of superior skill. They arise from the policy decision to follow a multiple-asset-class investment approach. Imagine for a moment that each of the 15 portfolios in Exhibit 10.1 represented the performance of a different stock manager actively engaged in trying to outperform his competitors through superior skill in security selection. We would want to know what the managers in the upper left portion of the graph were doing to generate such superior volatility-adjusted returns. We no doubt would be willing to pay them high investment management fees if we believed they could deliver similar relative performance in the future. Amazingly, the superior performance from the portfolios in the upper left portion of the graph did not rely on skill, but rather on a simple policy decision: Diversify!

Think of the 40-year period in the illustration presented in this chapter as a race similar to that between the tortoise and the hare.

Over any 1-year, 3-year, or 10-year period, one of the individual asset classes likely will lead the race. This lead hare, with its attention-getting pace, will grab the spotlight and obscure the progress of the tortoise, which runs faster than the *average* pace of its competitors. For example, commodity-linked securities led the first part of the race during the 1970s. The second leg of the race was run in the 1980s, when non-U.S. stocks ran the fastest. During the third leg of the race, the 1990s, U.S. stocks outpaced the other asset classes. During the last leg of the race in the 2000s, real estate securities took the lead. Yet the tortoise, our multiple-asset-class strategy, moved toward the front of the pack over the long run. We know the moral of the story: Slow and steady wins the race. In the end, patience and discipline are rewarded. To secure the reward, U.S. investors need to relinquish their domestic frame of reference and invest as citizens of the world.

> The Way of heaven does not strive; yet it wins easily.
> It does not speak; yet it gets a good response.
> It does not demand; yet all needs are met.
> It is not anxious; yet it plans well.
> The net of heaven is vast; its meshes are wide, but nothing slips through.
>
> —*Lao Tsu (604* BC*–?)*, Tao Te Ching

Chapter 11

Portfolio Optimization

All business proceeds on beliefs, on judgments of probabilities and not on certainties.

—*Charles W. Eliot (1834–1926)*

In theory, there is no difference between theory and practice. But, in practice, there is.

—*Jan L. A. van de Snepscheut (1953–1994)*

On two occasions I have been asked: "Pray, Mr. Babbage, if you put into the machine wrong figures, will the right answer come out?"

—*Charles Babbage (1791–1871)*[1]

This chapter is devoted to a discussion of portfolio optimization, also known as mean-variance optimization. It may be particularly valuable to readers who are interested in, or intend to use, computer programs that are designed to identify optimal asset allocations for various client situations. Those readers who are not interested in this technical aspect of asset allocation may want to proceed to Chapter 12.

In Chapter 8, we distinguished between good and bad ways to allocate assets when constructing investment portfolios. Good asset allocations are said to be *efficient*. An efficient asset allocation maximizes the portfolio's expected return, subject to a specific portfolio volatility level. Bad asset allocations are said to be *inefficient*. With inefficient portfolios, it is possible to increase the portfolio's expected return without increasing portfolio volatility (or, equivalently, to reduce portfolio volatility without sacrificing the portfolio's expected return) by simply reallocating funds among the various asset classes. Each asset class in a portfolio contributes to both the portfolio's expected return and its volatility. For a given level of portfolio volatility, an inefficient portfolio has some asset classes that make higher volatility-adjusted incremental contributions to portfolio expected return than do other asset classes.

For example, if the non-U.S. bonds in a portfolio contribute more incremental portfolio expected return per unit of portfolio volatility than do U.S. small company stocks, then we can improve the portfolio's expected return without increasing portfolio volatility by simply selling some U.S. small company stock holdings to provide additional funds for non-U.S. bond investments. Because such a swap changes the composition of the portfolio, each asset class's volatility-adjusted contribution to portfolio expected return also changes and therefore needs to be recalculated. If we again find differences in the volatility-adjusted incremental contributions to portfolio expected return for the various asset classes, the portfolio's expected return can be further improved (without increasing portfolio volatility) by swapping some of the asset class that now makes the smallest volatility-adjusted contribution to portfolio expected return for some of the asset class that makes the largest contribution. If we continue in this manner, we will eventually run out of advantageous swaps. The resulting asset allocation maximizes the portfolio's expected return for that particular level of portfolio volatility. Hence, the portfolio is efficient. As a condition of that efficiency, each asset class's volatility-adjusted incremental contribution to the portfolio's expected return is equal. (If this were not true, we could continue to improve the portfolio's expected return without increasing portfolio volatility by engaging in more swaps.) By analogy, you know that you are standing on the top of a mountain (i.e., you have maximized your altitude) when you lose altitude regardless of which direction you walk. Similarly, an efficient portfolio is like being at the top of a mountain in that the pursuit of any alternative asset allocation with equivalent portfolio volatility will result in a loss of portfolio expected return.

Any given set of asset classes has a unique efficient portfolio that corresponds to a given level of portfolio volatility. The collection of all efficient portfolios across the full range of portfolio volatility possibilities is known as the *efficient frontier*. Although all efficient portfolios on the efficient frontier are good because they maximize expected return for any given level of volatility, from a particular client's point of view they are not equally desirable because people vary in their volatility tolerance. The *optimal* portfolio for a client is that unique portfolio on the efficient frontier that maximizes the client's expected return subject to his particular level of volatility tolerance.

With the aid of computers utilizing sophisticated quadratic programming techniques, it is possible to identify mathematically the asset allocations that correspond to each portfolio on the efficient frontier. These portfolio optimization programs require, as inputs, estimates of the expected return and standard deviation of returns for each asset class, as well as estimates of the correlations of returns among all the asset classes. Hopefully, our discussions thus far have underscored the dangers of blindly using historical data to derive estimates of these variables. Incorporating measures of uncertainty into the inputs does not eliminate this danger. The difficulties are further compounded by the output's sensitivity to small variations in the input variables. The admonition often given to students in introductory computer programming courses is particularly relevant here: "Garbage in, garbage out!"

As a practical matter, most professionals who are experienced with portfolio optimization programs use historical correlations and standard deviations as departure points for developing estimates of future correlations and standard deviations.[2] Historical returns, however, are of less value in estimating future returns. For example, for the 10 rolling 20-year periods ending with 1978 through 1987, U.S. large company stocks usually had compound annual returns that were less than 2 percentage points greater than those of Treasury bills. Given the much greater volatility of U.S. large company stocks relative to that of Treasury bills, we would expect them to outperform Treasury bills in the future by a spread larger than 2 percentage points. Thus, anyone developing future return estimates based on these rolling 20-year periods would probably underestimate the incremental return expected from U.S. large company stocks. One way around this problem is to use longer-term historical relationships among asset class returns to develop estimates of future expected returns.

Chapter 4 discusses a more nuanced approach for developing estimates of future expected returns. For example, an unusually high valuation level for large company stocks argues for a below-average expected return estimate. An unusually low valuation level for large company stocks argues for an above-average expected return estimate.

Another approach utilizes the implications of modern portfolio theory to derive estimates of the expected returns for various asset classes. For example, modern portfolio theory suggests that it is optimal for an investor with average volatility tolerance to hold an investment portfolio with an asset allocation that mirrors the percentage allocation of assets of the world investable capital market. The estimation procedure first uses historical data as a basis for developing estimates of the standard deviations and correlations for the various asset classes. Then the allocation of the world investable capital market is determined. (See Exhibit 1.1 for an estimate of this allocation as of December 31, 2011.) Under an assumption that this asset allocation is optimal for an investor with average tolerance for volatility, it is possible to work backward to solve for the expected return for each asset class.

Once the inputs for expected return, standard deviation, and correlations have been estimated for the asset classes, it is a straightforward, although sophisticated, mathematical calculation to derive the asset allocations for portfolios on the efficient frontier. It is then necessary to select the specific portfolio along the efficient frontier that is most appropriate for the client in question. One method for doing this is to describe the expected return and volatility characteristics of a representative sample of portfolios from the efficient frontier and then have the client select one. The client's choice will be an indirect indication of his volatility tolerance. Because a client's volatility tolerance cannot be measured directly, this process of choosing an optimal portfolio will always have a subjective dimension.

Many portfolio optimization programs have a built-in feature that selects the optimal portfolio based on an input variable that attempts to describe a client's volatility tolerance. To do this, the computer identifies the efficient portfolio that optimizes the portfolio's *utility* for the client. Utility is an expression borrowed from economic theory that, loosely translated, means "psychological satisfaction." In an optimization program, utility is calculated as the portfolio's expected return minus a penalty for volatility. The volatility penalty in turn is a function of two things: the portfolio's volatility, which can be quantified mathematically, and the client's volatility tolerance, which can only be estimated subjectively. To indirectly assess a client's volatility tolerance, some optimization programs utilize a decision-making procedure like the one we developed in Chapter 7, which requires the client to choose a preferred portfolio allocation between Treasury bills and U.S. large company stocks. The percentage allocated to U.S. large company stocks serves as the input value for the client's volatility-tolerance variable. For example, a volatility-tolerance input of 80 corresponds to a preferred 80 percent commitment to U.S. large company stocks and hence indicates high volatility tolerance, whereas a volatility-tolerance input of 25 corresponds to a U.S. large company stock commitment of 25 percent, which indicates low volatility tolerance.

The portfolio optimization program described in the next section uses a different approach. The client is asked to specify how much additional expected return over Treasury bill yields he would require in order to actively choose a 50 percent Treasury bill/50 percent U.S. large company stock portfolio balance. A client with low volatility tolerance, for example, might require U.S. large company stocks to have an expected return that is 20 percentage points higher than that for Treasury bills in order to actively choose a 50/50 portfolio balance. The *volatility-premium* input variable therefore would have a value of 20. A client with higher volatility tolerance may require U.S. large company stocks to have an expected return only 3 percentage points higher than that for Treasury bills to actively choose a 50/50 portfolio balance. In this case the volatility-premium input variable would be assigned a value of 3.

Portfolio Optimization Programs

A portfolio optimization program is a very sharp tool that easily can cut the hand of an inexperienced user. The purpose of this discussion is to highlight the dangers and limitations of this powerful technology without losing an awareness of the contribution it can make to the portfolio management process.

Let us now observe a portfolio optimization program in action.[3] Although the reader is advised to exercise judgment in the specification of input values, for pedagogical reasons we simply will use unmodified historical performance statistics for our first optimization illustration. The input values shown in Exhibit 11.1 are based on the 22-year period from 1973 through 1994. In addition to the seven asset classes listed, I have included two specific investment alternatives—a real estate separate account and a precious metals mutual fund. I have included the real estate separate account to provide an example of the dangers of incorporating a nonliquid investment in a portfolio optimization. The precious metals mutual fund is included as an example of an investment that, historically, has been used as a hedge against inflation and/or political instability.

Exhibit 11.1
Portfolio Optimization Program Input Values

Expected Return Input Value	Standard Deviation Input Value	Asset Class	Correlation Matrix Input Values								
			(1)	(2)	(3)	(4)	(5)	(6)	(7)	(8)	(9)
7.34	0.81	(1) Treasury bills	1.00								
9.57	10.08	(2) U.S. long-term corporate bonds	0.05	1.00							
11.29	11.63	(3) Non-U.S. bonds	-0.09	0.35	1.00						
12.09	15.71	(4) U.S. large company stocks	-0.06	0.39	0.12	1.00					
17.83	21.51	(5) U.S. small company stocks	-0.08	0.24	0.02	0.79	1.00				
14.95	17.94	(6) Non-U.S. stocks	-0.09	0.24	0.64	0.48	0.38	1.00			
14.40	13.95	(7) Equity REITs	-0.09	0.27	0.13	0.65	0.75	0.41	1.00		
8.78	3.48	(8) Real estate separate account	0.32	-0.08	0.00	0.03	0.03	0.08	0.04	1.00	
23.03	33.78	(9) Precious metals mutual fund	-0.06	-0.02	0.20	0.21	0.19	0.31	0.16	-0.02	1.00

We will use the historical simple average return for the 22-year period rather than the compound annual return as the input value for the expected return of each asset class. The expected return is an estimate for a single-period return and is best approximated by the simple average return. Another reason for using the simple average return is that the standard deviation statistic is measured relative to the simple average return, not the compound annual return. In actuality, the size of the spread between the compound annual return and the simple average return contains information regarding the volatility of the returns. The erroneous use of the compound annual return statistic as the input value for the expected return would, in effect, double-count the volatility.

In the Appendix to Chapter 3 and at the beginning of Chapter 8, we discussed the fact that, for a variable pattern of returns, the compound annual return is always less than the simple average return. This difference occurs because it takes a larger above-average return to offset the impact of any given below-average return. Expressed another way, a given margin of above-average performance is not sufficient to offset an equal margin of below-average performance. An illustration will clarify this fact. Exhibit 11.2 shows three different investments. Each has a simple average return of 8 percent, an above-average return in year 1, and a below-average return in year 3. Although the three

Exhibit 11.2

Relationships Among Simple Average Return, Compound Annual Return, and Volatility

	Investment X	Investment Y	Investment Z
Year 1 return	10%	16%	22%
Year 2 return	8%	8%	8%
Year 3 return	6%	0%	-6%
Simple average return	8%	8%	8%
Compound annual return	7.99%	7.80%	7.39%
Volatility	Low	Medium	High
Future value of $1 in 20 years	$4.65	$4.49	$4.16

investments vary in terms of their volatilities, for each investment the margin of above-average performance equals the margin of below-average performance. In all three cases, the compound annual return is lower than the corresponding simple average return of 8 percent because the return for the above-average year was not sufficient to offset the return in the below-average year. Also note that investment X, which is the most stable, has the smallest spread between its simple average return of 8 percent and its compound annual return of 7.99 percent, whereas investment Z, which is the most volatile, has the largest spread between its simple average return of 8 percent and its compound annual return of 7.39 percent.

We saw the same relationship among the compound annual return, simple average return, and standard deviation statistics in Exhibit 3.1. Those asset classes with the highest standard deviations have the biggest spreads between their simple average return and compound annual return statistics. Conversely, those asset classes with the lowest standard deviations have the smallest spreads between their simple average return and compound annual return performance numbers.[4] This discussion regarding the relationship among the compound annual return, simple average return, and standard deviation provides further clarification of the issues reviewed in Notes 1 and 5 of Chapter 3 and Note 4 of Chapter 7.

Assume we have a client with whom we have thoroughly reviewed the concept of time horizon, and he understands the expected return and volatility characteristics of Treasury bills and U.S. large company stocks. We describe to him a portfolio composed of 50 percent Treasury bills and 50 percent U.S. large company stocks and ask him, "With Treasury bills currently yielding 7.3 percent, how much additional expected return would you require from U.S. large company stocks in order for you to actively choose a portfolio allocation of 50 percent Treasury bills/50 percent U.S. large company stocks?" The client's response will be an indirect measure of his volatility tolerance and will give us a value for the volatility-premium input variable in the portfolio optimization program. For our sample portfolio optimizations, we will assume that the client has responded that he would require U.S. large company stocks to have an expected return of 17.3 percent—10 percentage points higher than the 7.3 percent return for Treasury bills. Thus, the volatility-premium input will have a value of 10.

Exhibit 11.3 shows the portfolio optimization results for five sets of input assumptions. In each case, the computer identifies the optimal portfolio (based on the input variables and any specified constraints) for a client whose volatility tolerance corresponds to a volatility premium of 10 percent. The first optimization is unconstrained in that anywhere from 0 to 100 percent of the portfolio can be committed to any of the nine asset classes. Based on the inputs, the optimal portfolio has more than half its assets committed to real estate, with 41.9 percent and 15.6 percent, respectively, allocated to the real estate separate account and equity REITs (real estate investment trusts). The balance of the portfolio is allocated among non-U.S. bonds, U.S. small company stocks, and the precious metals mutual fund. The portfolio's expected return is 13 percent with a standard deviation of 7.6 percent. The probability is 96.3 percent that this allocation will achieve a positive one-year return.

Does this allocation make good sense? Yes, given the inputs. Although the expected return for the real estate separate account is the lowest among the equity asset classes, its standard deviation is extremely low. Its correlations with the other asset classes are also quite low, thus making it a very attractive building block for the portfolio. It is therefore not surprising that its allocation is so large. Any alteration in the allocation among the nine asset classes would produce a portfolio with less desirable expected return/volatility characteristics for this particular client.

Now, would we recommend this portfolio to our client? Perhaps we would if we had extremely high confidence in all our data inputs. Is there a basis for such confidence? The real estate separate account is an investment portfolio of nonliquid real estate properties managed by an insurance company. The performance measurement for the real estate separate account relies on a periodic appraisal of the current

Exhibit 11.3

Portfolio Optimization Results and Sensitivity Analysis for a Client Who Specifies a Volatility Premium of 10%

	Optimization 1 All 9 Asset Classes	Optimization 2 8 Asset Classes (Excluding Real Estate Separate Account)	Optimization 3 Expected Return of Equity REITs Decreased by 1%	Optimization 4 Standard Deviation of Equity REITs Increased by 1%	Optimization 5 Equity REITs Perfectly Correlated with U.S. Small Company Stocks
Asset Class					
Treasury bills	0.0%	26.6%	31.3%	29.7%	19.6%
U.S. long-term corporate bonds	0.0	3.0	4.3	3.6	4.2
Non-U.S. bonds	16.8	23.8	25.6	24.7	26.4
U.S. large company stocks	0.0	0.0	0.0	0.0	0.0
U.S. small company stocks	13.6	13.3	20.5	16.7	0.0
Non-U.S. stocks	0.0	0.0	0.0	0.0	0.0
Equity REITs	15.6	21.0	5.9	13.0	37.6
Real estate separate account	41.9	–	–	–	–
Precious metals mutual fund	12.1	12.3	12.4	12.3	12.2
	100.0%	100.0%	100.0%	100.0%	100.0%
Portfolio Characteristics					
Expected Return	13.0%	13.2%	12.9%	13.0%	13.1%
Standard Deviation	7.6%	8.4%	8.2%	8.3%	8.4%
Probability of achieving a positive one-year return	96.3%	94.8%	94.8%	94.8%	94.8%

Data Source: The optimization results shown were produced using Vestek Systems, Inc. software.

market values of the real estate properties in the portfolio. Considerable controversy exists over whether the appraisal process accurately reflects the actual variability of real estate values. (Just because you can't see the volatility of an investment doesn't mean it isn't there.) My judgment is that the appraisal process understates the magnitude of changes in property values and that the actual variability of returns from nonliquid real estate investments is much higher than the standard deviation statistic indicates. Likewise, although real estate may have low correlations with some financial asset classes, the appraisal process may result in correlation statistics that overstate the diversification effect to be expected from the inclusion of nonliquid real estate in the portfolio.

Also unsettling is the correlation statistic of 0.04 between equity REITs and the real estate separate account, which indicates that the returns of these two real estate investments are nearly uncorrelated! To the extent to which we lack confidence in the inputs, we should likewise lack confidence in the output. Given the inputs, it is not surprising that the optimal allocation for the client is heavily oriented toward real estate. Rather than concluding from the output that a portfolio heavily oriented toward real estate is best for the client, it may be more appropriate to consider the lopsided output as a warning signal to not take the input values too seriously.

Given the strong likelihood that the appraisal-driven standard deviation statistic misrepresents the actual volatility of the real estate separate account, we can choose to simply eliminate it as an investment alternative and rely on equity REITs to serve as the means of implementing the real estate asset class. Optimization 2 in Exhibit 11.3 does just that by constraining the allocation to the real estate separate account to 0 percent. For the same client, the optimal portfolio now shifts from one that is heavily oriented toward equities to one that slightly favors interest-generating investments. The most significant change is the addition of a 26.6 percent allocation to Treasury bills. The portfolio optimization program introduced Treasury bills to offset the impact of eliminating the real estate separate account investment alternative, which had a very low standard deviation.

This portfolio's expected return of 13.2 percent is actually higher than the first portfolio's, but the increase in expected return is accompanied by a higher standard deviation of 8.4 percent.[5] We can be somewhat more comfortable with this portfolio, because it is better balanced than portfolio 1. But at the same time, it is troubling to see that two major equity asset classes, U.S. large company stocks and non-U.S. stocks, are completely unrepresented, while the remaining real estate investment alternative, equity REITs, is now the largest equity asset class. Is this high commitment to equity REITs warranted? Again, the question is really how much confidence we have in the input variables for the various asset classes. Optimizations 1 and 2 estimate that equity REITs have an expected return of 14.4 percent with a standard deviation of 13.95 percent. These statistics indicate that the chances are approximately 2 out of 3 that equity REITs will give us a return over a one-year horizon between 0.45 and 28.35 percent (i.e., 14.4 ± 13.95 percent). Not a very specific estimate, is it?

Let us engage in some sensitivity analysis. Assume that our estimate of the standard deviation is perfectly accurate but that we have slightly overstated the expected return for equity REITs by 1 percentage point. The true typical range of returns is therefore between –0.55 and 27.35 percent (i.e., 13.4 ± 13.95 percent). For all practical purposes, this change in the estimated performance characteristics of equity REITs is not significant. If we revise the input for the expected return of equity REITs down by 1 percentage point, while keeping all other data inputs constant, what effect will this have on the output? Optimization 3 in Exhibit 11.3 describes the asset allocation and performance characteristics of the revised optimal portfolio. Note how this very minor change in one input variable radically alters the allocation among the asset classes. The commitment to equity REITs drops dramatically from 21 to 5.9 percent. As expected, the portfolio expected return drops, but the portfolio standard deviation is lower as well.

For optimization 4, instead of measuring the impact of using a lower estimate of the expected return for equity REITs, we increase the estimate of the standard deviation for equity REITs by 1 percentage point from 13.95 to 14.95 percent. In every other respect, the input variables are identical to those for optimization 2. Again, this very minor revision in one input variable triggers a pronounced redistribution of assets in forming a revised optimal portfolio. The commitment to equity REITs drops from 21 to 13 percent. Again, both the expected return and the volatility of this revised portfolio are lower than those of portfolio 2.

There is one more dimension along which we can alter the input data for the equity REITs asset class—its correlations with other asset classes. By examining the correlation matrix in Exhibit 11.1, we see that the equity REITs asset class has its highest correlation with the U.S. small company stocks asset class. For optimization 5, we will assume that equity REITs and U.S. small company stocks are perfectly positively correlated (i.e., no diversification effect between the two asset classes). The correlation of returns between equity REITs and every other asset class therefore will change to match the correlation of U.S. small company stocks with each of the other asset classes. All other input variables are identical to those for optimization 2. This time, the allocation to equity REITs jumps from 21 to 37.6 percent of the portfolio, accompanied by the complete elimination of U.S. small company stocks. As is the case with portfolios 2 through 4, there is no allocation to either U.S. large company stocks or non-U.S. stocks.

The sensitivity analysis we performed with optimizations 3, 4, and 5 should convince anyone that the output is indeed very sensitive to minor changes in the input variables. One reaction to this realization is to attempt to specify the input variables with even greater precision. In my judgment, this endeavor is futile. Exhibits 8.6 through 8.8 show the highly variable nature of rolling 60-month (5-year) returns, standard deviations, and correlation for two asset classes: U.S. large company stocks and U.S. long-term corporate bonds. These graphs underscore the extreme difficulty of trying to estimate optimization input statistics accurately. This argues for an approach that constrains the propensity for portfolio optimization programs to make extreme allocations to the various asset classes.

Exhibit 11.4
Constrained Optimization Results for a Client Who Specifies a Volatility Premium of 10.0%

	Constrained Portfolio Allocation	Permissable Range Minimum Holding	Permissable Range Maximum Holding
Asset Class			
Treasury bills	16.2%	5%	25%
U.S. long-term corporate bonds	16.0	16	25
Non-U.S. bonds	13.8	5	25
U.S. large company stocks	20.0	20	25
U.S. small company stocks	5.0	5	25
Non-U.S. stocks	5.0	5	25
Equity REITs	12.1	5	25
Precious metals mutual fund	11.9	5	25
	100.0%	66%	
Portfolio Characteristics			
Expected Return	12.8%		
Standard Deviation	9.0%		
Probability of achieving a positive one-year return	92.9%		

Data Source: The optimization results shown were produced using Vestek Systems, Inc. software.

Exhibit 11.4 illustrates a constrained optimization that specifies that a core 36 percent of the portfolio must be allocated between U.S. long-term corporate bonds and U.S. large company stocks—the traditional portfolio building blocks for a U.S. investor. Another constraint is that each asset class must have an allocation of not less than 5 percent nor more than 25 percent of portfolio assets. This approach blends aspects of a more traditional portfolio design with constrained minimum and maximum allocations for all eight asset classes, thus ensuring some breadth of diversification. Exhibit 11.4 shows the range of permissible portfolio commitments to each asset class and the constrained portfolio allocation. By summing the minimum holdings for the asset classes, we see that the constraints operate to prespecify 66 percent of the portfolio. The other 34 percent of assets are optimized subject to the constraints.

If we compare the constrained portfolio allocation in Exhibit 11.4 to the portfolio allocation for optimization 2 in Exhibit 11.3, which uses the same input assumptions without constraints, we see that the constraints have triggered a loss of 0.4 percent in the portfolio's expected return, with an increase of 0.6 percent in the portfolio's standard deviation. But, in exchange, we have a more broadly diversified portfolio with all asset classes represented. Although this constrained portfolio is mathematically suboptimal relative to the unconstrained portfolio, the benefits of diversification are still largely retained. For example, Exhibit 11.4 indicates that the constrained portfolio has a standard deviation of 9 percent based on the historical correlations of returns among the asset classes. If the asset classes were perfectly positively correlated, however, the standard deviation would be 14.2 percent—a volatility level that is more than 50 percent higher. Given the difficulties in deriving reliable estimates for each input variable and the sensitivity of the optimization output to small changes in the input variables, the constrained portfolio allocation shown in Exhibit 11.4 is a more sensible recommendation for the client than the unconstrained portfolio allocation shown in Exhibit 11.3 for optimization 2.

Richard and Robert Michaud have developed a different solution to this problem regarding the uncertainty inherent in the inputs used in portfolio optimization. Their approach, called *resampled efficiency*, uses a Monte Carlo simulation to create a variety of sets of alternative optimization inputs that are consistent with the uncertainty inherent in the input estimates. Each set of optimization inputs creates a different efficient frontier. These statistically equivalent alternative efficient frontiers are then averaged to create a "resampled efficient frontier." The Michauds argue that portfolios on the resampled efficient frontier are more stable, are better diversified, and have greater intuitive appeal than those arrived at with classical mean-variance optimization techniques that use only one set of input assumptions. For those interested in a fuller discussion of resampled efficiency, I recommend Richard Michaud's thought-provoking book, *Efficient Asset Management*.[6]

The Map and the Territory

Psychologically, it is easy to believe that a precise answer is more certain and therefore deserves a higher level of confidence than an approximate answer. For example, assume that an investor wants advice concerning what portion of her portfolio to commit to non-U.S. stocks. For guidance, she decides to consult two different investment advisors. The first advisor recommends exactly 19.3 percent of assets; the second advisor recommends about 20 percent. Even though there is no real difference in the recommended size of the allocation, wouldn't an investor tend to have more confidence in the first advisor's recommendation because it is more specific?

Portfolio optimization programs give asset allocation recommendations that are as precise as those of the first advisor. In addition, portfolio optimization programs can specify precise probability estimates of achieving various levels of return over different holding periods and format this information in either tabular or graphic form, with or without color pie charts! All this technology can be seductive to both investment advisors and their clients. Unfortunately, uninformed or unscrupulous investment advisors may encourage clients to blindly follow the "objective" recommendations generated by the technology. Knowledgeable investment advisors will maintain the proper perspective by keeping in mind that input variables are hard to specify with even a modest degree of confidence and that the output of portfolio optimization programs is highly sensitive to small changes in the input variables. Portfolio optimization programs cannot eliminate the uncertainty inherent in investing. Thoughtful consideration of the output makes this fact clear. For example, if the standard deviation of an optimized portfolio is 10 percent, what value is derived from knowing that the portfolio's expected return is not 8 percent but rather exactly 8.23 percent?

The portfolio optimization program inputs shown in Exhibit 11.1 and the portfolio optimization results and sensitivity analysis summarized in Exhibit 11.3 originally appeared in the second edition of this book. The illustrations were based on 22 years of asset class historical return data from 1973 through 1994. Seventeen years have elapsed since then. Did the subsequent performance of the asset classes conform to our prior modeling assumptions? How did the constrained optimal allocation of Exhibit 11.4 perform relative to its prior modeling? Exhibit 11.5 answers these questions. In this exhibit, columns 2 and 3 restate the expected return and standard deviation optimization inputs for each asset class based on historical return data from 1973 through 1994. (The data are the same as those contained in Exhibit 11.1.) Based on the expected return and standard deviation statistics shown in columns 2 and 3, we can estimate the future compound annual return in column 4 for each asset class and for the constrained portfolio shown in Exhibit 11.4.[7] Comparing these estimated compound annual returns with the actual performance that followed leads to a rather stark conclusion: The capital markets did not seem to care what we had predicted based on the prior performance of the asset classes. Comparing the estimated compound annual returns in column 4 of Exhibit 11.5 with the actual compound annual returns in columns 5 through 7 for the subsequent period from 1995 through 2011, we find:

1. Treasury bills underperformed significantly.
2. Contrary to expectations, U.S. long-term corporate bonds outperformed non-U.S. bonds.
3. U.S. large company stocks soared far above expectations from 1995 through 1999, then generated almost no return from 2000 through 2011.
4. Contrary to the optimization input assumptions, non-U.S. stocks underperformed U.S. large company stocks.
5. The precious metals mutual fund generated a huge negative compound annual return from 1995 through 1999, followed by a stellar positive compound annual return from 2000 through 2011.

Exhibit 11.5

Comparison of Portfolio Optimization Input Values with Subsequent Performance

	Modeled Performance Characteristics			Actual Compound Annual Return		
(1)	(2)	(3)	(4)	(5)	(6)	(7)
	Expected Return*	Standard Deviation*	Estimated Compound Annual Return	1995 – 1999	2000 – 2011	1995 – 2011
Asset Class						
Treasury bills	7.34%	0.81%	7.34%	4.99%	2.24%	3.05%
U.S. long-term corporate bonds	9.57	10.08	9.06	8.35	8.87	8.71
Non-U.S. bonds	11.29	11.63	10.61	5.90	6.36	6.22
U.S. large company stocks	12.09	15.71	10.86	28.56	0.54	8.08
U.S. small company stocks	17.83	21.51	15.52	18.49	7.34	10.51
Non-U.S. stocks	14.95	17.94	13.34	13.15	0.93	4.38
Equity REITs	14.40	13.95	13.43	8.09	11.78	10.68
Precious metals mutual fund	23.03	33.78	17.32	-16.33	19.23	7.43
Constrained Optimal Allocation (See Exhibit 11-4)	12.80%	9.00%	12.40%	9.74%	8.07%	8.56%

*Optimization input. See Exhibit 11.1.

Data source: *2012 Ibbotson® Stocks, Bonds, Bills, and Inflation® (SBBI®) Classic Yearbook*, Board of Governors of the Federal Reserve System, http://www.federalreserve.gov/release/h15/data.htm; and Morningstar® Principia®,

6. Indeed, each asset class underperformed relative to its optimization input assumption, and although we had modeled a compound annual return of 12.4 percent for the constrained optimal allocation shown in Exhibit 11.4, its actual compound annual return was a more modest 8.56 percent.

No matter how carefully we specify our optimization input values, we cannot eliminate the uncertainty in the markets. This uncertainty cuts both ways—sometimes generating unexpectedly generous outperformance with one asset class while producing significant underperformance with another. Accordingly, we should not expect the actual returns of optimized portfolios to conform to our prior modeling.

Admittedly, using portfolio optimizers poses real challenges. Over the past few years, however, I have witnessed considerable unjustified criticism of both mean-variance optimization and modern portfolio theory by a growing number of investment professionals. I believe it is no coincidence that the complaints grew louder following the 2000–2002 bear market and again after the Global Financial Crisis of 2008. Many advisors seemed shocked to discover that their optimized portfolios did not perform as they had modeled with their portfolio optimizers. A map is not the same as the territory it describes. A portfolio optimizer gives us a map of efficient asset allocation strategies. Based on our estimates of the expected returns, standard deviations, and correlations for the asset classes, the optimizer also gives us a snapshot of the expected returns and volatilities of portfolios that lie on the efficient frontier. This map is a static, simplified representation of capital market realities. The territory is the realized future returns and volatilities of these portfolios based on the actual subsequent returns, standard deviations, and correlations of the asset classes. This capital market territory is complex, fluid, and dynamic.

Even if we knew the exact distribution of possible returns for an asset class, we would still be uncertain about which returns would occur in the future. For example, rolling a die has only six specific possible outcomes. The chances are equal that you will roll a 1, 2, 3, 4, 5, or 6. Even though we know each possible outcome and its associated probability before rolling the die, we do not know which number will come up. Modeling capital market uncertainties is much more complicated. Unlike die rolling, we do not know in advance the exact distribution of possible outcomes for any given asset class. Many different returns are possible, and the likelihoods of the returns vary. Our expected return, standard deviation, and correlation input assumptions are simply educated guesses about the distribution and pattern of returns for an asset class. Relative to our simple die-rolling example, portfolio modeling is much more difficult because of the extra layers of uncertainty that must be considered.

Portfolio optimization modeling has one more source of potential misunderstanding and frustration. If the optimal portfolio outcome is defined as the short-term outcome with the highest realized return, an optimized portfolio will not lead to an optimal outcome. Before the fact, we do not know how the various asset classes will perform. *Given that uncertainty*, the portfolio optimizer generates an efficient frontier of optimal asset allocation strategies. A couple of years from now, the uncertainties will be resolved. We will know which asset classes had the best performance and which had the worst. With the benefit of retrospect, the optimal short-run strategy is probably the one that concentrated portfolio assets exclusively in the best-performing asset class. Hindsight is 20/20. Unfortunately, we must choose an investment strategy before we know how it will perform. Since portfolio optimization considers capital market uncertainties, optimal asset allocation strategies will not lead to optimal short-term outcomes. Ironically, yet understandably, by properly doing its job the portfolio optimizer diversifies away the possibility of an optimal short-term outcome.

Clients and investment advisors naturally want to eliminate the uncertainties of the capital markets. Given the difficulties that we have discussed regarding estimating the expected returns, standard deviations, and correlations of the asset classes used in an optimization, however, it should be obvious that an optimizer will not accurately predict future portfolio performance. Despite the fact that our prior models will not conform to subsequent reality, it would be a mistake to throw out the baby with the bath water. Charles Babbage said, "Errors using inadequate data are much less than those using no data at all." A portfolio optimization program makes the best use of the less-than-perfect information that we have to work with. When constructing a portfolio, we know that the return of each asset class is important. The volatility of each asset class is important. The correlations of each asset class with other asset classes in the portfolio are important. Within the limitations of the confidence that we have in our estimates of these variables, an optimizer specifies the asset allocation that maximizes portfolio expected return for a given level of volatility. An optimizer should not be the only tool in an investment advisor's toolbox; nevertheless this important tool accomplishes things that no other tool can. An optimizer's precise asset allocation recommendation need not be taken as the final portfolio solution for the client. Indeed, doing so may be dangerous since an optimizer does not address all the important behavioral issues involved with creating an asset allocation strategy that the client will not abandon. The optimizer cannot provide the education and coaching that the advisor gives the client in order to ensure that the final asset allocation strategy will be understood and embraced by the client and, in turn, implemented with discipline. An optimizer provides one, but not the only, source of input into the collaborative efforts of the advisor and client as they work together to design an appropriate asset allocation strategy.

Some investment advisors seek to alleviate the anxiety they feel about unknowable markets by embracing the idea of an efficient portfolio along with a misplaced hope that an optimizer will recommend portfolios that will behave properly and somehow protect them and their clients from bad outcomes. As in many areas of life, our expectations often will not match our experience. Our models are one thing; reality is another. Unfortunately, an optimizer is not a reliable fortune-teller. It models uncertainties; it does not eliminate them.

Additional Observations Regarding Portfolio Optimization

Consider an efficient portfolio of Treasury bills, U.S. long-term corporate bonds, and U.S. large company stocks that maximizes the portfolio expected return subject to a portfolio standard deviation of 9 percent. Now let us permit investment in a fourth asset class—for example, real estate securities. Depending on the expected return, volatility, and correlation characteristics of real estate securities, we may find a new asset allocation using all four asset classes that produces a higher maximum portfolio expected return consistent with a portfolio standard deviation of 9 percent. Assume that the optimal allocation to real estate securities for this four-asset-class portfolio is 30 percent of assets. Do we get the same increase in portfolio expected return from the first half of our optimal 30 percent commitment (as we increase the allocation to real estate securities from 0 to 15 percent) as we do from the second half of our commitment (as we continue to increase the allocation to real estate securities from 15 to 30 percent)? In other words, does the portfolio expected return increase linearly with an increase in the commitment to real estate securities until we reach the optimal allocation, or does the impact on portfolio expected return change as we incrementally increase the size of the allocation?

We can answer this question by performing a series of constrained optimizations that plot the expected returns associated with efficient portfolios with varying commitments to real estate securities. If graphed, the relationship between portfolio expected return and the percentage commitment to real estate securities might look like that shown in Exhibit 11.6. Note that the shape of the curve is steeper as we first introduce real estate securities into the portfolio. The initial steepness of this curve indicates that, as diversification into real estate securities begins, the initial beneficial impact on the portfolio's expected return is high. As the commitment to real estate securities

Exhibit 11.6
Portfolio Expected Return as a Function of Real Estate Allocation

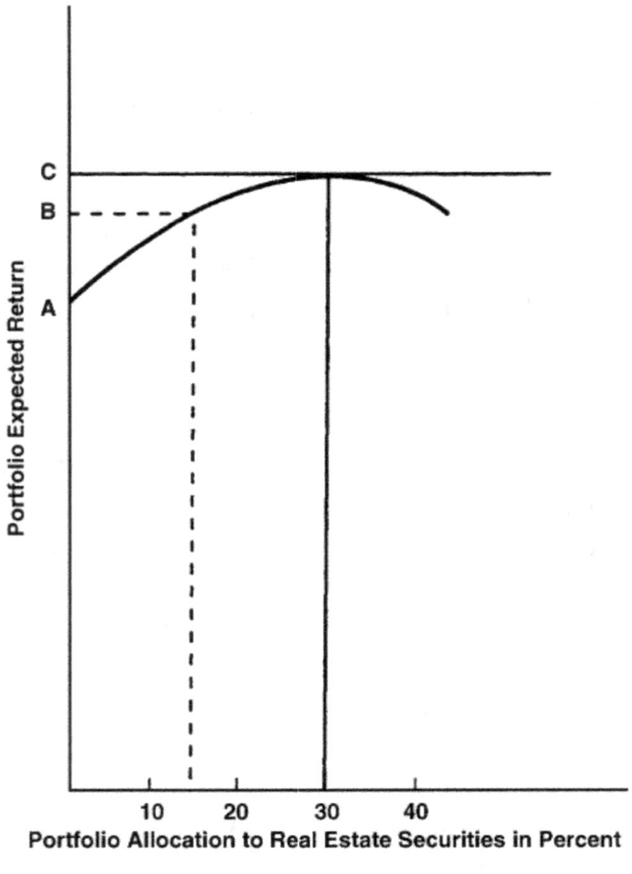

increases toward its optimal allocation of 30 percent of assets, the portfolio's expected return continues to increase, *but it does so at a diminishing rate.* The curve is relatively flat at and around the optimal allocation of 30 percent. This indicates that varying the size of the commitment to real estate securities by a few percentage points on either side of the optimal 30 percent commitment has a relatively small impact on the portfolio expected return. Beyond 30 percent, an increase in the commitment to real estate securities reduces portfolio expected return slowly at first, then more quickly.

Point A corresponds to the maximum expected return possible for a portfolio with a standard deviation equal to 9 percent, when investment choices are constrained to only Treasury bills, U.S. long-term corporate bonds, and U.S. large company stocks. Point C corresponds to the maximum expected return possible when utilizing real estate securities in addition to the other three asset classes. The distance AC is therefore the improvement in portfolio expected return made possible by an optimal allocation to real estate securities in the portfolio. Point B corresponds to the maximum expected return possible if the portfolio is constrained to a 15 percent commitment to real estate securities. We can see that most of the increase in the portfolio expected return is obtained by changing the allocation to real estate securities from 0 to 15 percent, with a smaller increase produced by changing the allocation from 15 to 30 percent.

This fact has very important investment implications. First, it removes some of the anxiety of trying to find the exact asset allocation that will maximize the volatility-adjusted portfolio expected return. In utilizing a portfolio optimization program, we know that we can have only limited confidence in our estimates of expected returns, standard deviations, and correlations used as input variables. Correspondingly, we can have only limited confidence in the optimal asset allocation generated as the output. We also know that even slight changes in the input variables result in rather drastic shifts in the portfolio asset allocation. Although at first this knowledge may seem somewhat discouraging, there is a bright side. It means that rather significant shifts of assets around the optimal portfolio may produce surprisingly little change in the portfolio's expected return and volatility characteristics. Thus, a range of alternative asset allocations may be found that produce similar, but not identical, portfolio expected return and volatility characteristics.

For example, earlier in this chapter, we performed an unconstrained optimization to identify the best asset allocation for a client who specified a volatility premium of 10 percent. (Refer to optimization

2 in Exhibit 11.3.) Although we knew that we had the mathematically correct answer given the inputs, it was uncomfortable to see that two major equity asset classes were completely unrepresented in the recommended asset allocation. By constraining the portfolio optimization program to maintain minimum allocations across all asset classes, we derived a more broadly diversified portfolio whose expected return and volatility characteristics were almost as attractive as those of the unconstrained alternative. It is advisable to hold the more broadly diversified portfolio, even though it is not mathematically optimal based on the inputs. The justification for choosing the suboptimal portfolio stems from a realistic acknowledgment that we have limited confidence in the output.

Although a variety of asset allocations may have similar portfolio expected return and volatility characteristics, after the fact the results can vary widely. This variance is expected, and for the strategic asset allocation investor, it reflects the chance element inherent in investing. For those who want to minimize the impact of chance (which means minimizing the potential impact of both bad luck *and* good luck), a more broadly diversified portfolio asset allocation makes sense.

The implications are no less important to a tactical asset allocation investor who periodically overweights or underweights an asset class. For example, consider a portfolio designed with a restricted range of allocations around an asset class's long-term strategic allocation. As long as the range is not too wide, the portfolio's expected return and volatility characteristics for the various allocations may be similar along this range. In essence, by committing most of the portfolio to a diversified core, a tactical asset allocation investor may be able to capture most of the advantages of diversification while still providing an opportunity to overweight or underweight an asset class in an attempt to generate a value-added incremental return. Although I am not an advocate of tactical asset allocation, an approach that uses a restricted range of asset class allocations at least eliminates the risk of being either entirely out of an advancing market or significantly over-committed to a declining market.

Using Optimization in Portfolio Management

The statistician and quality control expert W. Edwards Deming said, "All models are wrong. Some models are useful." Despite the caution with which it must be used, a portfolio optimization program is very useful in a variety of portfolio management contexts, including:

1. Determining the viability of a potential asset class as a portfolio building block
2. Testing for reasonable asset class input assumptions
3. Analyzing capital needs
4. Managing client expectations

A good asset allocation strategy should satisfy two conditions. The first condition is economic: The strategy should make good investment sense. That is, given the client's financial resources and reasonable capital market assumptions, the asset allocation strategy positions the client to realize her financial goals with the required level of confidence. The second condition is behavioral: The client will comfortably follow the strategy and not be tempted to abandon it, particularly during market extremes. To satisfy the second condition, both the client and her advisor should be knowledgeably and meaningfully involved in the portfolio design process. Without the education and coaching provided by the advisor, the client may not have an adequate frame of reference to assess the subsequent performance of her portfolio, or she may lack the patience and discipline needed to weather turbulent market conditions. Optimizers have important roles to play in satisfying both these conditions.

Determining the Viability of a Potential Asset Class

Let's begin by describing the defining characteristics of an asset class:

1. It is a broad grouping of investments that share common characteristics.
2. It has significant capital allocated to it.
3. Its performance cannot be replicated by other asset classes.
4. It has economic reasons for its performance characteristics.
5. It expands the efficient frontier. That is, including the asset class as a potential portfolio building block makes possible the creation of portfolios that offer more expected return for the same level of volatility.
6. Its value in a diversified portfolio does not depend on active management.

Although there is no hard and fast rule, with portfolio optimization and performance modeling I recommend using a more limited number of broad asset classes as opposed to a larger number of finely differentiated categories. In most modeling applications, 6 to 12 mutually exclusive asset classes are sufficient. Wall Street, however, continually creates an ever-expanding proliferation of new investment products. Usually, these new investment products are actively managed portfolios of securities from traditional asset classes or some type of strategy using derivatives of traditional asset class securities. As such, these new investment products usually do not create new asset classes as we have defined the term.

Occasionally, however, the possibility of a new asset class arises and, with it, the question of whether it is viable as a portfolio building block. For example, the Treasury Department first began issuing Treasury Inflation Protected Securities (TIPS) in 1997. Do TIPS constitute a new asset class, and do TIPS have a role to play in diversifying client portfolios? Because of the way TIPS behave, particularly relative to unanticipated inflation, they offer portfolios a unique pattern of returns that other asset classes cannot replicate. When modeled in an unconstrained optimization with other asset classes, TIPS expand the efficient frontier and therefore justify consideration as a portfolio building block.

Another example is commodity-linked securities. Over the past several years, mutual fund companies have launched funds that invest in commodity-linked securities. These funds usually are benchmarked to a recognized commodity index. For example, the Oppenheimer Commodity Strategy Total Return Fund is benchmarked to the S&P Goldman Sachs Commodity Index, and the PIMCO Commodity Real Return Strategy Fund is benchmarked to the Dow Jones-UBS Commodity Index. Do these funds give investors access to a new asset class? If so, should we use the commodities asset class as a portfolio building block? An investment benchmarked to a commodity index can be quite volatile, and when viewed in isolation, it easily can be rejected as a potential portfolio building block. When modeled in an unconstrained optimization with other asset classes, however, the commodities asset class emerges as an attractive building block due in large measure to its low to negative correlations with many traditional financial asset classes. It is difficult to evaluate the viability of an asset class as a portfolio building block without the help of a portfolio optimization program.

Testing for Reasonable Asset Class Input Assumptions

Earlier in the chapter, we engaged in a sensitivity analysis that altered the input assumptions used in a portfolio optimization example. (See Exhibits 11.1 and 11.3.) It was disconcerting to find that two major asset classes, U.S. large company stocks and non-U.S. stocks, were unrepresented in the optimization results. Since these two asset classes account for over one-third of the world's investable capital, we know they are viable asset classes for portfolio construction. (See Exhibit 1.1.) Accordingly, these asset classes should have meaningful allocations across a significant range of portfolios on the efficient frontier. Since these two asset classes are unrepresented in the unconstrained optimization, it is likely that their input assumptions are not reasonable relative to those of the other asset classes. For example, by increasing the expected return inputs for U.S. large company stocks and non-U.S. stocks, we may obtain more reasonable allocations to these asset classes in portfolios on the efficient frontier. An internally consistent set of asset class optimization inputs should lead to meaningful allocations to major asset classes in different parts of the efficient frontier.

Analyzing Capital Needs

The early members of the baby boom generation are entering retirement. Many boomers wonder whether they will have sufficient financial resources to meet their needs in retirement. A capital needs analysis seeks to answer this question. First, the advisor and client collaboratively determine a proposed portfolio asset allocation consistent with the client's time horizon, volatility tolerance, and asset class preferences. This portfolio's expected return and standard deviation can then be modeled by constraining the optimizer to match the proposed portfolio allocation. Next, the advisor uses the portfolio's expected return and standard deviation as inputs to a Monte Carlo simulation that models the likelihood that the client's financial goals will be met, given the size of the client's portfolio and the magnitude and timing of contributions to and withdrawals from the portfolio. If the proposed strategy does not result in a sufficiently high probability of success, the advisor can do a sensitivity analysis to determine various options the client has to increase the likelihood of success. For example, the client may:

1. Increase her savings rate between now and retirement
2. Postpone retirement to a later date
3. Reduce the portfolio withdrawal rate for living expenses in retirement
4. Change the portfolio asset allocation

The last alternative should be approached cautiously, since improving the likelihood of investment success through portfolio restructuring may require a more equity-oriented strategy. With more equity comes the possibility that the client may have difficulty sticking to the strategy during market extremes.

Managing Client Expectations

A knowledgeable, informed client who participates in the design of his portfolio will likely live more comfortably with its subsequent performance results. An optimizer is very useful in describing the likelihood and range of possible portfolio returns for a given asset allocation strategy. This information enables a client to hypothetically "road-test" the ups and downs of a proposed strategy prior to its implementation. Can the client live comfortably with the likely range of returns, particularly those returns on the downside? If not, the portfolio asset allocation should be modified.

Despite their limitations, if used properly portfolio optimization programs are powerful tools that can be of great value in the investment management process. They quickly and accurately perform very complex mathematical calculations, which are useful in portfolio sensitivity analysis and the comparison of alternative "what-if" scenarios. Many commercially available programs have features that also take into consideration such factors as transaction costs and the impact of income taxes. As an additional tool available to investment advisors, portfolio optimization programs improve the investment decision-making process by pointing toward alternative asset allocations that may be better suited to the realization of client objectives. They are also of significant educational value by enhancing the client's understanding of the probable performance results associated with different strategies.

Chapter 12

Know Your Client

The beginning is the most important part of the work.

—*Plato (c. 428–348* BC*),* Republic

Money is paper blood.

—*Attributed to Bob Hope (1903–2003)*

We will now discuss how to apply the ideas developed thus far to the dynamics of an ongoing client-advisor relationship. Exhibit 12.1 is a flowchart that describes the steps of the investment management process as an interactive loop that continually feeds back into itself. We will review each of these steps in detail in Chapters 12 through 14.

In this chapter we will cover the first two steps: gather client data and identify the client's needs, constraints, and unique circumstances. These two steps, grouped together under the heading "Know your client," are the foundation of the investment management process. The heading "Manage client expectations" includes the next four steps, which we will cover in the next chapter. The order of these steps is crucial. They build directly on the foundation of knowing your client and, out of necessity, *precede* the last four steps that constitute what we typically consider to be *portfolio management*. The process of managing client

Exhibit 12.1
Investment Management Process

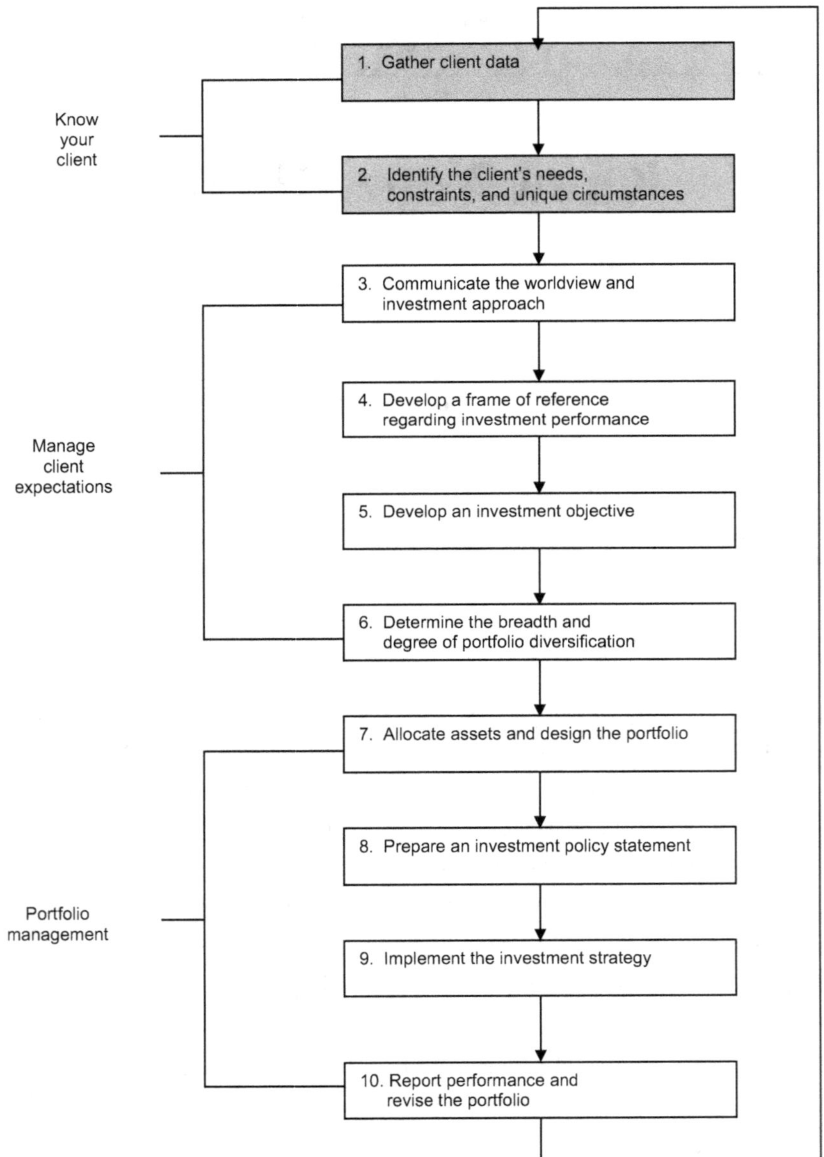

expectations is as important to the long-term realization of client objectives as the process of actually managing the portfolio. Many clients fail to reach their objectives as a result of simply not adhering to a sensible long-term strategy. Often, this failure is due to the client's unrealistic expectations. In essence, it is not enough for an advisor to properly manage a client's portfolio; it is also crucial that the client *understand* that the portfolio is being properly managed. Without that understanding, it is unlikely that the client will be able to adhere to an appropriate, long-term strategy through the pressures of extreme market conditions.

It is interesting to note that money is not actually invested until the next-to-last step in this flowchart. Unfortunately, many clients view the first eight steps of this process as requiring too much time and effort on their part. They prefer to limit their involvement to the initial selection of an investment advisor, who in turn assumes full responsibility for the last four steps under the heading "Portfolio management." Many investment advisors are likewise too quick to cut the process short and jump immediately to the last four steps. We greatly enhance the likelihood of a client reaching his objectives, however, by resisting the temptation to take shortcuts. This 10-step process requires the thoughtful commitment of both advisor and client and usually requires several meetings to complete. Given the importance of the decisions, it is time well spent.

Step 1. Gather Client Data

The client may be an individual, couple, or institutional account such as a trusteed retirement plan, endowment, or foundation. Regardless of the type of client, however, the goal of the data-gathering process is to know the client. Much of the data are factual or quantitative in nature. Beyond this is a realm of more subjective qualitative information, which attempts to assess what it is like "inside the client's skin."

Advisors who prefer to delegate the data-gathering process to a support person may be doing themselves and their clients a disservice.

It is important for data gathering to be handled by the advisor, preferably through face-to-face interaction with the client. The psychological bonding between the client and advisor begins here, and their conversation helps to establish a sense of comfort that facilitates making important investment decisions. The client also has the opportunity to begin to understand how the advisor thinks, and certainly the advisor will gain a level of understanding of the client that goes beyond the facts and figures written down in a data questionnaire.

Be alert for clues regarding the client's *present* volatility tolerance. The word *present* is italicized because, as we discussed previously, volatility tolerance is subject to modification within a rather broad range, based on providing the client with an informed framework for decision making. Without directly asking for volatility tolerance information, the advisor can infer a great deal from the current composition of the portfolio. If the client usually holds 90 percent of his portfolio in money market funds and bank certificates of deposit, indications are strong that he may be quite volatility averse. Another client who holds a disproportionately large portion of her portfolio in gold bullion, rare coins, diamonds, and other hard assets is likewise revealing something about her present investment attitudes. Occasionally, contradictory impressions emerge. For example, a person who describes himself as very volatility averse may have a large portfolio commitment to a small company traded over the counter. By asking more questions, the advisor learns that the client inherited the stock from his mother, who was the company's founder. This information is important because of the psychological and emotional issues that may be involved in the retention or sale of this stock.

When listing the client's assets and liabilities, it is helpful to organize the balance sheet in a format that supports the investment decision-making process. I recommend the following classifications:

1. Interest-generating investments
2. Equity investments
3. Lifestyle assets
4. Liabilities

As we concluded in Chapter 7, the most important decision a client makes is the balance he chooses between interest-generating investments and equity investments. This balance determines the general volatility and return characteristics of the portfolio. By gathering data using the above format, the advisor can quickly assess the client's current broad portfolio balance. Lifestyle assets include the client's primary residence and personal property as well as vacation homes. Occasionally, a client objects to the classification of a vacation home as a lifestyle asset, but unless it produces a positive cash flow by generating rental income in excess of the expenses of ownership, this classification is usually more accurate.

The balance between investment assets and lifestyle assets provides one indication of the client's financial discipline and thrift. The advisor can infer more information from an analysis of the client's cash flow. How much of his income is absorbed in lifestyle expenditures versus committed to building investment net worth? Since many investments generate taxable income, a client's income tax return serves as a useful source of information to double-check that the advisor has accounted for all assets.

The data-gathering process also provides a valuable opportunity to assess the client's level of investment knowledge and to begin the educational process. The advisor can share her observations regarding the strengths and weaknesses of the client's current investment portfolio and encourage the client to begin looking at his investment portfolio in the broadest possible terms. Frequently, a client initially seeks investment advice on what he should be doing with a small part of his portfolio, such as a certificate of deposit that will be maturing soon. He may not realize that he optimally should make the decision within the larger context of his entire portfolio and related financial goals.

Institutional clients likewise must learn to consider investing in a wider context. For example, for a corporate defined benefit pension plan, broad thinking entails consideration of the pension plan assets and liabilities within the larger context of the corporation as a whole.

After all, the corporate pension plan's sponsor has promised the benefit payments, not the pension plan itself. The risks and rewards of pension plan performance therefore are borne by the corporation, whose financial well-being is intimately tied to the performance of the pension plan assets.

Finally, the data-gathering session gives the advisor an excellent opportunity to provide an overview of the investment management approach that she will use to move the client toward the realization of his financial goals. For all these reasons, the data-gathering session is an important step of the portfolio management process that justifies the full involvement of both the client and advisor.

Step 2. Identify the Client's Needs, Constraints, and Unique Circumstances

Liquidity

The advisor should evaluate each client's situation for the need for portfolio liquidity. Nonliquid investments, such as direct ownership of investment real estate, should not be made if the client likely will need the funds to meet future expenditures. Even if the portfolio has sufficient liquidity elsewhere to meet such expenditures, the advisor should evaluate the size of nonliquid investments relative to the possible withdrawals from the portfolio.

For example, assume that, for a particular client, 15 percent of portfolio assets is the target allocation for nonliquid real estate investments, with the balance of the portfolio invested in a variety of liquid assets. If, within a short period thereafter, the client liquidates 25 percent of the portfolio to meet various expenditures, the commitment to real estate will rise above the target 15 percent allocation to 20 percent of the portfolio. As discussed here, liquidity is an issue separate from a client's yield requirements or cash flow needs.

Portfolio Cash Withdrawal Rate for Anticipated Expenditures

The advisor and client should quantify and plan for the magnitude and timing of required cash withdrawals from the investment portfolio. With the exception of situations involving regulatory or legal yield requirements, investment portfolios generally should not be designed to intentionally produce a certain yield or income stream. The issue of portfolio design is largely *independent* of the question of how to get cash out of the portfolio in order to meet necessary expenditures.

As we discussed in detail previously, the balance chosen between interest-generating investments and equity investments is an important determinant of an investment portfolio's volatility and return characteristics, and the client makes this most important decision in reference to his investment time horizon. A portfolio balanced on this basis reflects the best obtainable trade-off between the desire for stability on the one hand and the need for growth on the other. Assume that the yield on such a properly balanced portfolio is not equal to what the client needs for required expenditures. This inequality is not a good reason to reallocate the portfolio toward either more or fewer interest-generating investments. Doing so causes a mismatch between the portfolio structure and the investment time horizon, resulting in an overexposure of the portfolio to either inflation or volatility, depending on the direction of the reallocation.

Provided that the rate of withdrawal from the portfolio is not too high, most portfolios can maintain proper balance and broad diversification with more than adequate liquidity for necessary withdrawals. In practice, even portfolios implemented with passively managed investments like index funds need to be rebalanced periodically as the capital markets move. At these rebalancing points, cash can be set aside in a money market fund and earmarked for anticipated expenditures. This process is simple to execute and is conceptually sound from a portfolio management point of view.

Although it generally is true that the question of how to get money out of a portfolio should be considered independently of the determination of proper portfolio design, the two issues become intertwined when the withdrawal rate is unsustainably high relative to the size of the portfolio. For example, a client may have a 25-year investment time horizon, over which he intends to rely on his portfolio to meet his cash needs, but is withdrawing money so quickly that he likely will liquidate the portfolio within 5 to 10 years. In this situation, the portfolio cash withdrawal rate has triggered a reduction in the investment time horizon, which in turn will influence the portfolio balance decision. Recognize, however, that even in this situation, the portfolio balance decision still is made with reference to the relevant investment time horizon.

Tax Situation

Some clients, such as tax-qualified retirement plans, have been blessed by the tax code and provide a tax-sheltered environment within which investments can grow. Taxable clients are not so fortunate. To properly advise these clients, it is necessary to understand their tax situations. At minimum, this understanding requires a current-year tax projection that identifies the client's marginal tax bracket. Preferably, the advisor also will project the client's tax situation for a few years into the future. The most obvious use of this information is to determine the advisability of investing in federal income tax-free municipal bonds. For example, all other things being equal, it is more advantageous for an investor with a 35 percent marginal tax bracket to own a tax-free municipal bond yielding 2.7 percent than to own a taxable bond of similar quality and maturity date with a yield of 4 percent, over one-third of which she loses to income taxes, leaving her with a net yield of 2.6 percent.

The advisor should evaluate any decision involving the possible sale of an asset with respect to its tax impact. Often, investment issues take precedence over tax considerations. In other words, a client should not necessarily hold onto an inappropriate investment merely because its liquidation would trigger tax liabilities. These situations require an analysis to determine whether the economic benefits of the proposed sale exceed the tax liabilities that the sale would trigger. Consider the situation where a decision to sell an investment is made near the end of the year, and the client is expected to be in a lower marginal tax bracket the following year. Here, the advisor and client should weigh the benefit of selling the following year in order to save taxes against the economic risk of continuing to hold the investment in the interim. Similarly, it may make sense to postpone the sale of an appreciated investment if, within a short period, a short-term capital gain will become a preferentially taxed long-term capital gain.

These examples are only a few simple ones demonstrating the importance of understanding the tax dimension of a client's situation. Our current tax code is extremely complex, with no end to the variety and subtlety of the tax issues that can arise in the management of a client's investment portfolio. A full discussion of these issues is beyond the scope of this book. If the advisor does not have the requisite tax knowledge to handle such issues, he should enlist the help of other professionals who do.

Regulatory and Legal Constraints

Regulatory and/or legal constraints take a variety of forms and are more prevalent with institutional clients. For example, the Employee Retirement Income Security Act of 1974 (ERISA) governs many qualified retirement plans and contains provisions concerning such things as the preparation of written investment policy statements, portfolio diversification, and the use of "prudent experts" in the management of plan assets. If a client is an endowment or charitable foundation, minimum distribution rules may exist that must be adhered to. If the investment portfolio is a testamentary trust, the income beneficiaries may be different from the eventual inheritors of the assets. When designing the portfolio, the advisor and client need to consider the potentially adverse interests of these parties. The trust instrument may give guidance on these issues, as well as contain specific language regarding suitability standards for investments.

Individuals encounter similar constraints with IRAs that have detailed rules regarding contributions and withdrawals. Another example is restricted stock that can only be sold under certain stated conditions. These examples illustrate the kind of regulatory and legal constraints that clients and their advisors need to consider.

Time Horizon

The fact that an entire chapter of this book has been devoted to time horizon is a testament to its importance in investment management. Time horizon is the crucial variable that underlies the decision of how to allocate portfolio assets between interest-generating investments and equity investments. The two major risks confronting clients are inflation and volatility of returns. Over long time horizons, inflation is a bigger risk than market volatility. Investment portfolios with long time horizons should accordingly be weighted more heavily in equity investments to secure the long-term capital growth needed to build purchasing power. Over short time horizons, market volatility is more dangerous than inflation. Therefore, portfolios with short time horizons should be more heavily invested in interest-generating investments with more stable principal values.

Clients tend to underestimate their investment time horizons, resulting in portfolios that may be overexposed to the danger of inflation because of an underrepresentation of equities. Part of the problem is that a client may wrongly assume that his investment time horizon extends only to his date of retirement. This misunderstanding leads clients to the erroneous conclusion that equity investments are only appropriate while building net worth during preretirement years and that they should sell them at retirement and invest the proceeds in interest-generating investments that will produce the income needed in retirement. The problem with this line of thinking is that it ignores the fact that inflation continues to be a threat throughout the retirement years, when the client is relying on the portfolio to meet his cash flow needs. By definition, a person of average health has a 50 percent likelihood of living beyond his or her life expectancy. A conservative posture therefore requires an investment-planning horizon that extends well *beyond* the client's life expectancy. This time horizon can be quite long, and hence the need for capital growth to preserve purchasing power remains. The same argument holds for institutional portfolios, such as endowment funds or corporate qualified retirement plans, some of which expect to have perpetual existences.

Psychological and Emotional Factors

Ideally the investment decision-making process should be a series of logical steps that systematically build toward a conceptually sound, rational portfolio strategy. However, numerous psychological and emotional factors can impact the decision-making process, and advisors should therefore be aware of them. Most clients evaluating investment alternatives have preexisting preferences. The advisor should attempt to accommodate reasonable preferences in order to maximize the client's comfort with the portfolio. But if a client's preferences are based on misconceptions or result from a lack of investment knowledge, then the advisor should take the time to educate the client. Ultimately, it is the client's money, and the client may have limited willingness to endorse a recommended strategy. With a good understanding of a client's psychological and emotional factors, an advisor will be better able to present new ideas in a way that facilitates their acceptance.

The Decision-Making Dynamic

Institutional clients often have investment decision-making authority vested in a committee of trustees. The time horizons for these portfolios are often quite long, and trustees must assume the responsibility for making long-term investment decisions, even though their terms of office may be of limited duration. Given the many interested parties who may second-guess investment decisions, the temptation always is present for a committee of trustees to manage the portfolio for safe, short-term results. The practice of measuring institutional portfolio performance on a quarterly basis aggravates this tendency. Trustees need courage and confidence to do their job, and they deserve support and recognition for making tough decisions that have the potential to look bad in the short run but that are nevertheless wise in the long run. By contrast, an individual client affords more continuity in decision making. The money is the client's own, and she can make decisions with greater flexibility and freedom.

Chapter 13

Managing Client Expectations

There is no free lunch.

—*Anonymous*

Human wants are never satisfied.

—*J. Willard Marriott, Jr. (1932–),* Marriott

A six-inch line is short relative to an eight-inch line.
An eight-inch line is short relative to a ten-inch line.

—*Tibetan saying*

In this chapter we will cover steps 3 through 6 of the investment management process as outlined in Exhibit 13.1. Note that the four steps involved in managing client expectations follow the first two that deal with knowing your client and, of necessity, precede the last four steps that deal with what is more commonly thought of as portfolio management. This order is very important: First get to know your client, next manage his expectations, and only then manage his portfolio.

Exhibit 13.1
Investment Management Process

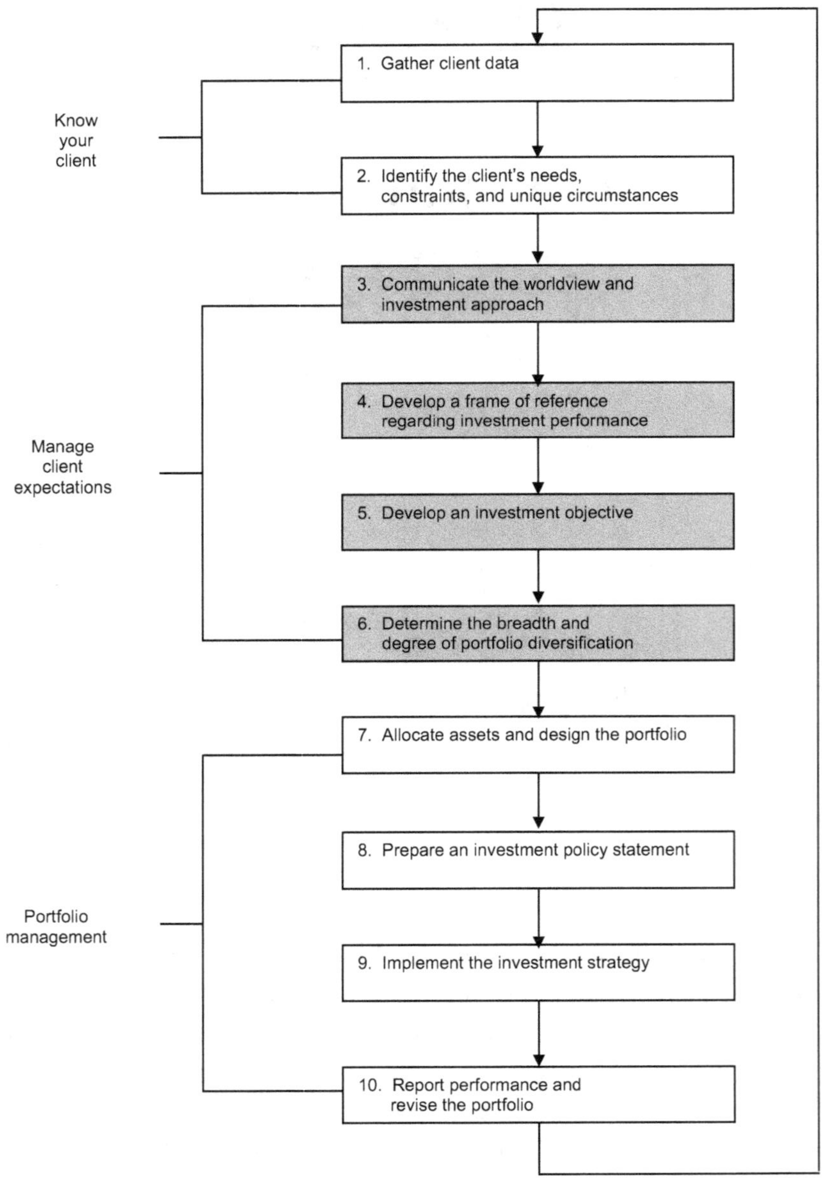

Step 3. Communicate the Worldview and Investment Approach

A sure prescription for trouble is a client who has a different investment worldview than her investment advisor has. For example, an investment advisor may believe it is impossible to engage in market timing successfully and therefore makes no attempt to do so. But if a client believes that part of the advisor's job is to protect her from bad markets, then it is only a matter of time until adverse market conditions strain and perhaps end the advisory relationship. Clients' expectations tend to err toward optimism; they believe that higher returns are possible with less volatility than may actually be the case. Managing client expectations prior to and throughout the investment management process provides important advantages to both advisor and client. When the client and advisor share the same investment worldview, they will be in agreement regarding the nature of the risks involved with and potential rewards of various strategies.

Worldview Determines Investment Approach

Before beginning the process of managing client expectations, an advisor must know where he stands. Every investment approach is built on an underlying investment worldview. In my judgment, the two most important worldview questions are:

1. Is successful market timing possible?
2. Is superior security selection possible?

Depending on how these two questions are answered, a 2-by-2 matrix of worldview possibilities exists, as shown in Exhibit 13.2. Although not all investors can be pigeonholed neatly into one quadrant, for our discussion we will assume that we have four different investors, each standing squarely in a different quadrant. The goals of this discussion

Exhibit 13.2
Worldview Determines Investment Approach

Is Superior Security Selection Possible?	Is Successful Market Timing Possible? YES	NO
YES	Quadrant 1	Quadrant 2
NO	Quadrant 3	Quadrant 4

Source:© Roger C. Gibson, 1995.

are to illustrate the close tie between worldview and investment approach and to emphasize the importance of a shared worldview between clients and their advisors.

Quadrant 1 Worldview

The first investor, John, answers "yes" to both questions and therefore has a quadrant 1 worldview: He believes that it is possible to both profitably predict the short-run movements of different asset classes and choose securities within each asset class that will outperform the asset class as a whole. What investment approach is consistent with this worldview? If successful market timing is possible, John will want to concentrate his entire investment portfolio in whichever asset class will now generate the highest returns. When a different asset class is poised to generate the highest returns, investments in the first asset class are sold, and the proceeds are repositioned in the next winning asset class, and so on. If it simultaneously is possible to engage in superior security selection, he will invest only in those securities that will outperform the asset class in which he is invested. If his investment strategy succeeds, he has it made. John does not need to worry about portfolio losses, since successful market timing will sidestep market declines. Simultaneously, he will maximize his returns by investing in the best-performing securities within whichever asset class is currently performing best.

Many unsophisticated investors hold this worldview and bring it to their investment advisory relationship. They expect their investment advisor to know which asset class will deliver the best returns and to choose the best-performing securities within that asset class. If the investment advisor shares that worldview, he is accountable to it, and his performance should be evaluated accordingly. Managing client expectations will not be the problem; delivering results that are consistent with that worldview is the challenge. The first time an advisor places a client's money in an underperforming asset class, he has failed. Or if the advisor chooses a portfolio of securities that underperforms the asset class, again he has failed. This worldview is easy to sell but very hard, if not impossible, to deliver. In my judgment, any investor or advisor who holds this worldview is setting himself up for failure.

Quadrant 2 Worldview

The second investor, Michelle, has a quadrant 2 worldview and therefore believes it is impossible to predict which asset class will outperform the others in the short run. She does believe, however, that it is possible to choose securities within an asset class that will outperform the asset class as a whole. Michelle will diversify her portfolio across multiple asset classes in order to mitigate the risks of markets that are unknowable in the short run. The good news with this approach is that, regardless of which major asset class generates the highest returns, she will participate by having a portion of her portfolio invested there. The bad news is that she also will have a portion of her portfolio invested in the major asset class that has the worst performance. Because Michelle believes superior security selection is possible, she will limit her investments in each asset class to those securities that she thinks will outperform the asset class as a whole. The majority of professional money managers and investment advisors have a quadrant 2 worldview.

Quadrant 3 Worldview

The third investor, Denny, stands in quadrant 3. He believes that the relative short-run performance of different asset classes can be predicted but does not believe that superior security selection is possible. His investment approach concentrates his portfolio first in one asset class, then another, based on his forecast of which asset class will generate the highest returns. Because Denny does not believe in superior security selection, he uses low-cost index funds to implement his strategy. An index fund is a passively managed, diversified portfolio of securities designed to mimic the performance of a specific market index. By using index funds, Denny minimizes the costs associated with active security selection and eliminates the possibility of significantly underperforming the asset class in which he is invested. This particular worldview has the fewest proponents. It is reserved for real market-timing purists.

Quadrant 4 Worldview

The last investor, Cass, stands in quadrant 4. She believes that markets are efficient: The current prices of securities reflect the relevant, publicly available information concerning them. This information includes factual data as well as consensus expectations about any uncertainties that are important in determining the prices of the securities. If this worldview is true, what moves security prices and markets in the short run? Basically, surprises. This worldview is known as the *efficient market hypothesis*. Considerable, though not all, academic investment research undertaken in the past 50 years supports this worldview. (The field of behavioral finance has perhaps levied the most successful challenges to the efficient market hypothesis by arguing that investors are subject to cognitive biases that lead to market inefficiencies.) The quadrant 4 investor follows a broadly diversified, multiple-asset-class investment strategy, using index funds as the building blocks. It is important to note that this investment approach is not a simple buy-and-hold strategy. As the markets move, the portfolio will stray from the allocation targeted for each of the asset classes, triggering a need to rebalance the portfolio back to its long-term, strategic asset allocation commitments.

A proponent of a quadrant 4 worldview faces three big issues. The first is proper asset allocation, because diversification is the primary means of mitigating investment risks. The second is cost minimization as the necessary prerequisite of obtaining performance that approaches the upper limit of what is achievable—that is, market returns. Minimizing costs can be accomplished by utilizing low-cost index funds and/or exchange-traded funds as portfolio building blocks. The third big issue is management of client expectations, since clients have no reasonable hope of outperforming the markets in which they are invested. Whereas quadrant 1 is easy to sell and hard to deliver, quadrant 4 is hard to sell and easy to deliver.

Comparing Alternative Worldviews

The worldviews of quadrants 1, 2, and 3 share one thing in common—the notion that skill has a positive impact on investment performance. With any of these worldviews, the investor does not have to settle for the underlying growth path of the market. He can beat the market in either one of two ways:

1. By moving into and out of a market as it gyrates on either side of its long-term growth path through successful market timing
2. By taking advantage of the divergent movement of securities within asset classes through superior security selection

By contrast, a quadrant 4 investor does not believe that skill can add value, and beating the market therefore is not a realistic investment objective. In other words, a quadrant 4 investor must accept the underlying long-term growth path of an asset class as the best outcome achievable from it.

Where Are We Going?

Even though intelligent investors may disagree about which of these four competing worldviews most accurately represents reality, competitive forces are moving us toward a quadrant 4 worldview. The more strongly investors adhere to either a quadrant 1, 2, or 3 worldview, the more strenuously they will attempt to beat the market through superior skill. Not surprisingly, many talented, hardworking, intelligent people are drawn to professional money management. This same pool of money management talent, however, makes it very difficult for any one person to consistently beat everyone else. The professionals are not competing with unsophisticated investors. They are competing against one another for the brass ring. If one money manager discovers a strategy that leads to superior results, his competitive advantage lasts only as long as others do not imitate the approach. Success, however, tends to encourage competitors to discover and replicate the strategy. As others compete, the rewards of the approach simultaneously begin to trend downward. In essence, the more vigorous the competition among money managers, the more quickly quadrant 4 becomes reality.

Implications of a Quadrant 4 Worldview

If quadrant 4 is the most accurate worldview, or if we indeed are heading inexorably in that direction, it is important to consider the implications. A quadrant 4 worldview undercuts the reason for the existence of the skill-based, active money management profession. If skill cannot be relied upon to add value, why pay fees and incur transaction costs in a futile attempt to beat the market? Consider a hypothetical efficient market without transaction costs and fees. In this world, buying and selling securities is a zero-sum game with an expected risk-adjusted net present value of zero. It is a zero-sum game in that one investor's wins are always exactly offset by another's losses. Buying and selling securities has a risk-adjusted net present value of zero, since you can only expect to get what you pay for. A security's price equals its risk-adjusted net present value.

Now consider a more realistic world—an efficient market with transaction costs and fees. In this world, trading securities is not a zero-sum game; it is a negative-sum game. In a negative-sum game, the participants expect to lose money by the mere act of playing it. A Las Vegas slot machine is an example of a negative-sum game. Even though you may get lucky and win more money than you put into the slot machine, on average the flow of money is from the players to the casino owner. (Slot machines are called "one-arm bandits" for a reason.)

We have evidence that the capital markets can be described as a negative-sum game. On average, most managers underperform the markets in which they invest. Before fees, the expected outcome is to match the market. After fees, therefore, the average participant will lag behind the market. The way to win a negative-sum game is not to play it. Those who adhere to a quadrant 4 worldview strategically expect to win the investment game by not playing it. They accept the return of an asset class as their upside and attempt to get as close to it as possible by minimizing their costs. Hence, index funds, which are designed to replicate the performance of an asset class while minimizing the associated costs, are preferred building blocks for their portfolios.

An investor with a quadrant 1, 2, or 3 worldview *fights* the forces of the markets by attempting to exercise skill. A quadrant 4 investor *uses* the forces of the market with the humble acknowledgment that the attempt to exercise skill will, in the long run, be a detriment to performance. Think of the trend line of an asset class's growth path as the signal, and think of the fluctuations of security prices around that growth path as the noise. Quadrants 1, 2, and 3 investors believe that the key to investment success lies in the noise, whereas the quadrant 4 investor believes that the key to success lies in the signal. The investment approach of the quadrant 4 investor can best be summarized by a quote from R. Buckminster Fuller: "Don't fight forces, use them."

As we increasingly move toward a quadrant 4 worldview, the importance of skill factors declines, and the importance of decision factors increases. Decision factors involve the choice of asset classes and the relative weighting of funds across those asset classes. These factors, in turn, shift the focus of attention from the investment professional, previously looked to for the exercise of skill, to the client, who is the locus of investment decision making. Once again we return to the importance of realistically managing client expectations. In a world where skill cannot protect them from bad outcomes, investors need to both make informed decisions *and* live with the consequences, with discipline, through good and bad times.

These different worldviews also contain important business implications for investment professionals. In a world where skill drives results, a successful money management firm separates the security selection and market-timing functions from the client service and marketing functions. Since investment genius is rare, the talented money manager's time and energy should be focused on the clients' portfolios of securities. Distracting her with responsibilities for maintaining client relationships or developing new business would be a waste of her talent. Those duties would be better handled by sales and account representatives whose job it is to bring new clients to the firm and hold their hands while the talented money manager beats the market through her superior skill. In this business model, the focus of attention is on the portfolio manager's skill.

By contrast, a quadrant 4 worldview spawns a different kind of investment organization. Where asset allocation decisions drive investment performance, the client-advisor relationship becomes central, given the importance of the decisions that the client must make regarding the structure of his portfolio and the necessity that the client live with results that are market driven. Within this business model, *the investment professional must be in relationship with the client*, because the client is the focus of attention. The client's perception of investment risks, his volatility tolerance, financial goals, asset allocation decisions, interpretation of investment results, patience, and discipline are the crucial variables determining his investment success.

A Conspiracy Against a Quadrant 4 Worldview

One final observation is pertinent to this discussion, and it impacts both the long-term viability of the investment advisory profession and the topic of managing client expectations. There is a conspiracy against a quadrant 4 worldview with three interlocking conspirators:

1. Investors
2. The skill-based, active money management profession
3. The financial press

Investors do not want to accept a quadrant 4 worldview because it means that they have no way to fully protect themselves from the sometimes harsh realities of the capital markets. If the quadrant 4 worldview is true, investors cannot rely upon skill to come to the rescue during a bad market. Successful investing will require the investor to knowledgeably make difficult decisions concerning portfolio volatility versus return trade-offs and then adhere to those decisions with discipline and courage. It is little wonder that investors prefer to embrace a different worldview. The skill-based, active money management profession rejects the quadrant 4 worldview, since its very existence is threatened by it. And finally, the financial press thrives on writing articles that, in one way or another, feed the notion that ways to beat the market exist. If the financial press fully embraced a quadrant 4 worldview, the press would have *much* less to write about. I am fascinated by how these three coconspirators have strong, mutually aligned interests in rejecting the evidence that supports a quadrant 4 worldview. To quote from Ecclesiastes 4:12: "A cord of three strands is not easily broken."

Summary

Many problems that occur in client-advisor relationships arise because the client stands in one quadrant while her advisor stands in a different quadrant. Most investors want to stand in quadrant 1, the majority of professional money managers stand in quadrant 2, staunch market timers stand in quadrant 3, and the proponents of the efficient market hypothesis stand in quadrant 4. These different worldviews involve radically different investment approaches, and a successful long-term client-advisor relationship, at minimum, requires that both parties be in agreement concerning what realistically is achievable in the management of the client's portfolio. Both parties should firmly and consciously acknowledge this agreement *before* money is invested. Lacking such an agreement, the advisor and client should not work together.

This book is based on the worldview that successfully engaging in short-term market timing is not possible. Most of the academic research on this subject supports that conclusion, and as Charles D. Ellis states in his book *Investment Policy*, "The evidence on investment managers' success with market timing is impressive—and overwhelmingly negative."[1]

Next we will cover step 4, "Develop a frame of reference regarding investment performance," which is important precisely because it is not possible to predict short-run market performance successfully. The jury is divided regarding whether superior security selection is possible. Many academicians maintain that superior security selection is not possible. The vast majority of professional money managers and investors believe otherwise, but their beliefs may not be the reality. A full resolution of the issue is not required for our purposes. Money can be managed within a strategic asset allocation framework with or without active security selection.

Step 4. Develop a Frame of Reference Regarding Investment Performance

On any given day, an investor can look up the value of her securities in the *Wall Street Journal* and calculate how much her portfolio is worth. She sees both her winners and losers in sharp relief. In a world where investors are exposed to the twin dangers of market volatility on the one hand and inflation on the other, they have no completely safe place to stand. The risks inherent in investing one's money are unavoidable. The pain of that realization can motivate investors to learn about capital market behavior and the principles of successful investing.

An investment advisor who spends time educating her clients about the nature of the capital markets empowers her clients to make wise decisions with greater equanimity. This educational process begins with a review of the long-term historical performance of Treasury bills, government bonds, corporate bonds, common stocks, and inflation, as presented in Chapters 2 and 3. The simple models of security returns that we developed provide the client with a sense of the comparative performance and relative payoff for assuming various forms of risk. By gaining an appreciation of all the risks confronting them, clients will understand that no ideal investment exists that is liquid, has a stable principal value, and generates returns sufficient to stay ahead of the combined impact of inflation and income taxes.

As the fantasy of the ideal investment dissolves, clients will understand the necessity of compromise in building an investment portfolio. Some investments will provide stable, predictable returns, but their stability is purchased at a price of lower returns. Other investments will provide the expectation of long-term growth of capital but necessarily entail the assumption of volatility. With all the uncertainty inherent in investment management, clients understandably look for some reliable constants. One constant is that people will continue to prefer stable returns over unpredictable returns. For this reason, clients can be confident that the buying and selling activities of investors will price volatile investments, like common stocks, to have higher expected returns than investments with stable principal values, such as Treasury bills. Without the uncertainty and volatility of common stock returns, equity investing would yield no incremental payoff.

Guiding clients through the concept of investment time horizon, developed in Chapter 6, teaches them that the passage of time significantly alters the magnitude of the possible penalty associated with volatility. The longer the investment time horizon, the more opportunities for good and bad years to offset one another, producing an average return that converges toward the long-term growth path of the asset class. Time thereby transforms the short-run enemy of volatility into a long-run friend that fuels the higher expected returns of equity investments.

Cultivating realistic expectations lays the foundation for developing realistic investment objectives. A client's volatility tolerance can shift within a rather broad range based on a proper understanding of investment time horizon and a greater familiarity with capital market behavior. As a result, she will more likely choose an investment portfolio structure appropriate for the realization of her financial goals. The goal of this process is to enable the client to make an informed decision regarding the proper portfolio balance between interest-generating investments and equity investments. The resulting portfolio will reflect the most satisfactory compromise between the desire for stability and the need for long-term capital growth.

Step 5. Develop an Investment Objective

When a client is asked to list his financial goals, his response might be something like: "A vacation home in an exclusive resort community, eight years of fully funded college and postgraduate expenses at the best private institutions for each of three children, and early retirement at age 55 with an annual income of $200,000 after taxes." A few quick calculations clarify that achieving these goals will require a very large investment portfolio. Given reasonable capital market assumptions, some clients have portfolios that are simply too small to achieve all their desired goals, regardless of how their portfolios are structured. Human desires tend to surpass the resources available for their fulfillment.

Structuring a portfolio capable of generating the return necessary to meet the client's financial goals may require the client to assume an unacceptable level of portfolio volatility. For this reason, it is generally more appropriate to focus on a client's volatility tolerance than his return requirement. Once the advisor determines the client's volatility tolerance, the upper limit on the portfolio's long-term expected return is defined. If this return is inadequate, the client will need to prioritize his financial goals and make the necessary compromises. If the return associated with the client's maximum volatility tolerance is greater than that necessary to reach his goals, the advisor can easily move down the volatility scale and structure a more stable portfolio with a lower return, if the client prefers.

Chapter 7 described the series of steps that enable an advisor to infer a client's volatility tolerance, based on the client's preferred portfolio allocation between two investment alternatives—Treasury bills and large company stocks. The choice of broad portfolio balance is an investment policy decision that requires the active involvement of the client. Without the guidance of a skilled investment advisor, few clients are equipped to make the best choices for themselves. Providing clients with a good frame of reference regarding investment performance and the importance of time horizon in investment management is crucial to their choices.

The beauty of the process described in Chapter 7 is that it forces the client to acknowledge and deal realistically with the trade-off between return and volatility that is inherent in the investment management process. The process also fosters the formation of realistic investment performance expectations. Generally, the advisor should encourage the client to choose a portfolio balance that places her near the upper end of her volatility-tolerance range, while simultaneously making sure that she can remain committed to her portfolio balance decision through market extremes. The goal of the process is to maximize the portfolio's expected return, subject to the client's need to sleep well at night.

Once the client has chosen a broad portfolio balance, the next step is to develop a qualitative statement of the corresponding investment objective. I do not use traditional investment objectives, such as "aggressive growth," "growth and current income," or "income." Rather, I prefer to word the objective in a way that acknowledges the trade-off between return and volatility. For example, based on my investment worldview, an objective of "long-term growth of capital with stability of principal value" is impossible. Examples of suitable investment objectives are:

1. Low portfolio volatility with low total return
2. Medium total return with medium portfolio volatility
3. High total return with high portfolio volatility

The first investment objective, "low portfolio volatility with low total return," would be appropriate for a client who chooses portfolio 2 in Exhibit 7.2. A client who chooses portfolio 3 would have an objective of "medium total return with medium portfolio volatility," and a client choosing either portfolio 4 or portfolio 5 would have an objective of "high total return with high portfolio volatility."

Step 6. Determine the Breadth and Degree of Portfolio Diversification

Once the client chooses a broad portfolio balance between interest-generating and equity investments and formulates the corresponding investment objective, the next step is to determine the breadth and degree of portfolio diversification. The *breadth* of portfolio diversification refers to the choice of asset classes used to construct the portfolio. The *degree* of portfolio diversification refers to the relative allocation of money across those asset classes. Since the equity side of an investor's portfolio is primarily responsible for both the best and the worst portfolio returns, we will focus our discussion on equity diversification issues.

Based on the discussion in Chapter 8, we concluded that the volatility of a diversified portfolio is *less* than the weighted average of the volatility levels of the investments comprising the portfolio. The difference is due to the diversification effect of partially offsetting patterns of returns among the investments. In Chapter 10, we reviewed the significant rewards of multiple-asset-class investing, both in reducing portfolio volatility and in potentially increasing long-term returns. The rewards of a multiple-asset-class investment approach, however, come with a price—a pattern of returns that is different from a U.S. capital market frame of reference.

Exhibit 10.2 (reproduced here as Exhibit 13.3) is wonderful for illustrating the surprisingly powerful benefits of equity asset class diversification. Given only the information in this graph, it is difficult to imagine anyone becoming infatuated with portfolio A (U.S. stocks). Of the 15 equity portfolios, portfolio A has one of the lowest compound annual returns and is the fifth most volatile. Every other one of the 11 multiple-asset-class portfolios had better volatility-adjusted returns as evidenced by their higher Sharpe ratios (as shown in Exhibit 10.10). Yet toward the end of the 1990s, many investors abandoned multiple-asset-class investment strategies in order to concentrate their equity holdings in U.S. stocks—a very costly mistake.

Exhibit 13.4 compares the growth of $1 investments in portfolio A (U.S. stocks) and portfolio ABCD (an annually rebalanced portfolio allocated equally to U.S. stocks, non-U.S. stocks, real estate securities, and commodity-linked securities). Portfolio ABCD had built a significant lead over U.S. stocks and then briefly lost it during 1998 due to the sharply negative returns that year from both real estate securities and commodity-linked securities. During the 2000-2002 U.S. stock bear market and subsequent recovery, however, portfolio ABCD once again regained a commanding lead. Both portfolios experienced negative returns in 2008. While the decline in that year for portfolio ABCD appears to be much larger than that of portfolio A, portfolio ABCD's loss of – 41.07 percent was only slightly worse than portfolio A's loss of −37.00 percent.

Exhibit 13.3

Fifteen Equity Portfolios (1972–2011)

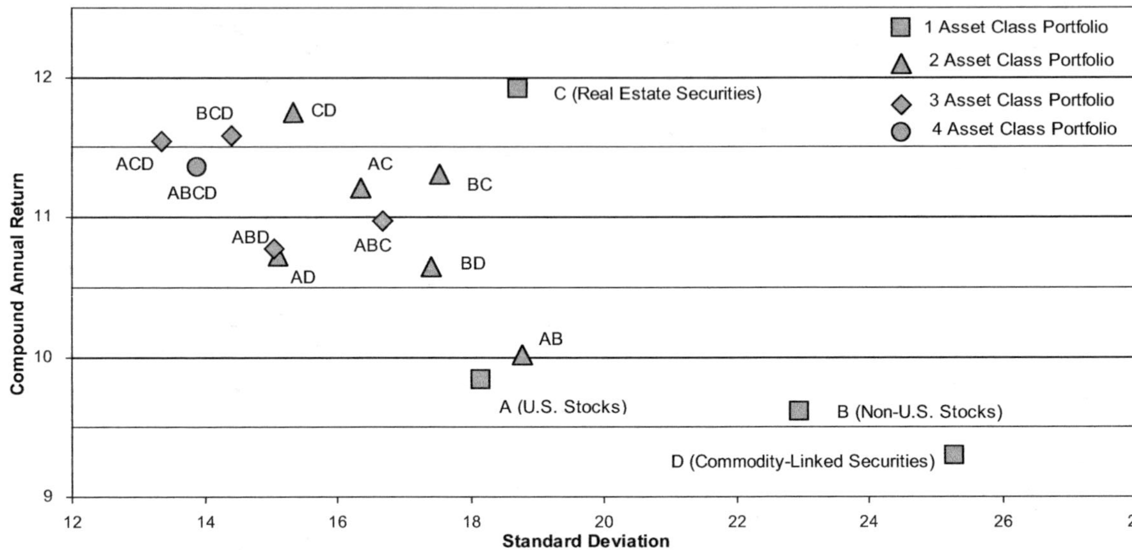

<u>Single-Asset-Class Portfolios</u>

A – U.S. Stocks (S&P 500 Index)

B – Non-U.S. Stocks (MSCI EAFE Index)

C – Real Estate Securities (FTSE NAREIT Equity REITs Index)

D – Commodity-Linked Securities (S&P GSCI Index)

<u>Two-Asset-Class Portfolios: Equally Allocated, Annually Rebalanced</u>

AB – U.S. Stocks, Non-U.S. Stocks

AC – U.S. Stocks, Real Estate Securities

AD – U.S. Stocks, Commodity-Linked Securities

BC – Non-U.S. Stocks, Real Estate Securities

BD – Non-U.S. Stocks, Commodity-Linked Securities

CD – Real Estate Securities, Commodity-Linked Securities

<u>Three-Asset-Class Portfolios: Equally Allocated, Annually Rebalanced</u>

ABC – U.S. Stocks, Non-U.S. Stocks, Real Estate Securities

ABD – U.S. Stocks, Non-U.S. Stocks, Commodity-Linked Securities

ACD – U.S. Stocks, Real Estate Securities, Commodity-Linked Securities

BCD – Non-U.S. Stocks, Real Estate Securities, Commodity-Linked Securities

<u>Four-Asset-Class Portfolio: Equally Allocated, Annually Rebalanced</u>

ABCD – U.S. Stocks, Non-U.S. Stocks, Real Estate Securities, Commodity-Linked Securities

Source: © Roger C. Gibson, "Asset Allocation and the Rewards of Multiple-Asset-Class Investing," 1998. Updated by author. Data source: Morningstar® Principia® © 2012 Morningstar. All Rights Reserved.

Exhibit 13.4

Growth of $1: Portfolio A (U.S. Stocks) Versus Portfolio ABCD* (Equal Allocation) (1972–2011)

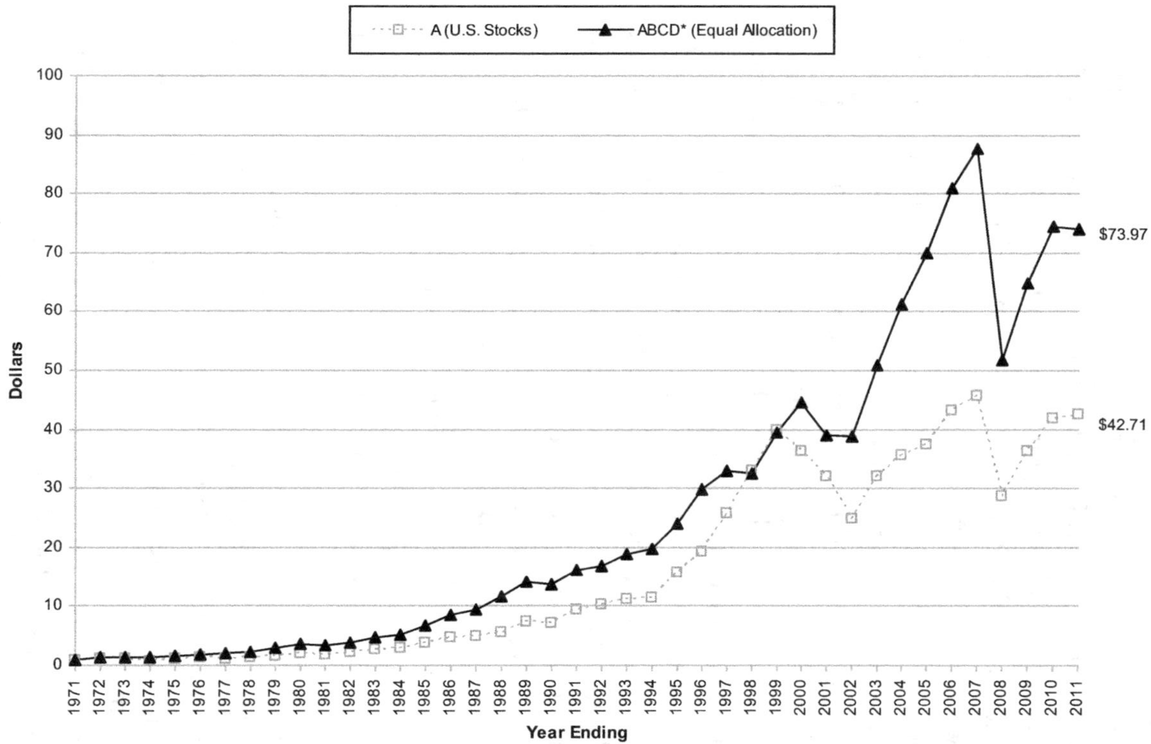

*An annually rebalanced portfolio equally allocated to:

A – U.S. Stocks (S&P 500 Index)

B – Non-U.S. Stocks (MSCI EAFE Index)

C – Real Estate Securities (FTSE NAREIT Equity REITs Index)

D – Commodity-Linked Securities (S&P GSCI Index)

Data source: Morningstar® Principia®,

Exhibit 13.5 compares the patterns of returns of portfolio A (U.S. stocks) with portfolio ABCD. Clearly portfolio ABCD usually has given the investor a smoother ride through time. It also has not been as susceptible to major losses. For example, Exhibit 13.6 compares annual return data for U.S. stocks versus the multiple-asset-class equity portfolio ABCD during three particularly painful U.S. stock bear markets. Over the 1973-1974 period, U.S. stocks were cumulatively down −37.27 percent, compared with a cumulative loss of only −0.56 percent for portfolio ABCD. Results were similar over the more recent 2000–2002 bear market years when U.S. stocks were cumulatively down −37.61 percent, compared with a cumulative loss of only −1.68 percent for portfolio ABCD. In the fourth edition of this book, written prior to the Global Financial Crisis, I commented that the next bear market might be different, and it certainly was. In 2008, U.S. stocks declined −37.00 percent, and portfolio ABCD posted a loss of −41.07 percent. Unlike the two prior bear markets, during the Global Financial Crisis investor fears turned into a panicked selling of all major equity asset classes. As an old Wall Street saying reminds us, "The only things that go up in a panic are the correlations!" Although generally true among equity asset classes, the correlations between high quality bonds and equity asset classes actually dropped during the Global Financial Crisis, as high quality bonds performed extremely well. The panic-driven flight to the perceived safety of high quality bonds underscores the value of diversification into interest-generating investments for most investors. Exhibit 13.6 gives a fuller picture of the value and limitations of multiple-asset-class equity investing. While multiple-asset-class equity investing is less susceptible to major losses, it does not guarantee downside protection in all market environments.

Despite the compelling evidence in support of multiple-asset-class investing, living with the strategy is not always easy. A U.S.-based investor typically will have a U.S. stock market index like the widely reported Dow Jones Industrial Average or the S&P 500 as his frame of reference for evaluating investment performance. During periods when

Exhibit 13.5

Portfolio A (U.S. Stocks) Versus Portfolio ABCD* (Equal Allocation) (1972–2011)

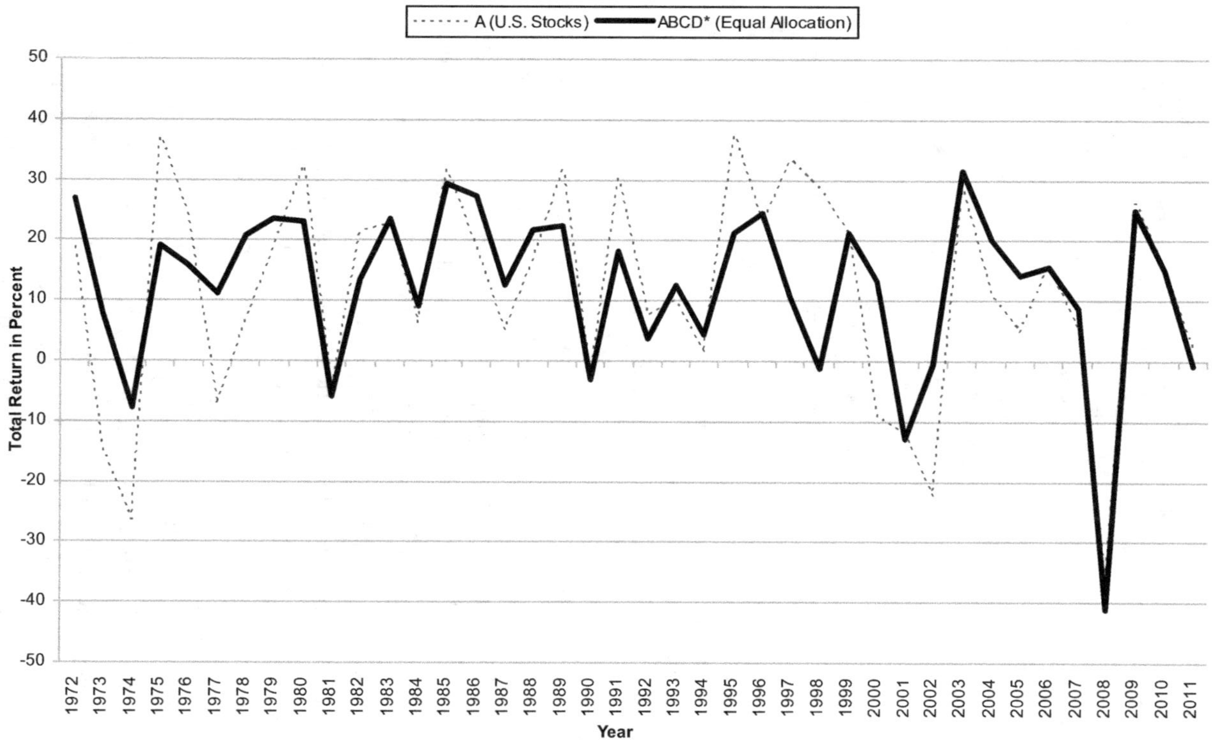

*An annually rebalanced portfolio equally allocated to:

A – U.S. Stocks (S&P 500 Index)

B – Non-U.S. Stocks (MSCI EAFE Index)

C – Real Estate Securities (FTSE NAREIT Equity REITs Index)

D – Commodity-Linked Securities (S&P GSCI Index)

Data source: Morningstar® Principia®, © 2012 Morningstar. All Rights Reserved.

Exhibit 13.6
U.S. Stock Bear Markets and the Multiple-Asset-Class Equity Portfolio

	Portfolio A (U.S. Stocks)	Portfolio ABCD* (Equal Allocation)
1973	-14.69%	7.65%
1974	-26.47%	-7.63%
Cumulative 2-Year Loss	-37.27%	-0.56%
2000	-9.10%	13.26%
2001	-11.89%	-12.78%
2002	-22.10%	-0.47%
Cumulative 3-Year Loss	-37.61%	-1.68%
2008	-37.00%	-41.07%

*An annually rebalanced portfolio equally allocated to:

A – U.S. Stocks (S&P 500 Index)

B – Non-U.S. Stocks (MSCI EAFE Index)

C – Real Estate Securities (FTSE NAREIT Equity REITs Index)

D – Commodity-Linked Securities (S&P GSCI Index)

Data source: Morningstar® Principia®,

U.S. stocks excel, portfolio ABCD understandably will generate returns that lag U.S. stocks as a result of the diversification into asset classes with lower rates of return. Managing this "frame-of-reference" risk involves significant challenges. I believe this risk is the biggest and most dangerous risk facing an investor who follows a multiple-asset-class investment strategy. Both advisors and their clients need to understand that their portfolio allocation decisions determine the amount of frame-of-reference risk that clients incur. More broadly diversified strategies have given investors higher volatility-adjusted returns but also greater frame-of-reference risk.

For example, Exhibit 13.7 compares the total returns of portfolio ABCD with those of portfolio A (U.S. stocks) from 1994 through 2005. This period is particularly interesting to examine when discussing frame-of-reference risk. U.S. stocks outperformed portfolio ABCD by a huge margin from 1995 through 1998. At the time, everyone was in love with U.S. stocks—particularly technology and large company growth stocks.

Exhibit 13.7
Frame-of-Reference Risk

Year	(1) Portfolio ABCD* (Equal Allocation)	(2) Portfolio A (U.S. Stocks)	(3) = (1) – (2) ABCD* minus A
1994	4.46	1.32	3.14
1995	21.18	37.58	-16.40
1996	24.63	22.96	1.67
1997	10.40	33.36	-22.96
1998	-1.09	28.58	-29.67
1999	21.16	21.04	0.12
2000	13.26	-9.10	22.36
2001	-12.78	-11.89	-0.89
2002	-0.47	-22.10	21.63
2003	31.43	28.68	2.75
2004	20.11	10.88	9.23
2005	14.16	4.91	9.25
Standard Deviation	12.71	19.56	
Simple Average Return	12.21	12.19	
Compound Annual Return	11.52	10.52	
Sharpe Ratio	0.65	0.45	
Future Value of $1	$3.70	$3.32	
Compound Return 1994-1999	13.05	23.55	
Compound Return 2000-2005	10.00	-1.13	

*An annually rebalanced portfolio equally allocated to:
A – U.S. Stocks (S&P 500 Index)
B – Non-U.S. Stocks (MSCI EAFE Index)
C – Real Estate Securities (FTSE NAREIT Equity REITs Index)
D – Commodity-Linked Securities (S&P GSCI Index)

Data source: Morningstar® Principia®, © 2012 Morningstar. All Rights Reserved.

Exhibit 13.8 traces the growth of $1 investments for portfolio ABCD and portfolio A over this 12-year period. By the end of 1999, the lead of U.S. stocks appeared to be insurmountable. During the 2000–2002 bear market and subsequent recovery, however, the performance advantage flipped in favor of portfolio ABCD. By the end of 2004, portfolio ABCD had pulled ahead.

The last two lines of Exhibit 13.7 compare the compound annual returns of portfolio ABCD and portfolio A for the first and second halves of this 12-year period. Note that portfolio ABCD had a higher compound annual return in the first half than it did in the second half.

Exhibit 13.8

Frame-of-Reference Risk—Growth of $1: Portfolio ABCD* (Equal Allocation) Versus Portfolio A (U.S. Stocks) (1994–2005)

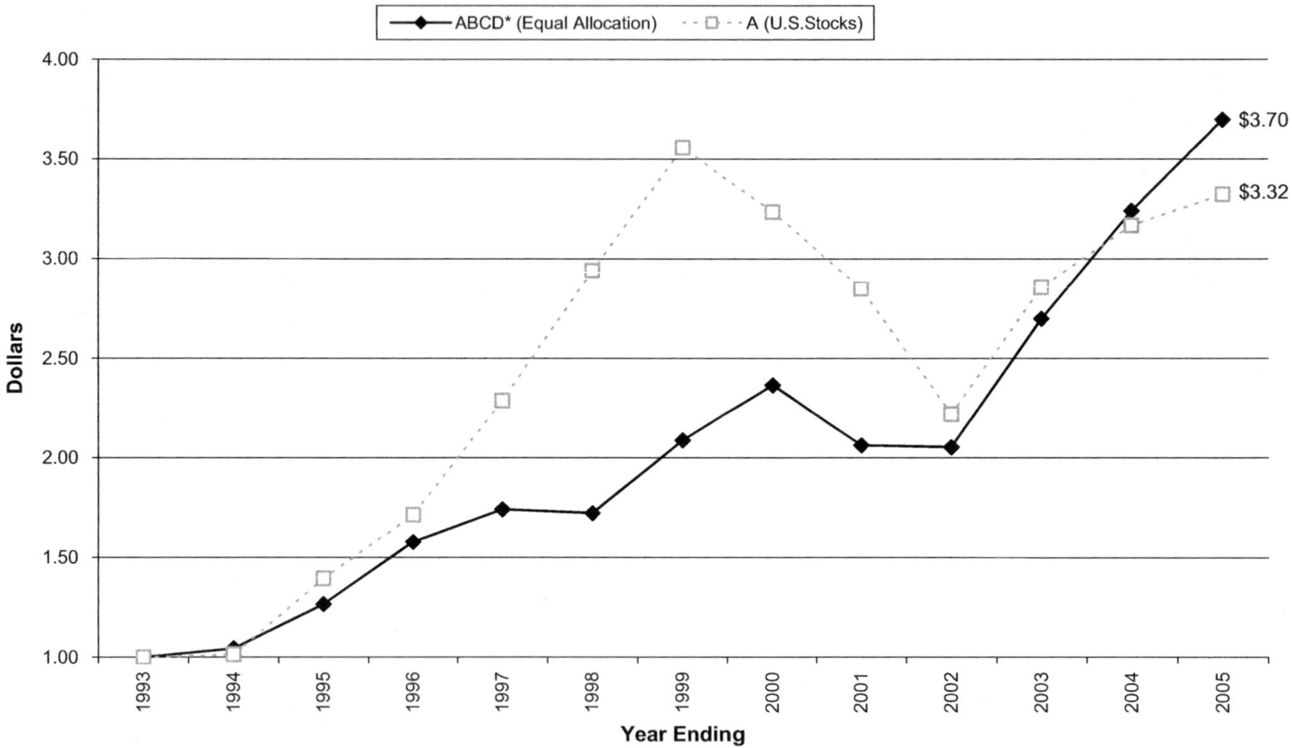

*An annually rebalanced portfolio equally allocated to:

A – U.S. Stocks (S&P 500 Index)

B – Non-U.S. Stocks (MSCI EAFE Index)

C – Real Estate Securities (FTSE NAREIT Equity REITs Index)

D – Commodity-Linked Securities (S&P GSCI Index)

Data source: Morningstar® Principia®,

This difference might lead you to believe that an investor in portfolio ABCD was happier in the 1994–1999 period, when his money compounded annually at 13.05 percent, than in the 2000–2005 period, when he earned 10 percent compounded annually. This definitely was *not* the case. Investors living in the United States will evaluate their equity results relative to the performance of U.S. stocks. Over the 1994–1999 period, the 13.05 percent compound annual return generated by portfolio ABCD paled in comparison to the eye-popping 23.55 percent compound annual return delivered by U.S. stocks (portfolio A). That difference in returns over a prolonged period was the source of mounting dissatisfaction with broadly diversified, multiple-asset-class investment strategies. Investors did not know that a bear market was just around the corner. Frustrated by the relative underperformance of their portfolios, many multiple-asset-class investors abandoned diversification right when they needed it the most. Later, during the 2000–2005 period, an investor in portfolio ABCD was delighted to earn a compound annual return of 10 percent against the backdrop of U.S. stocks losing money at a compound annual rate of −1.13 percent. To get the 10 percent compound annual return, however, that investor needed to have remained invested in portfolio ABCD.

It is interesting to note that when either non-U.S. stocks, real estate securities, or commodity-linked securities have a multiple-year winning streak, investors love diversification. It is only when U.S. stocks outperform the other asset classes for an extended period that investors encounter frame-of-reference risk, and diversification undeservedly gets a bad reputation. The multiple-asset-class equity investor is sometimes ahead of U.S. stocks and sometimes behind. He is at risk of abandoning the strategy during prolonged periods when his performance lags that of U.S. stocks, as occurred toward the end of the 1990s. On the other hand, he is also at risk of expecting too much from the multiple-asset-class strategy based on extended periods when his performance is significantly ahead of U.S. stocks, as occurred in the ensuing bear market and subsequent recovery.

A multiple-asset-class investor needs a longer time perspective to form realistic performance expectations. By accepting a pattern of returns that differs from that of U.S. stocks, the multiple-asset-class investor expects to reduce the volatility of his returns, which in turn contributes to a potentially higher long-term return. For example, note in Exhibit 13.7 that the simple average returns for portfolio ABCD and portfolio A were nearly identical over the 1994–2005 period. Portfolio ABCD, however, had a significantly lower standard deviation. As a result of that lower volatility, portfolio ABCD had a compound annual return a full percentage point higher than portfolio A. Although teaching illustrations typically do not work out this neatly, Exhibits 13.7 and 13.8 illustrate the challenges involved with frame-of-reference risk and the source of the superior long-term performance expectations that accompany multiple-asset-class investing.

Managing Frame-of-Reference Risk

In our firm's work with clients, we use a variety of illustrations to help our clients understand and manage this risk. Long-term investment success requires disciplined execution of the asset allocation strategy through widely varying market environments. If we can successfully inoculate clients against frame-of-reference risk, we will eliminate a major cause of strategy abandonment and increase the likelihood that they will safely realize their financial goals.

Sometimes a new client asks, "Does diversification really work?" I answer, "Yes, it works. But you actually may be asking a different question: That is, will you *like* diversification? The answer to that question is that sometimes you will, and sometimes you won't." I show Exhibit 13.9 to the client and say that we are looking at the year-end performance of four different asset classes W, X, Y, and Z. The returns range from a high of 29 percent to a low of –15 percent. If an investor had an equal allocation across those four asset classes, she would have earned an 8 percent rate of return. The above-average returns of W and X offset the below-average returns of Y and Z. Diversification worked. If I ask a client

Exhibit 13.9

Asset Class	Total Return
W	29%
X	16%
Y	2%
Z	-15%
Average	8%

how she feels when she looks at the relative performance of W, X, Y, and Z, she usually does not have much of a feeling one way or the other.

I then show her Exhibit 13.10, which associates specific asset classes with the same returns. Again, diversification works. When I ask the client if she likes what she sees, she usually says, "Yes. I like it. Diversification is a good thing." I then show her Exhibit 13.11, which shows the same return data but with the four asset classes in reverse order. But this time, when I ask the client if she likes what she sees, I often get a different response: "No. I don't like it." In this scenario, the client perceives

Exhibit 13.10

Asset Class	Total Return
Commodity-Linked Securities	29%
Real Estate Securities	16%
Non-U.S. Stocks	2%
U.S. Stocks	-15%
Average	8%

Exhibit 13.11

Asset Class	Total Return
U.S. Stocks	29%
Non-U.S. Stocks	16%
Real Estate Securities	2%
Commodity-Linked Securities	-15%
Average	8%

diversification as having impaired her portfolio performance. This simple exercise quickly shows the client that she instinctively benchmarks her portfolio's performance against the frame of reference of U.S. stocks. The goal is to move the client more toward the dispassionate response generated by Exhibit 13.9—a goal that is easier said than done.

All major equity asset classes have good times and bad times. The periods of underperformance and overperformance can persist for years. Exhibit 13.12 compares the performance of five equity portfolios: portfolio A (U.S. stocks), portfolio B (non-U.S. stocks), portfolio C (real estate securities), portfolio D (commodity-linked securities), and portfolio ABCD (an equally weighted, annually rebalanced portfolio comprised of all four equity asset classes). The top half of the table compares the performance of these portfolios over the 40-year period 1972–2011. In each row, the best performance statistic is boldface and shaded. For example, portfolio C (real estate securities) had the highest compound annual return and future value of $1. Portfolio ABCD, however, had the lowest standard deviation and the best Sharpe ratio and underperformed portfolio C by only 56 basis points.

The lower half of Exhibit 13.12 compares the compound annual returns of these five portfolios by 10-year subperiods. It is interesting to note that we have four 10-year subperiods shown in the table, and each asset class took a turn as the best-performing asset class in one of

Exhibit 13.12

Performance Statistics (1972–2011)

Entire Period

1972 – 2011	Portfolio A U.S. Stocks		Portfolio B Non-U.S. Stocks		Portfolio C Real Estate Securities		Portfolio D Commodity-Linked Securities		Portfolio ABCD* Equal Allocation	
	Return[1]	Rank	Return[1]	Rank	Return[1]	Rank	Return[1]	Rank	Return[1]	Rank
Compound Annual Return	9.84%	3	9.61%	4	**11.92%**	**1**	9.30%	5	11.36%	2
Future Value of $1	$42.71		$39.28		**$90.42**		$35.05		$73.97	
Standard Deviation	18.16%		22.96%		18.72%		25.30%		**13.88%**	
Sharpe Ratio	0.31		0.27		0.41		0.26		**0.47**	

By Ten-Year Sub-Period

Sub-Period	Portfolio A U.S. Stocks		Portfolio B Non-U.S. Stocks		Portfolio C Real Estate Securities		Portfolio D Commodity-Linked Securities		Portfolio ABCD* Equal Allocation	
	Return[1]	Rank	Return[1]	Rank	Return[1]	Rank	Return[1]	Rank	Return[1]	Rank
1972 – 1981	6.50%	5	10.62%	4	11.82%	3	**15.47%**	**1**	12.85%	2
1982 – 1991	17.59%	2	**18.50%**	**1**	14.06%	5	14.59%	4	17.06%	3
1992 – 2001	**12.94%**	**1**	4.76%	4	11.63%	2	2.11%	5	9.18%	3
2002 – 2011	2.92%	5	5.12%	4	**10.20%**	**1**	5.64%	3	6.62%	2
# of below-average returns	2		3		1		2		**0**	

[1]Compound Annual Return

Best performance numbers are in boldface and shaded.

*An annually rebalanced portfolio equally allocated to:

A – U.S. Stocks (S&P 500 Index)

B – Non-U.S. Stocks (MSCI EAFE Index)

C – Real Estate Securities (FTSE NAREIT Equity REITs Index)

D – Commodity-Linked Securities (S&P GSCI Index)

Data source: Morningstar® Principia®,

the subperiods. In the first 10-year subperiod, the commodity-linked securities asset class was in first place. Non-U.S. stocks had the highest compound annual return in the next subperiod. U.S. stocks won in the third subperiod, which included the strong returns of the late 1990s. In the most recent 10-year subperiod, real estate securities had the advantage. As we look down the column of 10-year returns for any asset class, we see an undesirable tendency to swing between boom and bust. For example, U.S. stocks did very well in the second and third subperiods but performed poorly in the 10-year subperiods ending with 1981 and 2011. Looking across the rows, we also see boom and bust variations in performance across the asset classes. In this case, however, the wide variations in performance are a good thing that the multiple-asset-class investor can advantageously harness to reduce portfolio volatility and improve longer-term returns. Unlike the individual asset classes, portfolio ABCD delivered a more consistent equity return from subperiod to subperiod and, in the process, earned a return for the entire period that was within 56 basis points of the asset class with the highest compound annual return—real estate securities. When evaluated in terms of volatility-adjusted returns, portfolio ABCD is the best, as evidenced by its Sharpe ratio.

Over any given investment horizon, each year's portfolio return is as important as any other's.[2] Investors, however, psychologically attach more significance to their recent investment experience. As a result, many U.S. investors found it increasingly difficult to follow the discipline of a multiple-asset-class investment approach during the multiple-year period of superior U.S. stock performance toward the end of the 1990s.

I have used the blindfolded exercise in Exhibit 13.13 to encourage clients to give more equal psychological weight to each year's portfolio return. This exhibit masks the identity of all five equity portfolios and then presents their annual returns ranked low to high. This format permits an easy comparison of the range of results for each portfolio, as well as the frequency and severity of negative returns. The client is told that, over the last 40 years, each of the five portfolios generated each of the returns listed for it but in a different order than is shown.[3] When

Exhibit 13.13
Annual Returns Ranked Low to High (1972–2011)

Year	Portfolio A	Portfolio B	Portfolio C	Portfolio D	Portfolio E
1	-37.00	-43.06	-37.73	-46.49	-41.07
2	-26.47	-23.20	-21.40	-35.75	-12.78
3	-22.10	-22.15	-17.50	-31.93	-7.63
4	-14.69	-21.21	-15.69	-23.01	-5.74
5	-11.89	-15.66	-15.52	-17.22	-3.14
6	-9.10	-14.17	-15.35	-15.09	-1.09
7	-7.16	-13.96	-4.62	-14.07	-0.63
8	-4.92	-11.85	-3.64	-12.33	-0.47
9	-3.10	-11.73	3.17	-11.92	3.70
10	1.32	-1.03	3.82	-6.13	4.46
11	2.11	-0.86	6.00	-1.18	7.65
12	4.91	2.06	8.01	1.05	8.53
13	5.25	3.74	8.28	2.04	9.03
14	5.49	6.18	8.84	4.42	10.40
15	6.27	6.36	10.34	5.29	11.27
16	6.57	7.87	12.16	9.03	12.58
17	7.62	8.06	13.49	10.01	12.59
18	10.08	8.21	13.93	10.37	13.26
19	10.88	10.80	14.59	11.08	13.46
20	15.06	11.55	15.27	11.56	14.16
21	15.79	11.63	19.10	13.48	15.06
22	16.61	12.50	19.16	16.26	15.66
23	18.61	14.02	19.30	17.28	15.84
24	18.67	19.43	19.66	20.33	18.14
25	18.99	20.33	20.26	20.72	19.10
26	21.04	20.70	20.93	23.77	20.11
27	21.55	24.43	21.60	25.55	20.71
28	22.56	24.61	22.42	27.93	21.16
29	22.96	24.93	24.37	29.08	21.18
30	23.93	26.86	26.37	31.61	21.66
31	26.46	27.30	27.95	32.07	22.40
32	28.58	28.59	27.99	32.67	23.10
33	28.68	32.46	30.64	33.81	23.52
34	30.47	32.94	31.58	33.92	23.62
35	31.69	34.30	35.06	38.28	24.63
36	31.73	37.10	35.27	39.51	25.10
37	32.50	37.60	35.70	40.92	26.76
38	33.36	39.17	35.86	42.43	27.45
39	37.23	56.72	37.13	49.74	29.39
40	37.58	69.94	47.59	74.96	31.43
Number of Negative Years	9	11	8	11	8
Number of 20+% Years	15	16	16	17	15
Standard Deviation	18.16	22.96	18.72	25.30	13.88
Sharpe Ratio	0.31	0.27	0.41	0.26	0.47

Data source: Morningstar® Principia®, © 2012 Morningstar. All Rights Reserved.

asked which portfolio they would prefer to own, clients almost always choose portfolio E:

1. It generated the best volatility-adjusted returns as evidenced by its Sharpe ratio.
2. It had the least severe negative return years.
3. Its volatility level was by far the lowest, as evidenced by its standard deviation.

Exhibit 13.14

Annual Returns in Chronological Order (1972–2011)

Year	Portfolio A U.S. Stocks	Portfolio B Non-U.S. Stocks	Portfolio C Real Estate Securities	Portfolio D Commodity-Linked Securities	Portfolio E ABCD Equal Allocation
1972	18.99	37.60	8.01	**42.43**	26.76
1973	-14.69	-14.17	-15.52	**74.96**	7.65
1974	-26.47	-22.15	-21.40	**39.51**	-7.63
1975	**37.23**	37.10	19.30	-17.22	19.10
1976	23.93	3.74	**47.59**	-11.92	15.84
1977	-7.16	19.43	**22.42**	10.37	11.27
1978	6.57	**34.30**	10.34	31.61	20.71
1979	18.61	6.18	**35.86**	33.81	23.62
1980	**32.50**	24.43	24.37	11.08	23.10
1981	-4.92	-1.03	**6.00**	-23.01	-5.74
1982	21.55	-0.86	**21.60**	11.56	13.46
1983	22.56	24.61	**30.64**	16.26	23.52
1984	6.27	7.86	**20.93**	1.05	9.03
1985	31.73	**56.72**	19.10	10.01	29.39
1986	18.67	**69.94**	19.16	2.04	27.45
1987	5.25	**24.93**	-3.64	23.77	12.58
1988	16.61	**28.59**	13.49	27.93	21.66
1989	31.69	10.80	8.84	**38.28**	22.40
1990	-3.10	-23.20	-15.35	**29.08**	-3.14
1991	30.47	12.50	**35.70**	-6.13	18.14
1992	7.62	-11.85	**14.59**	4.42	3.70
1993	10.08	**32.94**	19.66	-12.33	12.59
1994	1.32	**8.06**	3.17	5.29	4.46
1995	**37.58**	11.55	15.27	20.33	21.18
1996	22.96	6.36	**35.27**	33.92	24.63
1997	**33.36**	2.06	20.26	-14.07	10.40
1998	**28.58**	20.33	-17.50	-35.75	-1.09
1999	21.04	27.30	-4.62	**40.92**	21.16
2000	-9.10	-13.96	26.37	**49.74**	13.26
2001	-11.89	-21.21	**13.93**	-31.93	-12.78
2002	-22.10	-15.66	3.82	**32.07**	-0.47
2003	28.68	**39.17**	37.13	20.72	31.43
2004	10.88	20.70	**31.58**	17.28	20.11
2005	4.91	14.02	12.16	**25.55**	14.16
2006	15.79	26.86	**35.06**	-15.09	15.66
2007	5.49	11.63	-15.69	**32.67**	8.53
2008	**-37.00**	-43.06	-37.73	-46.49	-41.07
2009	26.46	**32.46**	27.99	13.48	25.10
2010	15.06	8.21	**27.95**	9.03	15.06
2011	2.11	-11.73	**8.28**	-1.18	-0.63
Number of Negative Years	9	11	8	11	8
Number of 20+% Years	15	16	16	17	15
Standard Deviation	18.16	22.96	18.72	25.30	13.88
Simple Average Return	11.45	12.04	13.61	12.35	12.36
Compound Annual Return	9.84	9.61	11.92	9.30	11.36
Sharpe Ratio	0.31	0.27	0.41	0.26	0.47
Future Value of $1	$42.71	$39.28	$90.42	$35.05	$73.97
Highest Annual Return Frequency	6	9	15	10	0

Highest annual returns are boldface and shaded.

Data source: Morningstar® Principia®, © 2012 Morningstar. All Rights Reserved.

By intentionally avoiding a chronological presentation of annual return data, the client cannot fall prey to frame-of-reference risk. Now we remove the blindfold and place the returns for each portfolio back into chronological order in Exhibit 13.14. Portfolios A, B, C, D, and E are, respectively, U.S. stocks, non-U.S. stocks, real estate securities, commodity-linked securities, and finally an annually rebalanced, equally weighted allocation of all four equity asset classes. Despite a clear vote in favor of the equally weighted equity portfolio E, clients still will tend to recoil from their choice when they compare the returns of this portfolio with those for U.S. stocks over the period from 1995 through 1998.

Investors evaluate their investment results against some backdrop or frame of reference, and for investors in the United States, that backdrop is the U.S. stock market. Frame of reference is reinforced every time an investor picks up a newspaper or listens to the evening news. Most of what he hears is oriented toward the U.S. economy and capital markets. The stock market report will talk about the Dow Jones Industrial Average, not the performance of a globally diversified portfolio. Frame of reference also is reinforced in investors' conversations with their friends at cocktail parties or over a round of golf. For investors who have a more traditional portfolio composed of U.S. stocks and bonds, what they hear on the evening news corresponds closely to the performance of their portfolio. The broadly diversified, multiple-asset-class investor, however, is still in the minority. His portfolio will not behave in the same way as the portfolios of his golfing buddies who do not follow a strategy with the same breadth and degree of diversification. If the multiple-asset-class investor knows that the U.S. stock market has been rising sharply over the past year, but his portfolio has not kept up due to diversification into other asset classes with lower rates of return, he experiences a painful dissonance between his investment performance and what he hears going on around him. This dissonance is frame-of-reference risk. Advisors should not underestimate the distress it causes investors.

Of course, at times the multiple-asset-class investor is ahead of the game, but there is not as much pleasure in being ahead as there is pain in being behind. It is worth repeating a comment made to me by a client: "I would rather follow an inferior strategy that wins when my friends are winning and loses when my friends are losing, than follow a superior long-term strategy that at times results in my losing when my friends are winning." Over the 1995 through 1998 period of dominance of U.S. stocks, a Japanese investor following a globally diversified, multiple-asset-class investment strategy would

Exhibit 13.15
Equity Asset Allocations

Equity Asset Classes	Greater Equity Diversification	Moderate Equity Diversification	Limited Equity Diversification
U.S. Stocks	30%	50%	70%
Non-U.S. Stocks	30%	22%	14%
Real Estate Securities	20%	14%	8%
Commodity-Linked Securities	20%	14%	8%
Totals	100%	100%	100%

have been delighted with the same investment results that a U.S.-based investor found so difficult to accept. Same results, same time period—different frame of reference![4]

As we discussed in Chapter 10, the equally weighted equity allocation is a teaching illustration. I do not recommend it for clients who live in the United States. Instead, I generally suggest that the U.S. stocks asset class be most heavily weighted, with smaller allocations to non-U.S. stocks, real estate securities, and commodity-linked securities. The reasons are psychological and behavioral: Investors will tolerate more easily the underperformance of familiar, widely held asset classes, and I therefore give larger allocations to these asset classes. Investors will be less tolerant of the underperformance of unfamiliar, less widely held asset classes, and so I give these asset classes smaller allocations. Exhibit 13.15 shows the allocations for three new equity portfolio structures. The "greater equity diversification" structure has the greatest degree of diversification across the four asset classes, with 30 percent allocated to U.S. stocks and the remaining 70 percent allocated across the other three asset classes. By comparison, the "limited equity diversification" structure has the least degree of diversification, with 70 percent of the portfolio concentrated in U.S. stocks and the balance diversified across the other three asset classes.

Exhibits 13.16 and 13.17 show the year-by-year patterns of returns and growth of a $1 investment for each of these three portfolios compared with that of U.S. stocks. Not surprisingly, increasing the percentage commitment to U.S. stocks causes the corresponding

Exhibit 13.16

Degrees of Equity Diversification (1972–2011)

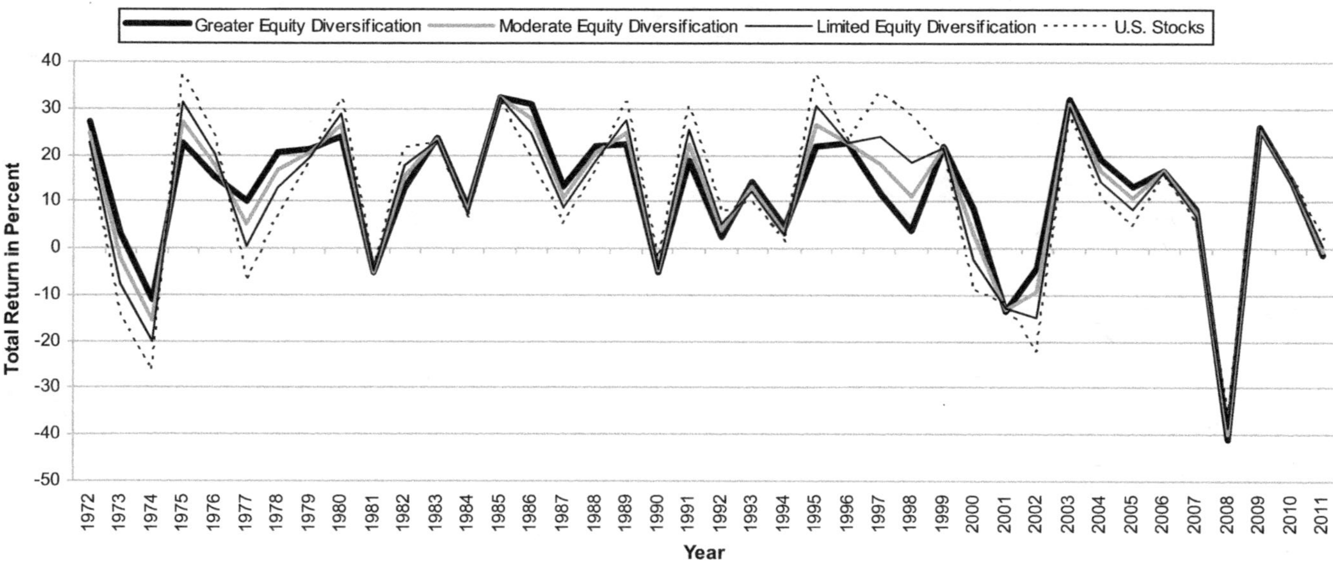

Exhibit 13.17

Growth of $1: Degrees of Equity Diversification (1972–2011)

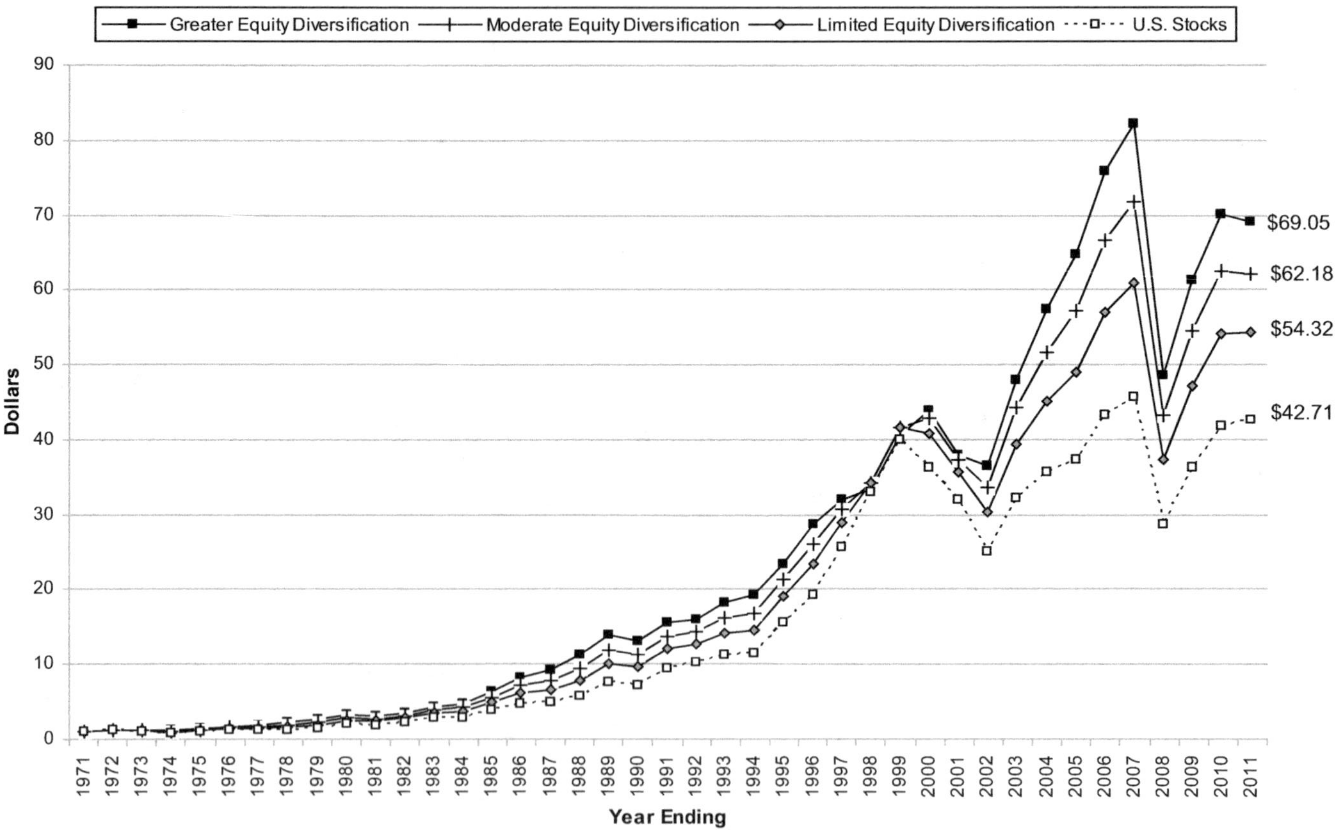

Data source: Morningstar® Principia®, © 2012 Morningstar. All Rights Reserved.

patterns of returns to approach that of U.S. stocks. This movement reduces frame-of-reference risk, but it deteriorates portfolio volatility-adjusted returns as a result of the lesser degree of diversification. Clients must deal with this trade-off: How much pain of dissimilarity in patterns of returns (i.e., how much frame-of-reference risk) can they bear in exchange for an expected improvement in long-term volatility-adjusted returns?

Exhibit 13.18 provides performance statistics for each of the portfolios described in Exhibit 13.15. Note that, as we move from the equally weighted equity allocation on the left to U.S. stocks on the right, the Sharpe ratios steadily decline, indicating the deterioration in volatility-adjusted returns. This decline is due primarily to the increasing level of portfolio volatility, as indicated by the rising standard deviation statistics. Exhibit 13.19 shows the total returns of each of the diversified portfolio structures relative to U.S. stocks. The standard deviation statistic at the bottom of each column measures the degree of dissimilarity in patterns of returns for each portfolio relative to U.S. stocks. As such, this standard deviation statistic is a measure of the degree of frame-of-reference risk inherent in each diversified equity allocation. The greater the degree of diversification, the greater the frame-of-reference risk. By comparing the relative returns for each portfolio structure over the period from 1995 through 1998, we can imagine the greater degree of pain experienced by the investor in an equally weighted equity allocation. That pain is the price paid for a pattern of returns that is, on average, much less volatile.

We find no right or wrong answer here, only a trade-off: Better volatility-adjusted expected returns are accompanied by more frame-of-reference risk. The advisor's job is to educate the client regarding the trade-off and provide a menu of portfolio structures with varying degrees of diversification. The client must then make an informed choice. If she chooses a broadly diversified, multiple-asset-class structure, she needs to simultaneously adopt a broadly diversified frame of reference.

Exhibit 13.18
Performance Statistics (1972–2011)

Year	Equally-Weighted Equity Allocation	Greater Equity Diversification	Moderate Equity Diversification	Limited Equity Diversification	U.S. Stocks
1972	26.76	27.07	24.83	22.59	18.99
1973	7.65	3.23	-2.14	-7.51	-14.69
1974	-7.63	-10.96	-15.57	-20.18	-26.47
1975	19.10	22.72	27.07	31.42	37.23
1976	15.84	15.44	17.78	20.13	23.93
1977	11.27	10.24	5.29	0.33	-7.16
1978	20.71	20.65	16.70	12.76	6.57
1979	23.62	21.37	20.42	19.47	18.61
1980	23.10	24.17	26.59	29.01	32.50
1981	-5.74	-5.19	-5.07	-4.95	-4.92
1982	13.46	12.84	15.23	17.62	21.55
1983	23.52	23.53	23.26	22.99	22.56
1984	9.03	8.64	7.94	7.25	6.27
1985	29.39	32.36	32.42	32.48	31.73
1986	27.45	30.82	27.69	24.56	18.67
1987	12.58	13.08	10.93	8.78	5.25
1988	21.66	21.84	20.39	18.94	16.61
1989	22.40	22.17	24.82	27.46	31.69
1990	-3.14	-5.14	-4.73	-4.32	-3.10
1991	18.14	18.81	22.12	25.44	30.47
1992	3.70	2.53	3.86	5.20	7.62
1993	12.59	14.37	13.31	12.25	10.08
1994	4.46	4.51	3.62	2.73	1.32
1995	21.18	21.86	26.32	30.77	37.58
1996	24.63	22.63	22.57	22.50	22.96
1997	10.40	11.86	18.00	24.14	33.36
1998	-1.09	4.02	11.31	18.59	28.58
1999	21.16	21.76	21.61	21.45	21.04
2000	13.26	8.30	3.03	-2.24	-9.10
2001	-12.78	-13.53	-13.13	-12.73	-11.89
2002	-0.47	-4.15	-9.47	-14.79	-22.10
2003	31.43	31.93	31.06	30.19	28.68
2004	20.11	19.25	16.83	14.42	10.88
2005	14.16	13.22	10.82	8.42	4.91
2006	15.66	16.79	16.60	16.41	15.79
2007	8.53	8.53	7.68	6.83	5.49
2008	-41.07	-40.86	-39.76	-38.67	-37.00
2009	25.10	25.97	26.18	26.38	26.46
2010	15.06	14.38	14.51	14.65	15.06
2011	-0.63	-1.47	-0.53	0.40	2.11
Standard Deviation	13.88	14.44	14.93	15.98	18.16
Simple Average Return	12.36	12.24	12.01	11.78	11.45
Compound Annual Return	11.36	11.17	10.88	10.50	9.84
Future Value of $1	$73.97	$69.05	$62.18	$54.32	$42.71
Sharpe Ratio	0.47	0.44	0.42	0.38	0.31

Data source: Morningstar® Principia®, © 2012 Morningstar. All Rights Reserved.

If the advisor has guided the client successfully to this point, he has accomplished much. The advisor and his client agree about how and why the capital markets behave as they do. The client has developed realistic investment expectations and a reasonable investment objective based on a broad portfolio allocation between interest-generating investments and equity investments that is consistent with her time horizon and capacity to tolerate volatility. She understands

Exhibit 13.19
Total Returns Relative to U.S. Stocks (1972–2011)

Year	Equally-Weighted Equity Allocation Minus U.S. Stocks	Greater Equity Diversification Minus U.S. Stocks	Moderate Equity Diversification Minus U.S. Stocks	Limited Equity Diversification Minus U.S. Stocks
1972	7.77	8.08	5.84	3.60
1973	22.34	17.92	12.55	7.18
1974	18.84	15.51	10.90	6.29
1975	-18.13	-14.52	-10.16	-5.81
1976	-8.10	-8.50	-6.15	-3.80
1977	18.43	17.40	12.45	7.49
1978	14.14	14.08	10.13	6.19
1979	5.01	2.76	1.81	0.86
1980	-9.41	-8.33	-5.91	-3.49
1981	-0.82	-0.27	-0.15	-0.03
1982	-8.09	-8.71	-6.32	-3.93
1983	0.96	0.97	0.70	0.43
1984	2.76	2.37	1.67	0.98
1985	-2.34	0.63	0.69	0.75
1986	8.78	12.15	9.02	5.89
1987	7.33	7.83	5.68	3.53
1988	5.05	5.23	3.78	2.33
1989	-9.29	-9.52	-6.87	-4.23
1990	-0.04	-2.04	-1.63	-1.22
1991	-12.34	-11.67	-8.35	-5.03
1992	-3.93	-5.09	-3.76	-2.42
1993	2.51	4.29	3.23	2.17
1994	3.14	3.19	2.30	1.41
1995	-16.40	-15.72	-11.27	-6.81
1996	1.67	-0.33	-0.39	-0.46
1997	-22.96	-21.50	-15.36	-9.22
1998	-29.67	-24.56	-17.27	-9.99
1999	0.12	0.72	0.57	0.41
2000	22.36	17.40	12.13	6.86
2001	-0.89	-1.64	-1.24	-0.84
2002	21.63	17.95	12.63	7.31
2003	2.75	3.25	2.38	1.51
2004	9.23	8.37	5.95	3.54
2005	9.25	8.31	5.91	3.51
2006	-0.13	1.00	0.81	0.62
2007	3.04	3.04	2.19	1.34
2008	-4.07	-3.86	-2.76	-1.67
2009	-1.36	-0.49	-0.28	-0.08
2010	0.00	-0.68	-0.55	-0.41
2011	-2.74	-3.58	-2.64	-1.71
Standard Deviation	11.79	10.48	7.45	4.43

Data source: Morningstar® Principia®, © 2012 Morningstar. All Rights Reserved.

the benefits of multiple-asset-class diversification and has determined the breadth and degree of her portfolio's diversification. Although the work was significant, the time commitment required of the client was not extraordinary. We now are ready to design the final portfolio structure.

Chapter 14

Portfolio Management

Don't fight forces, use them.

—*R. Buckminster Fuller (1895–1983),* Shelter, *1932*

Clients love to make money, and they hate to lose it. The most important conclusion of this book is that broad portfolio diversification among multiple asset classes in the long run will deliver better volatility-adjusted returns than traditional approaches that utilize fewer asset classes. The tendency of most money managers to underperform the market underscores the value of the performance advantages gained from a more broadly diversified approach. Remarkably, much of the improvement in portfolio performance flows from the simple *decision* to utilize a broader array of asset classes. Contrast this with improvements in portfolio performance that require the exercise of superior management *skill*. Although they are undoubtedly rarer than most people realize, money managers with truly superior skill exist, and their contributions to improved portfolio performance can be significant. Because of the inherent difficulty in conclusively identifying these managers, however, superior skill should not be relied upon as the driving force behind investment strategy. Rather, strategy should be grounded in realistic capital market performance expectations and implemented within a disciplined asset allocation framework. If superior skill in security selection adds value within an asset class, this will be the icing on the cake.

We now will cover steps 7 through 10 of the investment management process outlined in Exhibit 14.1. Step 7 describes a *process* for making asset allocation decisions and selecting specific investment positions. Advisors and their clients must consider a variety of issues when evaluating the choices at each level of decision making. The sample portfolios provide concrete illustrations of asset allocation strategies for clients with varying investment time horizons, volatility tolerances, and susceptibilities to frame-of-reference risk.

Step 7. Allocate Assets and Design the Portfolio

Allocate Assets

In Chapter 7, we discussed one of the client's most important investment decisions: the choice of broad portfolio balance between interest-generating investments and equity investments. This decision is the most general, and it determines the portfolio's basic growth path and volatility level. Chapter 10 described the impressive improvements in volatility-adjusted returns that multiple-asset-class equity strategies make possible. Chapter 13 tackled a variety of psychological and behavioral issues that need to be managed successfully in order to keep clients committed to their individually tailored portfolio strategies. These include determining the appropriate breadth and degree of portfolio diversification across different asset classes. Although more broadly diversified portfolios have better volatility-adjusted returns, those advantages come with a price—a pattern of returns that is different from one's customary frame of reference.

Exhibit 14.2 shows a format for progressing from the current cash value of the client's total investment portfolio to a detailed recommended portfolio structure. As the decisions proceed from the most general level to the more detailed levels of decision making, the probable impact of the decisions on long-term portfolio performance declines. Starting from

Exhibit 14.1
Investment Management Process

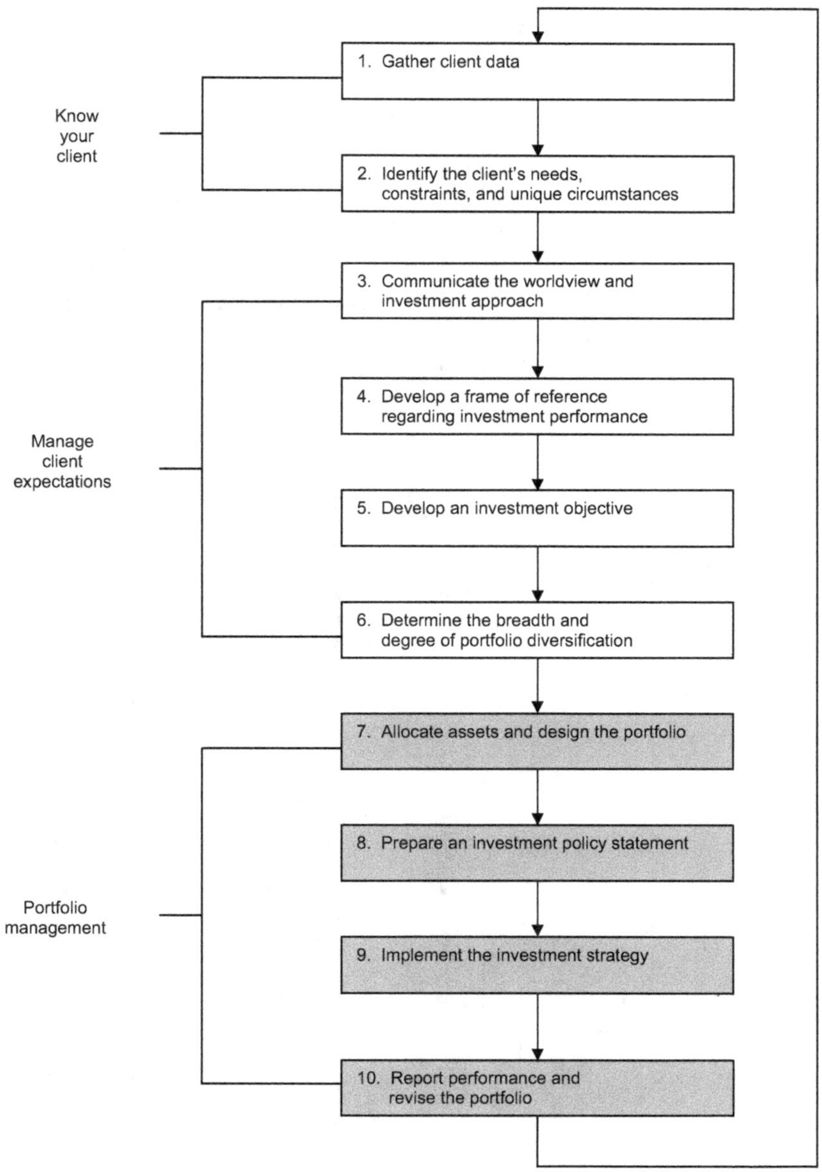

Exhibit 14.2
Investment Portfolio Design Format

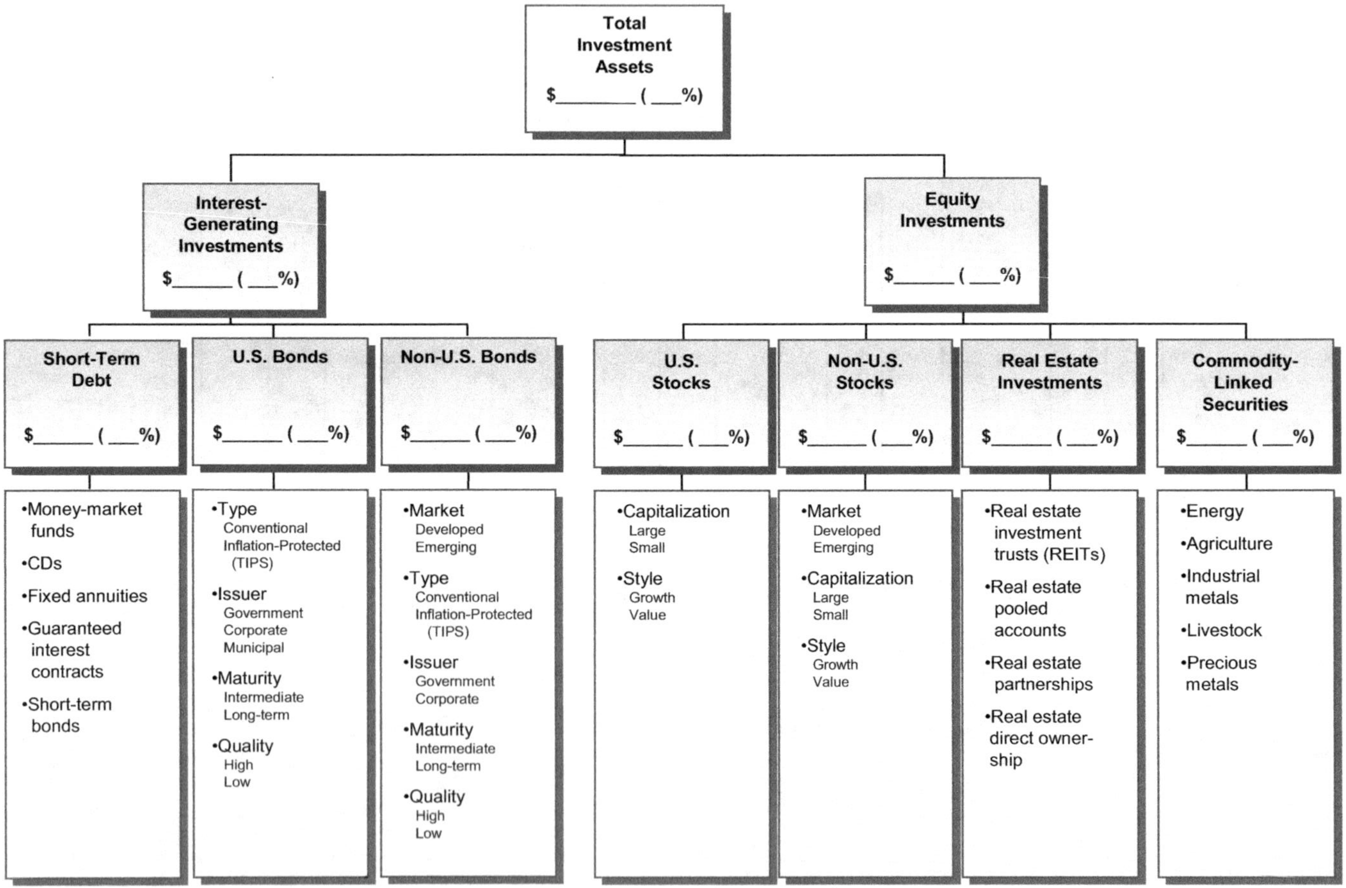

the top, the advisor begins by entering the current cash value of the client's total investment portfolio. Next, the advisor enters the percentages and dollar commitments to interest-generating investments and equity investments based on the client's broad portfolio balance decision, as described in Chapter 7. Once these percentages are set, they generally remain fixed, unless the client's volatility tolerance, investment time horizon, or financial circumstances change substantially.

Subject to the broad portfolio balance decision, the client and advisor then determine an appropriate asset allocation among seven asset classes:

1. Short-term debt investments
2. U.S. bonds
3. Non-U.S. bonds
4. U.S. stocks
5. Non-U.S. stocks
6. Real estate investments
7. Commodity-linked securities

Only after the asset allocation decisions have been made do the advisor and client choose specific investment positions.

I am a strong advocate of client involvement at each of these levels of portfolio design. Indeed, many of these decisions are the nondelegable responsibility of the client. The advisor's role is to point the client in the right direction and provide a frame of reference for improving the quality of the client's decisions.

If these decisions have been thought through with sufficient care and understanding, the resulting strategic asset allocation will be an individually tailored, all-weather investment strategy that will satisfy two criteria:

1. Given the client's assets, cash flows, investment time horizon, and financial goals, the strategy makes good investment sense. That is, in the informed judgment of a knowledgeable

investment professional, the portfolio's asset allocation is matched well to the client's goals and financial circumstances.

2. The strategy's pattern of returns (either volatility level or performance relative to the U.S. markets) will not cause the client to abandon the strategy during the widely varying market environments he is likely to experience in the future.

Both these criteria are essential for investment success. Good investment consulting is a blend of both art and science. Criterion 1 above is mostly science. For example, the advisor can test the portfolio strategy for its likelihood of success by doing a Monte Carlo simulation based on reasonable capital market assumptions, the investment time horizon, and the pattern of anticipated cash flows into and out of the portfolio. Criterion 2 is art—it requires a close working relationship between the client and advisor. The advisor's responsibilities (and greatest opportunities to add value) are to help the client accurately perceive both the risks and opportunities she faces, make informed choices that create the best opportunity for realizing her financial goals, and then, most importantly, encourage her to *stick to the strategy!* The art of good investment consulting requires an advisor to wear several hats: educator, psychologist, and coach.

To clarify the steps involved in determining the client's strategic asset allocation, we will create a matrix of sample portfolios and describe their historical performance attributes. Chapter 7 developed a model for determining the broad portfolio balance between interest-generating investments and equity investments. Exhibit 7.2 described five portfolio choices differentiated in terms of the relative commitments between Treasury bills (as a proxy for interest-generating investments) and U.S. large company stocks (as a proxy for equity investments). Let us consider the broad portfolio balances based on three of these choices:

1. *Portfolio 2:* 70 percent interest-generating investments/ 30 percent equity investments

2. *Portfolio 3:* 50 percent interest-generating investments/ 50 percent equity investments
3. *Portfolio 4:* 30 percent interest-generating investments/ 70 percent equity investments

These options do not cover the entire range of possible broad portfolio balance choices but are representative of the typical range of choices made by clients with varying volatility tolerances and investment time horizons. Each of these three broad portfolio balance choices can be implemented with either a "greater," "moderate," or "limited" degree of equity diversification as described in step 6 of Chapter 13 and summarized in Exhibit 13.15. Thus, there are 9 multiple-asset-class portfolio strategies that accommodate varying degrees of client volatility tolerance and susceptibility to frame-of-reference risk. Exhibit 14.3 shows the strategic asset allocations for these 9 portfolios compared with 3 traditional portfolios constructed exclusively with U.S. stocks, bonds, and Treasury bills. Exhibit 14.4 graphs the historical compound annual returns and standard deviations for these 12 portfolios. In these exhibits, each portfolio has an identifier. For example, "2MOD" identifies a portfolio corresponding to a broad portfolio balance choice of "2" from Exhibit 7.2 (i.e., 70 percent interest-generating investments/30 percent equity investments) with a "moderate" degree of equity diversification, as described in Exhibit 13.15. "3US" identifies a portfolio corresponding to a broad portfolio balance choice of "3" (i.e., 50 percent interest-generating investments/50 percent equity investments) composed entirely of U.S. stocks, bonds, and Treasury bills.

Given what we have learned thus far, the positioning of these portfolios in Exhibit 14.4 is consistent with what we might expect. For example, the number 2 portfolios with 70 percent interest-generating investments/30 percent equity investments lie in the lower left corner of the graph, whereas the number 4 portfolios with the opposite 30/70 portfolio balance lie in the upper right part of the graph. As we move

Exhibit 14.3
Strategic Asset Allocations

	Investment Objective (Chapter 13, Step 5)											
	Low Portfolio Volatility with Low Total Return				Medium Total Return with Medium Portfolio Volatility				High Total Return with High Portfolio Volatility			
Portfolio Balance Choice from Exhibit 7.2	2	2	2	2	3	3	3	3	4	4	4	4
Broad Portfolio Balance:												
Interest-Generating Investments	70	70	70	70	50	50	50	50	30	30	30	30
Equity Investments	30	30	30	30	50	50	50	50	70	70	70	70
Total	100	100	100	100	100	100	100	100	100	100	100	100
Diversification Degree Choice (Chapter 13, Step 6)	Greater	Moderate	Limited	U.S. Only	Greater	Moderate	Limited	U.S. Only	Greater	Moderate	Limited	U.S. Only
Portfolio Identifier for Exhibits 14.4 and 14.5	2GR	2MOD	2LTD	2US	3GR	3MOD	3LTD	3US	4GR	4MOD	4LTD	4US
Strategic Asset Allocation:												
Short-Term Debt	50	50	50	50	30	30	30	30	10	10	10	10
U.S. Bonds	12	14	16	20	12	14	16	20	12	14	16	20
Non-U.S. Bonds	8	6	4	0	8	6	4	0	8	6	4	0
U.S. Stocks	9	15	21	30	15	25	35	50	21	35	49	70
Non-U.S. Stocks	9	7	4	0	15	11	7	0	21	15	9	0
Real Estate Securities	6	4	3	0	10	7	4	0	14	10	6	0
Commodity-Linked Securities	6	4	2	0	10	7	4	0	14	10	6	0
Total	100	100	100	100	100	100	100	100	100	100	100	100

Exhibit 14.4

Historical Asset Allocation Performance (1973*–2011)

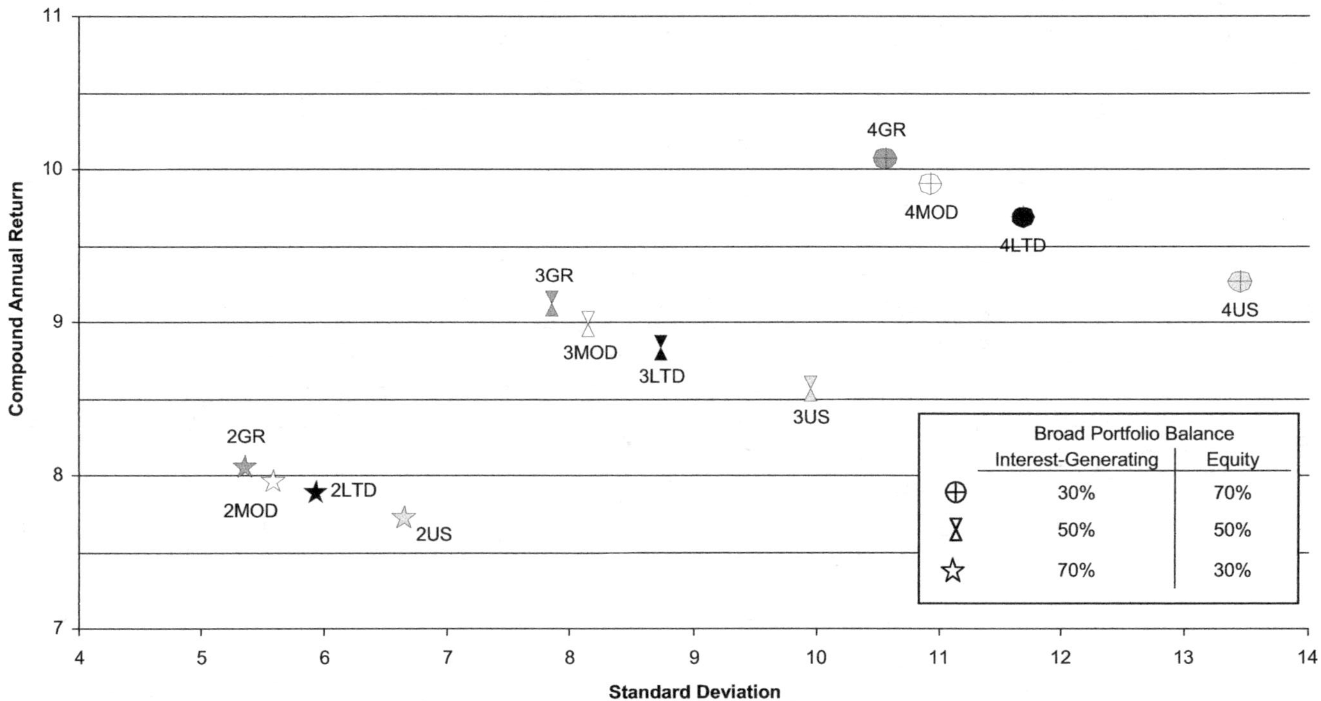

The compound annual returns and standard deviations of these asset allocations are based on an annually rebalanced weighted average composite of representative total return indices for the asset classes.

*1973 is the earliest year for which annual total return data is available for each of the asset classes.

Source: © Roger C. Gibson, 2011. Data source: Morningstar® Principia®, © 2012 Morningstar. All Rights Reserved.

from portfolio structures that are built entirely with U.S. asset classes through limited to moderate and, finally, greater degrees of portfolio diversification, volatility levels decline significantly and compound annual returns increase.[1]

This menu of portfolio structures presents us with some interesting alternatives. Let's start with the portfolio labeled "3US" in Exhibit 14.4. This portfolio has a broad portfolio balance of 50 percent interest-generating investments/50 percent equity investments and is composed exclusively of Treasury bills, U.S. corporate bonds, and U.S. large company stocks. If we add to this portfolio asset allocation non-U.S. bonds, non-U.S. stocks, real estate securities, and commodity-linked securities, it is possible to create portfolios with modestly higher returns but with much less volatility, such as those labeled "3LTD," "3MOD," and "3GR." Alternatively, we can create portfolios like "4MOD," or "4GR," which have a slightly higher volatility level but substantially higher returns as a result of their higher equity allocations of 70 percent. That is, by relying on the dissimilarity in patterns of returns among the expanded menu of asset classes, we can create higher-returning portfolios with 70 percent equity yet with only slightly more volatility than a traditionally diversified 50 percent equity portfolio composed exclusively of U.S. securities. As we discussed in Chapter 8, the diversification payoff made possible with a multiple-asset-class investment strategy can be taken in the form of either less portfolio volatility for the same return or more return for the same portfolio volatility.

Exhibit 14.5 lists a variety of performance metrics for the 12 portfolio structures. For each of the 3 broad portfolio balances, investment performance improves as the diversification degree increases from "U.S. Only" through "Limited" and "Moderate" to "Greater." That is, as diversification increases, the number of negative years declines, standard deviations drop, and the compound annual returns, Sharpe ratios, and future values of $1 all increase—accompanied, however, by increased exposure to frame-of-reference risk.

This method for determining the client's asset allocation is very different from one that simply relies on the output from a

Exhibit 14.5

Historical Asset Allocation Performance (1973*–2011)

Portfolio Identifier	2GR	2MOD	2LTD	2US	3GR	3MOD	3LTD	3US	4GR	4MOD	4LTD	4US
Broad Portfolio Balance:												
Interest-Generating Investments	70	70	70	70	50	50	50	50	30	30	30	30
Equity Investments	30	30	30	30	50	50	50	50	70	70	70	70
Total	100	100	100	100	100	100	100	100	100	100	100	100
Diversification Degree Choice	Greater	Moderate	Limited	U.S. Only	Greater	Moderate	Limited	U.S. Only	Greater	Moderate	Limited	U.S. Only
Number of Negative Years	2	3	4	5	3	4	5	7	5	6	6	8
Standard Deviation	5.36	5.59	5.94	6.65	7.86	8.17	8.75	9.97	10.57	10.93	11.70	13.45
Simple Average Return	8.20	8.12	8.06	7.94	9.40	9.29	9.19	9.02	10.61	10.47	10.33	10.11
Compound Annual Return	8.06	7.97	7.90	7.73	9.11	8.98	8.82	8.56	10.07	9.89	9.68	9.26
Sharpe Ratio	0.48	0.45	0.41	0.35	0.46	0.43	0.39	0.33	0.45	0.43	0.39	0.32
Future Value of $1	$20.58	$19.92	$19.40	$18.26	$29.96	$28.59	$27.06	$24.62	$42.13	$39.61	$36.67	$31.58
Exposure to "Frame-of-Reference" Risk	High	Medium	Low	None	High	Medium	Low	None	High	Medium	Low	None

*1973 is the earliest year for which annual total return data is available for each of the asset classes.

Data source: Morningstar® Principia®,

mean-variance portfolio optimization program. As we discussed in Chapter 11, the output from an optimization program is highly sensitive to small changes in the input variables, which cannot be estimated realistically with much precision. This limits the value of the recommended asset allocation generated by the optimizer. Assume for a moment that we can completely solve these problems, however, and we therefore have confidence that the optimizer's recommended portfolios on the efficient frontier are the optimal structures to maximize the expected return for each level of portfolio volatility. We still have no guarantee that the client will live with the pattern of returns of her optimized portfolio, even if the standard deviation of the portfolio is consistent with her volatility tolerance. The optimizer presumes rational investors who have no favorite asset classes, are not subject to frame-of-reference risk, and will not inappropriately abandon the asset allocation strategy during unusual market environments. When it comes to money, human beings are not completely rational. The growing field of behavioral finance has evolved in recognition of this fact. The investment decision-making process I advocate solves this problem first by educating clients in order to improve their investment decisions and then by intentionally accommodating client-specific behavioral risks by adjusting the portfolio asset allocation. This tailoring process increases the likelihood that the client will consistently follow the strategy. As we discussed in Chapter 13, even though alternative asset allocation strategies may be mathematically more efficient, they are of no value if clients abandon them after implementation.

Design the Portfolio

The bottom half of Exhibit 14.2 lists investment alternatives and classification criteria for the seven asset classes. Even though the specific decisions involved at this level of portfolio design are beyond the scope of this book, we will review briefly the choice points within each of the asset classes.

The "Short-Term Debt" asset class lists a number of investment alternatives that have little or no interest rate risk. The list is not exhaustive but provides a sample menu of possible choices. Investments with no interest rate risk are listed first, followed by those with low interest rate risk, such as short-term bonds.

The next asset class is "U.S. Bonds." The investment choices are differentiated along multiple dimensions: type, issuer, maturity, and quality. *Type* distinguishes conventional bonds, which promise nominal dollar returns, from inflation-protected bonds, which promise inflation-adjusted returns. From a diversification point of view, both conventional and inflation-protected bonds can often play a role in client portfolios. For example, inflation-protected bonds will respond positively to an unexpected surge in inflation, whereas conventional bonds will respond negatively.

The *issuer* of a bond can be the federal government, a corporation, or a municipality. Municipal bonds provide the advantage of a federal income tax–free coupon payment and are suitable for some investors with high marginal income tax brackets. The *maturity* of a bond is important because it defines the length of time the principal will be outstanding and is an approximate indicator of its price sensitivity to changes in interest rates.[2] The *quality* of a bond evaluates the likelihood of its timely payment of interest and principal. A bond manager may choose to vary the allocation between intermediate-term and long-term bonds based on the slope of the yield curve or on the basis of anticipated changes in interest rates. Similarly, the allocation between high-quality and low-quality bonds may be varied depending on the economic outlook and the size of the incremental return available from lower-quality bonds relative to higher-quality bonds.

Twenty years ago, the alternatives for investing in the next asset class, "Non-U.S. Bonds," were fairly limited for all but the very large investor. Fortunately, a significant number of non-U.S. bond mutual funds now exist that provide an efficient, low-cost means for any investor to gain access to this diversification alternative. Non-U.S. bonds can be differentiated geographically according to whether they originate with an issuer in a developed market or an emerging market. As with U.S. bonds, non-U.S. bonds also can be described along multiple dimensions: type, issuer, maturity, and quality.

The "U.S. Stocks" asset class includes the full range of U.S. common stock alternatives. For simplicity, U.S. stocks are typically classified across two dimensions: capitalization (large versus small) and style (value versus growth). *Capitalization* refers to the size of the company as measured by the price of its stock times the number of shares outstanding. A *value stock* is typically characterized by a low relative value for the stock's price/book ratio or price/cash flow ratio. A *growth stock* is usually characterized by a high relative growth rate for the company's long-term earnings, sales, and/or cash flow.

"Non-U.S. Stocks" provide a natural diversification complement to U.S. stocks. This form of diversification has been more widely implemented than non-U.S. bond diversification. Thus, a correspondingly greater number of implementation alternatives are available to investors, including professionally managed mutual funds, index funds, and exchange-traded funds (ETFs). As with the U.S. stocks asset class, non-U.S. stocks are classified according to capitalization (large versus small) and style (growth versus value). In addition, emerging market stocks are differentiated from developed market stocks in recognition of the increasing importance of rapidly growing third world economies.

"Real Estate Investments" take a variety of forms, and I list several alternatives. For many client situations, equity REITs or mutual funds that invest in REITs are effective choices for real estate diversification. Unlike direct real estate ownership, an equity REIT investor can easily diversify a relatively small sum of money both geographically and across different types of real estate investments, such as office buildings, apartments, regional malls, shopping centers, and industrial facilities. A personal residence or vacation home usually is not held primarily for investment purposes, nor does either generate cash flow, and accordingly they are not listed here. Instead, they are carried on the client's balance sheet under the heading of "Lifestyle assets."

Historically, the "Commodity-Linked Securities" asset class has been uncorrelated to many financial asset classes. Often, commodity-linked securities have delivered above-average returns when U.S. stocks generated below-average returns. During the 2000–2002 period when U.S. stocks were down cumulatively –37.6 percent, commodity-linked securities were up 34.6 percent. The prospect of such countercyclical performance makes the commodity-linked securities asset class a potentially powerful portfolio diversifier (see Exhibit 10.8). Until the late 1990s, commodity-linked securities diversification generally was available only within partnership structures that typically had expensive, incentive-based management fees. Now many mutual funds and exchange-traded funds that provide commodity-linked securities diversification are available.

Some investment advisors prefer to accommodate differences in client volatility tolerance at the level of investment position selection. For example, an advisor may recommend that a volatility-averse client build his portfolio with shorter-maturity, higher-quality bonds; more conservative, lower beta, large company stocks; and unleveraged real estate. For a client with high volatility tolerance, the advisor would recommend longer-maturity, lower-quality bonds; more aggressive, higher beta, small company stocks; and leveraged real estate.

Alternatively, I prefer to tailor portfolios for differences in volatility tolerance at the broad portfolio balance and asset allocation levels. There are several reasons for doing this. First, it directly involves the client in investment decision making by using the model described in Chapter 7 for determining the broad portfolio balance. Second, it is easy for clients to understand, which enhances their comfort levels. Third, it facilitates the design of portfolios to accommodate clients with either unusually high or unusually low capacities for tolerating volatility and/or frame-of-reference risk. Last, and most important, it permits a broader diversification of the portfolio for all clients regardless of volatility tolerance. That is, by handling the volatility tolerance issue at the level of broad portfolio balance and asset allocation levels, all clients can benefit from diversification with *both* high- and low-quality bonds, large company and small company stocks, and so on.

Occasionally, advisors or clients raise the issue of using stock options and/or futures to modify the volatility characteristics of a portfolio. If the advisor feels the need to modify the volatility characteristics of the portfolio, then one of two things is often true. First, the portfolio's asset allocation may have strayed from its targets, and rebalancing will restore it to its appropriate volatility level. The other possibility is that the portfolio's asset allocation is not matched to the client's volatility tolerance, in which case the broad portfolio balance or the breadth and degree of portfolio diversification should be reworked. In either case, options or futures are usually not the preferred solution.

Exhibit 14.2 shows several stages of decision making that link the broad portfolio balance decision to the final detailed target portfolio. Each of these steps can be characterized along an active versus passive dimension. Ultimately, both investment advisors and their clients share the responsibility to evaluate the likely gains and potential risks inherent in pursuing active strategies. For example, at the asset allocation level of decision making are seven asset classes. More active approaches presume pricing inefficiencies among the various asset classes that can profitably be exploited by overweighting undervalued asset classes and underweighting overvalued asset classes. By maintaining minimum and maximum percentage allocations for each asset class, the risk of errors in judgment can be kept within limits, while the attempt is made to add value. The passive alternative, which I strongly advocate, is simply to periodically rebalance the portfolio back to the target strategic allocation established for each asset class.

When choosing investment positions within each of the seven asset classes, more possibilities present themselves. An advisor may use passively managed, low-cost index funds or exchange-traded funds as portfolio building blocks. Alternatively, the advisor may choose actively managed funds with the hope that superior security selection will add value net of the incremental fees, transaction costs, and taxes.

An index fund seeks to replicate the performance of a specified market index by owning all or substantially all of the securities within the index. It does not attempt to outperform the market through superior security selection. The argument in favor of index funds rests on a simple and irrefutable premise: investors as a group *are* the market and therefore cannot outperform the market. Further, the attempt to beat the market through superior security selection comes with a price tag: higher expenses in the form of advisory fees, operating expenses, and portfolio transaction costs that result in a direct reduction of realized returns for the active investor. The problem would be eliminated if there were a reliable way to identify which money managers will outperform the markets, net of their expenses. But most research studies conclude that markets operate relatively efficiently and that the identification of tomorrow's superior money managers is a very difficult undertaking. An index fund, by minimizing costs and portfolio turnover, locks in an automatic performance advantage that may be small in the short run but becomes increasingly powerful over time. As John C. Bogle, founder of the Vanguard family of mutual funds, eloquently observed, "The fact is that indexers always win. That is, in any financial market—and any segment of any financial market—indexers owning all of the securities in that market at low cost *must* provide better returns than the other investors in the market in the aggregate, simply because the costs incurred by active investors—commissions, fees, taxes—are substantially higher."[3]

Advisors who choose to use actively managed mutual funds or separate accounts to build portfolios should evaluate money managers with rigorous due diligence. The *money manager evaluation* section of the sample investment policy statement in the Appendix to this chapter contains an example of such a due diligence process.

Step 8. Prepare an Investment Policy Statement (IPS)

We are almost ready to implement the strategy. Almost, but not quite. It is time to document the investment decisions and the parameters within which the advisor will manage the portfolio over time. If the portfolio is for a pension plan, foundation, or trust, legislation or regulations likely either require or strongly recommend a written IPS. Even in the absence of specific legal requirements, I highly recommend a formalized IPS. In addition to providing all interested parties with documentation regarding investment policies and procedures, the preparation of a well-written IPS has several advantages:

- It supports a disciplined, consistent execution of the portfolio's investment strategy. This is particularly important during extremely good or bad capital market environments.
- For institutional portfolios managed by investment committees, an IPS can provide continuity in the investment approach as new committee members replace those who are stepping down.
- An IPS provides a defense against "Monday morning quarterbacking," when prior investment decisions may be second-guessed.
- An IPS also provides evidence of investment stewardship and the fulfillment of fiduciary duties through proper oversight of the investment management process.

The Appendix to this chapter contains a sample IPS for an individual. The first section is "Background and Purpose," which contains key information concerning the client and details about the nature and size of the portfolio. The client's financial goals are itemized and linked to a qualitative investment objective that acknowledges the return versus volatility trade-off. The next section is "Statement of Investment Parameters," which documents the client's volatility tolerance, asset class preferences, investment time horizon, and information regarding any discretionary authority granted to the investment advisor. The "Portfolio Asset Allocation" section describes the portfolio's broad balance, asset allocation, and rebalancing guidelines. The "Modeled Portfolio Behavior" section estimates the portfolio's future return and upside versus downside volatility characteristics as a function of time. The "Duties and Responsibilities" section outlines the obligations of the investment advisor, money managers, and custodian. The "Money Manager Evaluation" section itemizes the due diligence criteria for selecting money managers. The last section, "Control Procedures," describes the procedures needed for monitoring money manager performance, measuring costs, and reviewing the IPS on an annual basis. "Appendix A" discusses the purpose and limitations of financial modeling. "Appendix B" documents the expected return, standard deviation, and correlation statistics for the asset classes used to diversify the portfolio. "Appendix C" describes the asset class peer groups and benchmark indices used in money manager due diligence.

The IPS is the most important document in the fiduciary process. It ensures that all the relevant aspects of the investment management process have been addressed, that roles are clearly defined, and that a proper frame of reference exists for evaluating the portfolio strategy over time. The litmus test for a well-written IPS is whether it contains sufficient detail and clarity for the portfolio strategy to be implemented by an investment advisor who is unfamiliar with the client.

Step 9. Implement the Investment Strategy

Moving from the Existing to the New Portfolio Strategy

After the client approves the blueprint for the portfolio and signs the IPS, it is time to implement the strategy. If the client's current portfolio balance differs from that of the recommended target portfolio, the question arises about the timetable for moving the portfolio to its target. For example, assume that a client currently has a portfolio balance of 70 percent short-term debt investments/10 percent longer-term bonds/20 percent equity investments. His target portfolio, however, is 35 percent/20 percent/45 percent. On the one hand, if his current balance is not appropriate given his investment objective and volatility tolerance, an argument exists for moving the portfolio quickly to its target. On the other hand, offsetting economic and psychological benefits can be gained by using a dollar-cost averaging strategy to gradually move the portfolio to its target.

Dollar-cost averaging is a simple technique that requires equal dollar investments to be made in an investment at regular time intervals. For example, if a client wants to invest $1,800,000 in common stocks, he can reach this target allocation by investing $100,000 per month for 18 months. When placing money in investments with variable principal values, such as common stocks, ideally you want to buy when prices are low. By following a dollar-cost averaging strategy, more shares are purchased when prices are low, and fewer shares are purchased when prices are high. At the completion of the strategy, the average cost per share will be less than the average price paid for the shares. We know that short-run returns from volatile investments can be very different from average long-term expectations. By establishing an investment position with equal dollar commitments at regular intervals, the probability increases that the client's investment experience will more closely resemble longer-term expectations.

Dollar-cost averaging has psychological advantages as well. A target portfolio may have decidedly different volatility and return characteristics than the client's current portfolio. By moving gradually to the target allocation, the client has a greater opportunity to become familiar with, and therefore more comfortable with, the new strategy. With greater comfort comes an increased likelihood that the client will remain committed to the strategy through good and bad market conditions.

The time frame chosen for establishing the target portfolio will be a compromise between the conflicting goals of establishing the target portfolio quickly and taking more time to mitigate the effects of possible adverse short-run market movements. In our example above, 35 percent of the client's short-term debt investments will be moved to longer-term bonds and equity investments. The more volatile the investment alternative to which you are adding money, the longer the period during which the investments should be dollar-cost averaged.

Because stocks are more volatile than bonds, it may be advisable to take 12 to 24 months to move the portfolio to its target common stock commitment but only 6 to 12 months to reach the target allocation for bonds.

Sometimes a client's current portfolio is already at or near the recommended allocation among short-term debt investments, longer-term bonds, and equity investments, but the new strategy will use a different mix of investment positions. In this case, the advisor can implement the new strategy more rapidly, provided the client is comfortable with the pace of implementation and appropriate consideration has been given to the transaction cost and tax issues involved.

Asset Location: Taking Optimal Advantage of Tax-Qualified Retirement Plans and IRAs

Some unique planning considerations are involved with clients who have a portion of their total investment portfolios committed to tax-qualified retirement plans and IRAs.[4] We first will consider the situation in which the client has discretion over how these funds are invested. Conventional wisdom says IRAs are long-term investment vehicles, and they therefore should be funded with long-term investments, such as common stocks. In this case, however, conventional wisdom may not lead to the best outcome. An IRA provides valuable tax-sheltering capability. To derive maximum advantage from this tax deferral, it is important to use IRAs to shelter those portfolio investments that, on average, generate the highest level of income taxes per dollar of investment value. These investments are not necessarily the common stock positions. I recommend a two-step process to facilitate the selection of investments for placement in the IRA. First, design the target investment portfolio without regard to the fact that an IRA will shelter part of the portfolio. Second, determine which investment position in the target portfolio generates the highest level of average annual income taxes per $1,000 of investment value. This investment is the first that should be positioned inside the IRA. If the IRA has room for more investments, select the investment that generates the next highest level of average annual income taxes per $1,000 of investment value from the remaining investments outside the IRA. By proceeding in this manner until the IRA is fully invested, the client will make good use of the tax deferral available from the IRA.

For example, let us consider a client with a $400,000 investment portfolio, as shown in Exhibit 14.6. Half of her portfolio is to be positioned outside of her IRA with the other half positioned within her IRA. For this illustration, we will assume that she is in a 25 percent marginal tax bracket with preferential 15 percent tax rates on qualified dividend income and long-term capital gains. The short-term corporate bond fund has a 3 percent yield, and the long-term corporate bond fund has a 5 percent yield. Both the bond funds generate small capital gains distributions. Each of the common stock funds has a 2 percent qualified dividend income yield and is expected to have a pretax total return of 9 percent. The S&P 500 stock index fund, however, has a significant portion of its total return in the form of unrealized capital appreciation. The client plans to retain this fund as a core portfolio holding for the rest of her life. Thus, this unrealized appreciation is a valuable form of tax deferral.

By contrast, the actively traded stock fund has a high portfolio turnover, which constantly churns out most of its total return in the form of short-term and long-term capital gain distributions, leaving a smaller component of average unrealized capital appreciation. By examining row (L) of Exhibit 14.6, we see that the actively traded stock fund generates the highest level of average annual taxes per $1,000 invested, followed by the long-term corporate bond fund, the total return of which is almost entirely taxed at the client's 25 percent marginal income tax bracket. Accordingly, the IRA should be funded with these two investment positions, with the short-term corporate bond fund and the S&P 500 stock index fund held in a taxable account outside the IRA.

In a data-gathering session with a new client, I often see municipal bonds held outside her IRA with stock positions inside her IRA. In

Exhibit 14.6

Comparison of Investment Alternatives for an Individual Retirement Account

	Investment Position			
	Short-Term Corporate Bond Fund	Long-Term Corporate Bond Fund	S&P 500 Stock Index Fund	Actively Traded Stock Fund
(A) Investment value	$100,000	$100,000	$100,000	$100,000
(B) Taxable interest	3,000	5,000	0	0
(C) = 0.25(B) = Taxes on interest	750	1,250	0	0
(D) Qualified dividends	0	0	2,000	2,000
(E) = 0.15(D) = Taxes on qualified dividends	0	0	300	300
(F) Average short-term capital gains distribution	120	120	0	4,000
(G) = 0.25(F) = Taxes on short-term capital gains distribution	30	30	0	1,000
(H) Average long-term capital gains distribution	60	120	500	1,500
(I) = 0.15(H) = Taxes on long-term capital gains distribution	9	18	75	225
(J) Average unrealized capital appreciation	0	0	6,500	1,500
(K) = (C) + (E) + (G) + (I) = Average annual total taxes	789	1,298	375	1,525
(L) = 1000 (K) ÷ (A) = Average annual taxes per $1,000 of investment value	$7.89	$12.98	$3.75	$15.25

most situations, the client would be financially better off holding stock positions outside her IRA while holding taxable bonds inside her IRA. Under the tax law at the time of this writing, stocks receive preferential tax treatment, with qualified dividends and long-term capital gains both taxed at 15 percent. In addition, unrealized appreciation is tax deferred. For similar quality and maturity, taxable bonds have higher yields than municipal bonds. By holding the higher-yielding taxable bonds inside her IRA, the client can increase the total return on her portfolio through a form of tax arbitrage.

Coordinating Personal Investments with Employer-Sponsored Retirement Plans

Sometimes, clients do not have discretion over the investment of money in an employer-sponsored retirement plan. Investment advisors occasionally ignore these assets because no decisions need to be made concerning them. This practice invites the creation of a less-than-optimal asset allocation. Consider a client who has a $1 million investment portfolio, $400,000 of which is in an employer-sponsored retirement plan. Assume that the appropriate portfolio balance for the client is 45 percent short-term debt investments/15 percent longer-term bonds/40 percent equity investments. Exhibit 14.7(A) shows the investment portfolio balance for the $600,000 that is under the client's control, if no consideration is given to the other $400,000 in the retirement plan.

Perhaps, however, the $400,000 in the employer-sponsored retirement plan is entirely invested in short-term debt investments. From the broader point of view of the client's entire $1 million portfolio, the actual balance is skewed heavily toward short-term debt investments, as shown in Exhibit 14.7(B)(1). Alternatively, if the $400,000 in the retirement plan is invested in common stocks, then the client's actual portfolio balance is equity oriented, as shown in Exhibit 14.7(B)(2). Exhibit 14.7(C)(1) and (C)(2) show the required allocation of funds outside the retirement plan in order to achieve the proper balance for

Exhibit 14.7

Portfolio Balance Where a Client Lacks Investment Discretion over a Portion of the Portfolio

Facts:

$600,000	Fully discretionary investment funds
400,000	Employer-sponsored retirement plan (no discretion)
$1,000,000	Total portfolio

(A) Portfolio balance if considering only discretionary funds

Short-term debt investments	$270,000	45%
Longer-term bonds	90,000	15%
Equity investments	240,000	40%
Discretionary funds	$600,000	100%

(B)(1) Total portfolio balance if the retirement plan is invested in short-term debt investments

	Discretionary Funds	Retirement Plan	Total	%
Short-term debt investments	$270,000	$400,000	$670,000	67%
Longer-term bonds	90,000	0	90,000	9%
Equity investments	240,000	0	240,000	24%
Total Portfolio	$600,000	$400,000	$1,000,000	100%

(B)(2) Total portfolio balance if the retirement plan is invested in equity investments

	Discretionary Funds	Retirement Plan	Total	%
Short-term debt investments	$270,000	$0	$270,000	27%
Longer-term bonds	90,000	0	90,000	9%
Equity investments	240,000	400,000	640,000	64%
Total Portfolio	$600,000	$400,000	$1,000,000	100%

(C)(1) Required positioning of discretionary funds to maintain proper portfolio balance if the retirement plan is invested in short-term debt investments

	Discretionary Funds	Retirement Plan	Total	%
Short-term debt investments	$ 50,000	$400,000	$450,000	45%
Longer-term bonds	150,000	0	150,000	15%
Equity investments	400,000	0	400,000	40%
Total Portfolio	$600,000	$400,000	$1,000,000	100%

(C)(2) Required positioning of discretionary funds to maintain proper portfolio balance if the retirement plan is invested in equity investments

	Discretionary Funds	Retirement Plan	Total	%
Short-term debt investments	$450,000	$0	$450,000	45%
Longer-term bonds	150,000	0	150,000	15%
Equity investments	0	400,000	400,000	40%
Total Portfolio	$600,000	$400,000	$1,000,000	100%

the portfolio as a whole. This example underscores the importance of always making portfolio decisions from a holistic point of view.

A subtler example of the same issue involves paying careful attention to the composition of the assets *within* an employer-sponsored tax-qualified plan. It is not enough to simply make sure that the broad portfolio balance is correct from the point of view of the client's total portfolio. If a significant portion of the client's equity investments is inside the employer-sponsored retirement plan and heavily oriented toward U.S. stocks, then it may be advisable for the client to invest his personally controlled equity money heavily toward non-U.S. stocks, real estate investments, and commodity-linked securities.

Heavily Constrained Portfolios

Similarly, constraints may occur if a large percentage of the client's portfolio is committed to nonliquid investments. The best way to handle these situations is nevertheless to go through the exercise of developing the ideal target portfolio as if the investment process could start from an all-cash position with no constraints. A comparison between the client's current, constrained portfolio and the ideal target will immediately clarify which modifications are most important and the order in which they should be implemented. The portfolio can then be moved toward the ideal target as the constraints permit.

At times, this will lead to what may appear to be strange investment advice. Consider an extremely constrained situation in which only 10 percent of a $1 million portfolio can be repositioned. Perhaps the client has at least modest diversification across all major asset classes except non-U.S. bonds and commodity-linked securities. The advisor's recommendation may be to invest $30,000 in non-U.S. bonds and $70,000 in commodity-linked securities. Considered in isolation from the point of view of the $100,000 available for investment, this advice is indeed strange, but it is nevertheless entirely appropriate from the point of view of the total portfolio. This situation presents some obvious problems regarding the evaluation of the investment advisor's performance results. It is thus essential that clients understand the context within which such recommendations are made.

A Word on Fees

Comprehensive portfolio management in today's world requires two separate levels of decision making. Each level can add value for the client if done properly, and each level therefore justifies appropriate compensation. The first level, which is the more important of the two, involves developing realistic investment objectives and appropriate asset allocation strategies. This requires that investment advisors have an in-depth knowledge of and close working relationships with their clients. The second level of decision making involves the selection of individual securities within each of the asset classes. We already have commented on the difficulties inherent in trying to beat the market through superior investment skill. Those who are capable of doing so usually specialize in one particular segment of the world's capital markets, and their continued success necessitates a full-time organizational commitment to their specialty. A successful U.S. small company stock manager, for example, will not likely become a leader in non-U.S. bond investing. Similarly, managers who specialize in security selection for a particular market segment will not have the means to develop the kind of relationship needed with a client in order to tackle issues at the asset allocation level of decision making.

The days of a client giving his investment portfolio to a single, balanced manager are over. Today, portfolio management requires the different skills and organizational commitments that correspond to the two levels of investment decision making just described. Mutual funds and separate accounts provide an excellent means of obtaining the desired breadth of diversification for an investment portfolio. This, of course, raises the issue of two layers of management fees. The two layers of fees are justified, provided that value is being added at each level of decision making. In the long run, the disciplined execution of the asset allocation strategy is more important with respect to its impact on long-term portfolio results than the selection of individual securities within each asset class. This is particularly true given the periodic temptations for the client to abandon the asset allocation strategy. If done well, these portfolio management tasks deserve compensation. If they are not done well, the client should terminate the advisory relationship. Similarly, at the level of individual security selection, the money management specialist should be paid for work well done. If a specialist does not perform adequately, the advisor should recommend a replacement who will be worthy of the compensation. Alternatively, index funds or exchange-traded funds can be used as portfolio building blocks.

In Chapters 12 through 14, we completed all but the last step of the investment management process outlined in Exhibit 14.1. Exhibit 14.8 shows a sample investment policy decision-making agenda, which guides the client through the steps to develop an individually tailored investment strategy consistent with her volatility tolerance and financial goals. Occasionally clients may express impatience with the time and energy commitments that this investment decision-making process demands. I strongly recommend, however, that the process not be rushed to a conclusion. Clients who invest the time required to participate thoughtfully in the design of their portfolios will be more sophisticated investors who are more likely to reach their financial goals.

Step 10. Report Performance and Revise the Portfolio

Performance Reporting

Performance measurement is a particularly troublesome issue for both investment advisors and their clients. One difficulty arises because the performance measurement interval, usually a calendar quarter, is much too short relative to the typical investment time horizon. The broad portfolio balance decision-making model in Exhibit 7.2 emphasized this fact by placing the modeled return in the context of its

Exhibit 14.8
Investment Policy Decision-Making Agenda

I. The Importance of Asset Allocation (Chapter 1)
II. U.S. Capital Market Investment Performance
 A. Historical Review (Chapter 2)
 B. Future Modeled Returns (Chapters 3 and 4)
III. Time Horizon (Chapter 6)
IV. Two Major Risks All Investors Face
 A. Inflation (Exhibit 6.1)
 B. Volatility (Exhibit 7.1)
V. The Broad Portfolio Balance Decision (Chapter 7)
VI. Diversification: The Third Dimension (Chapter 8)
VII. Expanding the Efficient Frontier (Chapter 9)
 A. Non-U.S. Bonds
 B. Non-U.S. Stocks
 C. Real Estate Investments
 D. Treasury Inflation-Protected Securities
 E. Commodity-Linked Securities
VIII. The Rewards of Multiple-Asset-Class Investing (Chapter 10)
IX. Asset Allocation Decisions and Final Portfolio Design
 A. Total Investable Capital Market Pie Chart (Exhibit 1.1)
 B. Investment Portfolio Design Format (Exhibit 14.2)
  1. Broad Portfolio Balance Decision (Chapter 7)
  2. Choice of Asset Classes (Chapter 14, Step 7)
   a) Short-Term Debt
   b) U.S. Bonds
   c) Non-U.S. Bonds
   d) U.S. Stocks
   e) Non-U.S. Stocks
   f) Real Estate Investments
   g) Commodity-Linked Securities
  3. Degree of Diversification: Allocation Across the Asset Classes (Chapter 13, Step 6)
  4. Choice of Investment Positions for Strategy Implementation (Chapter 14, Step 7)
X. Portfolio Modeling (Chapter 11 sections on "Analyzing Capital Needs" and "Managing Client Expectations")
 A. Modeling the Performance Characteristics of the Asset Allocation Design
  1. Are the return characteristics consistent with the financial goals?
  2. Is the downside volatility acceptable?
 B. Confirmation or Modification of the Asset Allocation Design
XI. Preparation of the Investment Policy Statement (Chapter 14, Step 8)
XII. Implementing the Investment Strategy (Chapter 14, Step 9)
 A. Logistics for Moving from the Existing to the New Portfolio Strategy
 B. Asset Location: Taking Optimal Advantage of Tax-Qualified Retirement Plans and IRAs
 C. Coordinating Personal Investments with Employer-Sponsored Retirement Plans
 D. Managing Portfolio Constraints
XIII. Establishing Procedures for Performance Reporting and Portfolio Revision (Chapter 14, Step 10)

associated typical annual range of results. The IPS should also contain information regarding the range and likelihood of possible portfolio returns. (See the "Modeled Portfolio Behavior" section in the sample IPS in the Appendix to this chapter.)

An additional performance measurement challenge arises from the dissimilarities between the returns of a broadly diversified multiple-asset-class portfolio and those of a more traditional portfolio composed exclusively of U.S. stocks, bonds, and cash equivalents. We discussed this frame-of-reference risk issue at length in Chapter 13. The S&P 500 index simply is not a suitable benchmark for a diversified multiple-asset-class portfolio. As an alternative, the advisor can construct a more appropriate evaluation benchmark by taking a weighted average of the portfolio's asset class index returns. Given the volatility inherent in the capital markets and the issue of frame-of-reference risk, clients should not attach too much significance to their short-term investment experience. The effectiveness and value of an asset allocation strategy can only be measured over longer time horizons.

An investment advisor pursuing a tactical asset allocation strategy can compare the actual results with the results that would have been achieved if the strategic asset allocation had been maintained. Finally, the advisor can compare returns for the various specific investment positions against appropriate benchmark indices' returns. For example, the performance of a U.S. large company stock manager can be measured against the performances of the S&P 500 and a peer group of other U.S. large company stock managers. An intermediate-term, high-quality U.S. bond manager's results can be compared with the Barclays Capital Intermediate U.S. Government/Credit Bond Index and a peer group of other intermediate-term, high-quality U.S. bond managers.

In the final analysis, the goal of portfolio management is the successful fulfillment of the client's investment objectives. In this context, the client should focus less on beating the market and more on evaluating the portfolio's performance in terms of its progress toward the realization of the client's financial goals.

Portfolio Revision

Strategic asset allocation seeks to identify and maintain a portfolio asset allocation appropriate for an investor's financial goals, investment objectives, time horizon, and volatility tolerance. Strategic asset allocation makes no attempt to predict the direction or magnitude of short-term market volatility. It is therefore characterized by a fixed target allocation to each asset class in an investor's portfolio.

Strategic asset allocation is not a buy-and-hold strategy. A buy-and-hold strategy involves no portfolio rebalancing. As a result, the relative proportions of the asset classes will vary over time as the capital markets move, producing an undesirable variation in the portfolio's risk and return characteristics. In the short run, it also will result in being wrong at every major market turn. For example, with a buy-and-hold strategy, a portfolio's allocation to U.S. stocks reaches its maximum as a U.S. stock bull market ends and a bear market begins. Conversely, the allocation to U.S. stocks will be at its minimum at the end of a bear market, as the next bull market gets under way. In the long run, a buy-and-hold strategy also likely will result in an increasingly greater percentage of the portfolio being committed to equities because of their higher expected returns. This produces an undesirable trend of increasing volatility exposure coupled with a shortening investment time horizon.

By contrast, strategic asset allocation requires periodic portfolio rebalancing in order to maintain the target allocation to each asset class. Portfolio cash flow activity can be used to facilitate this rebalancing. If a client is withdrawing money from her portfolio, it can be taken from the asset class that is most overweight relative to its target allocation. If a client is adding money to the portfolio, it can be first invested in whichever asset class that is most underweight relative to its target allocation. Absent cash flow activity, money is reallocated periodically from the most recent better-performing asset classes to the relative underperformers. For example, during a bull market for U.S. stocks, such as occurred during the 1990s, the portfolio's commitment to U.S. stocks will become larger than its target allocation. Returning to the target allocation thus necessitates selling U.S. stocks during the bull market. Conversely, to maintain the target allocation to U.S. stocks during the bear market accompanying the Global Financial Crisis of 2008, U.S. stocks must be bought. Strategic asset allocation is thus contrarian in execution and inherently "buy low, sell high."

Strategic asset allocation's rebalancing activity has several advantages:

- It is easy to understand and implement.
- It maintains a more consistent portfolio volatility level for the client.
- It preserves the multiple-asset-class diversification of the portfolio.
- It provides a strict discipline that prevents the portfolio from becoming overweighted in an asset class at its market top and underweighted at its market bottom.

Appendix

Investment Policy Statement

Prepared for:

Mary Thompson

Approved on January 3, 2012

It is intended that this investment policy statement be reviewed and updated at least annually. Clients are advised to have legal counsel review their IPS before it is approved. Any change to this investment policy statement should be communicated in writing on a timely basis to all interested parties.

TABLE OF CONTENTS

Background & Purpose

Key Information

Client:	Mary Thompson
Tax ID Number:	123-45-6789
Investment Advisor:	ABC Investment Group, Inc.
Custodian:	XYZ Custodial Services, Inc.
Accountant:	John Smith, CPA
Attorney:	Jane Doe, Esq.

The purpose of this IPS is to help the Client meet her financial goals. We hope to do this by focusing the Client's involvement on the areas of the investment process that have the most impact on portfolio return and volatility. The Client can then delegate the day-to-day implementation to trusted professionals within the framework of this written plan. The IPS also assists the Client and Investment Advisor (Advisor) in effectively supervising the management of the Client's assets. The Client's investment program is defined in the various sections of this IPS by:

1. Stating in writing the Client's attitudes, expectations, objectives, and guidelines in the management of her assets.
2. Setting forth an investment strategy for managing the Client's assets. This strategy diversifies the Client's portfolio across various asset classes and investment management styles in accordance with specified targets and acceptable limits for the asset class commitments. In designing the strategy, the Advisor has considered the Client's investment time horizon, volatility tolerance, tax status, financial goals and investment objective.
3. Encouraging effective communications between the Client and Advisor.
4. Establishing formal criteria to select and evaluate the performance of money managers on a regular basis.

This IPS describes the investment process that the Advisor deems appropriate for the Client's situation. The Client desires to maximize returns within prudent levels of volatility and to meet the following financial goals and investment objective:

Financial Goals

1. Retire in December 2020—The Client wants to maintain her current lifestyle during retirement by withdrawing an annual inflation-adjusted, after-tax cash flow of $200,000 (2011 dollars) from her portfolio to supplement her pension and social security benefits.
2. Private Foundation—The Client wants to create and fund a private foundation with $1,000,000 (2011 dollars) by December 2015.

Investment Objective

High total return with high portfolio volatility: Given the Client's current assets and expected cash needs, she has chosen to allocate 70% of her portfolio to equity investments and is willing to assume the associated portfolio volatility in seeking to achieve a higher long-term rate of return.

Assets Covered

Tax-deferred IRA account for Mary Thompson

Taxable individual account for Mary Thompson

Current Combined Market Value

$8,125,000

STATEMENT OF INVESTMENT PARAMETERS

VOLATILITY TOLERANCE

In determining the investment objective, the Client considered her ability to withstand short- and intermediate-term portfolio volatility. The Client's current financial condition, prospects for the future, and other factors suggest that interim fluctuations in portfolio market value and rates of return can be tolerated in seeking to achieve her financial goals.

The Client recognizes and acknowledges that volatility must be assumed in order to achieve her financial goals, and that there are risks and uncertainties associated with the investment markets.

ASSET CLASS PREFERENCES

Investment performance is determined largely by the portfolio's asset allocation. The Advisor has reviewed with the client the long-term performance characteristics of different investment alternatives in order to help her understand the various kinds of investment risks and the expected rewards associated with bearing those risks.

Historically, interest-generating investments, such as Treasury bills, have had the advantage of relative stability of principal value, but they provide little opportunity for real long-term capital growth due to their susceptibility to inflation. On the other hand, equity investments, such as common stocks, have a significantly higher expected return but have the disadvantage of much greater volatility of principal value. From the point of view of investment decision-making, this volatility is worth bearing, provided the time horizon for the portfolio is sufficiently long. The longer the investment time horizon, the more likely it is that equity investments will outperform interest-generating investments.

The Advisor has reviewed with the Client research concerning the advantages, as well as the "frame-of-reference" risk, associated with multiple-asset-class investing. The Client and the Advisor have agreed to follow a policy of diversification across multiple asset classes in order to mitigate the risks associated with the Client's investment objective.

The following asset classes were selected:

- Short-Term Debt Investments
- U.S. Bonds
- Non-U.S. Bonds
- U.S. Stocks
- Non-U.S. Stocks
- Real Estate Securities
- Commodity-Linked Securities

The performance characteristics (expected returns, standard deviations and correlations) for the asset classes are contained in Appendix B.

INVESTMENT TIME HORIZON

The investment guidelines are based upon an investment horizon of greater than 25 years. Therefore, interim portfolio volatility should be viewed with an appropriate perspective. The client anticipates minimal short-term need for liquidity.

DISCRETIONARY AUTHORITY

The Advisor will implement with discretion portfolio changes relating to rebalancing the portfolio, investing new deposits, and generating liquidity to cover withdrawals. The Advisor will review with the Client, prior to implementation, the addition of new positions or the elimination of existing positions.

Portfolio Asset Allocation

Broad Portfolio Balance

Interest-Generating Investments	30%
Equity Investments	70%
Total Portfolio	100%

Asset Allocation – Greater Diversification

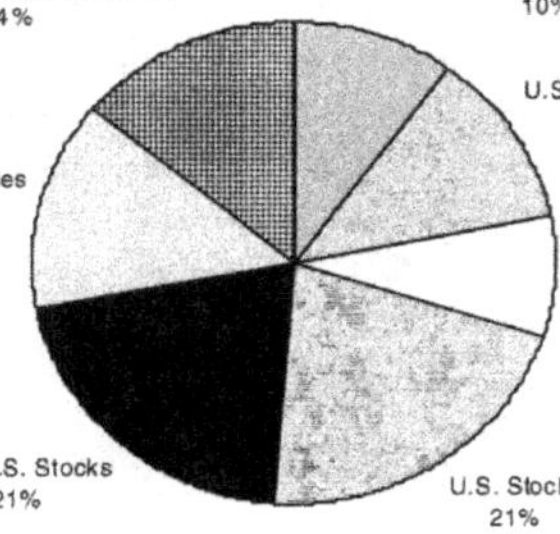

Portfolio Rebalancing

	Lower Limit	Strategic Allocation	Upper Limit
Short-Term Debt Investments	8%	**10%**	12%
U.S. Bonds	10%	**12%**	14%
Non-U.S. Bonds	6%	**8%**	10%
U.S. Stocks	17%	**21%**	25%
Non-U.S. Stocks	17%	**21%**	25%
Real Estate Securities	11%	**14%**	17%
Commodity-Linked Securities	11%	**14%**	17%

The Advisor will review the percentage allocation to each asset class at least quarterly. The allocations will be permitted to vary within the asset class ranges specified above. Portfolio contributions and withdrawals will be used to maintain or move the portfolio toward the strategic allocation.

MODELED PORTFOLIO BEHAVIOR

MODELED RETURN: 6.37%

The Client understands that, as of the date of this IPS, the portfolio has a modeled return of 6.37% with an equal likelihood of either outperforming or underperforming that return. The table and graph below describe the modeled range of probable returns from the portfolio. It also describes the likelihood of these returns. For example:

The portfolio's downside volatility for a 1-year horizon is modeled as follows:

- 25% likelihood of a return less than -1.73%
- 10% likelihood of a return less than -2.49%

Over the Client's 25-year investment time horizon, the portfolio's downside volatility is modeled as follows:

- 25% likelihood of a compound annual return less than 4.70%
- 10% likelihood of a compound annual return less than 3.21%

MODELED DOWNSIDE VOLATILITY

YEAR	10TH%	25TH%	50TH%	75TH%	90TH%
1	**-8.51**	**-1.73**	6.37	15.14	23.67
3	**-2.49**	**1.62**	6.37	11.35	16.04
10	**1.42**	**3.74**	6.37	9.07	11.56
15	**2.31**	**4.22**	6.37	8.57	10.59
25	**3.21**	**4.70**	6.37	8.07	9.63

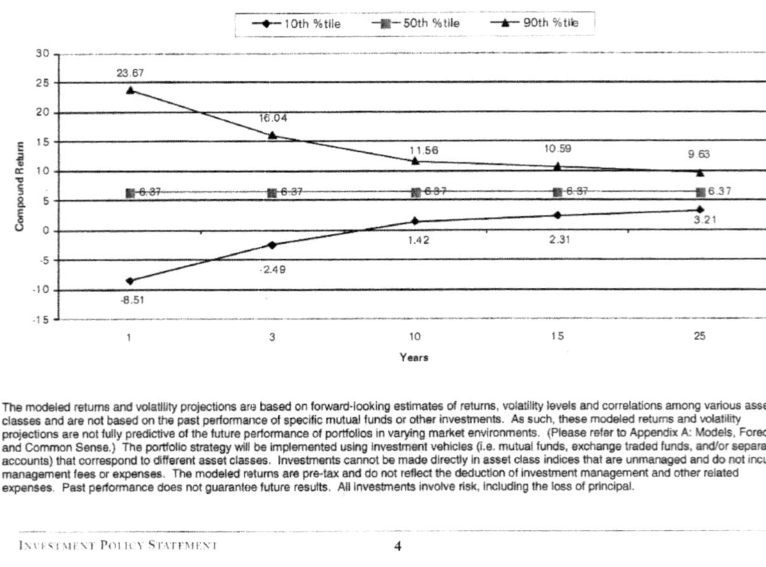

The modeled returns and volatility projections are based on forward-looking estimates of returns, volatility levels and correlations among various asset classes and are not based on the past performance of specific mutual funds or other investments. As such, these modeled returns and volatility projections are not fully predictive of the future performance of portfolios in varying market environments. (Please refer to Appendix A: Models, Forecasts and Common Sense.) The portfolio strategy will be implemented using investment vehicles (i.e. mutual funds, exchange traded funds, and/or separate accounts) that correspond to different asset classes. Investments cannot be made directly in asset class indices that are unmanaged and do not incur management fees or expenses. The modeled returns are pre-tax and do not reflect the deduction of investment management and other related expenses. Past performance does not guarantee future results. All investments involve risk, including the loss of principal.

Duties & Responsibilities

Investment Advisor

The Client has retained ABC Investment Group, Inc. as an objective, third-party Investment Advisor (Advisor) to assist in managing the investment portfolio. The Advisor will be responsible for guiding the Client through a disciplined and rigorous investment process in accordance with fiduciary standards of care. As a fiduciary to the Client, the Advisor's primary responsibilities are to:

1. Provide sufficient asset classes with different expected return, volatility, and correlation characteristics so that the Client can prudently diversify the portfolio.
2. Guide the Client in developing an appropriate portfolio asset allocation.
3. Prudently select investment options (e.g. money managers, indexed investments) for the Client's consideration.
4. Draft the investment policy statement and make recommendations for changes as appropriate.
5. Control and account for investment expenses.
6. Assist in monitoring and supervising all service vendors and investment options.
7. Monitor the portfolio's asset allocation and rebalance the portfolio in accordance with the Client's instructions.
8. Provide detailed portfolio performance reports and other tax and/or financial accounting reports as requested by the Client.
9. Avoid prohibited transactions and conflicts of interest.
10. Receive all proxy and related materials on behalf of the Client in lieu of forwarding such materials to Client, and vote such proxies on the Client's behalf.

Money Managers

As distinguished from the Investment Advisor, who is responsible for guiding the investment process and managing the portfolio as a whole, the Money Managers of the specific funds within the portfolio are co-fiduciaries responsible for security selection and price decisions. Each Money Manager focuses his attention on the market segment within which he invests and, accordingly, his responsibility is limited to that portion of the total portfolio that is under his management. The specific duties and responsibilities of each Money Manager are to:

1. Manage the assets under their supervision in accordance with the guidelines and objectives outlined in their respective Prospectus, Trust Agreement, or Contract.
2. Exercise full investment discretion with respect to buying, managing, and selling securities under his management.
3. Vote promptly all proxies and related actions in the best interests of the Client. The Money Manager shall keep detailed records of the voting of proxies and related actions and will comply with all applicable regulatory obligations.
4. Use the same care, skill, prudence, and due diligence under the circumstances then prevailing that experienced investment professionals, acting in a like capacity and fully familiar with such matters, would use in similar activities for like clients with like aims in accordance and compliance with all applicable laws, rules, and regulations.

DUTIES & RESPONSIBILITIES

CUSTODIAN

Custodians are co-fiduciaries responsible for safekeeping of the Client's assets. The specific duties and responsibilities of the Custodian are to:

1. Maintain separate accounts by legal registration (individual, joint, corporate, or in trust).
2. Hold title to the assets on behalf of the Client.
3. Value the assets.
4. Collect all income owed to the Client and make payments on behalf of the Client that are related to the assets held for the Client.
5. Settle transactions on behalf of the Client.
6. Report to the Client on a regular basis a detailed list of transactions, cash activity, and assets owned, including the number of units held, the unit price, and total value.

Money Manager Evaluation

The Advisor will perform the following due diligence process when evaluating each individual investment option:

Regulatory oversight
Recommends only those money managers that are registered with the relevant regulatory body. Such regulatory bodies may include the U.S. Securities and Exchange Commission (SEC), the Office of the Comptroller of the Currency (OCC), the Commodity Futures Trading Commission (CFTC), or the relevant state insurance regulatory body.

Correlation to style or peer group
The degree of correlation of the manager's investment product to an appropriate peer group and benchmark index. This is one of the most critical parts of the analysis, since most of the remaining due diligence involves comparisons of the manager to the appropriate peer group. (See Appendix C)

Performance relative to a peer group and benchmark index
The product's performance relative to its peer group and a benchmark index for annual and cumulative periods (1-, 3-, 5- and 10-year returns).

Performance relative to assumed risk
The product's risk-adjusted performance when measured against the manager's peer group as reflected by the fund's Alpha statistic, Sharpe ratio, and/or other risk-adjusted performance measures.

Track record
The product's inception date and the tenure of the money management team.

Assets under management
The level of assets under management within the screened product.

Holdings consistent with style
The percentage of the portfolio invested in "unrelated" asset class securities. For example, a U.S. stock fund will be reviewed for holdings in non-U.S. stock investments, cash equivalents, and bonds.

Expense ratios/fees
The screened product's expense ratio/fees relative to its peer group.

Stability of the organization
Perceived or known organizational problems. Examples include: personnel turnover, regulatory issues, assets coming in faster than the manager can handle.

Low cost, passively managed index funds that track asset class indices are viable investment options when available. Certain client-specific options that fall outside of our recommendations are not subject to this process. These options may include legacy positions, client-directed investment choices, and/or managed accounts with limited investment menu options.

Control Procedures

Monitoring of Money Managers

The Client is aware that the ongoing review and analysis of a money manager is just as important as the due diligence process followed for the initial manager selection. Recognizing that short-term market volatility will cause significant variations in return, the Advisor intends to evaluate manager performance from a longer-term perspective. On a quarterly basis, the Advisor will evaluate the ongoing performance of each of the approved money managers in accordance with the same due diligence process described in the preceding section.

In addition to the performance-based analysis above, the advisor will also evaluate other factors that may have an impact on a money manager's ability to perform in the future. Examples are:

- Changes in investment professional staffing
- Significant reduction or growth in assets under advisement
- Change in firm ownership
- Any legal, SEC, and/or other regulatory agency proceedings affecting the firm of which the Advisor is aware.

Ultimately, the decision to retain or terminate a manager cannot be made by a formula. It is a judgment based on the Advisor's and the Client's confidence in the manager's ability to perform in the future.

Measuring Costs

The Advisor will monitor, on an ongoing basis, various costs associated with the management of the Client's investment program, including:

- Expense ratios, or investment fees, of each investment option against the appropriate peer group.
- Custody fees: The holding of the assets, collection of the income and disbursement of payments.

Annual Review

The Client will review this IPS at least annually to determine whether stated financial goals and investment objective are still relevant. The Advisor will review the IPS at least annually to determine the continued feasibility of achieving the Client's financial goals and investment objective. The IPS is not expected to change frequently. In particular, short-term changes in the financial markets should not require adjustments to the IPS.

SIGNATURES

PREPARED BY:	APPROVED BY:
January 3, 2012	January 3, 2012
SIGNATURE:	SIGNATURE:
______________________	______________________
ABC Investment Group, Inc.	Mary Thompson

APPENDIX A: MODELS, FORECASTS, AND COMMON SENSE[1]

The modeled portfolio behavior contained in the IPS is not an absolute prediction of what will happen in the future. It is simply not possible to apply modeling techniques and conclude:

"If I adopt Portfolio X, in ten years I will have $Y."

If modeling techniques do not predict the future with precision, why use them? They are used not to *predict* the future, but rather to *explore* it. In this way, models provide useful support for decisions every investor is forced to make.

An investor cannot avoid making investment decisions just because the outcomes are uncertain. Inaction, such as remaining in cash, is itself an investment decision that carries its own risks and potential rewards. Despite the inability to predict the future with precision, sound investment decision-making is still possible.

The Advisor uses the tools of modern portfolio theory to aid the Client in making the best decisions possible without precise knowledge of the future. With these tools the Advisor can:

- Prepare reasonable *assumptions* about the future behavior of asset classes based on historical data.
- Use these assumptions to model the *relative* performance of various portfolio designs, including the range of outcomes inherent in each portfolio under consideration.

These comparative models are very useful in making asset allocation decisions. Again, these models are not predictions of outcomes in absolute terms.

The Advisor prepares the assumptions used in these models by analyzing historical data and applying the collective judgment of its investment professionals. Subjective elements are involved, such as the selection of the data sets and time periods. Common sense is used at each step, but in the end the assumptions are just that. Given these uncertainties, "past performance does not guarantee future results".

[1]Derived from the work of Mark Laskow.

Appendix B: Capital Market Assumptions

Modeled Performance Statistics

Asset Class	Expected Return	Standard Deviation
Short-Term Debt Investments	2.5	2
U.S. Bonds	3.5	8
Non-U.S. Bonds	3.5	10
U.S. Stocks	9.0	22
Non-U.S. Stocks	10.0	25
Real Estate Securities	8.5	25
Commodity-Linked Securities	7.0	18

Modeled Correlations

	(1)	(2)	(3)	(4)	(5)	(6)	(7)
(1) Short-Term Debt Investments	1.00						
(2) U.S. Bonds	0.09	1.00					
(3) Non-U.S. Bonds	-0.18	0.36	1.00				
(4) U.S. Stocks	0.25	-0.01	0.05	1.00			
(5) Non-U.S. Stocks	-0.10	-0.29	0.16	0.76	1.00		
(6) Real Estate Securities	-0.04	0.06	-0.12	0.46	0.45	1.00	
(7) Commodity-Linked Securities	0.03	-0.20	-0.09	0.24	0.37	0.51	1.00

Appendix C: Asset Class Peer Groups and Indices

Asset Class	Peer Groups	Representative Benchmark Indices*
Ultra-Short Bonds	Morningstar UltraShort Bond	3 Month T-Bill
	ABC UltraShort Muni Bond	6 Month CD
Short-Term Bonds	Morningstar Short-Term Bond	Barclays 1-3 Year Government
	Morningstar Muni-National Short	Barclays 1-5 Year Government
		Barclays Municipal 3 Year (2-4)
Global Bonds	Morningstar Intermediate-Term Bond	Citigroup Non-$ Wld Gov
	Morningstar Multi-Sector Bond	CSFB High Yield
	Morningstar Inflation-Protected Bond	JP Morgan Emerging Markets Global
	Morningstar Muni-National Intermediate	Barclays 5-10 Yr Govt/Credit
		Barclays Aggregate Bond
		Barclays Global Aggregate Bond
		Barclays Government
		Barclays Govt/Credit
		Barclays Interm Govt/Credit
		Barclays Municipal 10 Year (8-12)
		Barclays Municipal Bond
		Barclays U.S. TIPS
		Barclays U.S. Univ Bond
		BofA Merrill Lynch BB/B Global High Yield
U.S. Stocks	Morningstar Large Blend	MSCI KLD 400 Social Index
	Morningstar Large Value	Russell 1000
	Morningstar Large Growth	Russell 1000 Growth
	Morningstar Mid-Cap Blend	Russell 1000 Value
	Morningstar Small-Cap Blend	Russell 2000
	Morningstar Small-Cap Value	Russell 2000 Growth
	Morningstar Small-Cap Growth	Russell 2000 Value
		Russell 3000
		Russell Midcap
		Russell Midcap Growth
		Russell Midcap Value
		Standard & Poor's 500
		Standard & Poor's Midcap 400
		Standard & Poor's Smallcap 600
		Wilshire 5000

Appendix C: Asset Class Peer Groups and Indices

Asset Class	Peer Groups	Representative Benchmark Indices*
Non-U.S. Stocks	Morningstar Foreign Large Blend	MSCI AC World Free ID
	Morningstar Foreign Small/Mid Value	MSCI EAFE Gross USD
	Morningstar Diversified Emerging Markets	MSCI EM Gross USD
		MSCI World ex-US NR USD
		MSCI World NR USD
Real Estate Securities	Morningstar Real Estate	FTSE NAREIT Equity REIT Index
	Morningstar Global Real Estate	FTSE EPRA/NAREIT Global ex-US Index
		FTSE EPRA/NAREIT Global Real Estate Index
		Wilshire REIT
Commodity-Linked Securities	Morningstar Commodities Broad Basket	Dow Jones UBS Commodity Index
		Standard & Poors GSCI Index

* In some situations, other benchmark indices may be used.

Chapter 15

Resolving Problems Encountered During Implementation

> There is nothing more profitable for a man than to take good counsel with himself; for even if the event turns out contrary to one's hope, still one's decision was right, even though fortune has made it of no effect: whereas if a man acts contrary to good counsel, although by luck he gets what he had no right to expect, his decision was not any the less foolish.
>
> —*Herodotus (c. 485–425 BC)*, Histories

> Nothing astonishes men so much as common sense and plain dealing.
>
> —*Ralph Waldo Emerson (1803–1882)*, Art, *1841*

Imagine an advisor who has successfully guided a client through the multiple stages of portfolio design as outlined in this book. Together they have created an individually tailored asset allocation strategy and detailed plan for implementation. The new recommended portfolio structure has a decidedly different asset allocation that includes asset classes that are missing in the client's current portfolio. The new portfolio is also better diversified across securities within asset classes. With its better diversification, the new portfolio likely will generate higher volatility-adjusted returns than the old portfolio. As a result, the probability is greater that the client will reach his financial goals. Given that the client has meaningfully participated in the development of the new strategy, the client also should sleep better at night and be less likely to make poor investment decisions during market extremes.

In a world without financial constraints, such as transaction costs and/or capital gains taxes, a rational investor would embrace and comfortably implement the new portfolio strategy. People are not completely rational, however. A client may resist implementing the new strategy due to various psychological and emotional factors that muddy his thinking. Sometimes financial constraints, such as transaction costs and/or capital gains taxes, also must be considered before implementing the new strategy.

Recommendations to sell old, familiar investments in order to buy new, unfamiliar investments can generate client anxiety, even though the changes may substantially improve the risk and return characteristics of a portfolio. The fact that clients psychologically tend to equate familiarity and comfort with safety further complicates the situation. That which is unfamiliar brings with it discomfort and an associated misperceived riskiness. The result can be inertia. Although the recommended portfolio looks good, it is difficult for the client to implement the strategy fully.

Client Inertia

The field of behavioral finance studies how various cognitive errors and emotional biases influence the decisions made by investors. The field can be thought of as the psychology of financial decision making, with particular emphasis on the irrational thinking that leads to bad decisions.

The origin of behavioral finance is often traced to a landmark paper on *prospect theory* written in 1979 by Daniel Kahneman and Amos Tversky. Prospect theory describes, among other things, how investors experience more pain for a given size loss than they feel pleasure for a gain of equal magnitude. Since then, a number of other academics also have made significant contributions to the field of behavioral finance, including Dick Thaler (University of Chicago), Robert Shiller (Yale University), and Meir Statman (University of California at Santa Clara). In 2002, Daniel Kahneman received the Nobel Prize in Economic Sciences for his seminal work. This recognition further solidified behavioral finance as an important field of study.

Where there is a problem, there is an opportunity. Clients are usually unaware of the cognitive errors and emotional biases that lead to poor investment decisions. Through education and counseling, advisors are uniquely positioned to help clients understand and avoid these pitfalls.

If a client fails to adopt an improved asset allocation strategy, he may pay a price in the form of various potential opportunity costs:

1. By continuing to follow his old strategy, the client may be exposed to risks that the new strategy might otherwise mitigate.
2. The old strategy may increase the likelihood that the client makes bad investment decisions during market extremes.
3. The likelihood of reaching his financial goals may be lower with the old strategy than with the new strategy.
4. Although he may avoid transaction costs and/or capital gains taxes by continuing to follow his old strategy, he may forgo much larger financial rewards associated with the new strategy.

Occasionally, the source of client inertia is a highly appreciated, concentrated stock position. Let's assume an advisor works with a client, Mr. Smith, whose entire investment portfolio consists of BioTech stock that he inherited many years ago. Retaining this investment not only prevents adequate diversification across securities within the U.S. stocks asset class; it also precludes diversification into other asset classes in the recommended portfolio structure. A good portion of the total volatility of an individual stock can be diversified away simply by combining it with other stocks with dissimilar patterns of returns in a diversified portfolio. Because diversifiable volatility can be eliminated easily, the market does not pay a premium for bearing it.[1] In essence, the market prices securities to reward investors for bearing only that portion of a stock's volatility that cannot be diversified away. Thus Mr. Smith is exposed to an extra portion of volatility risk, which the market pays him no reward for bearing. In addition, his concentrated stock position does not take advantage of the significant improvements in volatility-adjusted returns made possible by better asset class diversification.

Imagine a hypothetical conversation between Mr. Smith and his advisor. Throughout the conversation, I will add parenthetical remarks that discuss problematic cognitive errors and emotional biases that have been researched in behavioral finance studies. These errors and biases may cause Mr. Smith to make a bad investment decision.

Advisor: "You have a very large percentage of your total portfolio committed to BioTech stock."

Client: "Yes, it has really done well over the years. I inherited two things from my Uncle Milty when he died 20 years ago—50,000 shares of BioTech stock and a bearskin rug. I really loved Uncle Milty. I love that bearskin rug, and I love my BioTech stock."

(*Attachment bias*: Holding onto an investment for emotional reasons.)

Advisor: "Your Uncle Milty sounds like he was a great guy. I'm concerned, however, about the diversifiable volatility you retain by continuing to hold such a large position. The marketplace does not provide any compensation for volatility that can be eliminated through broad diversification."

Client: "Yes, but the stock has performed really well over the years. It was worth only $10 per share when I inherited it. It is now worth $90 per share."

Advisor: "The new portfolio we have designed can accommodate a modest position in the stock if you prefer, but we recommend that you substantially reduce the commitment in order to free up the funds needed to move to the new strategy with its better diversification."

Client: "I understand what you are saying, but why should I get off a winning horse?"

(*Inappropriate extrapolation*: The tendency to assume that past performance has a momentum that will continue into the future.)

"I was pretty sure that you were going to recommend that I sell my BioTech stock, so I went onto the Internet and found several articles that say it is a great company and that the stock should continue to perform well."

(*Confirmation bias*: The tendency to accept information that supports a prior belief and to dismiss information that conflicts with it. In essence, we hear what we want to hear. Did Mr. Smith skip past any articles that had neutral or negative opinions about BioTech stock?)

Advisor: "Assume for a moment that you do not own the stock but have a sum of cash equal in value to your current stock commitment. Would you buy that much BioTech stock at today's price of $90 per share?"

(*Framing*: The way a situation is presented, or framed, can affect how someone responds to the information.)

Client: "No. I would never purchase a position that big if I had to buy it at today's price!"

(Investors tend to view highly appreciated investments as bargains, because they think of them in terms of their low acquisition prices. Of course, historical cost has nothing to do with whether BioTech stock will continue to perform well from its current market value of $90 per share.)

The advisor pauses for a moment to give Mr. Smith an opportunity to reflect on the inconsistency between wanting to hold onto all his shares of BioTech stock, yet at the same time acknowledging that he would not invest that much in BioTech stock if he did not already own it.

Advisor: "You see the inconsistency, don't you? I recommend you at least reduce your BioTech stock commitment to the lesser amount you would be inclined to purchase today at $90 per share, if you did not already own it."

(By considering the question in terms of how much BioTech stock he would purchase today at $90 per share if he did not already own the stock, Mr. Smith may discover that he actually prefers a more modest investment in BioTech. This insight may be sufficient to motivate Mr. Smith to reduce his commitment.)

Client: "I see your point, but what if I sell most of my stock and the price of BioTech stock subsequently soars?"

(*Fear of regret:* The tendency to take no action rather than implement a good recommendation that offers a higher likelihood of success yet still has some chance of looking bad in retrospect.)

Advisor: "I cannot promise you that that won't happen. Consider, however, that there are two ways to make a mistake. It is true that you can take action and that subsequent events may prove that you would have been better off staying put. It is also true, however, that you can stay put and that subsequent events may prove that taking action would have been better. We live in an uncertain world. Your better bet is to reduce your BioTech stock position and implement the new strategy with its broader diversification. I recommend that you go with the odds, don't look back, and do your best to emotionally detach yourself from the outcome."

(It is worthwhile rereading the quote by Herodotus at the beginning of this chapter.)

Client: "I made a good decision by not diversifying until now."

(*Self-affirmation bias*: The tendency to believe, when something works out well, that it is due to the intelligence of a prior decision. When things don't work out, the tendency is to chalk it up to bad luck. When Mr. Smith inherited the stock, did he make a conscious decision to hold it based on an informed evaluation of its future prospects and its role in his portfolio, or did he simply hold the stock by default?)

(*Hindsight bias*: The tendency to believe we understand why things happened as they did.)

"And I think that BioTech stock will continue to be a winner."

(*Overconfidence*: The tendency to overestimate one's skills and abilities. Does Mr. Smith have the investment knowledge to confidently form a conclusion regarding BioTech stock's future performance?)

(*Outcome bias*: The tendency to make a decision based on what you want to happen rather than on the likelihood of it happening.)

"I appreciate your advice, but for now, I am going to stay put."

(*Status quo bias*: The tendency to do nothing rather than take an action that would likely lead to a better outcome.)

A better strategy cannot work unless it is implemented and followed. A client's cognitive errors and emotional biases stand in the way of good investment decision making. Where there is a problem, there is an opportunity. Through education and good coaching, an advisor can help clients avoid the pitfalls of emotional decisions and muddled thinking. This is a very valuable part of the service a good advisor provides to clients.

Capital Gains Taxes and Transaction Costs

Of course, at times a client has a good reason to pause before selling a highly appreciated concentrated stock position—for example, capital gains taxes and/or significant transaction costs. Under the federal income tax laws in effect at the time of this writing, if an investor holds an appreciated stock at the time of his death, the inheritor of the stock receives a stepped-up tax basis. The capital gains taxes attributable to the appreciation that occurred during the deceased's lifetime are eliminated. Obviously, a client's age and health therefore need to be considered when evaluating the disposition of an appreciated security. If the client in the example above, Mr. Smith, were terminally ill, retaining this stock probably would be advisable. When an investor evaluates whether he should hold an appreciated stock until his death, the choice entails either paying or not paying capital gains taxes.

If, however, a client expects to eventually sell the appreciated stock at some point prior to his death, the choice is *not* to either pay the capital gains taxes or not pay the capital gains taxes. Rather, the choice is to either pay the taxes sooner or pay the taxes later. The question concerns the *time value of money*, where the economic cost involved with selling an appreciated security is equal to the difference between the taxes due if sold now and the discounted present value of the taxes due at the future time of sale—a much smaller economic cost to justify a move toward a better-diversified portfolio.

Although the taxes will not be paid until the security is sold, the government's claim on its share of the appreciation nevertheless exists. For this reason, it may be advisable to carry the security on the client's balance sheet at a lower value that adjusts for the anticipated taxes due upon sale. This accomplishes two things: First, it generates client awareness that the security should not be retained merely because its sale will trigger the current payment of capital gains taxes. Second, it avoids the perception of a decrease in net worth as a result of the sale of an appreciated security that is not expected to be held until death. When the issue is framed this way, a client may be less resistant to paying capital gains taxes in order to broaden the diversification of the portfolio and thereby improve its volatility-adjusted returns.

Another complicating factor exists when the appreciated security has a substantial income yield. Although the government has a claim on the unrealized appreciation, the client nevertheless gets the entire income stream from the security. Consider a stock with a $26-per-share tax basis, now selling for $100 per share. If the stock pays $4 per year in dividends, its current income yield is 4 percent. Assume that, upon sale, 15 percent of the realized gain will be lost to capital gains taxes. After-tax sale proceeds of $88.90 are available for repositioning. In order to generate the same $4 per share in income, we need to invest in a stock with a 4.5 percent yield ($88.90 × 0.045 = $4). This factor needs to be considered in the decision concerning retention or disposition.

Exhibit 15.1 lists a variety of factors to consider when evaluating the merits of diversifying out of a concentrated stock position. A Monte Carlo simulation is a very helpful modeling technique to quantify whether the financial rewards associated with a new portfolio structure are sufficient to justify paying the capital gains taxes and/or transaction costs involved with moving to the new portfolio structure. Monte Carlo simulation derives its name from random games of chance, such as roulette wheels and slot machines, found in Monte Carlo gambling casinos. Monte Carlo simulation techniques model the likelihood that a given portfolio strategy will successfully meet

Exhibit 15.1
Concentrated Stock Position: Diversification Decision Factors

These factors argue for retention of the concentrated stock:

1. Low cost basis
2. High tax rate on the gain
3. Future tax rates expected to be lower
4. Step-up in tax basis possible at death
5. Low volatility
6. Short time horizon
7. High expected return relative to the market
8. High risk-free interest rate
9. High dividend yield
10. No other planning options to manage tax liabilities

The opposite factors argue for diversification of the concentrated stock:

1. High cost basis
2. Low tax rate on the gain
3. Future tax rates expected to be high
4. No step-up in tax basis available
5. High volatility
6. Long time horizon
7. The same or lower expected return relative to the market
8. Low risk-free interest rate
9. Low dividend yield
10. Other planning options are available to manage tax liabilities

specific financial goals. A variety of factors determine this probability of success. All other things being equal, these factors increase the probability of success:

1. Larger portfolio
2. Higher portfolio expected return
3. Lower portfolio standard deviation
4. Larger contributions to the portfolio
5. Portfolio contributions that occur nearer to the present
6. Smaller portfolio withdrawals
7. Portfolio withdrawals that occur farther into the future

To perform a Monte Carlo simulation, the advisor first determines the size of the portfolio and the magnitude and timing of cash flows into and out of it. On the basis of the portfolio's expected return and standard deviation, the Monte Carlo program randomly simulates a set of future portfolio returns for the investment time horizon under consideration. The program then uses this sequence of simulated returns to calculate the changing value of the portfolio, taking into consideration the magnitude and timing of any contributions to or withdrawals from the portfolio. If money is left in the portfolio at the end of the investment time horizon, the portfolio strategy is a success for that particular trial simulation. If the portfolio runs out of money prior to the end of the investment time horizon, the portfolio strategy is a failure for that particular trial simulation. The process starts again with a new randomly simulated set of future portfolio returns and a determination of success or failure for that trial simulation. The Monte Carlo simulator runs thousands of such trial simulations and tabulates the percentage of trials that had money in the portfolio at the end of the investment time horizon. That percentage is the portfolio strategy's modeled probability of success.[2]

Let's use Mr. Smith's situation to illustrate a simplified Monte Carlo simulation. As we noted previously, he is resisting implementing the new multiple-asset-class portfolio strategy. Adding to his resistance is a $600,000 capital gains tax [50,000 shares × ($90 per share current market value −$10 per share tax basis) × 15% capital gains tax rate] that he must pay if he sells his 50,000 shares of BioTech in order to implement the proposed portfolio strategy. The proposed strategy has an expected return of 8 percent with a standard deviation of 10 percent. By comparison, BioTech has an expected return of 12 percent with a standard deviation of 40 percent. To meet his living expenses, he plans to withdraw annually from his portfolio $180,000 adjusted upward by an assumed inflation rate of 3 percent. What should he do? If he stays put, he continues to own a very volatile portfolio of BioTech stock currently worth $4,500,000. If he sells his BioTech stock, he will pay $600,000 in capital gains taxes and invest the remaining $3,900,000 in a much less volatile, multiple-asset-class portfolio.

Exhibit 15.2 summarizes the results of the Monte Carlo simulation. Despite the smaller initial portfolio value due to the payment of $600,000 in capital gains taxes, the multiple-asset-class portfolio has a higher probability of successfully generating an inflation-adjusted

Exhibit 15.2
Monte Carlo Simulation Illustration

	Concentrated Position in BioTech Stock	Multiple-Asset-Class Portfolio
Value	$4,500,000	$3,900,000
Expected return	12.0%	8.0%
Standard deviation	40.0%	10.0%
Inflation-adjusted annual withdrawal*	$180,000	$180,000
Initial withdrawal rate	4.0%	4.6%
Probability of success:		
10 Years	91%	100%
20 Years	64%	99%
40 Years	42%	70%

*Presumes an annual inflation rate of 3%.

Source: Monte Carlo simulation illustration used by permission of Wealthcare Capital Management, Inc., calculated using Wealthcare's Financeware wealth management application (http://www.financeware.com).

$180,000 annual cash flow. The initial 4 percent portfolio withdrawal rate from the concentrated BioTech stock position may seem modest, but the inflation adjustment will more than triple the annual withdrawal from $180,000 to $587,167 over the 40-year investment time horizon. The Achilles' heel of the concentrated stock position is the high standard deviation characteristic of most individual stocks. Despite a smaller initial portfolio value and lower expected return, the multiple-asset-class portfolio has one overriding advantage—its much lower standard deviation. By the end of the 40-year investment time horizon, the concentrated BioTech position has a probability of success of 42 percent—that is, given the modeling assumptions, the chances are greater than even that the portfolio will run out of money. By comparison, the multiple-asset-class portfolio has a 70 percent probability of successfully supporting the inflation-adjusted $180,000 annual cash flow.

Although it often makes most sense to simply pay the capital gains taxes in order to move to the new portfolio, other strategies are available to manage concentrated stock positions. An *equity collar* involves the simultaneous purchase of a put option and sale of a call option.

This strategy can protect the value of the concentrated position while waiting for a stepped-up basis or until the expiration of Securities and Exchange Commission restrictions in certain situations. The tax rules can be complicated, so advice from a tax professional is important.

A *prepaid variable forward contract* is an agreement with a financial institution in which an investor agrees to sell stock at a future date within a specified price range. It is similar to an equity collar in that the contract provides downside protection while limiting the potential gain on the upside. Although it enables immediate partial monetization of the stock position, the up-front payment to the investor is usually a significantly discounted percentage of the stock price.

An *exchange fund* enables an investor to dispose of low-tax-basis shares by contributing them to the fund along with other investors who hold low-basis stock in other companies. In exchange, the investor receives shares of the fund and thereby obtains an indirect interest in all the investments within the fund. Taxation of the capital gains is deferred provided that the investor holds his fund shares for at least seven years. After the seven-year holding period, the investor receives payment in the form of a prorated share of the securities in the fund, but with the original tax basis of the shares contributed by the investor. Tax law requires that 20 percent of the fund's assets be invested in relatively illiquid assets, such as real estate. There is also no guarantee that the fund will be adequately diversified.

Tax-managed index separate accounts exploit the price volatility of stocks to systematically harvest tax losses. These losses are available to offset taxable gains from other securities. In the process, funds are freed to move the portfolio toward the new portfolio strategy.

Although probably not the best course of action in most circumstances, concentrated stock positions can serve as collateral to borrow money on margin in order to invest in a more diversified portfolio.

An investor can also give appreciated securities to family members or friends. Even though the tax basis of the securities is transferred with the gift, if the new owner is in a lower tax bracket, she may be able to sell the security with a smaller tax cost.

For charitably minded investors, appreciated securities can be given outright to a qualifying charity, which can then liquidate them without tax consequence and thereby benefit from the full market value of the appreciated securities. Depending on the investor's tax situation, he may qualify for an income tax deduction. A gift of an appreciated security is usually a superior alternative to an equivalent cash bequest to a charity. Charitable remainder trusts, charitable lead trusts, or the formation of a private foundation may also be advisable for certain investors who want a tax-advantaged strategy for supporting charities.

Unrealized Capital Losses

Sometimes the advisor recommends selling an investment that has an unusually large unrealized capital loss. Cognitive errors and emotional biases may again cause a client to make a poor investment decision. Here, the conversation between the advisor and client may sound like this:

Advisor: "We recommend that you sell your Global Dynamo stock because it is not a preferred investment for the recommended target portfolio we designed together."

Client: "Yes, that stock has been rotten. I bought it for $50 per share, and now it's worth only $8 per share. But if I sell it now, I'll lose money."

(*Anchoring*: The tendency to become fixated on a specific price as the real value of a stock.)

Advisor: "You already have lost the money."

Client: "No, I haven't. It's just a paper loss."

(*Disposition effect*: The tendency to hold onto a stock that has lost value in order to avoid recognition of the loss.)

Advisor: "Assume for a moment that you do not own the stock but have a sum of cash equal to your current commitment. Would you buy it today at $8 per share?"

(*Framing*: The way a situation is presented, or framed, can affect how someone responds to the information.)

Client: "No way. I can't wait to sell it, and as soon as it gets back to $50 per share, I'm dumping it!"

The psychology underlying the "paper loss syndrome" is the erroneous conviction that no money is lost unless the security is sold and that paper losses have no economic substance. Again, apart from tax considerations, historical cost should have nothing to do with the decision to either retain or sell the security. What the client really is resisting is the admission of having made an investment that did not work out well. Once it is sold for a loss, the verdict is unavoidably apparent. But if the client holds the investment, he still can hope that some day the investment will break even.

These problems can often be overcome by the recommended exercise of having the client hypothetically assume that his or her entire portfolio has been converted to cash before designing the new target portfolio. This exercise frees the client from past decisions, with the result that new recommendations are no longer pitted against the sale of old and familiar positions. The entire range of investment options, including those positions the client currently owns, are available for consideration as building blocks for the target portfolio. With this approach, a client may still decide to retain some of the old familiar investments but likely will choose a more reasonable percentage allocation for them.

Investment decisions should be active. Traditionally, investment recommendations are classified as either *buy, hold,* or *sell*. I think hold recommendations often evade the responsibility to make active decisions, and the sell rule and buy rule should be one and the same.

The general rule stated simply is this: Hold in your portfolio only those investments that you would actively repurchase if you did not already own them. Subject to giving due consideration to tax and transaction costs, sell everything else.

Big Dollar Decisions

Investing large sums of money produces anxiety for many clients, particularly for unsophisticated clients who may suddenly have won the lottery or received a large inheritance. For the first time in their lives, they may be facing the need to make major investment decisions. Encouraging the client to think holistically regarding the entire portfolio and expressing investment recommendations as a percentage of the total portfolio can alleviate part of the anxiety. For example, a recommendation to invest 10 percent of a $5 million portfolio in commodity-linked securities sounds much less dramatic than investing $500,000 in the same position.

Resistance to Specific Investment Recommendations

The portfolio belongs to the client, and the client appropriately has veto power over any investment recommendation. Occasionally, however, a client rejects a specific investment for the wrong reasons. For example, a client may reject a recommended position in a non-U.S. stock mutual fund. As you dig deeper, it becomes apparent that she is not objecting to the specific investment recommendation. Rather, she is uncomfortable with non-U.S. stocks as an asset class. When this occurs, it indicates that a prior, more general level of decision making was not firmed up properly before proceeding to the next step.

The portfolio design process should proceed from the broad portfolio balance level to the more detailed asset allocation level and then finally to the specific investment positions. Each level of decision making should be firmly established before proceeding to the next. If done properly, this sequence will generate a positive momentum in the decision-making process and prevent a client's objection to a specific investment for reasons that should have been addressed at a more general level of decision making. It is fine for a client to object to a specific investment, as long as the objection relates to that level of decision making. If it does not, it is important to withdraw the recommendation and move back to the more general level of decision making that involves the source of the objection. The resolution may require a modification of either the broad portfolio balance decision or asset allocation strategy, which in turn will necessitate a redesigned target portfolio.

Obtaining Cash from the Portfolio for the Client's Expenditures

Advisor: "Here is the recommended target portfolio. It is broadly diversified among multiple asset classes and will maximize the portfolio's expected return subject to your volatility tolerance and time horizon."

Client: "Nice portfolio, but I couldn't possibly live on that yield. Why don't we cut down on the stock investments and reposition the proceeds in bonds until the portfolio yield matches my income needs?"

Exhibit 15.3 shows the components of return for three asset mixes of bonds and stocks. Assume that a particular client should have an asset mix of 50 percent bonds and 50 percent stocks, given her investment time horizon and volatility tolerance. This portfolio has an expected total return of 6 percent, composed of a 3 percent current yield plus a 3 percent average rate of capital appreciation. If the client has a $1 million portfolio, this mix will generate an income yield of $30,000. But what if her cash needs are $40,000 per year? Her higher cash flow needs require the invasion of principal. Most clients have had the advice to "never spend your principal" drilled into them. Although this advice

Exhibit 15.3
Components of Return

	Asset Mix 1	Asset Mix 2	Asset Mix 3
Bonds	100%	50%	0%
Stocks	0%	50%	100%
Total	100%	100%	100%
Asset mix yield	4%	3%	2%
Capital appreciation	0%	3%	6%
Asset mix total return	4%	6%	8%

is good in spirit, too literal an interpretation of the warning can result in a poor investment decision. A properly balanced portfolio maximizes the total return for a client subject to her volatility tolerance. If the income yield on the portfolio is less than what is needed for current expenditures, the client's first impulse often is to boost the portfolio yield by selling appreciation-oriented equity investments in order to buy more interest-generating investments. In our example, the client must move to a portfolio composed entirely of bonds in order to generate a current income yield sufficient for her needs. Ironically, if the client does so, she will subject herself to the very danger she was trying to avoid by not spending her principal. That is, increasing her income yield from 3 to 4 percent is accompanied by a 2 percent reduction in total return, thereby increasing her exposure to purchasing power erosion.

The solution is to educate the client to think in terms of total return (yield plus capital appreciation) rather than income yield. Within a total return framework, clients gain an appreciation that it may be better to spend a little principal to supplement the lower income yield from a portfolio with a higher total return than to choose a portfolio with a higher income yield but lower total return.[3] Creating an asset allocation strategy that can confidently support a client's future cash flow needs involves an intricate interplay among the portfolio's expected return, its standard deviation, the relevant investment time horizon, and the timing and magnitude of portfolio contributions and withdrawals. In the next section, we will illustrate how an advisor can use a Monte Carlo simulation to calculate the probability that the proposed asset allocation strategy successfully will meet the client's future cash flow needs.

Real Annual Portfolio Withdrawal Rates

In Chapter 2 we discussed the plight of a 50-year old widow with $2.5 million invested in certificates of deposit. In a world with even modest levels of persistent inflation, the purchasing power of a portfolio can erode significantly over time if too much of its average total return is used to meet living expenses. Sometimes, clients respond by saying that they do not want to leave a huge portfolio to their survivors, and so periodic invasions of principal are acceptable to them. The problem is that even an intentional full liquidation of principal may not increase sufficiently the cash flow available for meeting living expenses. For example, the widow with $2.5 million invested in certificates of deposit at 4 percent has an interest income of $100,000 per year. If, instead of spending only the interest, she systematically liquidates the principal over her 30-year life expectancy, her annual cash flow will increase to $144,575. This higher cash flow is not enough to compensate for a 3 percent inflationary environment that will increase the cost of living by 2.4 times over her remaining life expectancy.

Ideally, it would be advisable to choose a real (that is, inflation-adjusted) annual withdrawal rate that will maintain the purchasing power of the investment portfolio. At first blush, we seem to be able to achieve this goal by setting the annual portfolio withdrawal rate equal to the difference between the portfolio compound annual return and the inflation rate. To work reliably, however, the portfolio must have a constant rate of return—that is, a standard deviation equal to zero. For example, Exhibit 15.4 illustrates that, with a constant portfolio return of 5 percent and an inflation rate of 3 percent, the portfolio can sustain in perpetuity a real withdrawal rate of 2 percent. With volatile

Exhibit 15.4

Sustainable Real Portfolio Withdrawal Rate: Constant Returns

Initial portfolio value:	$1,000,000
Expected return:	5%
Standard deviation:	0%
Compound annual return:	5%
Minus inflation rate:	– 3%
Sustainable real portfolio withdrawal rate:	2%
Initial dollar withdrawal:	$20,000

	Dollar Values				Inflation-Adjusted	
Year	Beginning of Year Portfolio Value	Year-End Portfolio Value before Withdrawal	Year-End Withdrawal	Portfolio Ending Value	Portfolio Value	Withdrawal
1	$1,000,000	$1,050,000	$20,000	$1,030,000	$1,000,000	$20,000
2	1,030,000	1,081,500	20,600	1,060,900	1,000,000	20,000
3	1,060,900	1,113,945	21,218	1,092,727	1,000,000	20,000
4	1,092,727	1,147,363	21,855	1,125,509	1,000,000	20,000
5	1,125,509	1,181,784	22,510	1,159,274	1,000,000	20,000
6	1,159,274	1,217,238	23,185	1,194,052	1,000,000	20,000
7	1,194,052	1,253,755	23,881	1,229,874	1,000,000	20,000
8	1,229,874	1,291,368	24,597	1,266,770	1,000,000	20,000
9	1,266,770	1,330,109	25,335	1,304,773	1,000,000	20,000
10	1,304,773	1,370,012	26,095	1,343,916	1,000,000	20,000

Exhibit 15.5
Real Portfolio Withdrawal Rates: Volatile Returns

	Portfolio 1	Portfolio 2
Initial portfolio value	$1,000,000	$1,000,000
Expected return	9.5%	8.0%
Standard deviation	20.0%	10.0%
Estimated compound annual return	7.5%	7.5%
Investment time horizon	40 years	40 years
Inflation-Adjusted Withdrawals		
90% Probability of success		
Initial dollar withdrawal	$25,000	$37,000
Initial withdrawal rate	2.5%	3.7%
75% Probability of success		
Initial dollar withdrawal	$35,000	$44,000
Initial withdrawal rate	3.5%	4.4%

Source: Monte Carlo simulation illustration used by permission of Wealthcare Capital Management, Inc., calculated using Wealthcare's Financeware wealth management application (http://www.financeware.com).

returns, however, long-term real portfolio withdrawal rates are lower. To understand why, let's use Monte Carlo simulation to model long-term real portfolio withdrawal rates for the two portfolios shown in Exhibit 15.5. Portfolio 1 has a 9.5 percent expected return, a 20 percent standard deviation, and an estimated compound annual return of 7.5 percent. Portfolio 2 has an 8 percent expected return, a 10 percent standard deviation, and an estimated compound annual return of 7.5 percent.[4] For this illustration, I have placed the two portfolios on an even footing by giving each an identical compound annual return of 7.5 percent. This way, we can focus on the damaging impact of portfolio volatility. With a 90 percent probability of success, portfolio 1 can sustain an inflation-adjusted annual withdrawal of $25,000. With its considerably smaller standard deviation, portfolio 2 can sustain a higher inflation-adjusted annual withdrawal of $37,000. These withdrawal rates of 2.5 percent and 3.7 percent, respectively, are modest relative to each portfolio's estimated compound annual return of

Exhibit 15.6
Portfolio Withdrawals During a Bear Market

Year	Beginning of Year Portfolio Value	Return in Percent	Year-End Portfolio Value Before Withdrawal	Year-End Withdrawal*	Portfolio Ending Value
2000	$1,000,000	-9.10	$909,000	$50,000	$859,000
2001	859,000	-11.89	756,865	51,500	705,365
2002	705,365	-22.10	549,479	53,045	496,434

*Adjusted annually by an assumed inflation rate of 3%.

7.5 percent. If the client is willing to live with the lower probability of success of 75 percent, higher withdrawal rates of 3.5 percent and 4.4 percent, respectively, are possible.

It is not difficult to understand why volatility is so detrimental to portfolio withdrawal rates. Consider an investor who retired at the end of 1999 with his entire $1 million portfolio invested in an S&P 500 index fund—a highly volatile portfolio. To meet his living expenses, he planned to withdraw an inflation-adjusted $50,000 annually from his portfolio. Exhibit 15.6 shows that, by the end of 2002, the bear market coupled with portfolio withdrawals reduced his portfolio to only $496,434. At that point, it became very unlikely that his portfolio would be able to continue to sustain an inflation-adjusted $50,000 annual portfolio withdrawal for the long term. A multiple-asset-class equity strategy could have given this investor a similar long-term return with much less volatility. Less volatility means less downside risk and a greater probability of sustaining portfolio withdrawals for the long term.

Throughout the book, I have demonstrated that volatility is problematic. Investors are naturally volatility averse. That is, volatility is hard to tolerate psychologically. Volatility also impairs the rate at which money compounds. In Exhibit 15.5, for example, portfolio 1 has a higher expected return than portfolio 2, but because of the higher volatility of portfolio 1, each has the same estimated compound annual return of 7.5 percent. Now we have one more reason to disdain volatility: All other things being equal, volatility impairs sustainable portfolio withdrawal rates.

In practice, many clients face tough decisions when choosing portfolio withdrawal rates for their living expenses. Their portfolios may need to support them and their families over several decades. Their expenses may rise with inflation. They therefore will need equity in their portfolios to fight inflation. They also will need breadth of asset class diversification to mitigate the portfolio volatility that impairs portfolio withdrawal rates. Clients vary in their individual willingness and financial ability to accept lower portfolio withdrawal rates in exchange for increased probabilities that their portfolios will successfully meet their cash flow needs into the future. Advisors can help their clients design appropriate asset allocation strategies that mitigate the risks they face and model the probabilities of success of different courses of action. Clients must make the final decisions, bear the risks, and live with the consequences.

Chapter 16

The Global Financial Crisis of 2008

> History is the sum total of the things that could have been avoided.
>
> —*Konrad Adenauer (1876–1967)*

The Perfect Storm

Imagine an economic environment where equity asset classes are suddenly in trouble, big trouble, at the same time. This perfect storm happened during 2008. A combination of factors led to the crisis:

Securitization. I bought my first house in 1976 for $25,000. It was a two-story, brick Cape Cod. I put $5,000 down and took out a $20,000, 20-year mortgage at 8.5 percent fixed. My monthly mortgage payment was $174. The down payment made the bank more secure because it provided a protective cushion for the mortgage loan. The down payment also meant that I had money at risk in the transaction. The bank checked my creditworthiness and verified my assets and liabilities, income and expenses. The bank had an incentive to determine whether I would pay the loan back because the bank kept the loan on its books. If I defaulted, I could lose the equity I had in the house, and the bank might lose money as well. We were at risk together.

With the advent of securitization, mortgages are packaged and sold as securities to investors, severing the link between the financial institution, which originates the loan, and the investor, who bears the risk of the loan. With securitization, a bank or mortgage company that originates a loan no longer bears the risk of the loan once it is packaged and sold. The originator can make its money on the front end and need not be overly concerned about the riskiness of the loan.

Financial engineering. The slicing and dicing of securities makes possible the creation of tremendously complex financial instruments that modify and shift credit and interest rate risks among multiple parties. The complexity of the securities makes them difficult to value. The wide dispersion of these securities around the world, coupled with their complexity, made it all but impossible to assess the extent of the "toxic asset" problem. With the creditworthiness of financial institutions called into question, credit markets froze.

Excessive leverage. We can blame the federal government for policies that may have led to lax mortgage underwriting standards. We can blame the mortgage borrowers who took on debt they had little chance of repaying. We can blame the mortgage companies that peddled the "no documentation" subprime mortgages. We can blame the Federal National Mortgage Association (Fannie Mae) and the Federal Home Loan Mortgage Corporation (Freddie Mac), which should have been in a position to know what was going on and the accompanying risks involved. (Fannie Mae and Freddie Mac purchase and securitize mortgages in order to increase the funds available to institutions that lend money to home buyers.) We can blame the financial services companies—banks, investment banking firms, brokerage firms—which overleveraged their balance sheets and thus magnified the risks they were taking.

Misalignment of interests. Corporations, in theory, should be managed to maximize shareholder value in the long run. Unfortunately, executive compensation plans may tempt corporate executives to place short-term personal gain above long-term shareholder interests. Corporate boards of directors are also culpable in failing to provide sufficient governance on behalf of shareholders.

Greed. Plenty of blame exists to go around here as well: the mortgagor who borrows too much hoping to buy a house that will be worth a lot more a year later; the financial firms that originate, securitize, and sell the mortgage securities, without regard to the capacity of the mortgagors to service the debt; and corporate executives who are incentivized to line their own pockets while ignoring the risks to the shareholders.

Take away any one of these factors, and we might have avoided the depth and breadth of the crisis. Markets have largely recovered, but the economy will take longer to mend.

A Client's Question

After 2008's devastating equity asset class declines, a longtime client of our firm asked, "When you look back over the past 12 months, a year or two down the road, how do you think you will evaluate your asset allocation strategies?" It was a fair question. First, for the majority of our clients, including those who consider themselves volatility tolerant with long investment time horizons, we have always advocated diversification into interest-generating investments. Although interest-generating investments have lower long-term return expectations, they act like ballast in a portfolio and thus help to mitigate equity risk. This client had 40 percent of his portfolio allocated to interest-generating assets. Unfortunately, it didn't take a large equity allocation to turn portfolio results into negative territory for 2008, and for equity-oriented portfolio strategies the losses were very large.

Exhibit 16.1 shows that 30-day Treasury bills had a total return of 1.60 percent and investment-grade U.S. taxable bonds had a total return of 5.24 percent in 2008. In the panic-driven market environment of the Global Financial Crisis, Treasury bonds did markedly better, with the Barclays Intermediate Treasury Index and Barclays Long-Term Treasury Index generating 2008 total returns of 11.35 percent and 24.03 percent, respectively.

Exhibit 16.1 also shows the 2008 returns for the four equity asset classes we have discussed throughout this book. The year 1972 is the

Exhibit 16.1
Asset Class Returns

Asset Class /(Index)	2008 Total Return (%)	10 Years Ending 2008 Compound Annual Return (%)
30-Day Treasury Bills	1.60	3.22
Investment Grade U.S. Taxable Bonds (Barclays Aggregate Bond Index)	5.24	5.63
U.S. Stocks (S&P 500 Index)	-37.00	-1.38
Non-U.S. Stocks (MSCI EAFE Index)	-43.06	1.18
Real Estate Securities (FTSE NAREIT Equity REITs Index)	-37.73	7.42
Commodity-Linked Securities (S&P GSCI Index)	-46.49	7.35

Data source: *2012 Ibbotson® Stocks, Bonds, Bills, and Inflation® (SBBI®) Classic Yearbook*, © 2012 Morningstar. All rights reserved. Used with permission; and Morningstar® Principia®, © 2012 Morningstar. All Rights Reserved.

earliest for which performance data exist for all these asset classes. The return for 2008 was by far the worst for each of these asset classes over the 37-year period from 1972 through 2008. In fact, for each asset class the 2008 return was at least 10 percent worse than the next worst year during this 37-year period. Although these returns are admittedly awful, a 1-year period is much too short a time horizon over which to evaluate equity performance. In the short run, the highly volatile nature of annual equity returns overwhelms the incremental reward an investor expects to earn on average for bearing volatility risk. As a result, equity investing is appropriate only for longer time horizons during which good years can offset bad years and the equity return advantage has an opportunity to emerge. Just as an equity holding period should be longer term, an equity strategy likewise is most appropriately evaluated over longer time horizons. So I suggested to my client that we evaluate strategic asset allocation over the 10-year period ending with 2008.

The last column in Exhibit 16.1 shows the compound annual returns for each asset class over this 10-year period. Over intermediate periods, we expect (and hope) that the asset classes will have dissimilar patterns of returns. This dissimilarity in returns among the asset classes drives the long-term superior performance of a broadly diversified strategy. Of the four equity asset classes, U.S. stocks had the worst return—a compound annual loss of –1.38 percent with dividend income reinvested. (This 10-year return for U.S. stocks was the worst from 1926 to the time of publication of this book.) At the time it was only the third instance since 1926 that U.S. stocks had had a 10-year compound annual loss. Fortunately for the multiple-asset-class investor, other equity asset classes fared much better. Real estate securities and commodity-linked securities generated compound annual returns of 7.42 percent and 7.35 percent, respectively. An investment in either of these asset classes more than doubled in value over the 10-year holding period—even after sustaining huge losses in 2008.

I opened this section with our client's question about how I would eventually evaluate the effectiveness of our asset allocation strategy.

Here is my answer: Strategic asset allocation does a good job of mitigating risk, but it can't eliminate it. And the fact that returns were negative in 2008 doesn't mean that the strategy hasn't delivered on its promise. For over 25 years, I have advocated multiple-asset-class investing in my lecturing and writing and, most importantly, in advising our clients. Looking back, strategic asset allocation has rewarded investors with superior long-term volatility-adjusted returns. More specifically, long-term portfolio returns have been:

1. higher than the weighted-average return of the asset classes comprising the portfolio and
2. less volatile than the weighted-average volatility of the asset classes that comprise the portfolio.

In essence, broad diversification has enabled portfolios to perform better than the sum of their parts.

We cannot use short-term results to evaluate a longer-term strategy. We need a longer evaluation period. During the most difficult 10-year period for U.S. stocks since 1926, multiple-asset-class investing was a remarkable success. Interest-generating investments performed decently, and while U.S. stock and non-U.S. stock markets floundered, real estate securities and commodity-linked securities both doubled in value. The promise of strategic asset allocation was fulfilled—higher portfolio returns with less volatility. Multiple-asset-class investing worked.

Building a Context for 2008 Returns

Equity asset class returns were especially troubling during the Global Financial Crisis for two reasons. First was the record-setting magnitude of the 2008 losses. Second, the equity asset classes all dropped in value at the same time. Some investors believed that, with multiple-asset-class investing, at least one equity asset class always should be zigging when others are zagging. What went wrong?

Let's consider the first issue. Equity asset class losses in 2008 were certainly the worst that I had ever experienced. Exhibit 16.2 is a histogram of U.S. large company stock annual total returns from 1825 through 2011. Given this very long data series, the histogram displays a bell-shaped distribution. The return for 2008 is stacked with the return for 1937 at the interval for returns between −30 and −40 percent. U.S. large company stocks' 2008 return is thus one of the three worst returns since 1825. Yet the left side of this distribution looks like we expect it should. That is, the tail is thinnest for extremely bad returns and gradually fattens as we approach the middle portion of the distribution. Visually, we are not surprised to find two return observations in the −30 and −40 percent range.

Exhibit 16.2

U.S. Large Company Stock Annual Total Returns Histogram (1825–2011)

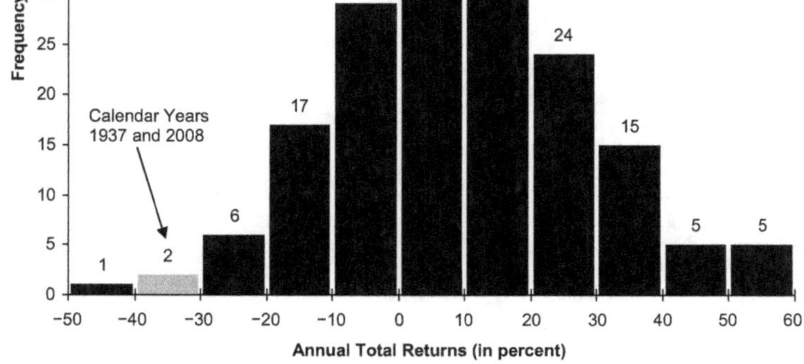

Data source for 1926–2011: *2012 Ibbotson® Stocks, Bonds, Bills, and Inflation® (SBBI®) Classic Yearbook,*

Data source for 1825–1925: William N. Goetzmann, Roger G. Ibbotson, and Liang Peng, "A New Historical Database for the NYSE 1815 to 1925: Performance and Predictability," *Journal of Financial Markets,* 2001.

Given a long enough view of history, a couple of losses of that magnitude are expected, and yet what a shock when one of those years was 2008!

Now we will examine the second issue. During 2008, the four equity asset classes simultaneously had devastating losses. Is this not a failure of multiple-asset-class equity diversification? In Chapter 8, we found that diversification payoffs are generated in a portfolio when one asset class's below-average return is partially offset by another asset class's above-average return. Therefore let's define a diversification failure as a year in which all four equity asset classes simultaneously have below-average returns or above-average returns—that is, no equity asset class is zigging while others are zagging. Exhibit 16.3 lists seven such failures—three are "positive failures," and four are "negative failures." The fact that all four equity asset classes had below-average returns in 2008 was unusual but not without precedent. Some might argue that it is not a failure of diversification when all equity asset classes deliver above-average performance; yet the "positive failures" meet our definition of failure since no asset class zigged while others zagged. These "positive failures" of diversification differ only in that no one complains about them.

Exhibit 16.3
Equity Diversification Failures (1972–2011)

Year	U.S. Stocks	Non-U.S. Stocks	Real Estate Securities	Commodity-Linked Securities	Positive Failure	Negative Failure
1981	-4.92	-1.03	6.00	-23.01		X
1983	22.56	24.61	30.64	16.26	X	
1994	1.32	8.06	3.17	5.29		X
2003	28.68	39.17	37.13	20.72	X	
2008	-37.00	-43.06	-37.73	-46.49		X
2009	26.46	32.46	27.99	13.48	X	
2011	2.11	-11.73	8.28	-1.18		X
1972-2011 Simple Average Return	11.45	12.04	13.61	12.35		

Data source: Morningstar® Principia®,

What Does the Future Hold?

Perhaps the most worrisome aspect of the Global Financial Crisis of 2008 is the "risk-on, risk-off" market environment that developed in the aftermath. The rewards of multiple-asset-class investing rely on dissimilarities in patterns of returns across the portfolio's asset classes. In a risk-on, risk-off market environment, investors tend to simultaneously buy all risky asset classes when turning optimistic and sell all risky asset classes when becoming pessimistic. This behavior is particularly acute when fear about the future is running high. As the old Wall Street saying goes: "The only things that go up in a panic are the correlations." With higher correlations among equity asset classes, the benefits of multiple-asset-class equity diversification are less. At the same time, however, when money retreats from the equity asset classes, it must go somewhere to seek safety. In the aftermath of the Global Financial Crisis, the retreat was a "flight to quality" to the perceived safety of U.S. Treasury securities. So while the correlations among equity asset classes rose during the Global Financial Crisis, the correlations between equity asset classes and very high quality bonds dropped, underscoring the value of diversification into interest-generating investments. At some point in the future, many of our current economic problems will find some sort of resolution, and we may once again find that equity asset classes will display more dissimilarity in their patterns of returns. We will have to wait and see.

Sir John Templeton, the great twentieth-century value investor, once said, "The four most dangerous words in investing are: This time it's different." I believe he was telling us that, regardless of the twists and turns of the market environment, the enduring principles of investing do not change. He was also warning us to be wary of new investment ideas. For example, during the late 1990s many argued that the "new economy" required a new investment paradigm that justified the stock market's extraordinarily high valuation level at the time. In retrospect, this was a dangerous idea. Despite Sir John's warning, however, I believe that this time something is indeed new. The capital markets never before have been in the hands of the world's politicians as much as is the case today. We must worry not just about the usual economic risks and market risks; we also must be concerned about the possibility that politicians will choose a path that takes us over a cliff. Policy makers face thorny issues that demand tough decisions: the burgeoning U.S. government debt, financial institutions that are "too big to fail and too complex to regulate," unresolved eurozone problems, to name a few. The best course of action is not always clear. For example, in the United States we currently have both a weak economy and a burgeoning debt crisis. Do we need more fiscal stimulus, or is it time for austerity? Even if agreement exists on the wisest course of action, do politicians have the political courage to enact policies that may be painful in the short run but necessary for longer-term economic health? Hopefully the world's policy makers will act preemptively with sufficient wisdom to prevent the unnecessary economic damage triggered by inaction. Too often, however, policy makers take action only when a crisis emerges that forces them to respond.

In addition to the economic risks and market risks facing investors, behavioral risks also introduce the possibility of self-inflicted wounds. In Chapter 5, we discussed the rise of tactical asset allocation following the Global Financial Crisis. Understandably, no one ever wants to again suffer equity asset class losses like those experienced in 2008. Hence, the promise of market timing and other tactical asset allocation strategies is appealing. For the reasons we discussed in Chapter 5, however, we think these tactical strategies most likely will be a detriment to portfolio performance. Investors and advisors look back at 2007 and berate themselves for not seeing the inevitable crisis that was developing. No doubt, there were people who saw and understood different aspects of the developing crisis, but the exact manner in which the crisis unfolded and the extent of the accompanying market and economic damage were not foreseen.

It is important to remember how few investors successfully sidestepped the market carnage. We examined the Morningstar database that tracks the performance of thousands of mutual funds covering a wide variety of investment strategies in both fixed-income and equity markets worldwide. Amazingly few mutual funds posted positive returns in 2008. Out of 3,734 funds that invest primarily in U.S. stocks, all but one lost money. (The single fund with a positive return was the Forester Value Fund with a total return of 0.4 percent. The fund was tiny, with only $60 million in total assets as of December 31, 2008.) The 978 funds that invest primarily in non-U.S. stocks all lost money. Every one of the 144 real estate security funds (both U.S. and non-U.S.) had negative returns. Out of 128 natural resource funds, which include those that invest in commodity-linked securities, all lost money. It was a tough year for equity investors, with all but one of the 4,984 equity mutual funds losing money. Fixed-income funds performed better but were also badly battered. Out of 1,730 bond funds, both taxable and municipal, 68 percent lost money. The bond funds with positive returns were mostly government bond funds and short-term bond funds. The scope and severity of the emerging crisis was clearly unforeseen by almost everyone.

I frankly do not like the current investment environment. Not much looks good to me right now. Risks are high and the expected returns are low for both interest-generating investments and equity investments. Nevertheless, as an investor and as an advisor, I must deal with the investment environment as it is and not as I want it to be. Despite my misgivings, as an investor I think I will be best served following a strategic asset allocation approach that utilizes multiple asset classes. As an advisor, I think this same approach will maximize the likelihood that my clients will reach their financial goals. Even though we can manage, mitigate, and modify risk, we cannot fully eliminate it. In the end, every portfolio still carries residual risk. As the former chairman of the Federal Reserve, Paul Volcker, said at a Chartered Financial Analyst conference many years ago: "You cannot hedge the world."

Conclusion

That's enough, Charlie. Don't show me any more figures; I've got the smell of the thing now.

—*Henry Ford (1863–1947) to Charles Sorenson, his lieutenant*

Certainty generally is illusion, and repose is not the destiny of man.

—*Oliver Wendell Holmes, Jr. (1841–1935),* The Path of the Law

The greatest gift is the power to estimate correctly the value of things.

—*Francois, Duc de La Rochefoucauld (1613–1680),* Maximes, *1664*

Investment management is simple but not easy. It is simple because the principles of successful investing are relatively few in number and are easy to understand. Although clients face a variety of risks in the management of their money, the two most important ones are inflation and portfolio volatility. The extent to which a portfolio is structured to avoid one of these risks unfortunately exposes it to the other. For this reason, clients must determine which risk is more dangerous to them. Time horizon is the relevant dimension along which clients make this judgment. For short investment time horizons, volatility is a bigger risk than inflation, and such portfolios should accordingly follow an asset allocation strategy that gives greater weight to interest-generating investments with stable principal values. For long investment time horizons, inflation is the more significant danger, and these portfolios should therefore have larger allocations to equity investments. Regardless of the investment time horizon, however, the risk-mitigating benefits of broad diversification argue for the utilization of multiple asset classes for all clients, regardless of volatility tolerance.

Because investment management is simple, all clients are capable of being meaningfully involved with the investment decision-making process. It is neither necessary nor advisable for a client to leave major investment decisions to the sole discretion of the investment advisor. It is the client's money, and she will have to live with the results. As a client becomes better educated regarding the investment management process, her volatility tolerance will change toward that which is most appropriate given the facts of her situation. With greater understanding, a client will make better decisions. The client also will benefit from having a realistic frame of reference for evaluating the portfolio's performance. Realistic expectations lead to greater equanimity and staying power, both of which are extremely important to the realization of financial goals.

Although investment management is simple, it is not easy. It is natural to fear the unknown and to want to reduce or eliminate uncertainty whenever possible. Uncertainties that cannot be avoided are inherent in the investment management process, however, and clients have a difficult time coping with them.

I toured Japan many years ago. Several people in our group wanted to see majestic Mount Fuji, and so a day trip by bus was organized. We were warned before we left that we had probably no better than a 50/50 chance of actually seeing the mountain peak because of typically poor visibility conditions during that time of year. When we arrived, Mount Fuji was nowhere in sight. Heavy fog and clouds blanketed the entire valley and mountain range. Having invested four hours by bus to get there, several people decided to take pictures anyway. Despite how carefully they focused their cameras, however, the fog did not go away. All they did was get a sharper picture of the fog. So it is with investment management. Clients often believe that, as professional advisors, we should have some method to eliminate the uncertainties that they find so difficult to live with comfortably. As we focus on the uncertainties inherent in investment management, however, all we can hope to accomplish is to get a better picture of the uncertainties—we cannot eliminate them. As a friend of mine who is an economist once said, "The window to the future is opaque."

As difficult as it is to accept, uncertainty is not necessarily bad. For clients with long investment time horizons, volatility is rewarded by the higher expected returns of equity investing. If we teach our clients to understand this relationship between volatility and return, they can use it to their advantage. Intellectually understanding investment concepts, however, is not the same as living with the ups and downs of an investment portfolio. Successful investing therefore always will be as much of a psychological challenge as it is an investment management endeavor.

Investment management is not easy because, without a very firm commitment to long-term investment policies within a strategic asset allocation framework, clients are easily distracted by investment schemes that promise high returns with little or no risk. Those who depart from long-term strategies in order to pursue these investments in the end will build portfolios in the same way that they collect shells at the beach, picking up whatever catches their eye at the moment. The bottom line is that no safe, quick, and easy way to build wealth exists.

Imagine that you are standing in the middle of a large group of slot machines at a Las Vegas casino. All around you, you can hear the sound of people winning as the jackpots from lucky pulls of the handle drop coins noisily into metal trays. Although it is always true at any point that some are ahead of the game (and these people always stand out from the crowd), on average the flow of money is from the pockets of those who play the game to the casino that owns the machines. Objectively we know this, but in the midst of the magic of a casino, our excitement can override better judgment as we win just often enough to make us believe that we can get ahead by continuing to play. Fueling our hope for beating this system is the evidence of our senses, which tells us that other people are indeed winning—if only we can find a "hot" slot machine.

The messages our clients receive from the day-to-day investment environment can be as distracting and misleading as the sounds of intermittently winning slot machines. Whether it is a new market-timing guru or an investment idea that seems to promise better results than a well-diversified portfolio, clients will always face temptations that encourage them to depart from a well-conceived, long-term strategy. At times, adhering to strategic asset allocation decisions may seem dangerous, such as urging our clients to allocate more money to common stocks during a bear market in order to restore the proper balance in their portfolios. At other times, the equity commitment may become too great as a result of a market rise. To persuade clients to rebalance their portfolios back to target asset allocations in the midst of a bull market may sound like a parent telling a child that he has to leave a party just when everybody really starts to have fun.

Historically, the money manager's job has been to enhance return and minimize risk by exercising superior skill in security selection and/or market timing. Success has been measured in terms of whether or not the manager has beaten the market. Since the superior talent of the money manager was presumed to be the engine driving portfolio performance, little attention was paid to the asset allocation decisions. Today, the capital markets are increasingly efficient, and it is dangerous to presume that superior skill can be safely relied on as the primary determinant of a portfolio's performance. If portfolio asset allocation decisions largely determine future performance results, then investment advisors and their clients should address issues of risk and return at the asset allocation level of decision making. The implication is that investment portfolio design and performance expectations should be based primarily on the risk and return characteristics of the portfolio asset class building blocks rather than on the often elusive positive impact of active management. As noted earlier in the book, we would do well to follow the advice of R. Buckminster Fuller, creator of the geodesic dome, who said, “Don't fight forces, use them.”

If investment management is simple but not easy, what are the implications for the investment advisory profession? Because it is simple, advisors have a tremendous opportunity to add value for clients by properly educating them. Knowledgeable clients more likely will choose and remain committed to those strategies that are most appropriate for realizing their financial goals. In addition to being educators, we also must be architects and general contractors, designing and implementing broadly diversified investment strategies that we create in collaboration with our clients. Because investment management is not easy, we have important work to do on an ongoing basis. As the capital markets move, our services will be needed to provide our clients with perspective regarding their investment experience. Particularly during extreme market conditions, clients may need the discipline and assurance of a steady hand that urges them to remain committed to their long-term strategies. We have witnessed many changes in the world capital markets over the past several decades, and more changes will undoubtedly occur in the future. In this evolving investment environment, clients do not need sporadic investment suggestions. They need and will value the comprehensive management of their portfolios by knowledgeable investment professionals who are committed to their clients' financial well-being and willing to always act in their clients' best interests.

Notes

Introduction

1. DALBAR, Inc., "Quantitative Analysis of Investor Behavior 2006," p. 5.
2. Peter L. Bernstein, *Against the Gods: The Remarkable Story of Risk,* New York: John Wiley & Sons, Inc.,1996, p. 265.

Chapter 1

1. Harry M. Markowitz, "Portfolio Selection," *Journal of Finance*, vol. 7, no. 1, March 1952.
2. In 1997, Congress passed the Uniform Management of Public Employee Retirement Systems Act. This legislation governs the management of public retirement plans and contains provisions similar to those contained in the Employee Retirement Income Security Act of 1974.
3. *Restatement of the Law/Trusts/Prudent Investor Rule*, St. Paul, MN: American Law Institute Publishers, 1992, p. ix.
4. John H. Langbein, "The Uniform Prudent Investor Act and the Future of Trust Investing," *Iowa Law Review*, vol. 81, no. 3, March 1996, pp. 646–647.
5. Langbein, "The Uniform Prudent Investor Act and the Future of Trust Investing," p. 655.
6. Langbein, "The Uniform Prudent Investor Act and the Future of Trust Investing," p. 655.

Chapter 2

1. Before 1978, the CPI (as opposed to the CPI-U) was used.
2. A new kind of U.S. bond, called a Treasury Inflation Protected Security (TIPS), was first issued by the Treasury in January 1997. Unlike a conventional bond that promises a known nominal return if held to maturity but unknown real return, a Treasury Inflation Protected Security promises a known real return but unknown nominal return. See Chapter 9 for a fuller discussion.
3. Duration is a better measure of interest-rate-risk sensitivity than maturity. The Appendix to this chapter contains a discussion of duration and an example of how it is calculated.
4. It is more proper to calculate the default premium as the geometric difference in returns calculated as follows:

$$\frac{(1+\text{Long-term corporate bond compound annual return})}{(1+\text{Long-term government bond compouund annual return})}-1$$

$$=\frac{1.061}{1.057}-1=0.38\%$$

5. There have been 77 rolling ten-year holding periods from 1926 through 2011. Large company stocks had cumulative total return net losses in only four of those 77 ten-year holding periods. Two of those periods occurred during the Great Depression (10-year periods ending with 1938 and 1939). The other two cumulative total return net loss 10-year periods, which were worse than those that occurred during the Depression, occurred during the 10-year periods ending with 2008 and 2009.
6. Treasury Inflation Protected Securities are an exception. See Chapter 9 for a fuller discussion.
7. Together, the stocks in the Large Company Stocks index and the Small Company Stocks index do not include all publicly traded U.S. stocks. As of December 31, 2011, the stocks in the Small Company Stocks index had a total market capitalization of less than 2 percent

of the market capitalization of all publicly traded U.S. stocks. They are truly small. By contrast, the stocks in the Large Company Stocks index comprise approximately 75 percent of the market capitalization of all publicly traded U.S. stocks. Thus midsized and small companies exist that are not included in either of the two indices.

Chapter 3

1. Do not use these models to develop inputs for a mean-variance optimization program. For that purpose, it would be more appropriate to develop models based on historical arithmetic spreads rather than differences in compound returns. For a full discussion of this issue, see Chapter 11 on portfolio optimization.
2. Alternatively, some researchers define the equity risk premium as the difference between stock returns and long-term government bond yields. Depending on the context, the equity risk premium may be expressed as the difference in either simple average returns or compound annual returns.
3. If you are unfamiliar with some of the statistical concepts used in this section, it may be helpful to review the Appendix to this chapter. It provides summary explanations of the terms *compound annual return, simple annual return, expected return, standard deviation,* and *probability distribution.*
4. For this reason, announcements of dividend changes—good or bad—are said to have *information content* and are of great interest to the investment community.
5. For example, the expected return inputs for mean-variance optimization models correspond to simple average returns. For a discussion, see Chapter 11 on portfolio optimization.

Chapter 4

1. As discussed in the previous chapter, the serial correlation statistic describes the extent to which the return in one period is helpful in predicting the return in the following period. A series of returns

with a serial correlation near 1.0, for example, would be highly predictable from one period to the next and indicative of a trend. If the serial correlation is near −1.0, the series is highly cyclical. If the serial correlation is near 0, then the series has no predictable pattern and is described as a *random walk*.

2. Description of the "long-term government bond" series from *2012 Ibbotson® Stocks, Bonds, Bills, and Inflation® (SBBI) Classic Yearbook, © 2012 Morningstar,* page 51:

> To the greatest extent possible, a one-bond portfolio with a term of approximately 20 years and a reasonably current coupon—whose returns did not reflect potential tax benefits, impaired negotiability, or special redemption or call privileges—was used each year. Where "flower" bonds (tenderable to the Treasury at par in payment of estate taxes) had to be used, we chose the bond with the smallest potential tax benefit. Where callable bonds had to be used, the term of the bond was assumed to be a simple average of the maturity and first call dates minus the current date. The bond was "held" for the calendar year and returns were computed.

3. From 1926 through 2011, the serial correlation in year-end yields to maturity for long-term government bonds was 0.95.
4. R^2 quantifies the proportion of variation in the dependent variable that is explained by the independent variable. R^2 ranges from 0 to 1. An R^2 of 1, for instance, means that all the variation in the dependent variable is explained by the independent variable.
5. Source for the long-term government bond yields to maturity: *2012 Ibbotson® Stocks, Bonds, Bills, and Inflation® (SBBI®) Classic Yearbook, © 2012 Morningstar.*
6. This valuation metric was popularized by Yale University professor Robert Shiller. (See Robert J. Shiller, *Irrational Exuberance*, Princeton, N.J., Princeton University Press, 2000, p. 7.) Shiller refers to this P/E ratio as a *cyclically adjusted price-to-earnings*

ratio, or CAPE for short. Decades earlier, the famous value investor Benjamin Graham proposed normalizing earnings by using an average of the prior five years of reported earnings. We use a normalized P/E ratio because it has been more predictive of future long-term stock returns than other (non-normalized) P/E ratios.

7. Due to the use of overlapping time periods, a question arises about the statistical significance of the relationship between these two variables. In a CFA Institute Research Foundation publication (*Behavioral Finance and Investment Management*, December 2010), Robert Shiller addresses the issue of statistical significance for a similar simple linear regression analysis:

> A regression would not indicate a terribly good fit, but it is a good enough fit to suggest that there is something to this model. I see a negative slope to that scatter, and what it shows is that when the P/E has been high, subsequent returns have been low, and when the P/E has been low, subsequent returns have been high. ("Irrational Exuberance Revisited," p. 52)

8. Source for the normalized P/E ratio for large company stocks: Robert Shiller's website, http://www.econ.yale.edu/~shiller/data.htm.

Chapter 5

1. The serial correlation for the annual total returns of large company stocks from 1926 through 2011 is 0.02.
2. Whether a surprise is good news or bad news is always defined relative to the market's prior expectations. For example, even though profits are always good, the price of a stock may drop on the news that the company had a profitable quarter, if the profits fell short of the market's expectations. Likewise, the price of a stock may

rise on the news that the company lost money in the last quarter, if the loss was not as big as the market expected it would be.

3. Trinity Investment Management Corporation provided the data through the bear market that ended December 4, 1987. Gibson Capital, LLC compiled subsequent bear and bull market data. Trinity Investment Management Corporation generally defines a bear or bull market as a price-only change of at least 20 percent over a six-month or longer horizon. Trinity defined two borderline situations with significant declines as bear markets even though they did not meet the duration requirement. These were the market declines that began on November 9, 1938, and August 25, 1987.
4. Imagine you are having drinks with friends at a bar when Bill Gates walks in the door. Suddenly, the simple average net worth of the people in the bar skyrockets. The median net worth of those in the bar, however, will be relatively unaffected. The median is more representative of the net worth of those in the room.
5. William F. Sharpe, "Likely Gains from Market Timing," *Financial Analysts Journal*, March–April 1975, pp. 60–69.
6. Robert H. Jeffrey, "The Folly of Stock Market Timing," *Harvard Business Review*, July–August 1984, pp. 102–110.
7. Annual returns in excess of 30 percent have occurred only seven times in the past five decades.
8. Jeffrey, "Folly of Stock Market Timing," pp. 107–108.
9. Jess H. Chua and Richard S. Woodward, *Gains from Stock Market Timing*, Monograph 1986–2 of *Monograph Series in Finance and Economics*, ed. by Anthony Saunders, New York: Salomon Brothers Center for the Study of Financial Institutions at the Graduate School of Business Administration of New York University, pp. 12–13.
10. Charles D. Ellis, *Investment Policy*, Burr Ridge, IL: Irwin Professional Publishing, 1985, p. 13.
11. Wei Jiang, "A Nonparametric Test of Market Timing," *Journal of Empirical Finance*, vol. 10, 2003, p. 415.

12. John R. Graham and Campbell R. Harvey, "Market Timing Ability and Volatility Implied in Investment Newsletters' Asset Allocation Recommendations," *Journal of Financial Economics*, vol. 42, 1996, p. 419.
13. Pu Shen, "Market-Timing Strategies That Worked," Federal Reserve Bank of Kansas City Research Working Paper RWP 02–01, May 2002, p. 1.
14. Shen, "Market-Timing Strategies," p. 12.
15. Chris Brooks, Apostolos Katsaris, and Gita Persand, "Timing Is Everything: A Comparison and Evaluation of Market Timing Strategies," October 2005, p. 8. Available at SSRN: http://ssrn.com/abstract=834485.
16. Sharpe, "Likely Gains," p. 67.
17. DALBAR, Inc., "Quantitative Analysis of Investor Behavior 2006," p. 12.
18. Ellis, *Investment Policy*, pp. 22–23.

Chapter 6

1. TIPS are an exception. See Chapter 9 for a fuller discussion.
2. Inflation compounded at 3 percent over both the 30-year period ending with 2011 and the 86-year period from 1926 through 2011.
3. The equity risk premium of 5.8 percent reflects an adjustment to large company stocks' historical compound annual return that eliminates the impact of an expansion in the price/earnings ratio from 1926 through 2011. See Chapter 3.
4. Large company stocks' compound annual loss of 1.4 percent occurred during the 10-year period ending with 2008.

Chapter 7

1. With a normal distribution, approximately two-thirds of the observations fall within one standard deviation of the arithmetic mean

(simple average), and approximately 95 percent of the observations fall within two standard deviations of the arithmetic mean.

2. The equity risk premium of 5.8 percent reflects an adjustment to large company stocks' historical compound annual return that eliminates the impact of an expansion in the price/earnings ratio from 1926 through 2011. See Chapter 3.
3. In later chapters, we will see that, with multiple-asset-class portfolios, incremental returns are possible with a smaller increase in volatility than is implied by the hypothetical world illustrated in Exhibit 7.2. In working with clients, however, it is better to avoid holding out such hope at this point in the decision-making process.
4. Another dilemma with the model is that the standard deviation is technically measured around the simple average return rather than the compound annual return. To use the simple average return in the model, however, may mislead clients into thinking that their money will compound at those rates. (As we discussed in the Appendix to Chapter 3, the simple average return will always be higher than the corresponding compound return for a variable pattern of returns.) Using the compound return number avoids this problem. In my judgment, the technical inaccuracy serves the more important consideration of clients' conceptual understandings. Within a time horizon context, clients naturally will think of compound returns, and yet their experiences of volatility will be in the near term. A fuller discussion of these issues appears in Chapter 11 on portfolio optimization.

Chapter 8

1. The *covariance* of two investments' returns is a weighted average of the products of the returns' deviations around their expected returns, where the probabilities of the deviations are used as weights. The *cross-correlation* of two investments' returns is equal

to their covariance divided by the product of their standard deviations.

2. Due to the diversification effect, in a situation with multiple potential investments, it is possible for the minimum-volatility portfolio to have a higher expected return *with less volatility* than the least volatile investment available as a portfolio building block.
3. I have modified the language normally used in discussing the CAPM by often substituting the word *volatility* for *risk*. This approach is consistent with my decision to carefully choose the contexts in which the words *volatility* and *risk* are used throughout the book.

Chapter 9

1. Although counterintuitive, diversification into an asset class with more volatile returns does not necessarily increase portfolio volatility. Depending on the magnitude of the difference in the volatilities and the correlations among the portfolio components, diversification into a more volatile asset class may actually *decrease* portfolio volatility. Similarly, diversification into an asset class with lower returns does not necessarily result in a lower portfolio return. Depending on the magnitude of the difference in the returns and the correlations among the portfolio components, diversification into a lower-returning asset class may actually *increase* portfolio return. We will see examples in Chapter 10, "The Rewards of Multiple-Asset-Class Investing."
2. Joseph L. Pagliari, Jr., Kevin A. Scherer, and Richard T. Monopoli, "Public versus Private Real Estate Equities," *Journal of Portfolio Management*. special issue, 2003.
3. In addition, healthcare REITs invest in medical offices, hospitals, assisted living facilities, and nursing homes. There are even specialty REITs that invest in car lots, golf courses, theaters, or prisons.

4. During the subsequent U.S. and non-U.S. stock market recoveries, real estate securities continued to deliver superior returns for several years.
5. Similarly, a non-U.S.-based investor may have a portfolio more heavily weighted in non-U.S. stocks and bonds. Non-U.S. stocks and bonds have lower correlations with U.S. real estate securities than with non-U.S. real estate securities. Therefore, a non-U.S.-based investor may get greater diversification benefits from U.S. real estate securities than from non-U.S. real estate securities.
6. Theoretically, for a given maturity, the yield spread between a Treasury Inflation Protected Security (TIPS) and a conventional Treasury bond consists of the expected future inflation rate plus an inflation risk premium embedded in the yield of the conventional Treasury bond.
7. The specific commodities chosen for inclusion in each index differ slightly. For example, the S&P GSCI includes very small allocations to cocoa, lead, and feeder cattle. These three commodities are not represented in the DJ-UBSCI.
8. *Backwardation* is a condition in the commodity markets in which a futures price is lower in distant delivery months than in near delivery months.

Chapter 10

1. The Sharpe ratio is a measure of reward relative to volatility. A portfolio's Sharpe ratio can be calculated easily using a simple spreadsheet program. The portfolio's returns are listed in one column and those for Treasury bills are listed in the next column. The differences between the portfolio returns and Treasury bill returns are computed in the third column. The Sharpe ratio is equal to the average of the differences in column 3, divided by the standard deviation of those differences. The Sharpe ratio affirms the notion that a portfolio should generate some incremental

reward for the assumption of volatility; otherwise, it would be better simply to own Treasury bills.

2. These equity diversification illustrations are based on data covering the period from 1972 through 2011. The year 1972 was chosen as the beginning point because it was the earliest year for which data were available for all four equity asset classes.
3. As we will see in Chapter 11, given a desirable asset class for portfolio diversification, the first dollars invested in the asset class have the biggest impact on improving portfolio volatility-adjusted returns. For example, half of the optimal allocation to an asset class delivers *more* than 50 percent of the total improvement in portfolio volatility-adjusted returns associated with the optimal allocation.

Chapter 11

1. Charles Babbage is known as the "father of computing" for originating the idea of a programmable computer in the 1800s. He designed machines that could mechanically calculate mathematical tables. He apparently also had an obsession with fire, once baking himself in an oven at 265 degrees Fahrenheit for four minutes "without any great discomfort" to "see what would happen." Later, he arranged to be lowered into Mount Vesuvius in order to see molten lava firsthand.
2. In using an optimizer, an asset class's input statistic for the standard deviation generally should be larger than its anticipated level of volatility in order to take into consideration the uncertainty in the level of future average returns for the asset class.
3. All portfolio optimizations were performed on Vestek Systems, Inc. software.
4. In decimal form, the compound annual return is approximately equal to the simple average return minus one-half of the variance. For example, in Exhibit 3.1, we see that large company

stocks had a compound annual return of 9.8 percent, a simple average return of 11.8 percent, and a standard deviation of 20.3 percent. The compound annual return of 9.8 percent is approximately equal to the simple average return of 11.8 percent minus one-half of the variance. The variance is equal to the standard deviation squared:

$$9.8 \text{ percent} = 0.098$$
$$\approx 0.118 - 0.5(0.203)^2 = 0.097 = 9.7 \text{ percent}$$

5. Note that, as we hold the volatility-premium input constant at 10 percent, the optimal portfolio under alternative input assumptions will have varying expected return and volatility levels. The optimal portfolio expresses a compromise between expected return and volatility that changes as the inputs are modified.
6. Richard Michaud, *Efficient Asset Management*, Boston: Harvard Business School Press, 1998.
7. In decimal form, the estimated compound annual return is approximately equal to the expected return minus one-half of the variance, where the variance is equal to the standard deviation squared.

Chapter 13

1. Charles D. Ellis, *Investment Policy*, Burr Ridge, IL: Irwin Professional Publishing, 1985.
2. For the purposes of this discussion, we will assume no contributions to or withdrawals from the portfolio.
3. The compound annual return associated with a series of numbers is the same regardless of the order in which the numbers are multiplied.
4. The multiple-asset-class investor may experience a different kind of pain when he is significantly ahead of the U.S. stock market—the disbelief of others. I have had a number of clients tell me that

their friends did not believe them when they said how good their returns had been throughout the 2000–2002 bear market and subsequent recovery.

Chapter 14

1. The historical returns of these portfolios are high relative to our estimates of future returns.
2. Duration is a better measure of a bond's sensitivity to changes in interest rates. See the Appendix to Chapter 2.
3. Excerpt from an address given by John C. Bogle at the Fourth Annual Superbowl of Indexing conference.
4. Throughout this discussion we will refer to IRAs, but the logic applies equally to tax-qualified retirement plans and other tax-deferred vehicles.

Chapter 15

1. Consider a well-diversified, no-load mutual fund with hundreds of different stocks. As a result of the dissimilarities in the patterns of returns of the various stocks, the mutual fund's volatility is much less than the average volatility level of the stocks in the fund. That is, the fund has eliminated considerable diversifiable volatility. The market does not pay a premium to investors for bearing diversifiable volatility. If the market *did* pay a premium to investors for bearing diversifiable volatility, an investor who wants to avoid it would be willing to pay a premium to other investors who are willing to bear it. It then would follow that a well-diversified, no-load stock mutual fund would sell at a price above its net asset value per share. The fact that no-load mutual funds do *not* sell at a premium to their net asset value is evidence that the market does not pay investors a premium for bearing diversifiable volatility.

2. The Monte Carlo simulations illustrated in this chapter define a trial as a success if the portfolio has some money left in it at the end of a specified investment time horizon. Alternatively, an advisor and client may want to define success as the preservation of the portfolio's dollar value, purchasing power, or some other predetermined amount at a specified time horizon. More sophisticated Monte Carlo simulation programs simultaneously model uncertainty in investor life expectancy.
3. The Uniform Principal and Income Act of 1997 confirms the wisdom of this approach as it pertains to the investment management of trusts. The act states that trustees should invest for total return and then allocate income and principal fairly, without regard to traditional notions of what constitutes income and principal.
4. In decimal form, the compound annual return is approximately equal to the expected return minus one-half the variance, where the variance is equal to the standard deviation squared.

Appendix

For exhibits produced using data from Morningstar® Principia®: © 2012 Morningstar. All Rights Reserved. The information, data, analyses and opinions contained herein (1) include the confidential and proprietary information of Morningstar, (2) may include, or be derived from, account information provided by your financial advisor which cannot be verified by Morningstar, (3) may not be copied or redistributed, (4) do not constitute investment advice offered by Morningstar, (5) are provided solely for informational purposes and therefore are not an offer to buy or sell a security, and (6) are not warranted to be correct, complete or accurate. Except as otherwise required by law, Morningstar shall not be responsible for any trading decisions, damages or other losses resulting from, or related to, this information, data, analyses or opinions or their use.

Index

About the Author

Roger C. Gibson, CFA, is chief investment officer of Gibson Capital, LLC (http://www.gibsoncapital.com), which advises high-net-worth individuals and institutional clients nationwide. An internationally recognized expert in asset allocation and investment portfolio design, Gibson speaks at conferences for financial professionals around the world and is quoted frequently in national media. He lives with his wife and business partner, Brenda, in a pre-Civil War farmhouse north of Pittsburgh, Pennsylvania.

www.ingramcontent.com/pod-product-compliance
Lightning Source LLC
LaVergne TN
LVHW052218200926
848481LV00001B/140

9781265801977